The Book of Proust

Philippe Michel-Thiriet

The Book of Proust

Translated by Jan Dalley

Chatto & Windus

LONDON

Published in 1989 by
Chatto & Windus Ltd
30 Bedford Square
London WC1B 3SG

Originally published as
Quid de Marcel Proust by Éditions Robert Laffont, S.A., Paris, 1987.
Conceived and directed by Dominique Frémy,
written by Philippe Michel-Thiriet.

A CIP catalogue record for this book is
available from the British Library.

ISBN 0 7011 3360 0

Photoset by Rowland Phototypesetting Ltd
Bury St Edmunds, Suffolk
Printed in Great Britain by
Mackays of Chatham plc, Chatham, Kent

Contents

Appendices

Translator's Note

In this translation of the *Quid de Marcel Proust* I have rendered all
quotations from Proust, whether they are from *A la Recherche du temps
perdu* or from other published or unpublished works, articles or letters,
into my own version. Readers who are familiar with C. K. Scott
Moncrieff and Terence Kilmartin's classic translation *Remembrance of
Things Past* (Chatto & Windus and Penguin Books) might wish to find
the equivalent passages there, in which case the synopses with page
numbers at the back of each volume give a useful indication, and an even
more convenient route is provided by Terence Kilmartin's *Guide to
Proust* (Chatto & Windus). The titles of all Proust's works have been left
in French in this book, to avoid possible confusion caused by references
to earlier versions under other titles, and so on.

The Book of Proust is essentially an informal reference book which
contains contemporary opinion, subsequent literary judgements, critical, anecdotal and historical background material, as well as a vast range
of factual material about Marcel Proust's life and work and the world he
created. The best guide to the various sections of the book, and a means
of quick reference, is the list of contents on page v; other readers may
prefer to browse at will.

Jan Dalley
London 1989

I

The Life

CHAPTER ONE

Biography of Marcel Proust

Main Stages in Proust's Life

Birth

To escape the Commune after the siege of Paris, Madame Adrien Proust spent her pregnancy at Auteuil with her uncle, Louis Weil, at 96 rue La Fontaine. In this peaceful house, after a very difficult confinement, Marcel Proust was born at 11 o'clock on the evening of Monday 10 July 1871, St Felicity's day. The birth certificate, signed by Marcel's father, Dr Adrien Proust, his grandfather, Nathé Weil, and his great-uncle, Louis Weil, was issued in the 16th arrondissement at 2 o'clock on 13 July. Proust was very frail and almost died at birth (all his life he attributed his sickly constitution to the fear and deprivation his mother suffered during the Commune, which had been established several months earlier, on 18 March, and lasted until 28 May 1871). But after a fortnight had passed, thanks to his father's care, his life was no longer in danger.

Baptism

On 5 August 1871, he was baptised at the church of Saint-Louis d'Antin, the parish church of his family home (his parents lived in the rue Roy). Although Madame Proust had kept her Jewish religion, the two parents had decided that their children would be Catholic like their father. Proust's godmother was Madame Houette, who died in December 1892.

Principal Events

1873: *24 May* The birth of his brother Robert at Auteuil. *1 August* His parents move to 9 boulevard Malesherbes. *19 December* His father becomes head doctor of the Sainte-Perrine hospice in Auteuil.

1874: *July* His father is sent as a delegate to the International Medical Conference in Vienna. *26 September* His uncle, the architect Moïse-Baruch Weil, dies in Beauvais.

1877: *June* His father is placed in charge of medical services at the Lariboisière hospital.

1878: *Easter* and *September* The Proust family spend their holidays at Illiers (where Philip Kolb places the incident involving Robert and the young goat reported in *Contre Sainte-Beuve*).

1879: His father is elected a member of the Academy of Medicine.

1880: *1 May* Proust breaks his nose in a fall in the Champs-Élysées. *5 September* The date of Proust's earliest surviving letter. *6 September* He leaves for Dieppe. *26 September* His first cousin, Jules Louis Émile Amiot, is born. Madame Beauvais embarks on a portrait in oils of Madame Adrien Proust.

1881: *Early spring* His first asthma attack, after a walk in the Bois de Boulogne. He was then at the Pape-Carpentier school, together with his friend Jacques Bizet. In the autumn he goes to the theatre for the first time. Marie Van Zandt, an American comic opera singer, dedicates a photograph of herself in male dress to his father: she was undoubtedly the model for Miss Sacripant in *A la Recherche*. *November* He goes to the wedding of his mother's cousin, Daniel Mayer, to Marguerite Lévy, at the temple in the rue de la Victoire.

1882: *27 February* Madame André Hamart, the only daughter of his Aunt Amiot, dies at the age of 33. *April* He and his brother are pages at the wedding of Jean Cruppi (a magistrate and future minister of Commerce) to Louise Crémieux. He spends the early autumn with his brother at the house of their great-uncle Louis Weil at Auteuil. *2 October* He is enrolled in Class 5 of the lycée Fontanes (as the lycée Condorcet was called until January 1883).

1883: *3 August* He wins second prize for natural sciences, comes fourth in the certificates of merit for Latin composition and fifth in French language. He takes his First Communion.

1884: *30 March* His father is appointed Inspector General of Health. *1 August* School prize-giving. *8 August* He receives his certificate of grammar. He leaves straight away for Houlgate where he takes lessons in Greek. *October* He joins Class 3A.

1885: *14 February* Although often ill, his name appears on the school's honours board. But he leaves the lycée immediately afterwards and is absent throughout the third term. *May* His father is a delegate to the International Conference on Health in Rome, and, on *14 July*, is awarded a medal of honour by the city of Toulon for his devotion to duty during the 1884 epidemic. *September* He spends his holiday at Salies-de-Béarn. *October* He goes into Class 2; his father is appointed to the Chair of Hygiene at the Faculty of Medicine. *31 December* He leaves the lycée, not to return for the rest of the school year.

1886: He answers a questionnaire in Antoinette Faure's album (see p. 57). *March* Away from Condorcet, he takes private lessons and does school work with his mother. He writes 'Les Nuages'. *1 June* Death of Madame Jules Amiot, the model for Aunt Léonie. *Autumn* The last stay at Illiers, where his parents are settling his aunt's estate. Whilst there he reads Augustin Thierry's *L'Histoire de la conquête de l'Angleterre par les Normans*. *October* He remains in Class 2 for a second year.

1887: *July* Almost every day he plays with Marie Bénardaky in the Champs-Élysées. *13 July* He sits the general history exam. *14 July* At Auteuil he goes to the military parade in honour of General Boulanger, whom he considers 'very common and a vulgar self-publicist'. *22 July* He competes in the inter-schools competition for Greek translation, but without success. *2 August* Prize-giving ceremony: he is mentioned four times (he comes fourth in the certificates of merit for French composition). *3 October* He goes into the second-highest class in the school, but he is absent a great deal. He becomes friends with Pierre Lavallée.

1888: *31 July* Prize-giving ceremony: he wins the *prix d'honneur* for French composition. Letters to his friends Jacques Bizet and Daniel

Halévy show his homosexuality for the first time. He spends his holidays reading Leconte de Lisle and Pierre Loti. *7 September* He goes to stay with his friend Édouard Joyant in L'Isle-Adam. *1 October* He enters the school's highest class in arts subjects, and contributes to *La Revue verte*, then *La Revue lilas*. *December* He courts Laure Hayman, the model for Paul Bourget's 'Gladys Harvey'.

1889: *17 January* After a dinner at the Prousts', Ernest Renan dedicates *La Vie de Jésus* to him. *19 March* The death of Madame François-Valentin Proust, his paternal grandmother. *15 July* He passes his *baccalauréat* in arts. *30 July* He wins the *prix d'honneur* for French essays. *September* He stays with the Finalys in Ostend. On his return, he is introduced to Madame Arman de Caillavet and to Anatole France. He also meets Gaston Arman de Caillavet. *11 November* He signs up for a year's voluntary service in the army, and, on the 15th of the month, joins the 76th Infantry Regiment in Orléans. He rents a room in the town, because his asthma attacks disturb his companions. *December* Madame Nathé Weil, his maternal grandmother, falls seriously ill.

1890: *3 January* She dies of uraemia. *February* At dinner with Monsieur Boegner, the Chief Commissioner of the Loiret district, he meets Robert de Billy. *September* He spends his leave in Paris and Cabourg. *14 November* He passes out into the army reserve. Back in Paris, he enrols in the Faculty of Law and in the École libre des sciences politiques, where he studies under Albert Sorel, Anatole Leroy-Beaulieu and Albert Vandal. Towards the end of the year he goes often to Madame Straus's salon, where he meets Maupassant.

1891: *21 March* At the Odéon with the Straus family, Jacques Bizet and Jacques Baignères, he is moved by seeing Réjane act in *Germinie Lacerteux* by Edmond de Goncourt. *1 May (?)* His first meeting with André Gide. *Summer* He is seen at the tennis club on boulevard Bineau with Jeanne Pouquet and her friend Gaston de Caillavet. *September* He writes to his mother from Cabourg, evoking 'those years at the sea when Granny and I, melted together, walked into the wind, chatting'. *October* He goes to stay with the Arthur Baignères in Trouville. Jacques-Émile Blanche does the first portrait of Proust, in pencil. *5 November* He re-registers at the law faculty and the École libre des sciences politiques.

At the end of the year he meets Oscar Wilde, who was passing through Paris, and is probably introduced to Maurice Barrès.

1892: *7 January* He is a page at the wedding of Henry Bergson and his cousin Louise Neuburger. The same month he makes friends with Fernand Gregh, and together with Robert Dreyfus, Louis de la Salle, Daniel Halévy, Horace Finaly and Jacques Bizet they found a monthly review called *Le Banquet*, in which he publishes several articles between March 1892 and February 1893. *Spring* He becomes a frequent visitor at the Hérédias' salon, where he meets Henri Barbusse, and at Princesse Mathilde's. He strikes up a friendship with Robert de Flers. *25 May* His review of *Voyage en Turquie d'Asie* by the Comte de Cholet, his former commanding officer, is published in *Littérature et Critique*. *June* He succeeds in passing three oral examinations at the École libre des sciences politiques. Every Saturday he visits Jacques-Émile Blanche, who is finishing his portrait in oils. *August* He goes to Princesse Mathilde's house in Saint-Gratien where he is introduced to Comte Benedetti, then stays with the Finalys in Trouville, at their estate Les Frémonts, the future model for Raspelière. Whilst there, Paul Baignères draws his portrait in an album. At the end of the year he answers another questionnaire in an album, entitled 'Marcel Proust, by himself'.

1893: *7 February Le Banquet* publishes 'Violante ou la mondanité' and 'La Conférence parlementaire de la rue Serpente'. *13 April* At Madeleine Lemaire's house he is introduced to Comte Robert de Montesquiou. *May* Jacques-Émile Blanche exhibits his portrait at the Champs de Mars salon. *July Gratis-Journal* publishes his review of *Cléopâtre* by Henri de Saussine. At about this time he first notices Comtesse Greffulhe at the Princesse de Wagram's. *July/August La Revue blanche*, in which he collaborates, publishes several pieces, including one of his first pastiches: 'Mondanité de *Bouvard et Pécuchet*'. *Summer* He plans to write a *roman à quatre* with Daniel Halévy, Fernand Gregh and Louis de la Salle; he drafts a short story, 'L'Indifférent'. In St Moritz, where he spends three weeks with Madame Meredith Howland, he writes 'Mélancolique Villégiature de Mme de Breyvet' (a short story published on 15 September in *La Revue blanche*). *Early September* In Évian, he writes an article on Montesquiou, then leaves for the Hôtel des Roches-Noires in Trouville with his mother. On his return to Paris he learns of the death of his friend Willie Heath on 3 October. *10 October* He is awarded his law degree and spends a fortnight working in the offices of Gustave Brunet. He begins a long correspondence about his future career with Charles Grandjean. *1 December La Revue blanche* publishes six pieces, 'Avant la nuit' among them.

1894: *January* He sends Madeleine Lemaire a poem in her praise: 'Vous faites plus que Dieu: un éternel printemps'. *February* Marie de Hérédia and he found the Académie des canaques. *March La Revue blanche* and *La Revue de Paris* both turn down his article entitled 'De la simplicité de Robert de Montesquiou'. *April* His poem 'Mensonges' is published by Heugel. *22 May* He probably meets Reynaldo Hahn for the first time at one of Madeleine Lemaire's parties. *30 May* Montesquiou gives a large party at Versailles in honour of his protégé, the pianist Léon Delafosse, whom Proust had introduced to him. *31 May* Proust reviews the event in *Le Gaulois* under the title 'Une fête littéraire à Versailles'. *August* Van Dyke's portrait of the Duke of Richmond inspires Proust to write a set of poems. *18 August* As the guest of Madeleine Lemaire, he goes to the Château de Réveillon, where he is joined by Reynaldo Hahn, and where the incident of the rose bushes related in *Jean Santeuil* and *Contre Sainte-Beuve* takes place. He writes a rebuttal of Tolstoy's 'Patriotism and the Christian Spirit' and drafts 'Mondanité et Mélomanie de *Bouvard et Pécuchet*'. *8 September* Robert, his brother, has a serious bicycle accident in Rueil. Shortly afterwards, Proust and his mother leave for Trouville, where he begins 'La Mort de Baldassare Silvande'. *October* Back in Paris, he works on three stories and some poems for *Les Plaisirs et les jours*. *December* After hearing Beethoven's 5th Symphony, he writes 'Un Dimanche au Conservatoire', which is published in *Le Gaulois* on 14 January 1895.

1895: *January* He submits a poem dedicated to Reynaldo Hahn to Suzette Lemaire. *Towards the end of winter* He becomes a regular visitor at the salons of the Montesquious, the Daudets, Madame Aubernon, the Princesse de Polignac, Madame Lemaire, Princesse Mathilde and the Comtesse Louis Cahen d'Anvers. He often goes to the Comédie-Française where he sees *Hernani* and the Concerts Lamoureux. *27 March* He is awarded his degree in philosophy, and leaves immediately to stay with Pierre Lavallée at the Château de Segrez for a rest. *23 April* At the

Princesse de Polignac's he hears Rameau's *Dardanus*; on *13 May* he goes to *Tannhaüser* at the Opéra. Despite Reynaldo Hahn's opinion, he makes no secret of his predilection for Wagner. During the course of this year, both his musical tastes and his intellectual interests deepen. He keeps up his visits to the Salle Érard and the Concerts Colonne. *29 May* He competes for a place as unpaid attaché at the Bibliothèque Mazarine; he wins the third of three places, and starts work in June. *21 June Le Gaulois* publishes his 'Portraits de peintres'. *July* He is allocated to the legal department of the Ministry of Education, and is allowed his first two-month holiday. He and his mother spend part of the summer in Kreuznach, a German spa town, where he works on *Jean Santeuil*. *10 August* He and Reynaldo Hahn go to Dieppe to stay with Madeleine Lemaire, who introduces him to the composer Camille Saint-Saëns. He writes 'Sous-Bois'. *September* Reynaldo Hahn and he leave for Brittany, first to Belle-Ile, then to Beg-Meil, where they stay at the Hôtel Fermont (a visit described in *Jean Santeuil*). He is reading Balzac's *Splendeurs et misères des courtisanes* and *The Heroes* by Carlyle, which will help him with his study of Ruskin. He works hard on his novel. *29 October* On his return to Paris *La Revue hebdomadaire* prints 'La Mort de Baldassare Silvande'. *End of November* Following a visit to the Loire, he writes an essay entitled 'Chardin et Rembrandt'. *8 December* He goes to a concert at the Conservatoire where Saint-Saëns plays a Mozart concerto; he records his impressions the next day in 'Camille Saint-Saëns, pianiste'. *14 December* In *Le Gaulois* he publishes 'Figures parisiennes: Camille Saint-Saëns', while Saint-Saëns' opera *Frédégonde*, which Proust attends, is being performed. *24 December* He gets a year's leave from the ministry. *31 December* He publishes three 'Portraits de peintres' in *Année des poètes*.

1896: *31 January* The première of *Bonne Hélène* by Jules Lemaitre, of which Proust writes a review called 'Éros et Vénus'. *March* He publishes 'L'Indifférent' in *La Vie contemporaine*. He drafts a few notes after reading *Histoires naturelles* by Jules Renard. *28 March* He receives the galley proofs of 'Château de Réveillon', whose title is changed to *Les Plaisirs et les jours* in April. *10 May* His maternal great-uncle, Louis Weil, dies of pneumonia. He becomes more and more friendly with Lucien Daudet. *12 June Les Plaisirs et les jours* is published by Calmann-Lévy. *15 July La Revue blanche* prints 'Contre l'obscurité'. *Early August* He and his mother leave for Mont-Dore. *16 September* On his return to Paris, he writes to his mother that his novel already fills '110 large pages' in a notebook he has just finished. He works on *Jean Santeuil* throughout the month. *October* To concentrate on the book, he installs himself at Fontainebleau, where he writes 'Jean à Beg-Meil I' and 'Le téléphonage à sa mère'. He reads Balzac, Shakespeare, Goethe and George Eliot. *3 November* He hears the appeal to Jaurès in the Chambre des députés on behalf of the Armenians massacred by the Turks; it is described in his novel. *December* At Reynaldo Hahn's, he meets Marie Nordlinger, Hahn's first cousin.

1897: *January* He publishes 'Silhouette d'artiste' in *La Revue d'art dramatique*. *3 February* He fights a duel with Jean Lorrain, who had alluded to Proust's homosexuality in an article in *Le Journal*. *End of March* His great-uncle Louis Weil's property in Auteuil is sold. *July* Through Reynaldo Hahn he meets the painter Alexander Harrison, the model for Bergotte (in *Jean Santeuil*) and one of the models for Elstir (in *A la Recherche*). *11 August La Presse* prints his article entitled 'Sur M. Alphonse Daudet', then he leaves for Kreuznach with his mother. He asks Lucien Daudet's advice about novels by Balzac, works by Michelet and Dickens, as well as *The Brothers Karamazov* and Boswell's *Life of Johnson*. *Autumn* He is in Dieppe with Léon Yeatman. *October* Dr Proust and Gilbert Ballet publish *L'Hygiène du neurasthénique*. *16 December* The death of Alphonse Daudet. *19 December* Proust publishes 'Adieux' in *La Presse*.

1898: *January* Major Esterházy, who was implicated in the Dreyfus affair, is acquitted. Fernand Gregh, Daniel Halévy and Robert Dreyfus draw up a petition in support of Colonel Picquart and collect writers' signatures; Proust gets Anatole France to sign. *14 January* The protest appears in *L'Aurore*. *20 January La Revue d'art dramatique* prints his article 'Robert de Flers', which raises the question of vocation. *From 7 to 23 February* He attends Zola's trial, which he uses as inspiration for parts of *Jean Santeuil*, written in April-May. *Early July* Madame Proust has an operation for cancer and remains in a clinic in the rue Bizet for almost three months. He then accompanies her to Trouville. *October* He travels to Holland, and in Amsterdam visits the Rembrandt exhibition; he alludes to it in a posthumous study of the painter. *November* He visits Gustave Moreau's house, which has been left to the State as a museum, and writes 'Notes sur le monde mystérieux de Gustave Moreau'. *End of*

November The petition on behalf of Picquart appears in *L'Aurore* bearing his signature. *31 December* He asks the ministry for a further year's leave of absence.

1899: *6 February* He is accorded a fourth year's leave from his post as a librarian. *May (probably)* Robert de Billy lends him *L'Art religieux du XIIIe siècle en France*, by Émile Mâle, which is useful for his work on Ruskin. *June* At Princess Alexandre Bibesco's he meets Antoine Bibesco, who becomes his great friend. Through Louis de Robert he also meets Colonel Picquart. *End of summer* He stays at the Splendide Hôtel in Évian with his parents, then in Geneva and Thonon with the Brancovans and Abel Hermant. Switzerland inspires 'Souvenirs de la mer devant le lac de Genève' in *Jean Santeuil*, as well as some landscape passages in *A la Recherche*. *19 September and 12 October* He publishes 'Lettres de Perse et d'ailleurs' in *La Presse*; later he reuses parts of it in his novel, notably 'Le Jet d'eau d'Hubert Robert'. *October* Back in Paris, he reviews Montesquiou's *Perles Rouges* for *La Presse*. He reads *The Seven Lamps of Architecture* by Ruskin in the Bibliothèque Nationale with François d'Oncieu; he decides to undertake a study of Ruskin commissioned by Gonderax, director of *La Revue de Paris*. *December* With his mother's help, he tackles the translation of the fourth chapter of Ruskin's *The Bible of Amiens* and begins a study of Reims cathedral.

1900: *January* He pays a visit to Rouen cathedral. *27 January* He writes an obituary of Ruskin, who had died in London on 20 January, in *La Chronique des arts*. *13 February Le Figaro* prints 'Pèlerinages ruskiniens en France' and announces a series of articles and translations that will begin with *The Bible of Amiens*. *14 February* He is formally summoned to return to his post at the law library. *1 March* He is considered to have resigned. *1 April* He brings out a further study of Ruskin in *La Gazette des beaux-arts* and 'Ruskin à Notre-Dame d'Amiens' in the April issue of *Le Mercure de France*. These two pieces appear in the preface to *La Bible d'Amiens*. *Early May* He and his mother leave for Venice, where he meets Reynaldo Hahn and Marie Nordlinger. He reads Ruskin's *St Mark's Rest* in St Mark's baptistry, and goes to see the Giotto frescoes in Padua (which he describes in *A la Recherche*). *1 August* In *La Gazette des beaux-arts* he publishes the second half of his study of Ruskin, the proofs of which Marie Nordlinger had corrected in Italy. *13 October* He goes back to

Venice without his mother. During his absence his parents move from 9 boulevard Malesherbes to 45 rue de Courcelles. On his return to Paris he visits the exhibition of Monet's *Nymphéas* at Durand-Ruel's. *7 December* He attends Bergson's opening course at the Collège de France.

1901: *5 January* A review of the work of Robert de Montesquiou, 'Le Pays des aromates', appears in *La Chronique des arts et de la curiosité*. He attends more society dinner parties, even though his asthma attacks are worsening. *19 June* He gives a dinner in honour of the Comtesse de Noailles. *10 July* During a visit to Léon Yeatman he shouts: 'I'm 30 years old today, and I've achieved nothing!' He doesn't go away on holiday but continues his evenings out at the Princesse de Polignac's or to the Opéra (where he hears Rossini's *William Tell*). *7 September* He goes to Amiens with Léon Yeatman, then to Abbeville, where he works in front of the church. *Autumn* He sees a lot of Antoine Bibesco, and unsuccessfully tries to interest Sarah Bernhardt in a play of Bibesco's entitled *La Lutte*. *December* He delivers his translation of *The Bible of Amiens* to Éditions Ollendorff.

1902: *Beginning of the year* For *Jean Santeuil*, which he had neglected, he writes a pen-portrait of the Baronne Deslandes under the guise of Madame de Réveillon. *15 March* Reynaldo Hahn dedicates *Les Muses pleurant la mort de Ruskin* to him. *30 April* The première of Debussy's *Pelléas et Mélisande*, which has a profound influence on his musical taste. *7 June* He goes to hear *Tristan und Isolde* with Antoine Bibesco and Bertrand de Fénelon. *Summer* He drafts the last part of *Jean Santeuil*, 'Madame Martial' (whose characteristics are drawn from the wife of the painter Hébert). *14 July* Charles Haas (the main model for Swann in *A la Recherche*) dies. *End of July and August* Dinners at Larue's or Weber's in the company of friends from the Faubourg Saint-Germain. *September* He spends a day at the Daudets' house at Pray, and another in Chartres. He writes an article about the Comtesse Greffulhe's salon, intended for the *New York Herald*. *3 October* He and Bertrand Fénelon go to Bruges, where they see an exhibition of Flemish primitives. He continues the journey through Anvers, Dordrecht, Rotterdam, Delft, Amsterdam, Haarlem (where he sees pictures by Frans Hals) and finally The Hague, where he admires Vermeer's *View of Delft*. He reads *Les Maîtres d'autrefois* by Eugène Fromentin. *11 November* He joins the territorial army. At the end of the month he attends several society dinners, despite his mother's complaints that he is neglecting his work. *End of autumn* He gives his translation of *The Bible of Amiens* to Alfred Vallette, editor of *Le Mercure de France*. He undertakes to finish it by 1 February and to edit a selection of Ruskin's work. *3 December* He goes to see Gallé (1846–1904), the glassmaker patronised by Montesquiou, to commission a vase for Fernand Gregh's wedding present. *6 December* He quarrels with Fénelon and stamps on his hat. Fénelon leaves for Constantinople at the end of the year, to Proust's great distress. *20 December* He writes to Antoine Bibesco about his awakening sense of vocation as a writer.

1903: Robert d'Humières helps him with his Ruskin translation at the beginning of the year. *2 February* Proust is best man at his brother Robert's wedding to Marthe Dubois-Amiot. *15 February* He publishes part of his translation of *The Bible of Amiens* in *La Renaissance latine*. *25 February Le Figaro* prints the first of his articles on the salons: 'Un salon historique. Le Salon de S.A.I. la princesse Mathilde', under the pen-name 'Dominique'. *7 March* In the *Chronique des arts et de la curiosité* he publishes a review of a study of Ruskin by Marie de Bunsen. *2 April* After seeing a show at the Folies-Bergère with Georges de Lauris, he writes an article for *Le Figaro* which is not used. *21 April* A motoring tour of Laon, Senlis and Coucy-le-Château with Lauris and the Bibesco brothers. *11 May* He publishes 'Le Salon de Madame Lemaire', under the pseudonym 'Dominique', in *Le Figaro*. At the end of the spring and throughout the rest of the year he often sees the Marquis d'Albufera and his mistress, the actress Louisa de Mornand. *27 July* His father makes a speech at the prize-giving at Illiers. *16 August* He spends a day with Madame Straus at Trouville. *End of August* He sets out to join his parents at Évian, stopping on the way at Avallon, Vézelay and Dijon. *6 September* He publishes 'Le Salon de la princesse de Polignac', under the name 'Horatio', in *Le Figaro*. This month, although Constantin de Brancovan has offered him a regular theatre column in *La Renaissance latine*, he goes to Chamonix and walks over the Sea of Ice with Louisa de Mornand and d'Albufera. *10 October* Before going back to Paris he visits the church at Brou and the hospice at Beaune. *7 and 14 November* The *Chronique des arts et de la curiosité* prints his 'Dante Gabriel Rossetti and Elizabeth Siddal', a review which also appears in the *Burlington Magazine*. *26 November* Dr

Proust dies of a cerebral haemorrhage which had struck him two days earlier. *28 November* He is buried in the Père-Lachaise cemetery. *Early December* Encouraged by his mother, Proust goes back to work and corrects the proofs of *La Bible d'Amiens*.

1904: *2 January* The *Chronique des arts* publishes a review by Proust, 'Charlotte Broicher, *John Ruskin und sein Werk*'. *4 January Le Figaro* publishes 'Le Salon de la comtesse d'Haussonville', a precursor to a similar piece about the Guermantes. *8 January* He attends Princesse Mathilde's funeral. A few days later he quarrels with Constantin de Brancovan, who has taken the theatre column of *La Renaissance latine* away from him. *18 January* He publishes 'Fête chez Montesquiou à Neuilly', a pastiche of Balzac, in *Le Figaro*. *February* With the help of Marie Nordlinger, he starts work on translating Ruskin's *Sesame and Lilies*, at the same time as his translation of *The Bible of Amiens* is published by *Le Mercure de France*. *March* He makes up his quarrel with Brancovan. *8 April Le Figaro* prints 'Antoine Bibesco', about his play *Le Jaloux*. *23 April* In the *Chronique des arts* he publishes 'Une miniaturiste du second Empire: Madame Herbelin', an obituary of Madeleine Lemaire's aunt. *13 May Le Figaro* runs 'Le Salon de la comtesse Potocka', signed 'Horatio'. He asks Marie Nordlinger to sculpt a bust for his father's tomb. *June* He reads Maeterlinck's *The Double Garden*, which he quotes in *Sésame et les lys* and in his article 'Les Éblouissements'. *1 July* He dines with his friend the Duc de Guiche at the Comtesse de Noailles' house, where he breaks a statuette by Tanagra. *8 August* Marie Nordlinger brings him the medallion bust of his father. *9 August* He sets off on a cruise along the Brittany coast on the yacht *Hélène*, which belongs to Paul Mirabaud, Robert de Billy's father-in-law. On the cruise he goes to Ouistreham, Cherbourg, Guernsey, Saint-Malo and Dinard, and returns to Paris on 15 August. *13 August* The *Chronique des arts* prints a review of *L'Île et l'Empire de Grande-Bretagne: Angleterre, Égypte, Inde* by Robert d'Humières. *16 August Le Figaro* publishes 'La Mort des cathédrales', which he later includes in *Pastiches et Mélanges*. About this date he replies to a survey conducted by the magazine *Les Arts de la vie* on the separation between the fine arts and the State. He still sees a lot of Louisa de Mornand, and comforts her about her romantic troubles. He has various medical tests because of his ill health, and consults numerous doctors until the end of the year. *October* His poor health prevents him from going to his friend d'Albufera's wedding. He complains to Bibesco of being 'very unhappy at the moment, in every way – morally, physically, intellectually'. *14 December* In *Gil Blas* he publishes a critique of *Étude sur Victor Hugo* by Fernand Gregh, signed 'Marc-Antoine'. At the end of the year he writes a letter to Gabriel de La Rochefoucauld in which he mentions his break with 'the mistress I loved the most'.

1905: *5 January* He gives a dinner party in honour of Bertrand de Fénelon. He drafts a preface to *Sésame et les lys* which prefigures *Contre Sainte-Beuve* and *Du Côté de chez Swann*. *1 March, 15 April and 15 May Les Arts de la vie* prints the first part of his translation of Ruskin's lecture 'Kings' Treasuries'. *End of winter* His application to the Cercle de l'Union is turned down. *March* His asthma troubles him, but the 'salons' series continues. *7 May* He publishes 'La Vie à Paris: la comtesse de Guerne', under the name 'Écho', in *Le Figaro*. *8 June* At the Comtesse Jean de Castellane's house he hears the young virtuoso pianist Arthur Rubinstein (1886–1982). At this date he drafts an important note for the preface to *Sésame et les lys* which gives a glimpse of the structure of his future work. *15 June* The preface to his new translation of Ruskin, 'Sur la lecture', is published in *La Renaissance latine*. He goes to an exhibition of the work of the American painter James McNeill Whistler (1834–1903), a friend of Montesquiou's and one of the future models for Elstir. *9 July* He sends his mother to Neuilly to enquire about the health of Montesquiou's secretary, Gabriel d'Yturri, but d'Yturri had died three days earlier. He rereads Homer, and writes about him in his pastiche of Renan. *August* He publishes an analysis of Montesquiou's style, 'Un professeur de beauté', in *Les Arts de la vie*. During this summer he writes a long letter to Bibesco, giving an early indication of the importance he would later place on masturbation. *Early September* He accompanies his mother to Évian, and she falls seriously ill with attacks of uraemia. Madame Catusse puts her on the train back to Paris, where she dies on *26 September*. 'She has taken my life away with her', Proust writes to Madame de Noailles. Her funeral takes place on *28 September*. *30 September* Charles Ephrussi, another of the models for Swann, dies. *9 November* The wedding of Germaine-Jeanne Aron, known as de Faucompré, to the Comte de Rafélis de Saint-Saveur, which Proust later uses for the marriage of Gilberte and Saint-Loup. *Early December* He is admitted to Dr Sollier's sanatorium in Boulogne-Billancourt (a stay he describes in *Le Temps retrouvé*).

1906: He retreats from Paris to try to forget his grief and writes very little. *About 24 January* He leaves the sanatorium and returns to the family home at 45 rue de Courcelles, but doesn't start seeing his friends again until the end of the following month. He is still bedridden and very depressed. *March* A visit from the handsome Illan de Casa-Fuerte. *May* He is very interested in the Gustave Moreau exhibition at the Georges-Petit gallery, but is unable to go. *5 May* The *Chronique des arts* publishes his review of *The Stones of Venice*, translated by Madame Crémieux, a relation of his. The article was also to appear in the *Revue générale de critique et de bibliographie* of 25 July. *12 May* The printing of his translation of *Sesame and Lilies* is complete: he sends out the copies himself. *June* He establishes the daily routine – living at night and sleeping by day – that he would continue all his life. *July* He reads Francis Jammes, whom he finds 'charming', and André Gide, whom he finds 'irritating'. *6 August* After making some fruitless travel plans, he settles into the Hôtel des Réservoirs at Versailles. On a visit back to Paris to see his uncle, Georges-Denis Weil, who is unwell, he feels faint at the Gare Saint-Lazare. *7 August* His uncle dies of uraemia; Proust is too ill to attend the burial. *September* René Péter pays him a visit at Versailles, and Proust suggests to him a play whose theme is later used in 'Confession d'une jeune fille' and the scene with Mademoiselle Vinteuil at Montjouvain. *Early October* He decides to rent his great-uncle Louis Weil's flat at 102 boulevard Haussmann. *5 November* He is distressed to learn that his niece Adrienne has diphtheria. He and René Péter collaborate on a 'little fairy play' which they send to Reynaldo Hahn. With *David Copperfield* he plunges into Dickens for the first time, but he finds the little orphan 'appalling'. *Early December* He sends Reynaldo Hahn a poem, probably a pastiche of *The Tales of Hoffmann*. *27 December* He leaves Versailles and moves into 102 boulevard Haussmann.

1907: He starts once again to write pieces that foreshadow *Contre Sainte-Beuve* and *A la Recherche*; he reads a study of the Italian painter Carpaccio (1460–1525), who later finds a place in his work. *24 January* Henri van Blarenberghe, a relation of Proust's, kills his mother then commits suicide. *1 February* At the request of Gaston Calmette, he publishes 'Sentiments filiaux d'un parricide' in *Le Figaro*, but without the ending, which the sub-editor Cardane considered 'immoral' and which Proust was particularly keen on (he evoked Orestes, Oedipus and Freud). *March* He hires Nicolas Cottin as his valet. His asthma attacks begin again. *9 March* He publishes a review (signed 'M.P.') of *Gainsborough*, by Gabriel Mourey, in the *Chronique des arts*. It contains numerous references to Ruskin. *Mid-March* In only three hours he writes his article on 'Les Éblouissements' by Madame de Noailles, which appears in *Le Figaro* on 15 June. He suppresses one page, and it becomes part of *A l'ombre des jeunes filles en fleurs*. *20 March Le Figaro* publishes his 'Journées de lecture', on the memoirs of the Comtesse de Boigne which had begun to appear under the Émile-Paul imprint; he later reuses numerous passages in *A la Recherche*, such as the telephone scene in *Le Côté de Guermantes*. *April* He supports the candidature to the Cercle de l'Union of Illan de Casa-Fuerte, for whom he feels an 'affection' which is 'growing swiftly and sweetly'. *11 April* The Baron Doazan, one of the models for Charlus, dies. Proust attends the Princesse de Polignac's 'Beatrice d'Este ball' which Reynaldo Hahn has organised; his lasting impressions of it are used in *Le Temps retrouvé*: 'How all the people I know have aged', he writes to Hahn. *Early May* He takes Céline Cottin into his service. *1 July* Félicie Fitau and Ulrich (his secretary-cum-valet) leave his service. That evening Proust gives his first big dinner at the Ritz, to thank Gaston Calmette for publishing his articles. *7 July Le Figaro* runs a piece by Paul Bourget, 'Charles de Spoelberch de Lovenjoul', which inspires in Proust some thoughts on Sainte-Beuve's methods. *23 July* He publishes 'Une grand'mère' in *Le Figaro*, following the death of Robert de Flers' grandmother. *Early August* He leaves for Cabourg, and takes a trip with Lauris to Trouville, passing through Houlgate. He pays a visit to the Guiches in Bénerville, and he and Paul Helleu motor through Bayeux, Caen, Balleroy and Dives. At night, he asks Alfred Agostinelli, the chauffeur, to shine the headlights at the Balleroy rose bushes and at the churches so that he can contemplate them better. *15 August* Following an article in *La Revue des Deux-Mondes* on Tolstoy and Shakespeare, he writes a reply in which he once again talks about Sainte-Beuve. *End of August* He pays a visit to Vuillard, another model for Elstir. *September* At the Straus's house in Trouville he meets Robert Dreyfus, and talks to him about the Eulenbourg affair. He visits Evreux (whose stained-glass windows are an inspiration for those at Combray) and the church at Conches. Before returning to Paris, he spends an evening with the Clermont-Tonnerres in Glisolles. *7 October* He goes to hear the singer Mayol, who is to be found in *A la Recherche*. *19 November Le Figaro* publishes his 'Impressions de route en automobile'. One part reappears in 'Combray', describing the Martinville steeples, and a passage on Wagner is used again in *La Prisonnière*. Alfred Agostinelli, whose death he eerily foresees, is transfigured into 'Sainte Cécile'. *26 December* He writes an obituary (signed 'D') for *Le Figaro* on the death of Gustave de Borda (who was his second in the duel with Jean Lorrain).

1908: He begins an essay entitled 'Contre la méthode de Sainte-Beuve' whose final form is still unclear, and which is not published until 1954 under the title *Contre Sainte-Beuve*. *Early January* He drafts 'Robert et le chevreau, maman part en voyage', which appears in the Bernard de Fallois edition of *Contre Sainte-Beuve* and is transformed into the 'adieux aux aubépines' in *A la Recherche*. *9 January* The start of the Lemoine affair, the subject of future pastiches. Madame Straus gives him five precious small oblong notebooks in which he writes headings for his work in progress. On 2 February he thanks her, confiding: 'I would like to get down to a fairly long task'. *22 January* The literary supplement of *Le Figaro* carries the first series of his pastiches (those on Balzac, the Goncourts, Michelet, Faguet). *Late February* He pays a visit to Helleu, who later sends him a picture, *Automne Versaillais*. *March* In *Le Figaro* of *14 March* he publishes the pastiches of Flaubert and Sainte-Beuve; the one of Renan appears on *21 March* in the same paper. *21 April* He writes to d'Albufera that he is going to 'begin a very important piece of work'. *Early May* He becomes more specific, saying he has 'under way: / a study of nobility / a novel about Paris / an essay on Sainte-Beuve and Flaubert / an essay on Women / an essay on pederasty / (not easy to publish) / a study of stained-glass windows / a study of tombstones / a study of the novel . . .' *Spring* Thanks to the Duc de Guiche, he is made a permanent member of the Polo de Paris. He offers his pastiches to Éditions Calmann-Lévy for publication. *1 July* He renews the lease on his flat. *18 July* He leaves for Cabourg, where his social life continues. In one of his notebooks he lists his novel's chapter titles under the heading 'pages written'. During *August* he meets Gaston Gallimard in Bénerville, and invites him to dinner at the Grand Hôtel in Cabourg with Louisa de Mornand and Robert Gangnat. *September* He goes to a film show in his hotel. He talks to his new friend Marcel Plantevignes about the 'cinematographic Guignol' which gives a 'dismal but magical display'. *8 September* Under the pseudonym 'Marc el Dante' he writes a review for *L'Intransigeant* of Lucien Daudet's first book, *Le Chemin mort. End of September* He settles into the Hôtel des Réservoirs in Versailles. Agostinelli is in his employ. In a letter to Georges de Lauris, who had a bad leg at the time, he alludes to his unhappy love affairs: 'Oh, I've been treated so cruelly and with so little understanding …' *27 October* He confides the problems with his health and his difficulty in getting down to work to Madame Straus: 'In my least bad moments I've started some work (for twenty minutes, on two occasions)'. His financial affairs are worrying him. *Early November* He returns to Paris. *Mid-December* He concentrates on writing his study of Sainte-Beuve, and asks advice from Madame de Noailles and Lauris on the form it should take. He writes a pastiche of Chateaubriand and buries himself in Saint-Simon's *Mémoires*.

1909: The year begins badly. Proust is very ill. He works on the early versions of *A la Recherche*. To help with the work he borrows the seven volumes of Sainte-Beuve's *Port-Royal* from Lauris. *6 March Le Figaro* carries the last of the pastiches which later appear in *Pastiches et Mélanges*: 'L'affaire Lemoine, par Henri de Régnier'. He reads a chapter of Romain Rolland's *Jean-Christophe*, and remarks on its banality in his notebook. *May* He attends one of the performances of the 'Russian season' at Châtelet. *23 May* He asks Lauris if the name Guermantes is still in use. *About 23 June* He writes to Lauris: 'I am so exhausted from starting Sainte-Beuve (I'm working flat out …)', but in fact he was referring more to the essay than to the novel. *Towards the end of June* He finishes the pastiche of Ruskin, 'La Bénédiction du sanglier', but too late for publication in *Le Figaro. July* He tells Comtesse Greffulhe that he has given up writing articles for the time being. He works relentlessly at his novel, worried that it will not please Madame Lemaire who, according to Philip Kolb, began to provide the model for Madame Verdurin. *Mid-August* He talks to Lauris about the walks in the Bois de Boulogne he loves so much (and which he often evokes in *Du Côté de chez Swann*).

In a letter he tells Alfred Vallette that he has offered his novel to Mercure de France: 'I've just finished a book provisionally called "Contre Sainte-Beuve. Souvenir d'une matinée". Despite the title it's a real novel, and an extremely explicit one in parts.' That submission was unsuccessful, but Gaston Calmette offered to publish it in serial form in *Le Figaro*. *15 August* He sets off for Cabourg. In Villers-sur-mer he hears an act of Massenet's *Werther* which he enjoys. *Towards the end of September* He is disturbed by building work at the Grand Hôtel, and leaves Cabourg earlier than planned. *Early October* Very unwell, he has the first part of his novel typed. *Mid-November* He estimates that his work will fill three volumes. He reads the first 200 pages to Reynaldo Hahn, who is encouraging, and to Lauris, who is enthusiastic (he returns *Port-Royal* to him). He wants Lauris to lend him *L'Art religieux de la fin du Moyen Age* by Émile Mâle to help him with descriptions of churches in 'Combray'. *Early December* The first three typed notebooks of 'Le Temps perdu' are delivered to *Le Figaro*.

1910: *Early January* No reply from *Le Figaro*. *13 January* Deeply distressed by the death of Madame Arman de Caillavet, he writes to her son Gaston and to Anatole France, whom he met through her. A few days later he writes to Simone de Caillavet, the daughter of Gaston and Jeanne Pouquet, asking for her photograph for his collection: 'My memory has been ruined by all my medication, and is now so faulty that photographs are especially precious to me ... When I was in love with your mother I did extraordinary things to get hold of a picture of her'. He is still working on 'a long novel' and spends a lot of time with Lionel Hauser organising his affairs. *28 January* The Seine overflows its banks and the floods rise as far as the Gare Saint-Lazare and boulevard Haussmann. 'I might die by drowning yet,' is his joking response. The drying-out processes cause him violent asthma attacks. *13 February* He attends the dress rehearsal of Reynaldo Hahn's *La Fête chez Thérèse* at the Opéra. *March* He tells Robert de Billy of his taste for Anglo-Saxon literature (he has just read *The Well-Beloved* by Thomas Hardy). He is also deeply immersed in *Matter and Memory* by Bergson, which he uses for the passage about sleep in *Sodome et Gomorrhe*. After receiving some critical comments from Beaunier, of *Le Figaro*, to whom he had entrusted the first three notebooks of the novel the previous year, he reworks the beginning of his novel. *18 March* He meets Jean Cocteau for the first time, at a party given by the Strauses. *Early June* He goes to a performance by the Ballets Russes at the Opéra, at which Nijinsky surpasses himself in Fokine's production of *Schéhérazade*. *11 June* He accepts the Comtesse de Greffulhe's invitation to see *Cléopâtre* and *Les Sylphides*. *11 July* At one o'clock in the morning, he collects his manuscript from *Le Figaro*. *17 July* Roadworks in the boulevard Haussmann make him leave suddenly for Cabourg, losing his baggage on the way. *18 August* He writes to Jean-Louis Vaudoyer that he counts on finishing his novel as soon as he is in better health and on seeing it published in the *Grande Revue*. At the Grand Hôtel he sees a lot of the Vicomte d'Alton (whose two daughters become models for Albertine). *21 September* His only article of the year is published in *L'Intransigeant*: 'Autour d'un livre: le prince des cravates', a review of a collection of Lucien Daudet's work. In it he writes about Whistler, Balzac and Cocteau. *End of September* He returns to Paris in a taxi. On the advice of Anna de Noailles, he has the walls of his room lined with cork to keep out noise. *November* He works on 'Un amour de Swann' (for which he looks out a short story he wrote in 1893, 'L'Indifférent'), and on 'Matinée chez la princesse de Guermantes'. In *Le Journal des débats* he reads *A Pair of Blue Eyes* by Thomas Hardy; he later mentions it in *La Prisonnière*. Three characters appear in the notebooks of 1910: Albertine, Elstir and Bergotte.

1911: Badly affected by his asthma, he publishes nothing during this year, but works hard on his novel, which he considers dividing into two parts: 'Le Temps perdu' and 'Le Temps retrouvé'. *10 January* After reading *Barbara* he tells Lucien Daudet: 'I'm completely recovered from Thomas Hardy'. He has a 'théâtrophone' installed in his room (an instrument for transmitting an opera direct from the theatre by means of a telephone). *20 February* Through this device he listens to one act of *Die Meistersinger*, and during the next few days *Pelléas et Mélisande*, 'a delightful revelation', transmitted from the Opéra-Comique. He writes a little pastiche on the subject at the end of the month, and often refers to it later in *A la Recherche*. *During February* Antoine Bibesco gives him a subscription to *Nouvelle Revue Française*, 'Gide's review'; he reads Gide's *Isabelle* without much enthusiasm. His health is no better; in a letter to Lauris he says: 'I can't sleep, I can't eat. I can't work, and there are plenty of other things I can't do either, but that's been the case for a long time now'. *March* He sends Cocteau 50 francs for Verlaine's monument. His friendship with Louis de Robert, who sends him his *Roman du malade*, is rekindled. *21 May* He and Montesquiou go to the Châtelet to see *Martyre de saint Sébastien*, a mystery play by d'Annunzio set to music by Debussy. His report of it to Reynaldo Hahn was: 'I found the play rather tiresome despite some good moments, and the music pleasant enough but very thin'. *11 July* He sets off for Cabourg with Robert Nahmias, whom he has employed as his secretary. Miss Cecilia Hayward continues with the typing of his manuscript, which has reached a 'mad length'. On the cover it is entitled: 'Les intermittences du coeur, le temps perdu, 1er partie'. It is the second version of 'Combray', in which the famous sentence 'Longtemps je me suis couché de bonne heure' appears for the first time. He becomes interested in the little Japanese game mentioned in *Du Côté de chez Swann* for Combray's resurrection in the teacup. *16 September* The army notifies him that he has been removed from its lists. *End of September* He leaves Cabourg. The first of the two volumes he plans is typed. During the year he has also put in many hours of work on 'L'Adoration perpétuelle'. *15 November* His maternal grandmother, Madame Baruch Weil, dies in Beauvais. *5 December* He goes to an exhibition of Chinese painting at Durand-Ruel's, where he meets Georges Rodier, a 'rich dilettante' on whom he bases the character of Legrandin. *End of the year* A 'huge piece of speculation' on the stock exchange results in enormous losses.

1912: *Early January* He entrusts the rest of 'Le Temps perdu' to Miss Hayward for typing. *19 January* Madame Peigné-Crémieux dies. *End of winter* More unfortunate investments lose him 40,000 francs. During the coming year Nahmias is the intermediary through whom he sends his manuscript to Miss Hayward for typing. *21 March Le Figaro* publishes an extract from 'Combray' under the title 'Au seuil du printemps: Épines blanches, épines roses'. Calmette promises he will take the book to Fasquelle. Proust reckons at the time that his book will run to 800 or 900 pages. *End of March* He is considering the publisher Fayard, but sends the manuscript to other publishers. *April* Using Odilon Albaret's taxi, he visits Rueil to see the apple blossom; his impressions are recorded in *Sodome et Gomorrhe*. *24 May* The styles of dress of the Comtesse

Greffulhe and Madame Standish at the Vaudeville theatre give him the inspiration for the Princesse and Duchesse de Guermantes' contrasting styles. *4 June Le Figaro* publishes further extracts from 'Combray', one under the title 'Rayon de soleil sur le balcon'. He gets up to go to an exhibition of Monet's work. *End of June* He spends an evening with Cocteau, who recites 'La Danse de Sophocle' to him. *Early July* He is considering offering his novel to Mercure de France. *7 August* He leaves for Cabourg, where he meets Philippe Soupault, and sees Calmette and Madame Straus in the casino. *3 September Le Figaro* publishes 'L'Église de village'. Two days before his return to Paris he meets up with Madame Straus in Trouville and goes to Honfleur with her. *1 October* He goes to see *Hérodiade*, by Massenet, at the Gaîté-Lyrique. *During October* He considers Nouvelle Revue Française (N.R.F.) for his novel and confides to Madame Straus his impatience with the lack of response from Calmette and Fasquelle. *28 October* On Calmette's advice he sends Fasquelle the typescript of 'Le Temps perdu'. He also allows Louis de Robert to put in a word for him. *Early November* He sends the second typescript of 'Le Temps perdu' to Gallimard, after writing to him three times. From this date appears the title of the second volume – *A l'ombre des jeunes filles en fleurs*; he envisages a third called 'Le Temps retrouvé', the overall title of the work being 'Les Intermittences du coeur'. At the same time he sends an extract of the book to Coupeau for publication in the *Nouvelle Revue Française*, but it is rejected. He also hopes *La Revue de Paris* will publish selected pieces. *About 23 December* Gallimard rejects the book. According to Céleste Albaret, the mansucript, which was sent to Gide through the intermediary of Antoine Bibesco, was never even opened: the package was intact. At this time Gide considered Proust 'a snob, a society amateur'. *24 December* Fasquelle in turn sends back the manuscript (*Le Figaro littéraire* of 8 December 1966 published the report written by Fasquelle's reader, Jacques Madeleine, which led to the rejection of the book). Proust immediately wrote to Louis de Robert, asking him to suggest the book to Ollendorff for publication at their expense.

1913: *Early January* He sends the manuscript to Humblot, the head of Ollendorff. *14 January* He goes to *Le Figaro* to give Calmette an expensive cigarette-case to thank him for his efforts; Calmette doesn't even thank him for the present. *End of January* He spends hours contemplating the Sainte-Anne door of Notre-Dame, with a coat thrown over his nightshirt. *About mid-February* He attempts a series of articles to be published by Fasquelle. Humblot announces his rejection of the book about now: 'I may be narrow-minded, but it is incomprehensible to me that someone can take thirty pages to describe how he tosses and turns in bed before falling asleep.' (Louis de Robert, *Comment débuta Marcel Proust*, p. 13). *About 20 February* Proust asks René Blum, an editor at *Gil Blas*, to ask Bernard Grasset to publish the book at the author's expense. *24 February* Proust tells Grasset that he has sent off the manuscript. *End of winter* He plans a trip to Switzerland and Florence, for a rest. One evening he pays a visit to Count Joachim Clary, who is half-paralysed and half-blind. *11 March* The contract with Grasset is signed. *25 March Le Figaro* prints 'Vacances de Pâques', extracts from what will become *Du Côté de chez Swann* and *Le Côté de Guermantes*. *31 March* The first proofs of *Du Côté de chez Swann* are printed at Mayenne; he corrects them during April. *19 April* He hears Enesco and Goldschmidt playing César Franck's sonata for piano and violin, and it becomes the inspiration for the sonata by Vinteuil (a character he has just created). *End of April* He loses a great deal of money on his financial speculations. *Sets of proofs* 1st set: Proust sends back corrected to Grasset in mid-May, and writes to Jean Louis Vaudoyer: 'There isn't one line in twenty left intact from the original text (which has itself been replaced by another).' 2nd set, dated 30 May to 1 September; 3rd set, dated 31 July to 28 August; 4th and 5th, dated 13 to 27 October. *15 May* At a performance given by the Ballets Russes at the Champs-Élysées theatre he notices Madame Scheikévitch, who makes him think of a 'stabbed dove'. For a while he considers giving the title 'Colombes poignardées' to the last part of his novel. *17 May* He watches *L'Après-midi d'un faune* danced by Nijinsky, and afterwards dines with him and Maurice Rostand. *22 May* He meets the Comtesse Anna de Noailles and Jacques Coupeau at the première of *Boris Godunov* at the Champs-Élysées. *29 May* After the première of *Le Sacre du printemps* he has supper at Larue's with Stravinsky and Cocteau. *30 May* Alfred Agostinelli, his former chauffeur, has lost his job and asks Proust to employ him. Proust installs him and his mistress Anna in the flat and entrusts the rest of the typing to him. In spring he writes a review of *La Colline inspirée* by Maurice Barrès and sends it to Adrien Hébrard, the editor of *Le Temps*, but it is not published. *26 July* He leaves for Cabourg with Agostinelli at short notice. *4 August* Equally suddenly, he returns to Paris after a trip to Houlgate, following a crisis in their love affair (the same crisis appears at the end of *Sodome et Gomorrhe* between the narrator and Albertine). *Towards the end of August* He submits to Lucien Daudet the proofs of *Du Côté de chez Swann*, which he has already sent to Louis de Robert. *Early September* Much weakened by illness, he claims to have lost 30 kilos in weight. His money troubles persist, and in October he is forced to sell shares in order to pay his quarter's rent. *Early November* He promises to extract a short story from his novel for *Gil Blas*. *8 November* Two chapters – 'Autour de Madame Swann' and 'Noms de pays: le pays' – have to be cut from *Du Côté de chez Swann*. *13 November* *Le Temps* publishes an interview with him by Élie-Joseph Bois, a large part of which he has written himself. *14 November* *Du Côté de chez Swann* appears in the bookshops, and Proust does his utmost to get newspaper coverage for publicity. *16 November* Robert Dreyfus writes a short piece for *Le Figaro*. *18 November* *Gil Blas*, which announced 'A Novel by Marcel Proust' on the 9th of the month, publishes an extract called 'Une soirée de musique'. On *21 November, Le Temps*, and *Les Annales*, on *23 November*, both bring out an extract from *Swann* about Gilberte. *23 November* Cocteau contributes an article to *Excelsior*, and Lucien Daudet does the same for *Le Figaro* of *27 November*. Since Céline Cottin is undergoing surgery, performed by Proust's brother at the Broca hospital, Proust starts using Céleste Albaret to deliver copies of the book. *1 December* Agostinelli, who has been taking flying lessons at Buc, not far from Paris, leaves for Antibes to perfect his technique. Proust sends Nahmias to Nice to bribe Agostinelli's family to persuade him to come back, but Nahmias returns to Paris alone. *9 December* Paul Souday writes a 'hateful' piece in *Le Temps*, to which Proust replies with a personal letter. *21 December Le Miroir* runs an interview with Proust by André Arnyvelde and gives the warmest acclaim to 'the resounding appearance of this new novel'.

1914: *1 January* Dissatisfied with the reviews of *Du Côté de chez Swann* and hurt by Agostinelli's departure, Proust writes to Jacques Copeau: 'I'm so unhappy and so ill that I can't get out of bed'. The *Nouvelle Revue*

Française, to which he is so attached, prints an ironic piece on *Du Côté de chez Swann* by Henri Ghéon. Proust reacts in a point-by-point reply the next day. *11 January* Gide writes a letter of support: 'The rejection of this book will prove to be N.R.F.'s gravest mistake,' and a eulogistic correspondence with Jacques Rivière follows soon afterwards. *End of January* Using Maurice Rostand as an intermediary, Fasquelle declares that he is prepared to publish the rest of *A la Recherche*. *20 March* N.R.F. informs him, through Gide, that it is ready to do the same. This provokes long discussions between Proust and Grasset, who agrees to free Proust from his contract. *Early April* Proust is still with Grasset, but sends parts of his book to N.R.F. *About 14 April* He is introduced to Jacques de Lacretelle, who questions him about the sources for his novel. *15 April* Jacques-Émile Blanche writes a review praising *Du Côté de chez Swann* in *L'Écho de Paris*. Proust, very pleased, writes news snippets about this for *Le Figaro* and *Gil Blas* on *18 April*, and *Le Journal des débats* on *24 April*. *May* Fearing financial difficulties after more unsuccessful investments, he offers Robert de Flers a regular column in *Le Figaro*. He takes his new friend, Comte Hubert de Ganay, to the Opéra to see the Ballets Russes. *30 May* Alfred Agostinelli, who had enrolled in the brothers Garbero's flying school near Antibes, crashes into the sea and drowns. *7 June* Agostinelli's body is found by fishermen. Proust suffers intense grief. *During the first six months of the year* Proust has continued work on *Sodome et Gomorrhe* and on what will become *La Fugitive*. He has also spent time on a quartet by Vinteuil which will become the septet in *La Prisonnière*. *6 June* The first proofs of the rest of his novel begin to arrive, but he feels unable to correct them. *1 June and 1 July* Nouvelle Revue Française prints extracts from *Le Côté de Guermantes* which in fact belong in *A l'ombre des jeunes filles en fleurs*, but the war interrupts its publication. *2 August* He drives to the Gare de l'Est with his brother Robert, who has been called up to serve in Verdun as a military doctor. Since Odilon Albaret and Nicolas Cottin have also been conscripted, he asks Céleste to move in with him. She will never leave. Proust is exempted from military service because of ill health, and stays in Paris. *Early September* In a letter he mentions a walk in the moonlight which he later describes in *Le Temps retrouvé*. *3 September* He and Céleste leave for Cabourg accompanied by his new Swedish valet, Ernst Forssgren. This turns out to be his last visit. Whilst there he experiences 'the first stage of detachment from his misery'. At the Grand Hôtel he distributes playing cards to wounded soldiers. He goes on working at his notebooks. *About 13 October* He returns to Paris, having run out of money. Ernst then departs, and Proust begins in earnest his life as a recluse, by having his telephone disconnected. *November* Frightened of being called up, he asks several doctors for medical certificates. He tries to find a job for Alfred Agostinelli's brother. *17 December* Bertrand de Fénelon is killed at the front (official notification arrives in March 1915). *31 December* Proust refers to 'this appalling year' in a letter to Madame Catusse.

1915: *14 January* Gaston de Caillavet dies. Proust writes to his wife: 'The dead are still alive, for me. And for me, this is equally true of those I loved and those who were my friends. I can't explain it in a letter. When the whole of my "Swann" comes out, if you read it, you'll understand what I mean.' His work on the novel continues. The edition of *Le Côté de Guermantes* is cancelled (Grasset is at the front); the volume eventually supplies parts of *Sodome et Gomorrhe, La Prisonnière* and *La Fugitive*. *January* He goes to a party at Misia Edwards's. *March* Talking to Lucien Daudet about the war, he says: 'It's true that the word Boche doesn't feature in my vocabulary and that things don't seem as clear-cut to me as they do to some people'. He had already discussed the subject in a letter to Daudet of 1 November 1914: 'If instead of being at war with Germany we were at war with Russia, what would people be saying about Tolstoy and Dostoyevsky?' *15 March* The official announcement of Fénelon's death appears in *Le Figaro. 13 May* Robert d'Humières is killed at the front. *Spring* Proust immerses himself in the *Journal des Goncourt*, of which he writes a pastiche in *Le Temps retrouvé. June* He sends Lucien Daudet a letter with an early version of pages which appear in *La Fugitive*. Always very sensitive to new movements in the arts, he enthuses about *Le Mot*, a journal produced by Jean Cocteau and Paul Iribe and illustrated by artists like Léon Bakst and Raoul Dufy. He sends Léon Daudet a letter containing lines from a pastiche of Wagner that he must already have written, but which has never been traced. At this time his judgement of the literature produced by the war is harsh: 'I've received a volume by Léon Daudet called "Hors du sang allemand" and another by Montesquiou called "Les Offrandes blessées" (188 elegies about the war). He must have started writing them on the first day of the call-up. What fertile minds! I hope I'll be allowed simply to admire their efforts, without copying them,' he wrote to Madame Anatole Catusse. *July* He confides to Montesquiou: 'I'm saving what little strength I have left for the work I'm about to finish, God willing'. *September* After consultations with a number of senior doctors his conscription is again deferred for six months. *November* The essential elements of *Sodome et Gomorrhe*, *La Prisonnière* and *La Fugitive* are already complete, as is shown by the dedication to Madame Scheikévitch written in a copy of *Du Côté de chez Swann*, which contains the story of Albertine in outline. At the end of this year Proust feels more alone than ever. He writes to Antoine Bibesco: 'These very sad days remind us that the years roll round, bringing us all the beauties of nature once again, but without bringing back the people. In 1916 there will be violets, and apple blossom, but there will be no Bertrand de Fénelon.'

1916: Proust changes his publisher. *24 February* After he writes to Gide, 'to make peace', Gide comes to see him and asks him to let *A la Recherche* appear in N.R.F., as the committee later asks him on 14 April. *Spring* He goes to Versailles to hear Reynaldo Hahn's new opera. In a letter he tells Lucien Daudet that he is rereading Tallemant des Réaux, whom he quotes in *La Prisonnière*, and plans to reread *The Thousand and One Nights*, to which he alludes in the nocturnal walks in *Le Temps retrouvé*. At about this time he returns home from a visit to Francis Jammes on foot, at night, through a bombardment. He puts the finishing touches to *Le Temps retrouvé* (he probably made five or six visits to the rue de l'Arcade, to a brothel set up by Albert Le Cuziat in 1915 or 1916, and made use of several esoteric details in describing Jupien's brothel). Simultaneously, he reworks his notebooks, adding details; he writes to Maria de Madrazo, Reynaldo Hahn's sister and the couturier Fortuny's aunt, to perfect the description of the Duchesse de Guermantes' and Albertine's clothes: 'Do you know whether Fortuny has ever used as a motif for his dressing gowns those mating birds drinking from a vase which are so common in St Mark's, on the Byzantine capitals?' René Blum is to become the intermediary for the break with Grasset. *27 May* Walter Berry sends him a book dating from 1709 bound with the coat of arms of Paulin Prondre de Guermantes, which he has just found in Belin's bookshop. *31 May* Proust claims to be 'bankrupt' and to have seen no money from *Du Côté de chez Swann*, despite five editions, since April 1914. *June* He goes to stay with Jacques-Émile Blanche in Auteuil to work on the proofs of 'Cahiers d'un artiste'. He talks until the small hours about the 'architectural structure' of his novel. *July* René Blum discovers Grasset, who was previously untraceable, in a clinic in Neuchâtel. Proust justifies his stubbornness: 'In everything to do with my book I am as provident as a bee, even planning beyond my death, which is probably none too distant.' *29 August* After lengthy negotiations, Grasset replies to Proust personally: 'Naturally I wouldn't want to sever my links with an author of whom I think so highly without expressing my regret, and there was certainly no reason for you to take offence about that, but I don't want to add to your worries and your troubles by any action of mine. And, whatever it costs me to do this, I renounce my option to publish the second part of "A la recherche du temps perdu".' Proust is now free to be published by Gallimard. He pays a visit to the Comtesse de Chevigné and to Jean Cocteau at 10 rue d'Anjou, and undertakes a long friendly correspondence with Paul Morand, whom he saw again in the spring at Bardac's. *August* At dinner at Larue's he catches a glimpse of Saint-Saëns and Tristan Bernard. *September* He visits the house of Madame de la Béraudière, the mistress of the old Comte Greffulhe (models for Odette and the Duc de Guermantes). *November* He invites to his flat the Poulet quartet, who play him some César Franck. At the end of the year he goes to see the Princesse Lucien Murat, whom he admires. During this year Nicolas Cottin has died of pleurisy at the front. With 1916 ends an important period which sees the editing of the manuscript which runs from *Sodome et Gomorrhe* to *Le Temps retrouvé*.

1917: There are very few documents, apart from several letters, to enable us to follow Proust's life during 1917. He works mainly on *Le Temps retrouvé*, fired by the events of the war. He begins the year by thanking Paul Morand for his good wishes: 'In doing me the "honour" of sending me a line you have added some "sweetness" to this sorry 1 January' (Paul Morand, *Le Visiteur du soir*, p. 40). He also writes to Lucien Daudet, to whom he describes himself, at the beginning of the year, as 'some strange character out of Wells' who 'hasn't slept for fifty hours'. He leads a more social life, as if his work, now almost complete, preoccupies him less, needing only some supplementary information. *January* He visits the Rothschilds, where he is 'recognised by the old butler as if by Eurydice' (Morand, p. 41). Morand comes to see him often, bringing news of the war and of diplomatic activity; Proust talks to Morand about his work and his life. He makes friends with the Princesse Soutzo, who later marries Morand. *4 March* He dines with her at Larue's, and studies 'the princess's ermine muff like an entomologist absorbed by the veins on a firefly's wing' (Morand, *Journal d'un attaché d'ambassade*, pp. 185–6). That evening he searches unsuccessfully for the Poulet quartet to play some Franck for his friends. After this he regularly dines several times a week at the Ritz, where the Princesse Soutzo has a suite. *30 March* To Morand he expresses his fears for Laon cathedral, and it may be at this time that he sets Combray and Tansonville close to that town. *All spring* The young Emmanuel Berl, like Proust a relation by marriage of Bergson's, visits Proust. *12 April* His last meeting with Emmanuel Bibesco, whose face is deformed by paralysis, takes place in a coach. *22 April* At the Ritz he dines with Morand, the Princesse Soutzo and Madame de Chevigné, who shows her jealousy of the princess's special relationship with Proust. He writes her a harsh letter: 'When someone you have loved seems stupid ... ' *May* He writes a piece on Dostoyevsky which is to be found in *La Prisonnière*. *27 July* From a balcony at the Ritz he watches the great air raid on Paris. He describes it to Madame Straus: 'I went out on to the balcony and stayed more than an hour watching this wonderful apocalypse, in which the aeroplanes going up and down made and unmade different constellations'. This scene also features in *Le Temps retrouvé*. *22 August* Emmanuel Bibesco commits suicide in London. About this time Proust lies inert, without displaying any sign of life, for two days. He may have been experimenting with veronal, to see how far he could go. *13 October* Morand is appointed secretary to the Rome embassy. The proofs of *A l'ombre des jeunes filles en fleurs* begin to arrive from N.R.F.'s printers, La Semeuse, at Étampes. But the typographers are called to the front. *November* Louis de Talleyrand-Périgord marries a rich widow, Cecilia Blumenthal; this wedding inspires that of the Prince de Guermantes and Madame Verdurin. *Mid-November* Robert Proust leaves for the Italian front, which is very dangerous. Montesquiou starts writing his autobiography, having decided to spare no one. Proust, who has mislaid his certificate of exemption from military service, is afraid every night that he will be arrested as a deserter. To pay the interest on a loan taken out in 1911, he asks his friends to sell some valuable furniture and two fine carpets. *24 December* He and Jacques de Lacretelle are among the guests at a supper following midnight mass given by Princesse Marie Murat in honour of the Infanta of Spain. *Night of 31 December – 1 January* He takes two young American soldiers 'à la recherche de l'hôtel Bedford', as he writes to Walter Berry. This long night-time walk features in *A la Recherche*. In 1917, Céleste seems to have burnt 32 'black notebooks' in the kitchen furnace. According to Henri Bonnet they were probably rough drafts for volume 1, 'Le Temps perdu', which he had offered to Fasquelle.

1918: Proust and Walter Berry exchange New Year wishes for 'peace with victory'. At the same time he confides his feelings about the war to the Princesse Soutzo: 'For me the war is not so much an object (in the philosophical sense of the word) as a substance which interposes itself between me and other objects. I see in war what one used to love in God ... As for the guns and the German aircraft, I promise you I've never given them a moment's thought; I am afraid of much less dangerous things – mice, for instance'. *30 January* Leaving a party at the Duc de La Rochefoucauld's, he walks casually about in the midst of a German air raid, which he describes in *Le Temps retrouvé*. *Early in the year* He takes on a new secretary, a young Swiss named Henri Rochat, a former employee at the Ritz, who stays with him for two years. *3 February* His first meeting with François Mauriac at a reception in honour of Francis Jammes. At this time he sees a lot of the Abbé Mugnier, the confessor of the Faubourg Saint-Germain, with whom he exchanges a long mystical correspondence. *Early April* New symptoms give him premonitions of death – a sort of facial paralysis and some difficulties with speech lead him to consult Dr Babinski and ask him to perform a trepanation. The doctor refuses, and Proust later uses this situation in *Le Temps retrouvé* to emphasise the narrator's sense of urgency about writing. *10 April* Jacques-Émile Blanche, his childhood friend, offers to dedicate to Proust the first volume of his *Propos de peintre, de David à Degas*; in exchange, Proust is to write a preface. He agrees, and sets about the task in May, borrowing elements from the *Contre Sainte-Beuve* notebooks. *Mid-April* After a four-month interval, he receives the rest of the proofs of *A l'ombre des jeunes filles en fleurs*. He then has five volumes of *A la Recherche*. The process of making corrections continues into the autumn. Gallimard passes through Paris in *June*, on his way back from America. He visits Proust and suggests that he goes back to the project that finally becomes *Pastiches et Mélanges*. Gallimard also negotiates to buy back *Du Côté de chez Swann* from Grasset 'for a fairly steep price'. However, Grasset claims compensation for the copyright Proust demands. *20 April* Proust writes Jacques de Lacretelle a long letter on a copy of *Du Côté de chez Swann*: 'There are no originals on which the characters in this book are based, or rather there are six or seven for each . . . There is no doubt that reality reproduces itself by division as well as by amalgamation'. *18 July* In a long letter to Grasset, Proust expresses his indignation about the publisher's behaviour; he also mentions his plan to collect in one volume his pastiches of the Lemoine affair and a selection of articles and prefaces published between 1900 and 1908. Since he kept no copies, he asks Robert Dreyfus, who has gone back to his job as editor of *Le Figaro*, and Lucien Daudet for the originals. This letter mentions the chapter about the war in *Le Temps retrouvé* which he completed at the beginning of the year. Although Madame Straus goes to Trouville, Proust stays in Paris rather than going to Cabourg, and dines often at the Ritz. There he is introduced to Madame Ritz, and to the Princesse Soutzo's brother, 'a young oriental prince amid all the beauties of the Thousand and One Nights'. His social circle becomes wider. He often sees the Comtesse de Pourtalès, now remarried to the Comte Rehbinder, the Comtesse Jean de Lubersac, Mademoiselle Thérèse d'Hinnisdal and the Duchesse de Clermont-Tonnerre, who later writes two essays on Proust. *September* His brother Robert, who has had a serious car accident at the front, comes back to Paris to convalesce. They see each other every day. On the advice of Henri Bardac, Proust goes to consult Madame de Thèbes, a famous clairvoyant, whom Saint-Loup talks about in *Le Côté de Guermantes*. On the coming of the 'miraculous, dizzying peace', as he calls it, he sends a long, prophetic letter to Madame Straus: 'The kind of peace I like best is the kind that leaves no rancour in anyone's heart. But since this peace is not like that, and since its legacy will be a desire for vengeance, it might be best if that revenge were made impossible.' He tries again to sell some of his furniture, using the Strauses and Walter Berry as intermediaries. *30 November* La Semeuse finishes printing *A l'ombre des jeunes filles en fleur* in one volume. *December* Proust envisages six volumes in all, as he plans a 'Sodome et Gomorrhe III'. He also receives the first six galley proofs of *Le Côté de Guermantes*. But Gallimard changes the printer, choosing Louis Bellenand at Fontenay-aux-Roses. *Pastiches et Mélanges* is sent to the printer straight away. Proust is still keeping back the pastiche of Saint-Simon, unfinished and greatly added to since the 1904 version. He worked hard on it during the summer, and added the theme of the nobility of Empire with the Murats. These new friends feature in it as part of a vast satire on Parisian society towards the end of 1918.

1919: *Mid-January* Proust has to move, because his aunt Weil has sold the building at 102 boulevard Haussmann to the Varin-Bernier bank, who are to start alterations in February. Thanks to Armand de Guiche, he receives substantial compensation from the bank, and sells some of his furniture; then he asks his friends to find him a new apartment. *Early March* In a state of anxiety, he again experiences trouble with his speech related to his asthma. At about this time Montesquiou pays him a two-hour call in the middle of the night, his last visit. *March* Jacques-Émile Blanche's *Propos de peintre* appears, with a preface by Proust: a sort of farewell to painting: 'I will certainly never again in my life have the chance to talk about painters.' *25 April* Despite Gallimard's promise to publish his three books at the beginning of May, Proust agrees to delay the publication until early June to allow Jacques Rivière, who has recently returned from imprisonment in Germany, the chance to bring out an extract from *A l'ombre des jeunes filles en fleurs* in the *Nouvelle Revue Française* of 1 June. His is the leading piece in the first issue of this new series, reappearing after a five-year break. He also asks Rivière to indicate that 'the other volumes of "A la Recherche du temps perdu" ("Le Côté de Guermantes", "Sodome et Gomorrhe" and "Le Temps retrouvé") will appear only a few months later.' Until the end of his life he continues to believe in the possibility of publishing his works simultaneously at short notice. *May* He gives Gallimard a stinging defence of his author's corrections: 'When you asked me to leave Grasset to come to you, you were aware of this, because you were present when Copeau saw the alterations on Grasset's proofs and cried, "This is a completely new book!" ... Since you are good enough to find in my books something special, which you like, bear in mind that this is due precisely to the rich nutrition I infuse into them by a lively sense of what is materially added by the changes I make.' He searches for a new apartment, but also dreams of going to Perugia, Sienna or Pisa, of renting Madame Catusse's villa in Nice or of going to stay in London with Antoine Bibesco, who married Elizabeth Asquith on 30 April. *30 May* The day before his lease expires he moves to 8 bis, rue Laurent-Pichat, to the fourth floor of the town house owned by the actress Réjane. Jacques Porel, Réjane's son, through whom this transaction took place, later becomes one of Proust's intimate friends. *1 June Nouvelle Revue Française* publishes extracts from *A l'ombre des jeunes filles en fleurs*, while Proust corrects the proofs of *Le Côté de Guermantes*. *27 June Pastiches et Mélanges* (which was printed by 23 March), the new edition of *Du Côté de chez Swann* (printed by 14 June) and *A l'ombre des jeunes filles en fleurs*, which had waited since 30 November, appear simultaneously in the bookshops. The publication does not meet with immediate success. Proust lets his novel find its own way, without asking friends to review it. *1 July Nouvelle Revue Française* prints extracts from *Le Côté de Guermantes*. *7 July* Using the pseudonym 'Bartolo', Robert Dreyfus writes on *A l'ombre des jeunes filles en fleurs* in *Le Figaro*. The literary supplement of *Le Figaro* prints 'Pour un parti de l'intelligence', a nationalist manifesto echoing the views of Action française, signed by some of Proust's friends, such as Halévy and Vaudoyer. Proust indicates to Jacques Rivière his disagreement on the subject of France as an upholder of civilised values, and shows his literary determinism. *15 August* He considers going to Cabourg, but decides to give it up for good. *During the summer* He sees Boni de Castellane (one of the models for Saint-Loup), who is now bankrupt. *September* He tells Louis de Robert that he is putting himself in for the Prix Goncourt. *1 October* He moves 'temporarily' to a furnished apartment on the fifth floor of a building near Madame Standish, 44 rue Hamelin. It proves to be his last home. *10 December* Léon Daudet tells him he has won the Prix Goncourt by six votes to four over Dorgelès's *Croix de bois*. This honour proves exhausting as it entails increased correspondence and numerous social functions. The 5000-franc prize money quickly disappears on 'thank-you dinners'. To Paul Souday he writes: 'This prize has dragged me down a little, but if it makes people read me I prefer it to any other honour!' and to Jacques-Émile Blanche: 'The day before the prize (I had no idea when it would be announced) I found out from a "cutting" that someone had written that I didn't deserve to win because I was 47 years old. The next day I was unworthy of it because I was 50. Now they've got up to 58, so I'm resigned to becoming a centenarian very soon ... According to some I won the prize because I was brought up at Stanislas with Léon Daudet – in fact I've never been to Stanislas and I met Léon Daudet when he had already left his first wife. According to others, Daudet and Élémir Bourges (whom I've never met) wanted to reward my anti-Dreyfus position. In fact I was the most ardent supporter of Dreyfus ...'

1920: *1 January* In the *Nouvelle Revue Française* he publishes 'A propos du "style" de Flaubert', a critical essay written in 1909 which he mentioned to Antoine Bibesco in 1913. *20 January* When questioned by the journalist Louis Handler from *Comœdia* about his 'Hommage à Madame Réjane, Chevalier de la Légion d'honneur', he criticises a submissive attitude towards public taste: 'How relaxing it would be to think less about the public, and not to feel oneself obliged alternately to produce operas that last three days, and, as soon as fashions change, others whose length must not exceed ten minutes.' *22 February* Jacques Rivière suggests an article on Sainte-Beuve to appear in April's *Nouvelle Revue Française* but Proust, feeling short of time, declines the idea. Tired and suffering from insomnia, he falls behind with correcting the proofs of *Le Côté de Guermantes*. He plays draughts with Henri Rochat, as the narrator does with Albertine in *La Prisonnière*. *February* N.R.F. employs the poet André Breton (1896–1966) to correct the proofs of *Le Côté de Guermantes*, but he doesn't concentrate on the job. *28 February* Proust replies to questions put by *L'Opinion* in 'Une tribune français au Louvre?': 'I am not, in principle, a great believer in Art trying to suit itself to the convenience of the art-lover, rather than insisting that the art-lover goes to it'. *March* He writes an article called 'Un esprit et un génie innombrables: Léon Daudet' on the publication of the fifth volume of Daudet's memoirs. *19 March* Comte Pierre de Polignac marries the Duchesse de Valentinois, the adopted daughter of the Prince of Monaco. (In *Le Côté de Guermantes* he becomes the inglorious Comte de Nassau, heir to the

Grand Duke of Luxembourg.) *End of March* Because of the delay in the proof corrections of *Le Côté de Guermantes*, Gallimard requests Rivière to ask Proust to let them publish the first half separately. Proust agrees, but feels forced to alter the book: 'I have turned the content of this volume completely upside down. There were situations I set up which would have been resolved in other volumes that came out at the same time but which will make no sense when the first part of "Côté de Guermantes" is published alone.' *Early April* The de luxe edition of *A l'ombre des jeunes filles en fleurs* is published. Despite the high cover price, Walter Berry buys three and the Princesse Soutzo one. *4 May* Proust goes to see the Ballets Russes at the Opéra, where he catches sight of the old Comte d'Haussonville, who serves as a model for the Duc de Guermantes at the end of *A la Recherche*. *About 23 May* He returns the final proofs of the first part of *Le Côté de Guermantes*. *14 June* He attends the dress rehearsal of Gide's translation of *Antony and Cleopatra*. At the interval he hears the news of Réjane's death, and rushes to her house in the rue Laurent-Pichat. *16 June* He writes to Porel: 'At the moment these words will mean nothing to you, as they are perhaps inconsistent with painful thoughts. But you will find them true and sweet and strengthening when the process of tearing yourself away from your memories is complete, a process whose appalling twists and turns, alas, no one can spare you.' He suggests writing a homage to Réjane in the *Nouvelle Revue Française* but cannot find the strength. *Summer* He is invited to Monaco by the Duc de Valentinois and considers accepting, but decides against it. *3 August L'Intransigeant* prints his reply to 'Une petite enquête: Si vous deviez avoir un métier manuel': 'You make a distinction between manual and spiritual occupations which I cannot endorse. The mind guides the hand . . . the manual occupation I would choose would be precisely that which I exercise at present: that of writer.' *28 August L'Intransigeant* prints his reply to a 'Petite Enquête des Treize' on reading-rooms: 'People who have very little money, and people who have a lot, are both prevented from buying books, the former through poverty and the latter through avarice. So they borrow them . . . if people have to hire books, perhaps they will end up buying some, if not reading them.' *25 September* He is made Chevalier de la Légion d'honneur on the same day as Comtesse Anna de Noailles and Colette. He receives the diamond-studded cross, awarded by the painter Jean Béraud, from the hands of his brother

Robert. *30 September* He is a member of the Comité Blumenthal and has the prize awarded to his friend Jacques Rivière. *About 21 October Le Côté de Guermantes 1* (which was printed by 17 August) is published. Proust writes the preface to a book of comic drawings, *Au royaume du bistouri*, by Rita de Maugny, the wife of one of the friends of his youth. He evokes delightful memories of the shores of Lake Geneva with Clément de Maugny; he also describes 'a nice little railway' from Geneva to Évian which is reminiscent of the Balbec railway in *Sodome et Gomorrhe. 15 November* In *La Revue de Paris* he publishes 'Pour un ami: remarques sur le style' which, in 1921, becomes the preface to *Tendres Stocks* by Paul Morand. (At the beginning of the year Morand himself published a collection of free verse called *Lampes à arc*, which contained a malicious ode 'To Marcel Proust'.) In the piece Proust writes of his new obsession, death: 'A stranger has taken up residence in my brain,' a sentence which echoes 'This sense of death settled inside me once and for all, as love does,' at the end of *A la Recherche. End of the year* He suffers from otitis; Dr Wicart cures him. During this year he has consulted an oculist and acquired a pair of glasses.

1921: *1 January Nouvelle Revue Française* publishes 'Une agonie', an extract about his grandmother's death. *8 January La Renaissance politique, littéraire, artistique* publishes an 'Enquête sur le romantisme et le classic- isme'. Proust makes his reply in a letter to Henriot: 'I believe that all true art is classical, but the dictates of the soul rarely allow it to be recognised as such when it appears. In this, art is just like life.' *January* The second volume of Jacques-Émile Blanche's *Propos de peintre, Dates*, appears in the bookshops. A long dedication mentions the similarity between Montesquiou and Charlus. In it Blanche prophesies that Proust will be made a member of the Académie Française, a wish Proust himself expressed to Rivière in May 1920. He speaks of it again in June to Barrès. *11 January* He writes to Gallimard about the publication of *Le Côté de Guermantes II* and *Sodome et Gomorrhe I*, in two volumes. After that he is thinking of *Sodome II, Sodome III, Sodome IV*, and *Le Temps retrouvé*, four long volumes to follow each other at fairly lengthy intervals. For the first time he has given up the idea of simultaneous publication which was always so dear to his heart. *20 January* He sends off the manuscript of *Sodome I. 1 February Nouvelle Revue Française* prints 'Un baiser', the story of Albertine's first visit. *26 February La Revue hebdomadaire* publishes 'Une soirée de brouillard', describing Saint-Loup's dinner with the narrator. *March Tendres Stocks* by Paul Morand is published by N.R.F. with a preface by Proust. *2 May Le Côté de Guermantes* II and *Sodome et Gomorrhe* appear in a single volume (of which the printing was completed on 30 April). *13 and 14 May* André Gide comes to see him in Odilon Albaret's taxi. *About 24 May* In the morning he and Jean Louis Vaudoyer go to see the exhibition of Dutch painting at the Jeu de Paume. He feels unwell as he is going to look at Vermeer's *View of Delft* – an incident which later provides the inspiration for Bergotte's death. D'Albufera, who recognises himself in the character of Saint-Loup, in his relationship with Rachel, breaks off his friendship with Proust. The Duchesse de Chevigné, who is unflatteringly reflected in the Duchesse de Guermantes, also quarrels with him. He replies to Robert de Fitz-James: 'By making her a powerful vulture I at least prevented people from thinking she was an old magpie.' Cocteau consoles him by saying: 'Fabre wrote a book about insects, but he didn't ask the insects to read it.' *1 June Nouvelle Revue Française* publishes 'A propos de Baudelaire', a critical study which stands out because of its novelty, although it takes certain elements from *Contre Sainte-Beuve*. Rivière asks him to write an article on Dostoyevsky, but Proust prefers to reserve his analysis of that writer for *La Prisonnière*. *4 June* His secretary Henri Rochat leaves to go to Argentina, where he has found a job in a bank. *16 June* Proust dines with Madame Hennessy, who is celebrating the Duke of Marlborough's engagement to an American, Miss Gladys Deacon, a keen reader of Proust's work. Proust is too ill to take up the ensuing invitation to Blenheim. *Autumn* As always, his health is poor. *September* He has a fall in his bedroom: symptoms of uraemia begin to appear. *Early October* Through a pharmacist's error, he accidentally overdoses himself with veronal by taking seven tablets of a gramme each (instead of tablets containing a tenth of a gramme). *1 October Nouvelle Revue Française* prints 'Les Intermittences du coeur'. Montesquiou sends him his latest book, *Élus et Appelés*, with the dedication 'To Marcel Proust, an author I believe justly valued, a friend I believe well loved'. *November Les Oeuvres libres* bring out 'Jalousie', the story of the narrator's tormented love for Albertine. Proust sends Gallimard the manuscript of *Sodome et Gomorrhe* II, which he envisages as two volumes; in fact it becomes three (he starts work on *Sodome et Gomorrhe III* immediately). Pleased with the ending, he confides to his publisher that it is the thing he has 'written best (Albertine's death; the forgetting)'. He pays a visit to Miss Barney, but the meeting is not a success. *1 December Nouvelle Revue Française* prints 'En tram jusqu'à La Raspelière'. *11 December* Montesquiou dies in Menton, alone and forgotten. Proust ends the year at the Beaumonts' ball.

1922: *15 January* He attends the Ritz ball with Mademoiselle d'Hinnisdal and Paul Morand, and meets the famous Polish harpsichordist Wanda Landowska (1879–1959). *7 February* At the Princesse Soutzo's he meets Maurice Martin du Gard, then director of *Écrits nouveaux*, who later describes him in *Les Mémorables*. *26 February* In reply to questions in *Annales politiques et littéraires*, 'Voyage en zigzags dans la République des lettres', he talks about the 'novel of adventure' and the 'analytical novel', which he prefers to call the 'introspective novel'. Yvonne Albaret, Céleste's niece, moves in to the rue Hamelin to type *Sodome et Gomorrhe III*, later called *La Prisonnière*. Three typed drafts are needed because of the continual corrections. *March* He writes a long letter to Philippe Berthelot, general secretary at the Quai d'Orsay, and is given a 'non-executive' role for ten years. He also begins a brilliant correspondence with the German critic Ernst-Robert Curtius, who is one of the first to make a penetrating critique of his work. *Early spring A la Recherche* is finished. He calls Céleste: 'Great news: tonight I wrote the words "The End".... Now I can die' (Céleste Albaret, *Monsieur Proust*, p. 403). *2 May* Publication of *Sodome et Gomorrhe II* (the printing was complete by 3 April). That day, keen to meet the Schiffs, an English couple who were patrons of the arts, he takes an overstrong dose of adrenalin and burns his stomach. *18 May* After the première of Stravinsky's *Renard* he attends a supper at the Ritz given by his English friends in honour of Diaghilev, Picasso, Stravinsky, Joyce and himself. *12 June* During an evening at Madame Hennessy's, he is mistaken for 'the famous Marcel Prévost, author of "Don Juannes"!' At the same place he meets Jeanne Pouquet, his erstwhile love. When she says 'au revoir' to him, he replies, with a sudden premonition: 'No, Madame, adieu! I shall never see you again!' Shortly afterwards his friend Lucien Daudet pays his last visit. The two Princesses Bibesco, Marthe and Elizabeth, the wife of Prince

Antoine, also come to see him, but only Antoine is admitted to his bedroom. Céleste explains that: 'Monsieur is terrified of princesses' perfume.' *13 July* He goes to 'Le Boeuf sur le toit' with Paul Brach and Edmond Jaloux. After a quarrel, Proust considers fighting another duel. At about this time, the publication of a translation of the poet Rabindranath Tagore (1861–1941) entitled *La Fugitive* makes him decide not to use that title, but it is restored after his death. Another project on Flaubert is stillborn. *22 July La Renaissance politique, artistique, littéraire* prints his reply to 'Une enquête littéraire: Sommes-nous en présence d'un renouvellement du style?'. *14 August* He replies to *L'Intransigeant*: 'Une petite question: Et si le monde allait finir ... Que feriez-vous?' *August* His work is discussed at the Pontigny 'décade'. *September Swann's Way*, the first volume of *Remembrance of Things Past*, appears in England. Proust is dissatisfied with the translator, Charles K. Scott Moncrieff, whom he believes to be insensitive to the subtlety of the French title. To Gallimard he writes: 'I care about my work, and I shall not allow it to be demolished by the English.' But his health is rapidly deteriorating. *2 and 3 September* Violent asthma attacks overwhelm him. *4 September* Dizzy spells cause him to fall several times in his room. He writes the last notes in notebook 59 and on the typescript of *La Prisonnière*. He prepares a number of extracts from his work which are to appear in 1923 in *Nouvelle Revue Française* and *Les Oeuvres libres*. *Early October* Already suffering from 'flu, he catches cold when leaving a party at Étienne de Beaumont's and develops bronchitis. He is treated by Dr Bize, who prescribes injections of camphorated oil which Proust refuses. He scarcely eats anything now, consuming only warm milk, coffee, stewed fruit or cold beer. The fever gets worse. Dr Bize goes to Professor Robert Proust to convince him that he should treat his brother, but Robert cannot persuade Marcel to go to the rue Piccini clinic. Marcel rudely orders Robert away and makes Céleste promise never to let anyone give him any injections. *19 October* Proust goes out, but comes back almost immediately, exhausted. *24 October* He finishes *La Prisonnière* and sets to work on the revisions of *La Fugitive*. *1 November Nouvelle Revue Française* publishes 'La regarder dormir. Mes réveils'. The copy the *Revue* sends him has the pages of articles by Thibaudet (on 'composition in the novel'), Léautaud and Rivière cut: these pieces are certainly the last things he read, together with Rivière's novel *Aimée*, which had just been published. *2 November* His last letter to Gallimard, which says: 'At the moment I think the most urgent thing is to deliver all my books to you.' *About 8 November* He contracts pneumonia. Jacques Rivière pays him a last visit to collect the manuscript of *La Prisonnière*. Proust is so exhausted that he speaks as little as possible, communicating with Céleste on scraps of paper. Despite this, when he hears that his former Swedish valet, Ernst Forssgren, is passing through Paris, he gets up and goes to the Riviera Hôtel to wait for him, in vain, until 3 o'clock in the morning. Knowing that the end is close, he completes various tasks he considers indispensible. He asks Céleste to return to Marie Scheiké-vitch, after his death, a cigarette-lighter made of two English coins which she gave him in 1917. He intends Reynaldo Hahn to have a watercolour of Senlis painted in 1898 by Marie Nordlinger, which has never left his bedside. He thinks about his soul, too: 'When I am dead, says he with a mixture of reverence and irony, you can ask Abbé Mugnier to come and say the prayers for the departed at my bedside ... You can place in my folded hands the rosary that Madame Lucie Félix-Faure Goyau brought me from Jerusalem.' *From 15 November* His brother Robert is with him constantly. *16 November* He suffers a terrible attack. *17 November* He feels better and asks for a fried sole. *Night of 17–18 November* He calls Céleste to him 'Settle down there, in the armchair, and we'll work together.' He adds: 'If I get through the night, it'll prove to the doctors that I am stronger than them.' (C. Albaret, *op. cit.*, p. 421). At half past three he stops, exhausted: the abcess in his lung has burst. At about seven o'clock he asks for some coffee. He talks to Céleste of a 'fat woman dressed in black, horrible' who is threatening him in his bedroom. He clutches the sheets and makes movements as if gathering up his papers, a reflex of the dying. Céleste disobeys his instructions and sends Odilon to get Dr Bize; then she goes to the baker's to telephone Robert Proust. At ten o'clock in the morning Dr Bize arrives and gives him an injection in his thigh; Proust grabs his housekeeper's wrist and pinches it, murmuring, 'Ah, Céleste ... Ah, Céleste!' They had just given him, quite uselessly, the thing he most feared. After Dr Bize, his brother Robert stays by his bed until midday, and returns an hour later, when he applies cups without success. As Proust's breathing becomes more and more laboured, Robert uses oxygen cylinders, which give him some relief: 'Is that doing you good,

my dear Marcel?' – 'Yes, Robert.' Those are his last words. He never
said 'Maman', as some people claim. About half past two, Dr Bize
returns and, with Robert's consent, calls in the great Professor Babinski.
But there is nothing more to be done, and Babinski leaves again,
preceded by Dr Bize. Robert stays alone with Céleste beside his brother,
whose eyes never leave their faces. Proust dies, silently, at half past four
in the afternoon of *Saturday 18 November 1922*, Saint Eudes' day, at the
age of 51.

Death

FINAL ARRANGEMENTS At Robert Proust's request, Céleste cut a lock of
hair for him and another for herself. In her memoirs (published in 1973),
she left this account: 'The professor and I tidied what there was on his
bed, silently, as if we were afraid of waking him up. It felt strange to me:
I was moving things and tidying up in his presence for the first time.
There were newspapers, papers, an issue of the *Nouvelle Revue Française*
with a note scribbled on it. Then Professor Robert Proust said to me:
"Céleste, you will do him one last service, with me. We shall lay him
out." I came back with clean linen; the professor put a clean nightshirt
on him and we changed the sheets and pillowcases. I wanted to put
Monsieur Proust's hands together, like the dead people of my village I'd
seen on their deathbeds. I was so overwhelmed that for the moment I
forgot the wish he'd expressed: that I should place in his fingers the
rosary brought back from Jerusalem by Lucie Faure. If I hadn't forgotten this, the professor would probably have let me do as I wanted, and
wouldn't have said: "No, Céleste. He died at work. Let's leave him with
his hands outstretched." After which, he placed the arms accordingly . . .
The professor asked me whether Monsieur Proust had expressed any
preferences about his funeral. I replied that he'd never spoken of it to
me. He said: "Well then, I shall do what we both did for our parents." I
mentioned Monsieur Proust's wish that the Abbé Mugnier should be
asked to come and pray beside his deathbed. The professor saw to this,
but the Abbé Mugnier was ill himself and couldn't come.' Mugnier
wrote in his *Journal* the following day (19 November): 'Visit yesterday
from the adorable niece, dressed in violet. I gave her to read the letter
Reynaldo Hahn had written me that morning. Marcel Proust dead,
Saturday evening. His friend fulfilled his request and asked me to spend

a little while beside his body. Niece went to rue Hamelin with Princesse Lucien Murat. She thought he looked wonderful on his deathbed – black beard, deep rings under the eyes, arab-type looks. She took violets. She'd never seen him when he was alive.'

Reynaldo Hahn, who arrived shortly after the death, telephoned and sent telegrams to Proust's close friends. Then he kept Céleste company sitting with the body all night. Fernand Gregh and Léon Daudet also came on the 18th. Robert decided that the burial would take place on 22 November. On 19 November the visitors to rue Hamelin were: Suzy Proust and her mother, Robert Dreyfus (who was too upset to enter the bedroom), Madame de Noailles accompanied by Henri Gans, Lucien Daudet, Georges de Lauris, Robert de Billy, Proust's cousins, Valentine and Marguerite Thomson, Edmond Jaloux, Paul Morand, Jacques Morel, who slipped on to the dead man's finger a cameo that Anatole France had given Réjane at the première of *Lys Rouge*, and Jean Cocteau. Céline Cottin, malicious as always, commented: 'Thin and white as ever, legs like two matchsticks, nothing has changed much.'

LAST PORTRAITS At about two o'clock in the afternoon, at Robert's invitation, the painter Paul Helleu came to make a dry-point etching (he later complained that he was hindered in his task by the reflection of a bulb on his leather sheet). He made two copies for Robert, who gave one to Céleste. Dunoyer de Segonzac, who didn't know Proust, came on the chance that he would be allowed to make some sketches; he completed several drawings from different angles over the next two days. The American painter and photographer Man Ray took a photograph. The sculptor Wlérick was also invited. Until the body was laid in the coffin, in the afternoon of 21 November, Céleste, Reynaldo Hahn, Robert Proust and two nuns watched over it.

BURIAL It took place on Wednesday 22 November, St Cecilia's day, in the chapel of Saint-Pierre-de-Chaillot. As a Chevalier de la Légion d'honneur Proust had the right to military honours. Among the large number of people who attended were Marie Nordlinger, Serge Diaghilev, Antoinette Faure-Berge, Comte Greffulhe, Pierre Lavallée and Princesse Marie Murat. The Abbé Delepouve said the funeral mass and gave the absolution. Ravel's *Pavane pour une infante défunte* was played.

Maurice Martin du Gard, in *Les Mémorables*, described the funeral as follows: '[it] took place in the chapel of Saint-Pierre-de-Chaillot. Barrès, his bowler tipped slightly over his eyes, watched the people coming in ... "I'd always thought he was Jewish, little Marcel Proust; what a fine funeral!" And really, what a collection of top hats! Dukes, princes, ambassadors, members of the Jockey Club and the Union, in buttoned boots, monocles, morning suits ... in the crowd were representatives of both the grand Russian Jewry and the grand Parisian pederasty past their prime, complete with make-up, nail varnish and prying eyes. Dominating the front row was the patron of the ballet and the fêtes du Paris de la Victoire, Comte Étienne de Beaumont, weeping. Writers, everyone who mattered or was going to matter, everyone who was part of the 'Proust bluff', as Bourget – now as bad a critic as he had been a good one in his day – wildly called it. Gide's absence was noticed. The music was heavenly. And several critics who had had reservations about Proust were moved to tears by the tide of the organ and the violins.'

On the way to the cemetery, Gabriel Astruc and Léon Daudet – sworn enemies – shared a taxi and had a reconciliation. Maurice Barrès, his umbrella hooked over his forearm, said on meeting François Mauriac: 'Ah well, well, well ... that was our young man' (André Maurois, *A la Recherche de Marcel Proust* p. 310).

TOMB Proust is buried in the Père-Lachaise cemetery (85th division), in the family vault crowned by the medallion portrait of Adrien Proust sculpted by Marie Nordlinger (this medallion was removed from the stele on 11 April 1966 and placed on the house in the rue du Cheval-Blanc, in Illiers, where Proust's father was born). For several years the Abbé Mugnier said an anniversary mass at Saint-Pierre-de-Chaillot.

Names

FIRST NAMES Valentin Louis Georges Eugène Marcel: Valentin and Louis came from his paternal grandfather, Louis François Valentin Proust, and Georges from his maternal uncle, Georges-Baruch Denis Weil.

NICKNAMES When he was a child his mother called him *little yellow one, my little canary, my little silly, little dopey.* She began her letters with *my dear little boy, dear wolf, my dear little wolf.* His brother Robert, knowing his tastes, called him *the great prophet of the theatre.*

Reynaldo Hahn called him *Poney* and especially *Buncht, Buls, Bunibuls, Buntchnibuls, Genstil.* The brothers Bibesco and Bertrand de Salignac-Fénelon, using the coded language of their secret society, gave him the name *Lecram*, an anagram and palindrome of Marcel (Salignac-Fénelon was Nonelef; the Bibesco brothers were known as Ocsebib). Antoine Bibesco also called him *the Toady* and Salignac-Fénelon *the Saturnine* (which meant homosexual in their vocabulary).

Regular visitors to the salon of Princesse Mathilde nicknamed him *Popelin Junior* at the start of the 1890s (she had just left her last lover, the master enameller Claudius Popelin). Laure Hayman was to call him *my dear Marcel*, as everyone did, or, more particularly, *my little psychological Saxon.* Paul Bourget, Laure's lover, wrote to her: 'Your psychological Saxon, the young Marcel, as you call him, is absolutely exquisite, judging by the letter you were good enough to send me'. Abbé Mugnier, famous father confessor of the Faubourg Saint-Germain, dubbed him *the honey-bee of heraldic flowers.*

The tearful behaviour Proust sometimes adopted brought accusations of 'Proustification'. But his memorable dinners in the great Parisian hotel also earned him the soubriquet *Proust of the Ritz.* That was the final image he gave of himself.

PSEUDONYMS From the time he began to write in newspapers and periodicals Proust used a number of pen-names. He did so not out of political timidity, or the lure of anonymity, or from a love of mystery. Was their use ironic? The witty pastiches he elaborated would make one think so; above all, the pseudonyms reflect the many facets of his personality.

In August 1893 he embarked on an epistolary novel with three old schoolfriends from Condorcet, and wrote 'l'Abbé' (Daniel Halévy) a series of letters which he signed with the name of the heroine, *Pauline Gouvres-Dives.* On 31 May 1894, his article for *Le Gaulois* was signed *Tout-Paris.*

On 19 and 20 September and 12 October 1899 he wrote some fictional letters which appeared in *La Presse* under the name of *Bernard d'Algouvres.* Robert de Flers, who took part, signed himself Françoise de Breyves, the fictional mistress of this man-about-town. On 27 January 1900, to mark Ruskin's death, he published an obituary in the *Chronique des arts et de la curiosité* signed only with his initials. It was in *Le Figaro*, however, that he most often used pseudonyms. The article he published there on 25 February 1903, 'Un salon historique: le salon de S.A.I. la princesse Mathilde', carried the byline *Dominique*, a name he borrowed from a character in 'L'Étranger' in *Les Plaisirs et les jours*. For the pieces entitled 'Le salon de la princesse de Polignac', on 6 September 1903, 'Le Salon de la comtesse d'Haussonville', on 4 January 1904, and 'Une fête chez Montesquiou à Neuilly' on 18 January, he chose the name *Horatio*. On 14 December 1904 he published a review of Fernand Gregh's book *A Study of Victor Hugo* in *Gil Blas* under the name *Marc-Antoine*. On 7 May 1905 *Le Figaro* carried 'La Vie à Paris: la comtesse de Guerne' with the pseudonym *Écho*. He signed the obituary of Gustave de Borda, on 26 December 1907, with the initial *D*, and from time to time he used the name *Laurence*.

Physical Appearance

His military service record, begun 11 November 1889, carried this description: 'Hair: brown; Eyebrows: dark brown; Eyes: brown; Forehead: low; Nose: medium; Mouth: medium; Chin: round; Face: oval; Height: 1.68 metres.' His nose, which he broke when he was 8 in a fall in the Champs-Élysées, remained slightly bent (this fracture might have been the cause of his asthma).

The pallor of his complexion was accentuated by the colour of his thick hair – which had a rebellious lock that always fell over his forehead – and his moustache. He wore a beard, and a longish moustache curled at the tips hid his upper lip (he changed its shape once, after the war, having it trimmed much shorter, in the style of Charlie Chaplin). As he grew older his emaciated white face contrasted even more sharply with his large dark eyes, sunken in their sockets and baggy from many wakeful nights.

Photographs

The first photograph we have shows him at the age of 5, wearing a dress and holding his brother Robert protectively in his arms. As he told Céleste Albaret, he was quite blond, and already had a perfectly oval face. 'His big eyes under their long lashes, like a lacquer surface which catches reflections, were his mother's. His thick hair was well brushed'

(É. de Gramont, *Marcel Proust*, p. 28). This photograph was taken on 1 March 1876. Two years later the boys were photographed again, together with their paternal grandmother, *née* Virginie Torcheux. Proust's face hadn't changed. A photograph taken with his brother in 1885 shows Robert squeezing his brother's arm with the deferential attitude which had been obvious earlier. Proust had already experienced ill health. For George D. Painter, 'Marcel's face has a frozen frenzy which recalls the young Rimbaud, a timidity masked by arrogance and anger. It is about the time of his first attack of asthma in the Bois de Boulogne' (George D. Painter, *Marcel Proust*). It was also, perhaps, a photograph of a nervous child trying to pose for the camera.

Céleste Albaret owned a snapshot of the same date of Proust dressed 'en petit prince'. This was his grandmother Weil's favourite, and she had it framed with the 'laurels of fame'. His thick, often unruly hair is shiny and falls in a fringe. Balancing a cane across his knees, he is sitting on the studio balustrade with an expression of poetic intelligence and nostalgic melancholy. Some biographers doubt the authenticity of this retouched photograph. He has the same anxious look in a picture taken in the Parc Monceau with Antoinette Faure, in which he wears a boater. He places his hero in *Jean Santeuil* in that period; Proust makes him a complaisant admirer of his own good looks. After seeing the Van Dyck painting he considers himself 'a little Duke of Richmond, just as thoughtful and handsome, and likely to die fighting a duel'. Later, he talks of 'his pride in being young, being beautiful, being powerful and rich'. He sees himself in the mirror looking 'more handsome than usual', and he continually mentions his 'care of his good looks'.

At Condorcet there is a photograph of him in M. Darlu's philosophy class in 1888; he is in the second row on the left. His physical features are certainly inherited from his mother and his Jewish ancestry. His thoughtful expression makes him lean his head slightly to one side, as Céleste Albaret observes later.

A rather pathetic portrait taken during his military service, in 1890, shows him standing in front of a garden trellis, 'in a loose greatcoat, his beautiful Eastern prince's eyes hidden by the peak of a flower-pot shaped kepi' (A. Maurois, *op. cit.*, p. 42). He still has the same large, questioning eyes and was beginning to grow a moustache.

The year 1892 found him in the boulevard Bineau, at the feet of Jeanne Pouquet. He is smiling, and looks, in the words of Paul Desjardins, like 'a Persian prince with the huge eyes of a gazelle'. He has ivory skin, black hair, and his mother's slimness and expressive dark eyes. On 29 August, at Les Frémonts, Paul Baignères did a drawing in an album of Proust sitting in a rocking chair, his hair parted in the middle, cradling his left cheek in his hand with a dreamy look. Only a month earlier Jacques-Émile Blanche had completed his famous portrait, in which we can see the perfect oval of his face and his 'Assyrian' gaze; 'the cheeks a little too pink (he was pale), the mouth lightly reddened under the fine Sarazin moustache' (É. de Gramont, *op. cit.*, p. 28).

This was also the time of his friendship with Lucien Daudet and Robert de Flers, beside whom he posed with a cynical look and his moustache provocatively ruffled. Madame Proust forebade him to show anyone this photograph: she considered it too revealing. Élisabeth de Gramont had previously called him: 'Too beautiful, with the pallid beauty of a weakling and big Oriental eyes which were too luminous' (É. de Gramont, *op. cit.*, p. 30). We can complete the picture with a description by Léon Pierre-Quint: 'Marcel Proust at 20: large, shining black eyes with heavy lids that drooped a little at the sides; a very gentle gaze which lingered on whatever it encountered; an even gentler voice that was slightly breathless, slightly hesitant, verging on affectation but always just avoiding it. Long, thick black hair that sometimes fell over his forehead, and would never have a single white strand. But one always returned to the eyes – huge, weary, nostalgic, endlessly mobile eyes ringed with purple shadows, which seemed to follow the secret thoughts of whoever was speaking. A perpetual smile, amused and welcoming, played around his mouth before settling there; his ivory skin was nonetheless fresh and healthy-looking. Despite his fine black moustache, he brought to mind a large, lazy, clever child' (L. Pierre-Quint, *Marcel Proust*, p. 40).

A picture of 1896 shows him in another elegant pose, sitting on a Louis XVI sofa, propped on his left elbow. This was taken at the time he published *Les Plaisirs et les jours*. At about the same date he posed, standing, with his mother seated between her two sons. His position is the same as in Jacques-Émile Blanche's portrait and he looks like 'a

Neapolitan prince in a novel by Bourget', according to Fernand Gregh. In a photograph dated 1905 he is sitting in Reynaldo Hahn's garden; the 'gull's eye' of the young man-about-town Élisabeth de Gramont describes is in evidence.

Céleste Albaret gives an account of Proust's physique in 1914: 'Because of his gracefulness some people thought him smaller than he was, but he was as tall as me, and I'm not small: I'm almost one metre seventy-two' (C. Albaret, *Monsieur Proust*, p. 17). Later, she goes into more detail: 'I've said he was fairly tall. He was also thin, and he walked with his back slightly arched, his head held high in a grand manner, which made him look even taller – although he didn't throw out his chest from affectation. It's common for asthmatics to walk in this way, as if it relieves the pressure on their breathing' (p. 107). The housekeeper also remarked on the beauty of his skin even when he was tired, and the way in which it was set off by his black hair, eyes and moustache. His teeth were very white and quite intact, unlike those of his friend Montesquiou, who hid his teeth when he laughed. Proust imitated him, without any reason. He never dyed his hair, and never wore make-up, as some people claimed. During the war, Mugnier likened him to Carnot.

The last photographs we have of him were taken on the terrace of the Jeu de Paume in 1921. He is fatter, and his face is puffy, like Jean Lorrain's. His eyes are still very gentle, sparkling with amusement but always watchful, as if he was going to turn everything he saw into words. He has the same expression in another photograph which Paul Morand mentions, in which he closes his eyes but keeps one half-open, watching. The people who were present at his deathbed in 1922 also described this slight lifting of one eyelid.

Dunoyer de Segonzac's drawing of him after his death shows an emaciated white face. The new growth of his black beard gave him back a 'frankly Assyrian' look, the face of an 'Arab storyteller' in the words of Maurice Barrès, or of a 'Jewish prophet' in those of Edmund Wilson.

From Accounts Given by His Friends

In Adolescence

COLETTE: 'He was a young man when I was a young woman, and that was not the time I came to know him well. I met Marcel Proust one

Wednesday at Madame Arman de Caillavet's, and I found his over-elaborate politeness and the excessive attention he paid his interlocutors, especially if they were female – the sort of attention that made the age difference between himself and them too obvious – not much to my taste. He seemed remarkably young, younger than all the other men, younger than all the women. Great, dark, melancholy eye-sockets, a complexion sometimes healthy and sometimes pallid, an anxious look in his eyes and a mouth that, when it was silent, pouted tightly as if for a kiss ... Formally dressed, and a lock of hair always out of place.'

FERNAND GREGH: 'Proust was a very pretty young man of 20 at the time, with a regular oval face, bright cheeks, and eyelids half-closed over black eyes which seemed to see out of the corners. He complained, coquettishly, of a small bump in the middle of his nose – a bump I saw again when I leant over his magnificent corpse, crowned with that thick black hair without a single white thread. [...] I've said that at the age of 23 Marcel Proust was handsome, handsome in a slightly Oriental, or perhaps rather Italian way: he laughed complacently when I told him he looked like a Neapolitan prince in a novel by Bourget. [...] After he had let his beard grow for a while, the charming Marcel we knew suddenly seemed to turn into an ancestral rabbi' (*L'Age d'or*, pp. 156, 161).

RAMON FERNANDEZ: 'That marvellous voice – careful, absent-minded but emphatic, muffled in tone – seemed composed of sounds formed somewhere beyond his lips and teeth, beyond his throat, at the very seat of his intelligence' ('A la gloire de Proust', *Nouvelle Revue critique*, 1944).

In Manhood

EDMOND JALOUX: In 1917: 'He always seemed to have come out of a nightmare, from another age, perhaps even from another world – but which? He had never discarded the fashions of his youth: a very high straight collar, a starched shirt-front, deeply cut waistcoat and narrow, sailor-knotted tie. He moved with a sort of troubled languour, a kind of shy stupefaction: he simply seemed to materialise in front of you. It was impossible not to turn and look at him, not to be struck by that extraordinary physiognomy, which had a kind of natural excess.

'He was rather stocky, and had a full face. What one noticed immediately were his eyes: fine, feminine, Oriental eyes, with an expression that was tender, caressing, even passionate, but as passive as those of a doe or an antelope. His upper eyelids were slightly hooded (like Jean Lorrain's), and the whole eye was set in a dark ring so marked that his face looked both agitated and sickly. His bushy black hair, always worn too long, formed a thick helmet around his head. The development of his chest, which he thrust forward when he walked, was also surprising; Léon Daudet likened it to a chicken's breast, and remarked that this was another feature he had in common with Jean Lorrain' (*Avec Marcel Proust*).

PAUL MORAND: 'A man with a very pale face, bundled in an old pelisse [. . .], thick black hair cut low on the neck in the style of 1905 pushed up the back of his grey bowler hat; his hand, in its slate-coloured patent kid glove, clutched a cane; his ivory cheeks darkened into a soft blue towards the jaw [. . .]; he had large, fine teeth, a moustache that set in relief his heavy lips, and dusky eyelids which weighed heavy over his deep, velvety gaze and half-veiled its magnetism' (*Le Visiteur du soir*, p. 9).

ANDRÉ GIDE: In 1921: 'He was fat, or rather bloated; he reminded me a little of Jean Lorrain [. . .]. From time to time he stroked the sides of his nose with the edge of his dead-looking hand, its fingers bizarrely stiff and splayed: nothing could have been more striking than this awkward and maniacal gesture, which seemed to be that of a lunatic or an animal' (*Journal 1889–1939*, pp. 692, 694).

In Death

ÉLISABETH DE GRAMONT: 'There he lay, his face white and emaciated, his mouth slightly contorted by a last sarcastic smile, his abundant hair as black as his beard, without a single strand of grey even though he was 51 years old. Between the handsome youth and the recumbent Christ had come his work, the whole *Recherche du temps perdu*' (*Marcel Proust*, p. 282).

LUCIEN DAUDET: 'Marcel Proust was at rest; all traces of wear and tear and the rings under his eyes had disappeared. The candlelight glimmered over the grave face, which still bore a smile that was neither bitter nor haughty, the kind of smile that follows a hard-won victory: the rejuvenated features showed that, after suffering so much and putting up with so much, Marcel Proust had at last found Eternity – and rediscovered the Time he was searching for' (*Autour de soixante lettres de Marcel Proust*, p. 242).

Health

Principal Ailments

ASTHMA His first serious asthma attack took place in the spring of 1881, when he was 9, in the Bois de Boulogne. His parents were frantic with anxiety. In an attempt to treat his condition, his father made him take cold baths and advocated an open-air life. As soon as he noticed that holidays in Illiers affected his son's health, he gave up going there, and from then onwards summer holidays were spent in Tréport, Dieppe, Houlgate and finally Cabourg. Proust was often absent from his classes at Condorcet because of his asthma attacks.

Every year, in spring, he suffered from hay fever: the sore eyes, sneezing fits and other respiratory troubles, which were exacerbated by heat, bright light and flowering plants exhausted him, and sometimes prevented him from visiting his great-uncle Louis, whose gardens at Auteuil were filled with fine trees and extended for 1500 square metres. Between 1885 and 1894 he enjoyed several years of remission, after which the asthma returned and remained with him until he died. However, it was a condition which suited his taste for obscurity and the life of a recluse.

On 31 August 1901, Proust wrote to his mother: 'After I'd written to you yesterday I had an attack of asthma and an incessantly running nose, which forced me to tramp about, lighting cigarettes at every tobacconist, etc. And worse was to come: I went to bed about midnight, feeling all right after spending a long time inhaling smoke, but three or four hours later came the real attack of the summer, specially designed for me . . .'

Some people have claimed that this illness hid a strong need for love. The psychoanalyst Milton L. Miller talks of 'the appeal to the mother' (*Psychanalyse de Proust*, p. v). He believes that the young Proust had to compete with his father and younger brother for his mother's affection, and that this illness served to bring her closer to him.

Treatment. Proust mostly treated his ailment with inhalations of smoke. As soon as he woke up, he lit some Legras powder in a saucer. Since the smell of a match could suffocate him, 'he used to light the powder with a small square of white paper, which in turn he lit from a candle' (C. Albaret, *op. cit.*, p. 43). Because of this, he had to have a candle burning day and night. Each attack left him exhausted and bathed in sweat; afterwards he would feel very cold and would have to replenish his hot water bottles, which he referred to as his *boules.* He cared little for medical prescriptions, but liked to have both veronal and caffeine at hand. One required the other: after an attack, when he was tired but wanted to work, he would take the caffeine; in the mornings, when he needed rest, he would swallow some veronal. But both were used in very small quantities. According to Céleste, he never used adrenalin.

CLAUSTROPHILIA In his room the windows were invariably closed and the walls were lined with sheets of cork to shut out noise – an idea he took, according to the Comtesse de Noailles, from Henry Bernstein.

PROUST AND MEDICINE Proust had no faith in medicine: he even laughed about it, defining it as 'a compendium of successive and contradictory mistakes on the part of doctors'. None the less, through his father he met several doctors: Dr Cazalis, Dr Pozzi, Professor Dieulafoy, Dr Cotard and Dr Chambon in Cabourg.

Proust's Doctors

Regular Doctors

DR HENRY CAZALIS (1840–1909): A poet of the symbolist school and friend of Mallarmé, who wrote under the name Jean Lahor.

DR SAMUEL POZZI (1846–1918, when he was killed by a demented patient): A friend of Montesquiou and the best-known medical practitioner of the *haute bourgeoisie*, he was nicknamed 'the Love doctor' by Madame Aubernon because of his famous infidelities. It was at his house that Proust went to his first 'society dinner'. Robert Proust became his assistant at the Broca hospital. He was the chief model for Cottard in *A la Recherche*.

PROFESSOR GEORGES DIEULAFOY (1839–1911): Head of the department of internal medicine at Hôtel-Dieu. Like Pozzi, he was doctor to and a social acquaintance of Princesse Mathilde; also a model for Cottard. In *Le Côté de Guermantes* he appears under his own name, when he comes to certify the death of the narrator's grandmother.

Other Doctors

JULES COTTET (1871–1959): A houseman in Paris hospitals, he settled in 1899 in his native Évian. Proust consulted him about a swollen wrist in the same year.

DR PIERRE MERKLEN (1852–1906): A doctor at the Laënnec hospital and a heart and lung specialist who believed that asthma was a nervous condition. In 1904 he referred Proust to the clinic of Dr Paul Dubois in Berne. He attended Proust's mother when she was dying.

DR GEORGES LINOSSIER (1857–1923): A Vichy doctor. In September 1904 he received a long letter from Proust about his physical condition.

DR NICOLAS VASCHIDE (1874–1907): A Romanian doctor who was head of Experimental Psychology at the École des Hautes Études. On 17 July 1904, during a dinner at Madame de Noailles's house, Proust talked to Vaschide about his asthma, but found his theories ridiculous.

PROFESSOR HENRI VAQUEZ (1860–1936): A specialist in cardiac medicine whom Proust consulted for the first time in 1902, and who diagnosed his tachycardia as nervous, not organic, in origin.

DR WIDMER: In 1905 Proust decided to take a rest cure with Widmer at Valmont, near Montreux.

DR EDOUARD BRISSAUD (1852–1909): Proust consulted him in the summer of 1905. He became the model for Professor E. in *A la Recherche.* In 1921, Proust confided to Lucien Daudet that in du Boulbon there was also 'a touch of the Brissaud type of doctor, more eloquence and scepticism than clinical medicine'.

DR JULES DÉJERINE (1849–1917): Director of the nursing home of the Sisters of the Holy Family where Proust considered taking a rest cure after his mother's death. Déjerine promised to cure him in three months of complete isolation. Proust booked a room there in December 1905, but very soon gave it up.

DR PAUL SOLLIER (1861–1938): Head of the clinic at Boulogne, with whom Proust came into contact on 6 December 1905. Sollier's promise of a cure in six weeks made Proust go into the clinic that very evening, but when he came out he was no better.

DR MAURICE BIZE (1870?–1962): An excellent general practitioner whom Robert Proust (a friend of Bize's from their student days) recommended to his brother in 1906. Dr Bize came to see Proust every Friday, and Céleste said: 'His favourite was Dr Bize, a small man with greying hair, very calm and serious, as well as very sympathetic and courteous – he called Monsieur Proust 'Maître'. [...] When he called him in – and Dr Bize always came immediately – it was usually for particular reasons to do with his book and because, with Bize, he was sure that the information he needed to draw on would be sound' (C. Albaret, *op. cit.*, pp. 82–84).

Dr Bize also looked after Proust's servants, Nicolas Cottin and Odilon Albaret. He attended Proust on his deathbed. He prescribed various medicines which Proust refused to take, and advocated injections of camphorated alcohol to help the congestion of his chest. Proust refused these too, but on 18 November 1922, when Bize gave him an injection in the thigh, Proust no longer had the strength to resist.

DR JOSEPH BABINSKI: Leading medical authority whom Proust consulted in June 1918 following problems with his speech and the onset of facial paralysis. He wanted to undergo a trepanning operation, but Babinski assured him it was unnecessary and the operation was avoided. Robert Proust called in Babinski on 18 November 1922 to certify Proust's death.

Psychological Portrait

Proust's Personality

HYPERSENSITIVITY Proust suffered from a need for constant affection and protection. In *Jean Santeuil* and *A la Recherche*, the reiterated theme of the 'goodnight kiss' reveals a morbidly sensitive child. His mother remained indispensable to him, and they lived together until her death; he was then almost 35 years old. In *Jean Santeuil*, Proust describes himself as an adolescent at Condorcet: 'He didn't understand that his need for sympathy and his morbid over-sensitivity, which made him overflow with love at the smallest kindness, seemed like shocking hypocrisy and an irritating pose to those young people, whose colder temperaments were reinforced by the toughness of youth.' In the same novel, however, the adolescent has a violent outburst against his parents, who never knew how to behave towards him, and who veered from extreme strictness to rare indulgences. The young despot also knew how to make himself liked by those around him. The servants at the Beg-Meil hotel clustered round him. In *Du Côté de chez Swann* and the rest of *A la Recherche*, the narrator is softer. Like him, Proust seems to have been naturally good: his friends considered him as such. His tips were legendary, he gave numerous presents, and his letters overflow with tenderness, despite his highly susceptible nature. His unfailing devotion demanded unconditional friendship from other people.

Proust was aware of this hypersensitivity, and that it was the strength behind his genius: 'For a nervous temperament like mine (that is, one in which the nerves fulfil their job as intermediaries very badly, and let through to my consciousness the cry of the humblest and most fugitive elements of myself – distinct, exhausting, limitless and agonised) the anxiety and fear that I felt beneath that high, strange ceiling [...] was only a manifestation of the fondness for a familiar, low ceiling that lingered in me' (*A l'ombre des jeunes filles en fleurs*).

Proust's hypersensitivity gave him an extraordinary capacity for joy as well as for suffering. He could play a symphony of pleasure by involving every one of the senses, and by touching the most extreme intellectual feelings with the same fleshly voluptuousness. In 1894, Reynaldo Hahn described Proust contemplating Réveillon's rose bushes: 'With his head bowed and a grave face, he screwed up his eyes, frowning slightly, as if he were making an impassioned effort of concentration; his left hand kept pushing the tip of his small black moustache between his lips while he nibbled at it' (*Hommage à Marcel Proust*, pp. 39–40). Contemplating the depths of his being in this way also made him suffer terribly from his difference from other people, his feminine sensibilities and his latent homosexuality. His life was a long succession of self-reproach and compensatory behaviour, which explained his snobbery and eventually gave birth to *A la Recherche*.

Handwriting

The first impression Proust's writing makes is that of a soul in torment. His over-sensitivity shows up in the many dented or deformed letters, indicating, in his case, more vulnerability than affective warmth.

In the typology of Carl-Gustav Jung, it is the graphic expression of Intuition, firmly established by writing that is rythmic, subtle, light, airy, juxtaposed, combined with a relatively ample form. The writing is also irregular, like that of Bonaparte, Marx and Mauriac. The characteristic features are differences in form, slant, size and direction, without being discordant.

Proust's graphology is positive, overall, as his writing is condensed, well-ventilated, irregular, subtle, flowing and firm. It reveals his sensitivity and emotional nature, as well as an intelligence that is ingenious, witty, intuitive, inventive and perspicacious; it also shows a sense of the appropriate and a fertile imagination which enjoys intellectual speculation. Its quality of 'airiness', which might seem to indicate a lack of weight and firmness, actually shows adaptability. His is a lively personality constantly open to new impressions: his social behaviour is engaging and attractive, he is artistically and psychologically gifted, his enthusiasm and attitude to life lend him a powerful charm. He also has something of the dandy, a fastidious, sparkling side to his nature. Thus his writing displays an elastic personality, agile, resilient and cheerful.

Proust's Questionnaires

In about 1886, when he was 15, Proust answered a questionnaire put to him by Antoinette Faure, in which he reveals his already acute sensitivity. The handwriting is still childish, but some of the replies ˆstify to a fully developed intelligence.

Your favourite moral quality: The universal qualities; all those that are not specific to any one sect.

Qualities you admire in a man: Intelligence; moral sense.

Those you admire in a woman: Gentleness, naturalness, intelligence.

Your favourite occupation: Reading, daydreaming, poetry, history, theatre.

Your chief characteristic: (Proust did not reply.)

Your idea of happiness: To live close to the people I love, surrounded by the charms of nature, plenty of books and musical scores, and not far from a French theatre.

Your idea of unhappiness: To be away from Mummy.

Your favourite colours and flowers: I like all colours; as for flowers, I don't know.

Who would you like to be, apart from yourself?: Not having to ask myself the question, I prefer not to answer it. However, I would have liked to be Pliny the Younger.

Where would you most like to live?: In the realm of the ideal, or rather of my ideal.

Your favourite prose writers: George Sand, Aug. Thierry.

Your favourite poets: Musset.

Your favourite painters and composers: Meissonnier, Mozart, Gounod.

Your favourite real-life heroes: A mixture of Socrates, Pericles, Mahomet, Musset, Pliny the Younger and Aug. Thierry.

Your favourite real-life heroines: A woman of genius who lives like an ordinary woman.

Your favourite fictional heroes: The romantic, poetic heroes, who are an ideal rather than a model.

Your favourite fictional heroines: Those who are more than women without departing from their sex, everything tender, poetic, pure and beautiful in every genre.

Your favourite food and drink: (No reply.)

Your favourite names: (No reply.)

Your 'bête noire': People who are incapable of feeling what is good, and who are ignorant of the sweetness of affection.

Which historical characters do you hate most?: (No reply.)

What is your present state of mind?: (No reply.)

Which fault do you feel most indulgent towards?: The private life of geniuses.

Your motto: One which cannot easily be summed up because its most simple expression is all that is good, beautiful and great in nature.

In about 1892, at the age of 21, after his voluntary service, Proust answered another questionnaire. He once again reveals his sensitive nature and his insatiable craving for tenderness, but also his hidden remorse, feelings.of anguish and some irresistible impulses. His spirit and his critical sense have both evolved. When he cites Pierre Loti and Anatole France, he shows the influence Madame de Caillavet's salon had on him at that time, but he indicates that his tastes might change by using the qualifier 'today':

My main character trait: The need to be loved; more precisely, a need to be petted and spoilt more than a need to be admired.

The quality I want to see in a man: Feminine charm.

My favourite quality in a woman: The virtues of a man, and openness in friendship.

What I most appreciate in my friends: Their feelings of tenderness towards me, if they are beautiful enough to set a high value on that tenderness.

My greatest fault: Not knowing, not being able to 'want'.

My favourite occupation: Loving.

My dream of happiness: I'm afraid it wouldn't be sufficiently elevated: I daren't express it, and I'm afraid of destroying it by expressing it.

What my greatest unhappiness would be: Not to have known my mother or my grandmother.

What I would like to be: Myself, as the people I admire would like me to be.

The country I would like to live in: A place where certain things I want would come about, and *where feelings of tenderness would always be shared*.

My favourite colour: Beauty doesn't reside in colours, but in the harmony between them.

The flower I like best: The flower of one's self – after that, all of them.

My favourite bird: The swallow.

My favourite prose writers: Today they are Anatole France and Pierre Loti.

My favourite poets: Baudelaire and Alfred de Vigny.

My favourite fictional heroes: Hamlet.

My favourite fictional heroines: Bérénice (he crossed out Phèdre).

My favourite composers: Beethoven, Wagner, Schumann.

My favourite painters: Leonardo da Vinci, Rembrandt.

My heroes in real life: Monsieur Darlu, Monsieur Boutroux.

My heroines in history: Cleopatra.

My favourite names: I only have one at a time.

What I hate most of all: All that is bad in me.

The character in history I most despise: I haven't enough knowledge to answer this.

The military action I most admire: My voluntary service!

The reform I most admire: (No reply.)

The natural gift I would most like to have: Willpower, and charm.

How I would like to die: Better – and well loved.

My present state of mind: Bored of thinking about myself in order to answer all these questions.

Failings towards which I feel most forgiving: Those I understand.

My motto: I'd be afraid it would bring me bad luck.

CHAPTER TWO

Childhood

Early Childhood

Proust spent his early childhood in a warm family atmosphere. His parents then lived near the Madeleine, at 9 boulevard Malesherbes. The birth of his brother Robert on 24 May 1873 shattered his exclusive relationship with his mother. His parents spent the spring and early summer at Auteuil, in his great-uncle Louis's house. (Rue La Fontaine was the scene of the goodnight kiss which inspired the famous episode in 'Combray'.) During the Easter and summer holidays, the Proust family used to go to stay with their Uncle Amiot, at 4 rue du Saint-Esprit in Illiers. Marcel and Robert used to play in his garden, or in the nearby garden of the Pré Catelan, and anecdotes from this time swarm through Proust's work. *Contre Sainte-Beuve*, notably, contains the story of the younger brother who wanted to take a young goat back to Paris; in *Swann* we find sessions with the magic lantern or the visits to 'Aunt Léonie'.

In the spring of 1881, at the age of 9, he suffered his first asthma attack, during a walk in the Bois de Boulogne. Throughout his life he was to fear gusts of wind and the scent of flowers. Adrien Proust, his father, felt it was bad for him to stay in the countryside near Illiers, so from 1880 to 1890 he spent his holidays with his mother or his grandmother on the Normandy coast, at Houlgate, Tréport, Dieppe or Trouville, but most often at Cabourg. When he was 14 he also accompanied his mother to Salies-de-Béarn, in the Pyrenees.

In Paris, he played almost every afternoon in the Champs-Élysées. On 1 May 1880 he broke his nose playing 'prisoner's base' along an avenue of trees. Later, thanks to Princesse Bibesco, the avenue was named 'Marcel Proust'. Robert Dreyfus remembers: 'In the Champs-Élysées garden, near the Restaurant des Ambassadeurs, a passer-by coming from the avenue Gabriel first skirts a fairly large lawn with a fountain surmounted by a statue of a bathing woman knotting her hair, then encounters two merry-go-rounds, after passing an avenue of trees which runs alongside the old summer Alcazar ... It was there I used to see Marcel Proust as a child playing "prisoner's base", or preferably chatting to the young boys of his age, already reciting us his verse, but leaving us quickly enough as soon as he saw his favourite young girl approaching' (R. Dreyfus, *Souvenirs sur Marcel Proust*, pp. 11–12).

It was his mother he most resembled. His face already displayed 'the luminous gifts of his magnificent artistic intelligence and delicious sensitivity. An exceptional being, a child of dizzying precocity and originality, he charmed his young companions' (Dreyfus, pp. 13–14).

His legendary generosity was already apparent. At the age of 7, his mother sent him to take a 5-franc coin to a relative's cook for the New Year, but on the way he gave it to a poor shoeshine boy. Another day, taking advantage of his parents' absence, he and his brother made a sumptuous tea for the delivery boy from the Belle-Jardinière. But it was with elderly people that he showed himself most amiable, always finding the appropriate way to chat about their health or their problems. Comtesse Martel, better known under her pseudonym of Gyp, used to watch him: she was amused by his ability to enjoy children's games in the Champs-Élysées, and a few days later to buy the complete works of Molière or Lamartine at the Calmann-Lévy bookshop in the rue de Gramont, then the favourite meeting-place of Charles Haas (the model for Swann) and Anatole France (the model for Bergotte).

READING He read incessantly (George Sand, Dickens, Théophile Gautier and Balzac), on the advice of his mother and grandmother. George Eliot's *The Mill on the Floss* made him cry. He couldn't tear himself away from Théophile Gautier's *Capitaine Fracasse* or *The Thousand and One Nights*. 'Perhaps no part of our childhood did we live as fully as those days we thought we had let go by without living them at all, those we spent with a favourite book' (*Pastiches et Mélanges*).

He amazed his friends in the Champs-Élysées gardens: 'Racine,

Hugo, Musset, Lamartine and Baudelaire already rang through his prodigious poetic memory, and I remember having first heard from him the name Leconte de Lisle. If I wasn't afraid of committing an anachronism of several years, I'd say he also spoke with rapture of *Anna Karenina* and the novels of George Eliot. And I'm certain of his enthusiasm, while still a child, for Mounet-Sully and for Madame Sarah Bernhardt, whose genius he transmuted into the character of the tragic actress Berma' (R. Dreyfus, p. 16).

THEATRE In the autumn of 1881 he went to the theatre for the first time. It was to be one of the great passions of his life. His favourite heroes were Hamlet and Bérénice. His grandmother talked to him for hour after hour about Rachel, whom she had known in the Crémieux's salon.

Education

The first volumes of *A la Recherche* give us little information about Proust's life at school and university. When the narrator alludes to 'all my conversations with my school friends' (*Du Côté de chez Swann*), he does not specify which institution he was attending. In *A l'ombre des jeunes filles en fleurs* he is questioned by Monsieur de Norpois, who 'asked me a number of questions about what my life and education had been and about my tastes'. These questions remain unanswered in the novel.

Jean Santeuil offers more information. The young hero is not a brilliant pupil: although a great lover of the French dramatic poets like Hugo and Musset, whom he quotes from memory in long tirades of verse, he is nonetheless very lazy. Like Proust, Jean is talkative in class; the teacher notices this and gives him an hour's detention, which is imposed in spite of heartfelt pleas from the rest of the class on his behalf. Jean is often punished and never features among the prize-winners in his class.

In *Jean Santeuil*, Proust describes one of his Philosophy masters, M. Darlu, in the guise of Monsieur Beulier. Unlike real life, the hero is disappointed in the first lesson the latter gives, but Darlu's thoughts are clearly conveyed: 'Since at that time the spiritualist doctrines associated with Monsieur Beulier's powerful intelligence had refuted, in Jean's mind, the sophisms of materialism and scepticism, a materialist and sceptical rationale could not interest him.'

Establishments Attended

PRIMARY SCHOOL When very little he spent a year or two at an elementary school called Pape-Carpentier, where his brother Robert also went.

SECONDARY SCHOOLS He was a day-boy at a public 'établissement d'enseignements secondaire' in the rue Caumartin, ten minutes' walk from his parents' home in the boulevard Malesherbes.

From 2 October 1882 to 30 July 1889. In October 1882, at the age of eleven, he went into Class 5 of the lycée Fontanes – named after the Grand Maître de l'Université under the First Empire. (This lycée had changed its name many times: 1804, lycée Bonaparte, then lycée Impérial Bonaparte; 1814, collège Royal de Bourbon; 1815, in March, lycée Impérial Bonaparte; in July, collége Royal de Bourbon; 1848, lycée Bonaparte; 1853, lycée Impérial Bonaparte; 1870, lycée Condorcet; 1874, lycée Fontanes, and finally on 27 January 1883, lycée Condorcet.) The pupils could 'run about in the meagre shade of the trees in the cour du Havre, waiting for the drum roll which advised us, rather than ordering us, to make our way to lessons. The discipline wasn't strict; our parents even thought it a little too relaxed' (R. Dreyfus, p. 20).

The lycée was housed in a former Capuchin monastery designed by Brongniard in 1779. In 1864, the original plan was changed by the building of the rue du Havre over the large gardens of the Pères Capucins. Even though the buildings were severe and monastic, the atmosphere differed from that of the military lycées on the left bank. Condorcet, unlike Saint-Louis, Louis-le-Grand or Henri-IV, did not prepare students for the 'grandes écoles', and Proust didn't suffer the intellectual exhaustion of the pupils of the *khâgne*, the class which prepared for the entrance exam of the École Normale Supérieure. The students were different too. The left-bank schools attracted a large number of provincials, bent on conquering Paris by means of the Polytechnique or the École Normale. Condorcet, on the right bank, was attended by the children of smart Paris society, which included many Jews, or half-Jews like Marcel. Education was not considered a means to social advancement or a brilliant professional future but the affirmation of an already solid intellectual heritage: the honours awarded to Condorcet pupils in the Concours général were proof of this. A number of future celebrities passed through the lycée: men of letters (the Goncourts, Eugène Labiche, Théodore de Branville, Abel Hermant); philosophers (Taine, Sainte-Beuve, Bergson); scholars (Ampère, Becquerel); a society painter (Jacques-Émile Blanche) and even three Presidents of the Republic (Sadi Carnot, Casimir-Périer and Paul Deschanel). In 1882 the headmaster was Julien Girard (he remained there from 1878 to 1892). 'The lycée's administration took our preferences into consideration' (R. Dreyfus, p. 22).

FURTHER EDUCATION *1890–1893* After his military service, Proust enrolled in the *Faculté de droit* (20 November) and also in the *École libre des sciences politiques* (founded in 1874 and housed since 1881 in the rue Saint-Guillaume). He attended both establishments until the end of 1893. *Until 1895* He also attended the *Sorbonne* for his Bachelor of Arts degree in Philosophy.

In 1887, he went to the Sorbonne for the examinations of the Concours général on 13, 18 and 22 July. *In 1893*, he decided against the École des Chartes and hankered after the École de Rome; *in 1900*, he went to the Collège de France to attend Bergson's 'cours d'ouverture' on 7 December.

Principal Teachers

BEFORE CONDORCET The Abbé Marquis, in Illiers, gave him the rudiments of Latin. It is very likely that he had other private tutors, as this was common practice among the affluent and educated bourgeoisie his mother belonged to. Passages in *Jean Santeuil* describe the private lessons of a Monsieur Jacomier.

AT CONDORCET *In Class 5*. The lycée's archives give no information.

In Class 4 (1883–1884). German: M. Schmitt. Geography: M. Launay. History: M. Gazeau. Letters (French, Latin and Greek): M. Legouëz, who had been teaching at the lycée since 1852. In 1883, he was 64 and approaching retirement. In 1869 he received the cross of the Légion d'honneur, and was a member of the 'jury d'agrégation de grammaire'. He was a kindly man whose colleagues appreciated his talents. Despite repeated absences, Proust followed his lessons enthusiastically and profitably, but Monsieur Legouëz's comments, though appreciative, didn't predict his pupil's future talent. Natural sciences: Georges

Colomb (1856–1945), a humanist educated at the École Normale who ended his career as assistant director of the botany laboratory at the École des Hautes Études and went on teaching at the Collège Sévigné until 1936. He was best known for his sense of humour and the clownish side of his personality, and for three books: *La Famille Fenouillard* (1895), *Le Sapeur Camember* (1896) and *L'Idée fixe du savant Cosinus* (1899), which he published under the pseudonym 'Christophe', after leaving Condorcet. He was a good communicator and full of enthusiasm, and his attractive and precise teaching had a strong effect on Marcel, who was already drawn to botany and the natural sciences.

In Class 3 (1884–85). Physical sciences: M. Merlier. German: M. Sigwalt. Mathematics: M. Sestre. History: M. Régis Jallifier (at 38 the youngest of the teachers at Condorcet). He and Proust kept up a friendly relationship, as their correspondence shows. Letters: M. Guillemot (aged 54, a graduate of the École Normale Supérieure), had been teaching in Paris since 1861. He held degrees in Grammar and in Letters. A brilliant grammarian, his lessons were rather dry and cold, and he didn't succeed in arousing the interest of his class.

In Class 2 (1885). German: M. Sigwalt. History-Geography: M. Vast. Mathematics: M. Henet. Physics: M. Merlin. Letters: M. Claude Courbaud (aged 53, a native of the Jura, who graduated from the École Normale Supérieure with degrees in Grammar and Letters). He was awarded the Légion d'honneur in 1886, while Proust was attending his lessons. Contrary to all educational programmes and despite the opposition of the general inspectors, he used to set exercises in style: this allowed a pupil to develop his literary personality without constraints and without following a particular plan. However, his stolid teaching lacked liveliness and sparkle. Nevertheless, Marcel remembered his name and used it in *A la Recherche* for the tutor of Palamède, the future Baron de Charlus, and his brother Basin de Guermantes. He was 'Le vieux père Courveau' (*Sodome et Gomorrhe*). Drab, with a pedantic voice and lacking in ambition, Courbaud also provided the characteristics of Brichot, whose name was taken from M. Brichet, the mathematics teacher when Proust repeated Class 2.

Proust repeated a year in Class 2 (1886). Physics: M. Seignette, who might have lent his name to the archivist Saniette, habitué of the Verdurin salon. History: M. Alexandre Gazeau, graduated top of the

École Normale Supérieure in 1874, at the lycée since 1880, awarded the Légion d'honneur in 1885 at the age of 36. A brilliant and lively teacher, he became head teacher in 1893 and directed the school from 1907 to 1915. Although he had little enthusiasm for geography, he fascinated his pupils with his intriguing history lessons. Well liked by his students, he had a special regard for Marcel, whom he entered for the Concours général in 1887.

In 'Rhétorique B' (1887–88). Latin: Victor Cucheval, born in Rennes in 1830 and at the lycée since 1860, had also given Latin classes at the Sorbonne since 1878. In 1888, the year when Proust was in his class, he was decorated with the cross of the Légion d'honneur. His name, pronounced like *cul-cheval* (horse's arse), must have attracted many jibes, like that of Cambremer in *A la Recherche*. In an article signed 'Horatio' in *Le Figaro*, his former pupil makes a joke of it: '... meanwhile, the user announced each visitor.

"Your name, Monsieur?"

"Monsieur Cucheval."

"No, Monsieur, I asked you your name."

"What cheek! Monsieur Cucheval."

And the usher referred the matter to the master of the house' ('Le Salon de la princesse de Polignac', *Le Figaro*, 6 September 1903).

A strict Cartesian, Cucheval allowed no room for fantasy. To Proust he was 'vehemently and expansively vulgar. A schoolmaster in the raw, crude, unpolished – but all in all I assure you he's very agreeable. That Brunetière, so green, so "direct", certainly isn't lacking in flavour ... A dose of Cucheval wouldn't do you any harm' (Letter to Robert Dreyfus, August 1888).

French and Greek: Maxime Gaucher, born in 1829, graduate of the École Normale Supérieure, who came to the lycée in 1860, the same year as Cucheval. He wrote elegant, ironic reviews for *La Revue littéraire* and *La Revue bleue*. During a general inspection one day, according to Robert Dreyfus and André Maurois, Gaucher asked Proust to read a piece aloud for Eugène Manuel. This mediocre poet indignantly demanded: 'Isn't there a single pupil in your class who can write more clearly and correctly in French?'

'Monsieur Inspector General,' Gaucher replied, 'none of my pupils writes French like a manual worker.' (A play on Manuel's name.)

(André Maurois, *A la Recherche de Marcel Proust* p. 27). Unfortunately, André Ferré, in his study 'Années de collège de Marcel Proust', has checked the dates and casts some doubt on the authenticity of the story.

Gaucher, a delicate and witty man with a non-conformist mind, had a deep influence on Proust, whose literary promise he was able to nurture. He was aware of Proust's gifts and used to make him read his excellent compositions aloud, to encourage his classmates. Lesson notes of Proust's which have survived testify to brilliant teaching, solid and perfectly structured. Gaucher stimulated his students' abilities, and to do so he set them a large number of essays. Proust considered him 'by far the best teacher in "Rhétorique"' (R. Dreyfus, *op. cit.*, p. 27). In the third term Gaucher fell seriously ill and was replaced by M. Dupré: 'He has a very affectionate and delicate soul whose qualities I have managed to discern inside his old buffer's body. But he is boring. It's true he knows Dierx and Leconte de Lisle (the works) – but what's the use of being told about modern authors by someone who has so many reservations about them?' (R. Dreyfus, *op. cit.*, p. 28). Gaucher died as a result of his illness on 24 July 1888. At the beginning of the next school year he was replaced by a younger teacher, M. Dauphiné. He had a surprising and 'strange pronunciation in which the "r"s were softened, as in creole people. He used to say "monsieur Duouand", "monsieur Gouegh". And he'd say, "monsieur Halévy, monsieur Bizet, vous passeouez à la pôte"' (F. Gregh, *L'Age d'or*, p. 136). Proust must have known him well, as his friend Robert Dreyfus asked for information about him. Had Dauphiné acted as Dupré's assistant in replacing Gaucher at the end of the school year 1887–88? Had Proust had private lessons with him? In this letter, written in August 1888, Proust wrote an assessment of him that showed great intuition: 'The gentleman in question is a small thin man, dry and formal. Extremely intelligent and well read. A marvellously acute and agile mind. Almost subtle in its shrewdness. Teaching very distinctive, very rich, very lively. Strict and virtuous soul. Much more intelligent and particularly more intellectual than artistic . . . All in all, Dauphiné is a course, Cucheval a lesson, Dupré often a conversation. But the course is very remarkable, the lesson very good, and the conversation boring.'

History: M. Choublier. Afflicted by a heavy limp, graduated top in 1860, lacking in life and dynamism. German: M. Catala.

In 'Philosophie' (1888–89). Philosophy teacher: Alphonse Darlu, born 20 March 1849 in Libourne, the accent of which he kept all his life. He took his *baccalauréat* in Letters and Sciences at the age of 16, was schoolmaster at the Collège de Bergerac, obtained a degree in 1868, top honours in philosophy in 1871, without having taken the courses of study. After Périgueux, Angoulême and Bordeaux, he was appointed to a teaching post in Paris and went to Condorcet in January 1885. He also gave classes at the écoles normales supérieures in Fontenay-aux-Roses and Sèvres. Created Chevalier de la Légion d'honneur in 1891, inspector general of public education in 1900, he retired in 1919 and died on 5 May 1921. In 1893 he participated in founding the *Revue de métaphysique et de morale.* His philosophy can be summed up as a rationalism which was spiritual but essentially secular; his position resembled and influenced that of Proust in *A la Recherche.* The narrator realises that 'only crude and erroneous perception places everything in the object, when everything is in the spirit' (*Le Temps retrouvé*).

Darlu wielded 'a real charm', as the headmaster Girard put it, and a strong and fertile influence over Marcel, who wrote him a long and hopeful letter, signed 'Your pupil and profound admirer', on the evening of his first lecture. (H. Bonnet, *Alphonse Darlu: maître de philosophie de Marcel Proust*, p. 63). In 1894, in the dedication to *Les Plaisirs et les jours,* Proust refers to: 'Monsieur Darlu, the great philosopher whose inspired words, more certain to last than any piece of writing, engendered in me, as in so many others, the ability to think.' In a letter to Madame Straus written in 1908 Proust even considers him a candidate for the Académie française. Fernand Gregh, another of Darlu's pupils, remembers 'the image of Darlu placing on the lectern in front of him his top hat, which he always used when he needed an object to demonstrate a point, and producing philosophy from inside it as if he were a conjurer' (F. Gregh, *op. cit.*, pp. 142–3). Robert Proust, who was taught by Darlu the following year, described his vivid and imagistic way of speaking: 'Darlu's methods were personal and intuitive, and he had an almost poetic way of explaining things which Marcel loved' (R. Proust, 'Hommage à Marcel Proust', *Nouvelle Revue Française*, January 1925). Marcel took private lessons with him, and enjoyed them so much that he prolonged them by accompanying Darlu on his journey home to 20 rue de la Terrasse. Even there he would keep Darlu talking on the doorstep and make him late for meals, to the great amusement of the master's family. Darlu maintained a great respect for Proust, whose literary career he followed with interest; a speech he gave at the Condorcet prize-giving in 1907 praised Proust's translation of *Sesame and Lilies*, which had appeared the year before. Nevertheless, Proust wrote in 1909: 'No man has had any influence on me except Darlu, and I know that influence to have been a bad one.'

Natural sciences: M. Seignette. History and geography: M. Chamblis. Mathematics: M. Ducatel. Physics and chemistry: M. Aubert. French: M. Cucheval.

FURTHER EDUCATION *At the École libre des sciences politiques* Proust was greatly interested in the courses given by Albert Sorel, Anatole Leroy-Beaulieu and Paul Desjardins. He was less impressed by those given by the witty Albert Vandal, as this quatrain quoted by Robert de Billy shows:

> Vandal, exquis, répand son sel.
> Mais qui s'en fout, c'est Gabriel,
> Robert, Jean et même Marcel
> Pourtant si grave d'habitude.

> (Vandal, the fop, parades his wit,
> Gabriel and Jean don't give a shit,
> Nor does Robert, nor even Marcel
> Who's much less solemn than usual.)
> (R. de Billy, *Marcel Proust*, p. 24)

Vandal was afflicted with a nervous tic which made him blink one eye like Dr Cottard. During the Dreyfus affair he became part of the Ligue de la Patrie Française founded by Charles Maurras.

At the Faculty of Law Proust, who had little interest in the subject, resorted to private lessons with Monsieur Monnot.

At the Sorbonne In 1894–95 he followed M. Egger's philosophy lectures with great interest. He went back to taking private lessons with Alphonse Darlu, and also took a home study course from M. Mossot, one of the 'Rhétorique' teachers at Condorcet. He also enjoyed attending Charles Secrétan's philosophy seminars from time to time, as we know he did on 6 January 1893. However, he was never taught by

Bergson, who lectured at secondary level until 1897, then in 1900 took a post at the Collège de France (where Proust attended his inaugural lecture on 7 December).

In a questionnaire probably dated 1892, to the question: 'Who are your real-life heroes?', Proust replied: 'Monsieur Darlu, Monsieur Boutroux.' Bergson was not among them, as his *Essai sur les données immédiates de la conscience*, published in 1889, had not yet made its impact on Proust.

Results Obtained

SECONDARY SCHOOL *Class 5* In 1882 Proust proved to be an intelligent pupil who worked well and quickly. His family and his private lessons also helped him. He was very interested in literature; he read voraciously. The only surviving honours list of this class shows that on 3 August 1883 he was awarded: 5th certificate of merit (the lowest) in French; 4th in Greek composition; 2nd prize for natural sciences. Top of the class was Pierre Leroy-Beaulieu.

In Class 4, section A. In the honours list of 1 August 1884 he obtained 3rd certificate of merit in natural sciences. It was his only prize. He had only attended lessons for two terms, during which he obtained the highest assessment marks out of the class of 25. In the first term, Monsieur Colomb, his teacher, wrote: 'Behaviour: VG [Very Good]; Application: VG; Progress: G [Good]'; in the second: 'Behaviour: VG; Application: G; Progress: F [Fair]'. History: Monsieur Gazeau gave him G for each of the three sections and in each term. French: Proust's lively mind was displayed in the rough drafts he has left from this period, which are very neat and almost without crossings-out. He threw himself into his homework, which was often written at a sitting. But he only worked at what he liked. His first piece of French homework, hastily written over seven pages, begins poetically: 'The air is heavy with the scent breathed by a fresh lilac ...' His characteristic love of quotation, literary comment, digressions and notes was already making itself felt. The same year he handed in another piece of homework: 'Pison's trial before the Roman Senate', a perfect rendering of the style of Tacitus. His teacher Monsieur Legouëz noted, in the first term: 'VG, good student, very willing' (an expression he used for boys who were hard-working but without great brilliance). In the second term his mark was 'G'; in the third 'F, inadequate work'. None the less, Proust followed his lessons carefully, and his behaviour earned him VG for the first two terms and G for the third. Latin: G and F for the three terms; Greek: G and F in the first two terms and F and P [Passable] in the third. German: Monsieur Schmitt continued to give him G for behaviour, but P for effort and progress in the first term, Med. [Mediocre] in the second and third. Geography: Monsieur Launay marked his behaviour as Mediocre in the second term, Passable in the third. For effort and progress he went from Good to Passable. Mathematics: Marcel didn't like mathematics. 'When he was at the lycée, my father did Marcel's maths homework. He wanted to help him, but, since his urge to teach was strong, he also wanted Marcel to understand; Marcel used to say: "Stop, stop, I'm completely at sea" (Claude Francis, *Marcel Proust et les siens*, p. 146). Behaviour: VG all year; effort: VG in the first term, P in the second and third; progress: P in all three terms.

On 8 August Marcel received his 'certificat d'aptitudes de grammaire', having passed in the subjects taught in Class 4 of the lycées – French language, Latin language, Greek language, German language, Roman history, French geography, arithmetic (basic theory), plane geometry (elementary), geology, botany.

In Class 3 Marcel was often absent during 1884. For the third term he was given no mark at all. His name was not included in the honours list, where P. Leroy-Beaulieu and Benjamin Küss figured prominently. Despite his illness, his marks in the other two terms were good. In mathematics (M. Sestre) and in German (M. Sigwalt), he got Good throughout; in history, Very Good; in literature (M. Guillemot), the general assessment for the first term was: 'A good pupil, very willing; lively and spirited but with little knowledge of Greek'; 2nd term: 'A good pupil'. Some of his written work still exists, among which is a 'French composition' written in rough with many crossings-out, dated 1er Xbre 84, and entitled 'The dying gladiator'. The second 'French composition', on the sacking of Corinth by the Romans, already shows the 13-year-old author to have a precise and confident style.

In Class 2 During 1885, his absences from class hampered his studies increasingly. His name didn't appear in the honours list, in which Gaston Haas, perhaps a relation of Charles Haas (the main model for Swann), carried off all the prizes. However, a fine story about

Christopher Columbus, dated March 1886 and entitled 'The Eclipse', survives from this period.

In 1886, Marcel had to repeat the year. He was then 15. Two pieces of work prove that he was making up the time he'd lost. The first is a translation from Cicero on the discovery of Archimedes' tomb, whose firm and accurate style shows a noticeable improvement. The second piece of work, unmarked like the others, is an 'exercise in style'. Even though this sort of written work was meant to be limited to twenty lines or so, Marcel wrote four pages on 'Clouds'. Mathematics: M. Brichet's comment on the first term was: 'Could do better'; in the second: 'Does no work'; at the end of the year: 'Poor'. History: M. Gazeau's marks throughout the year were Very Good for behaviour and Good for work and progress.

On 13 July 1887, he entered the Concours général at the Sorbonne. There were twelve boys from Condorcet; Proust was eighth on the list. There were 120 or 130 entered altogether. The subjects examined were 1) Philip II and the decline of Spain. 2) Asian Russia, with map. Joseph Harmann, from Louis-le-Grand, gained first place. Boys from Condorcet achieved 2nd prize (Louis Boulle), 4th merit award (Dufourcq) and 6th merit award (Manheimer). Proust was named 'runner-up', in case anyone dropped out of the French composition test, on 18 July, or Greek translation on 22 July. He didn't have to take the exam on 18 July, but on 22 July he replaced a candidate called Lazard. He didn't appear on the honours list of the Concours général.

At the prize-giving on 2 August, Proust took second prize in history and (for the first time) an honourable mention with second merit award in Geography, in Latin the top merit award, and in French a 4th merit award for French composition.

In 'Rhétorique B' In 1887–1888, for Latin, M. Cucheval's second-term comment was: 'uneven work, a daydreamer'; and in the third term: 'homework often not done, although more willing'. His non-conformity and the already very idiosyncratic style which his friends tried to imitate did not always please the rigorous Cucheval: 'By the end of the first two months the upshot was that a dozen idiots were writing in the decadent manner, Cucheval saw me as the source of the rot, I'd started a war in the classroom, and several people regarded me as a poseur. Luckily it was all over in a couple of months, but even a month ago Cucheval was still saying: he'll pass because he's just a fraud, but he'll cause fifteen others to fail.' (Letter from Proust to Robert Dreyfus, August 1888.) French/ Greek: his teacher (M. Gaucher) made him read his homework aloud. And Proust was able to enjoy well-structured lessons, as a draft entitled 'Second-rate comedies of the eighteenth century' shows. Comments in the first term: 'Very good pupil', with Good throughout for French and Greek; in the second: 'A bit too fanciful', but the Good mark stayed constant, apart from progress in Greek, for which he got F. Gaucher was ill in the third term, and was replaced by M. Dupré, who gave Proust F for effort and progress in French and Greek. He also wrote: 'Uneven work, but has some talent'. However, other subjects were somewhat sacrificed to the demands of the arts. History: M. Choublier's marks for the first term were F for effort and progress, passable in the second term. Behaviour was given G, however. Mathematics: Brichet noted 'P for behaviour' in the first term and G in the two other terms. 'Bad' was the verdict for effort and progress, with the following remarks in term order: 'A very poor student', 'hopeless', 'very poor'.

As in other years, Proust did not shine in German either. His name was not on the honours list at the end of the year, but thanks to M. Gaucher he won first prize for French composition at the awards ceremony on 31 July. He also achieved an 8th merit award for Latin language and 7th for Greek. That year he passed the first part of his *baccalauréat* easily but without special mention.

In 'Philosophie' In 1888, this was a small class of twenty. There exists a six-page dissertation by Proust, complete with deletions, entitled 'The spirituality of the soul', reflecting the influence of M. Darlu, his strongly moralistic teacher. Darlu was not an easy teacher. He often marked his students' work with comments like: 'Fantasy of a sick mind' or 'Sganarelle philosophy' (F. Gregh, *op. cit.*, p. 142). But he appreciated Proust's qualities. In the first term, he gave him G for behaviour, effort and progress. In the second term, the remarks had changed to: 'Has a great deal of ability and taste. Cannot work very much.' His behaviour earned him VG, effort and progress G. The third term's appreciative comments were: 'Good work. Sure to succeed', although Marcel had G marks throughout. In Natural sciences M. Seignette gave him VG throughout in all three terms, but mathematics were still out of favour. In the first term, even though he achieved G for behaviour he only got F for effort and progress. In the second term his behaviour was only Fairly Good and progress and effort were rated Passable, as in the third term, when only behaviour got a G mark. M. Aubert in physics and chemistry still found him a difficult pupil: in the first term his behaviour was Good but effort and progress were Poor, as they remained in the second term although his behaviour improved a little to Fair. Proust therefore made an effort for the third term, when he got G for behaviour and F for the rest. The archives of the lycée do not give that year's marks for French from M. Cucheval. At the prize-giving on 30 July 1888 Proust won the top *Prix d'honneur* in French composition, and 3rd *accessit d'excellence*. He passed the second part of his *baccalauréat* successfully, and received the grade of *bachelier ès lettres* on 15 July and the diploma on 26 October.

HIGHER EDUCATION *École libre des sciences politiques* (1890–1893). On 22 June 1892, Proust sat an oral exam on the course given by Albert Sorel: 'Diplomatic history from 1818 to 1878'. His marks were 4¾ out of 6, with the comment: 'Extremely intelligent'. On 23 June, in the oral exam on Albert Vandal's course, 'Eastern Affairs', he got 5 out of 6, with the remark: 'Good replies overall'. On 25 June, in the oral on Anatole Leroy-Beaulieu's course, 'Picture of Contemporary Europe', he got 4¼ out of 6.

Faculty of Law (1890–1893). In 1892, on 4 and 5 August, Proust sat a series of exams of which he passed the first set but failed the rest. In 1893, on 1 March, he received his diploma of Bachelor of Law. On 29 and 30 July, he resat his exams brilliantly and on 10 October received the diploma of his degree in law.

At this time he was more absorbed by his articles for *Le Banquet* and thought of his studies at Condorcet with nostalgia. He wrote to his father: 'I always hoped that in the end I would be able to go on with the literary and philosophical studies to which I believe I am best suited'.

Sorbonne (1894). Although the problem of his career was worrying his parents, Proust enrolled in a philosophy course at the Sorbonne in 1894. After deciding against entering the *license de philosophie* in October, he followed a course given by Egger. In the notebook where the latter kept his students' marks, an entry for December 1894 mentions an essay Proust had handed in, apparently late ('only handed in 17 Dec.'), on Socrates' philosophy: 'Difficult to read, handwriting too English and not separated enough. It's all of a block, with hardly a chink to divide different parts.' However, he added, 'Nevertheless ingt' (probably 'intelligent') and 'Has used Boutr [Boutroux], but others too, and has understood everything.' This piece of work rated 11 out of 20, which was a very high mark. The notebook mentions the first session of the degree examinations, dated March 1895. There were two written subjects, the first given by Janet: 'The unity and identity of self', the second by Boutroux: 'Descartes' opinion on some of the ancients'. For the two tests, the notebook gives four marks, which perhaps correspond to a double marking system: '6,12 and 10,14'. Proust passed. In the oral, he got 15 and 10. After the extra German exam at the end of March he was awarded his *license de philosophie*, in 23rd place with 118 points. He could leave for Brittany with Reynaldo Hahn.

Problems at School

His health was a handicap to his scholastic life. Like the hero of *Jean Santeuil*, Proust suffered from insomnia and fevers. He was very susceptible to cold, and used to stuff his pockets with hot potatoes or chestnuts to keep his hands warm.

His absences from class were very frequent. In Class 4, M. Legouëz (French) made a note for the second term: 'Absent for three weeks'; in the third: 'absent since the month of May'. The mathematics teacher mentioned the same thing: 'Absent for a long time'. In Class 3 M. Guillemot (literature) commented in the second term: 'Illness has spoilt his work; his success will return with his health'. His condition worsened and he seems not to have come back to school in the third term (judging by the lack of teachers' marks). In Class 2 he was absent even more often. He had to take private lessons. In the first term he hardly attended Condorcet. M. Courbaud (literature) gave him nothing but zeros, signifying his non-attendance. M. Vast (history and geography) put nothing in his columns, but observed: 'always absent', as did M. Henet and M. Sigwalt. In the second term it was the same. At the end of the school year, his name did not even appear on the teachers' lists. Consequently, Proust had to repeat the year.

In 'Rhétorique', Cucheval remarked in the first term: 'often ill'.

Apart from his illness, which explained his lack of progress, his character and an already strong personality prevented Proust from fitting into the scholastic mould. When he came out of Condorcet he had the habit of dawdling in the street, treating himself to cakes and chatting for hours with the concierge.

In 'Philosophie', M. Aubert (physics and chemistry) noted: 'Does absolutely nothing'. But Darlu, who knew about Proust's terrible handicap, his asthma, commented: 'Works as hard as his health allows.'

At the École libre des sciences politiques, Proust did not shine through diligence. As the quatrain about Vandal he composed about this time suggests, he didn't 'give a shit'. Society affairs interested him more. On 26 January 1893 he absent-mindedly lost the list of four law examinations he had to sit, and had to ask his friend Robert de Billy for it between two pieces of social gossip.

Friends

COURS PAPE-CARPENTIER Jacques Bizet, Daniel Halévy (son of the playwright and novelist Ludovic), Robert Dreyfus, Henri de Rothschild.

LYCÉE The same. As lessons finished at three o'clock, they played together in the afternoons in the Champs-Élysées gardens. These friends, children of the Jewish haute bourgeoisie which Proust's mother's family mixed with, would later enable Proust to become a regular guest at the Parisian salons. From this small group the following made distinctive careers: a philosopher, Léon Brunschwicg, who later gave private lessons to Robert Proust; a member of parliament, Paul Bénazet; an ambassador, Maurice Herbette; men of letters, Louis de la Salle, Jean de Tinan and Paul Leclercq.

Proust was faithful to his friends. *In Class 6*, we find the name of Daniel Halévy. *In Class 5*, Maurice Brunschwicg (brother of Léon), Horace Finaly (son of Hugo Finaly with whom Proust later stayed at Ostend), Charles Gans (son of the banker) and Élie Halévy. *In higher classes*, in 1883, Édouard de Rothschild, Léon Brunschwicg, Gaston Arman; this little clan remained his friends. Added to it were the brothers Jacques and Paul Baignères, Fernand Gregh, Robert Dreyfus and Robert de Flers, Henri Rabaud, Marcel Boulenger, Gabriel Trarieux, Alfred Athis. *In Class 2*, Proust, who was then 16, still spent time in the Champs-Élysées, where he used to meet Marie Bénardaky,

Lucie Faure and her younger sister Antoinette, the daughters of the Le Havre member of parliament, Félix Faure, later President of the Republic. Proust wrote to Antoinette Faure: 'I have nothing to tell you about the Champs-Élysées. Blanche is still very sweet, with an angelic, mischievous face. Marie Bénardaky is very pretty and more and more high-spirited. She had a "fist-fight" with Blanche, who was "beaten" . . . Should I give your friends any message from you? I go to the Champs-Élysées almost every day'.

In 1886, when he *repeated Class 2*, Proust teamed up with Daniel Halévy, whom he had known in Class 6. *In 'Rhétorique'*, in October 1887, he made friends with Pierre Lavallée, Édouard Joyant and Jacques Bizet who had just arrived at Condorcet. He dedicated his photograph to him: 'To my dearest friend (jointly with Daniel Halévy), 18 February 1889, J. Bizet.' The grandfather of both these boys, the composer Jacques Fromental Halévy (1799–1862) was a regular guest at the Crémieux salon. The two cousins and Robert Dreyfus were the 'three most intelligent boys in the class' (*Jean Santeuil*), but also, according to Fernand Gregh, the most undisciplined: 'The two cousins competed in making a "din". The naïve teaching assistant, M. Martin, who wore blue spectacles, said to them one day: "You know perfectly well that with your names, you'd never be expelled . . . They abuse their privilege, the cowards!"' (F. Gregh, *op. cit.*, p. 136).

Relationships with Friends

At the lycée, Proust was already difficult and exclusive. His friends appreciated this, recognising his originality, but were easily exasperated by his femininity and gentleness. Daniel Halévy recalled: 'We loved him, we admired him, but we remained amazed and rather embarrassed by the sense of difference, distance, by something immeasurable and invisible but real that divided us. There we were in the lycée yard, three or four noisy boys, Jacques Bizet, Fernand Gregh, Robert de Flers, and suddenly we felt a presence, a breath close to us, a light touch at our shoulder. It was Marcel Proust, who had come up as silently as a ghost; it was him, with his big oriental eyes, his high white collar, his floppy tie. There was something about him that we didn't like, and we'd reply with a cross word, or mime a slap on the back. We would never have actually given Proust a dig in the ribs: that was unthinkable: but we pretended to, and that was enough to hurt him. He was undoubtedly not boyish enough for us, and his kindness, his capacity for caring, his caresses, just seemed to us (incapable as we were of understanding such a delicate soul) like mannerisms and affectation, and we even said so to his face sometimes. Then his eyes were even more tragic than ever. But nothing stopped him being amiable.'

Proust was always 'amiable', whatever happened. Halévy also quoted a sonnet in which Proust described himself, and which began: 'His eyes are like the shining black night'. But his relationships were already stormy. Proust complained about Halévy to Robert Dreyfus: 'What's the matter with him? Why, after being so affectionate towards me, did he drop me completely, and make me so clearly aware of it, and then come up and say hello after he'd stopped speaking to me altogether for a whole month? And what about his cousin Bizet? Why did he say he was my friend, and then desert me even more suddenly? What are they trying to do to me? Get rid of me, annoy me, confuse me, what? I thought they were so nice!'

Proust then left for Isle-Adam to stay with his friend Édouard Joyant, the son of Madame Joyant, née Duchauffour. He was beginning to get more experience of friendship, of cruelty and perhaps of love, the perpetual themes of *A la Recherche*. Some of Proust's letters of the time raise questions about the kind of relationship he wanted. He wrote to Daniel Halévy: 'The fact that you are delicious, and have pretty light eyes which reflect the subtle grace of your spirit so purely that it seems I can't love your soul completely unless I kiss your eyes, and if your body and your eyes are as graceful and supple as your mind, so that it seems I would sink deeper into your thoughts if I sat on your knee, and if I feel that the charm of your self, the you in which I can't separate your lively mind and your lithe body, would be even stronger for me if it included "the sweet joys of love", does not mean I deserve the sort of con-temptuous words better suited to someone who is tired of women, and looking for new thrills in the experience of pederasty.'

In the spring of 1888, Proust wrote to Jacques Bizet, who may have rejected his advances: 'So I accept the superb, cruel yoke you impose upon me. Perhaps you are right. Nevertheless, I still find it sad not to pluck the delicious flower which soon we will not be able to pluck – for it will already have become forbidden fruit.'

Proust loved to pastiche his friends, and remarks such as this of Robert Dreyfus – 'the portrait of you I have in my mind, swathed in your contempt for the vulgarian and giving him a display of an imaginary, very ironical Dreyfus' – show his analytical powers and his lack of indulgence. For him: 'Another pleasure is that of speaking ill of one's friends.'

In 'Philosophie'. He met two future philosophers, Élie Halévy (1870–1937), Daniel's brother, and Xavier Léon, who was to be a founder of the *Revue de métaphysique et de morale.*

After the lycée. Proust kept his friends from Condorcet. He also became friendly with Robert de Billy, with whom he later studied *sciences politiques.* Gabriel Trarieux (born in 1870), a future symbolist poet, and Jean Boissonnas, who followed a diplomatic career, went with them. In 1895 he gained his philosophy degree, but his friends Bazaine and Léon Yeatman failed. On 9 May 1892, Yeatman invited him to Neuilly, with Fernand Gregh, to a party in honour of Maurice Barrès, then a young member of parliament for Nancy.

École des sciences politiques. At the beginning of 1893, Proust asked Yeatman to a ball at the Finalys' where he introduced him to Anatole France. In the spring of 1893, he gave a dinner party for his friends hosted by his parents. That summer, he considered writing a '*roman à quatre*' with Louis de la Salle, Fernand Gregh and Daniel Halévy. He also saw a good deal of Pierre Lavallée (1872–1948) and spent his holidays at the latter's château at Segrez. The École des sciences politiques was a sympathetic environment for the society events (dinners and performances) that Proust and his friends liked to attend. According to the custom of the time they exchanged photographs (Robert de Billy gave his to Proust on 7 January 1895).

Proust began to flit through the salons of his friends' mothers.

CHAPTER THREE

Military Service

By enlisting before he was called up, Proust took advantage of the system of voluntary service, then in its last year. Since 1872 five years' military service had been compulsory, but this was reduced to one year for volunteers.

Proust enlisted on 11 November 1889 and on 15 November joined the 76th Infantry Regiment, 1st Battalion, 2nd Company, at the Coligny barracks in Orléans. (These had been so named in 1887 by General Boulanger, and had previously been called the Bannier barracks.)

Volunteers were supposed to live in barracks. However, like many of his friends, Proust rented a room in the town from Madame Renvoizé at 92 Faubourg Bannier, 300 metres from the barracks, close to the cathedral and the church of Saint-Euverte (whose name he gave to one of the characters in *A la Recherche*).

Thanks to his father, he was exempted from morning roll-call and the hardest and most tiring physical exercise; but he practised riding, fencing and swimming as well as marching. He liked military life and made friends. During a dinner party at the house of the *préfet* of the Loiret, Paul Boegner (father of the future Pastor Boegner, president of the Protestant Federation), he met up with Robert de Billy, himself doing voluntary service in Orléans, in the 30th Artillery Regiment. In his brief moments of depression, letters from his mother (to whom he wrote practically every day) were a comfort. On 14 December 1889, she wrote: 'Well, my darling, a whole month has passed, so you only have to swallow eleven more pieces of the cake, of which a couple of slices will be consumed by leave. I've thought of a way to make the time pass more quickly for you. Take eleven pieces of your favourite chocolate, and tell yourself you'll only eat one on the last day of each month – you will be amazed to see them disappear, and your exile with them.'

He spent his leaves in Cabourg and almost every Sunday in Paris, at Madame Arman de Caillavet's house (he was very friendly with her son Gaston). Gaston often drove him to the station to catch the 7.40 p.m. train to Orléans. On 13 December 1889, Horace Finaly came to see him.

He enjoyed the company of his comrades, whose backgrounds were often humble; he envied their moral and physical health: 'the simplicity of some of my peasant comrades, whose bodies have stayed more beautiful and agile, whose minds are more original, hearts more spontaneous and characters more natural than those of the young people I had known until then [...], all this came together to make that period of my life now seem like a series of little pictures full of happy truthfulness and charm' (*Les Plaisirs et les jours*). He later wrote about his life in the army in *Jean Santeuil*.

The military uniform he had had made to measure was packed away in a box by his mother; he kept it in his wardrobe all his life.

On 16 December 1889, he was *admis à suivre le peloton d'instruction* (he was graded 63rd out of 64). On 3 March 1890 he was admitted to the company college and became *officier d'administration de 2e classe* in the territorial army. In the summer of 1890 he became *secrétaire au quartier général* in the division, but not for long, because the chief of staff couldn't stand his handwriting.

Superior Officers

COLONEL ARVERS, commander of the regiment. At the request of Proust's father (whose political connections were far from negligible), he softened the regime Proust had to follow. In June 1890 he became deputy director of infantry at the ministry and was replaced by Colonel Delbos.

CAPTAIN CHARLES WALEWSKI (4 June 1848 – 2 October 1916). Napoleon's grandson (his grandmother, Marie Walewska, was the Emperor's mistress; his mother, Countess Walewska, was the mistress of Napoleon III). Proust based the Princesse de Borodino in *Le Côté de Guermantes* on her, and Captain de Borodino at Doncières on her son. In 1914 Walewski was the colonel in command of the Versailles garrison.

CAPTAIN SALVRIN. He was close to some of Madame Proust's friends and used to pass her news through them.

LIEUTENANT PIERRE ARMAND DE CHOLET (26 April 1864 – 9 May 1924). Proust was directly under his orders. He later made Cholet one of the models for Saint-Loup in *A la Recherche*, and for Lieutenant de Brucourt and the Comte de Saintré in *Jean Santeuil*. Cholet gave Proust his photograph, with the dedication: 'To Marcel Proust, volunteer, from one of his torturers.' Proust's review of *Voyage en Turquie d'Asie*, which Cholet published early in 1892, appeared in *Littérature et Critique* on 25 May 1892. Chabannes La Palice painted Cholet's portrait.

Return to Civilian Life

In November 1890, Proust wanted to stay in the army for a few more months, but Colonel Delbos refused his request. On 14 November he became an active army reservist and went home to Paris. He subsequently managed, apparently, to avoid his period of military service every year, thanks to his father's friend, Dr Simon Duplay, who gave him a medical certificate. On 11 May 1894, he was excused from his 28-day period of training in this way. Called up once again in August 1896, he sent in his recruitment card to be exempted from duty, claiming a 'minor asthma attack'. On 11 November 1902 he was transferred to the territorial reserve. On 13 June 1904, he asked for a deferment of his training period, and was granted it on 4 July. On 31 July 1908, he once again obtained a deferment.

On 6 September 1911, following the intervention of Gaston Calmette, the director of *Le Figaro* (whose brother Émile was head of the health service of the Paris military command), he was finally removed from the lists of the territorial army, with the rank of *officier d'administration du service de santé*, on the grounds of ill health. Although he was invalided out in 1914, he was afraid of having to pass a military health review in November 1914 and asked several different doctors for medical certificates.

During World War I he underwent a medical examination on 25 August 1915; the military doctors granted him six months' deferment. In 1917 he lost his certificate of exemption from military service and was afraid of being arrested as a deserter if asked for his papers.

CHAPTER FOUR

Literary Beginnings

From his days at the lycée, Proust had started to write. His style was sometimes 'mannerist', influenced by Paul Bourget and Jules Lemaitre, masters of the time. He described himself as 'decadent' in a letter to Robert Dreyfus of 10 September 1888: 'I should like to say [...] to whoever is interested that I am a decadent.' For Daniel Halévy, Proust was: 'Our master, our guide in matters of taste in a school full of civil servants' (D. Halévy, *Pays parisiens*, p. 118). Proust was to make corrections to Halévy's first poems.

Proust was instrumental in creating several small duplicated pamphlets, all short-lived.

First Periodicals

Lundi: revue artistique et littéraire. Founded at the beginning of 1887. Its cover was white, with a design showing two lovers holding up a folio with a boastful motto inspired by Verlaine: 'The triumphant eclecticism of Beauty'.

La Revue de seconde (February 1887 to March 1888). This was intended to be the vehicle of Halévy's literary school, 'subtilitisme'. Proust composed various affected verses for it, some of which were dedicated to Albert Cuyp and later used in *Portraits de peintres*.

La Revue lilas. A small magazine printed in 1888 at Condorcet. Its name came from 'the pale mauve covers of the thin notebooks costing two or three sous which we chose for it in the stationers in the passage du Havre' (R. Dreyfus, *Souvenirs sur Marcel Proust*, p. 56). Robert Dreyfus owned a manuscript, 'notes de théâtre' – a pastiche of Jules Lemaitre – which had been written for it. Proust was a contributor; in October he wrote a pen-portrait of the 'charming Glaukos' which his friends suppressed, considering it too scandalous.

La Revue verte. Composed on green paper – the same as that which the Class 2 teacher Eugène Lintilhac made his pupils use in order to rest their eyes – only a single copy was planned. It was to circulate among its readers at Condorcet. Halévy, who was the editor, wanted to keep it, but Proust, as editorial secretary, vetoed this: 'Mr Secretary formally opposes Mr D. Halévy's request, which he was in ignorance of. His opposition is not unconstitutional (that is the first point). The reason for it is to prevent the bad impression that could be formed at a later date, by attributing to a few hastily written journalistic pieces an importance they never claimed to have.' (R. Dreyfus, *op. cit.*, p. 70). Did the magazine ever appear? All that remains is this protest, written on the green paper. Halévy made up for it later by founding, in 1920, the series of 'Cahiers verts' at Grasset, whose number 26, which came out in 1926, was entitled: *Souvenirs de Marcel Proust* by Robert Dreyfus.

Le Banquet

The Founding of the Magazine

Le Banquet was founded in 1892 by Fernand Gregh (then studying law at the Sorbonne) and Proust (who was then enrolled at the Faculty of Law and at the École des sciences politiques), Louis de la Salle, Jacques Bizet (a medical student at Hôtel-Dieu), Daniel Halévy (studying Arabic at the École des langues orientales), Robert Dreyfus, Henri Rabaud (who was studying under Massenet at the Conservatoire de musique) and Robert de Flers. They were joined by Gabriel Trarieux, Léon Blum, Henri Barbusse, Amédée Rouquès and Gaston Arman de Caillavet. Each of them contributed ten francs a month to bring out an issue. The magazine was printed at the printworks of *Le Temps* by a friend of Jacques Bizet, Eugène Reiter. The editorial office was in the basement of the Rouquette bookshop, 71 passage Choiseul, Paris 11. They had considered calling it *Le Chaos*, and various other titles had been suggested: *Les Divergences, Opinions et Variétés, L'Anarchie littéraire, Varia, Revue timide, Revue des Opinions, L'Independence, Le Toupet périodique, Revue des Futurs et Conditionnels, Aperçus littéraires et artistiques, Chemins dans la Brume, Les Tâtonnements, Vers la Clairière, Les Guitares* and others. They decided on *Le Banquet* as a reference to Plato. Daniel Halévy, Robert Dreyfus and Proust were in charge of collecting material. Fernand Gregh quickly took overall charge and became the 'Director'.

The cover was bluish with the title in red. Publication was monthly, but only eight numbers appeared between March 1892 and March 1893. By that date the coffers were empty, and each of the contributors had made their literary début. The first issue had a print-run of 440 copies; the subsequent ones were each 200. A complete survey of *Le Banquet* appears in the *Bulletin d'Informations Proustiennes*, No. 4, 1976.

Proust's Contributions

Number 1 (March 1892). 'Un conte de Noël'. Reflections on 'Les Petits Souliers' by Louis Ganderax, which was published in January in the *Revue des Deux Mondes*.

Number 2 (April 1892). Four *Études*. They were later to reappear in *Les Plaisirs et les jours*: 'I. Les Maîtresses de Fabrices. II. Cydalise. III. Les Amies de la comtesse Myrto. IV. Heldémone, Adelgise, Ercole', and 'Un livre contre l'élégance: Sens dessus dessous', reflections on an anonymous work on elegance and fashion (in fact by Édouard Delessert), in which Proust defends the feminine toilette.

Number 3 (May 1892). Five *Études* that reappeared in *Les Plaisirs et les jours*. Only the third had a title, 'Esquisse d'après Madame ***', in which pen-portraits of Madame Straus and the Comtesse de Chevigné (both future models for the Duchesse de Guermantes) are recognisable. There was also an attack, signed 'Laurence', on *L'Irreligion d'État* and socialism.

Number 5 (July 1892). Three *Études* which reappeared in *Les Plaisirs et les jours*. Robert Dreyfus published an ambitious and clumsy article on 'La Situation en Littérature'. In the same month Proust wrote to him: 'I've read your spirited piece in *Le Banquet*, and felt you were rather laughing at us in writing it. However, since I'm not quite sure, I'd like to talk to you about it [...] Unless it's a complete hoax, I can't understand a word of it.' Dreyfus accepted this criticism from an old friend, who was already an important influence. That year Proust also wrote him a note: 'I'd like to do something in collaboration with Gregh or Halévy, in a fairly distinct collaboration: each giving an academic lecture, for instance, Halévy (Daniel) admitting me to the Academy.'

Number 6 (November 1892). Two *Études*, of which only the first would reappear in *Les Plaisirs et les jours* : 'La Mer', dedicated to Louis de la Salle, and 'Portrait de Madame ***' (in fact Madame Guillaume Beer). Also a note, signed 'M.P.', on *Tel qu'en songe* by Henri de Régnier.

Number 7 (February 1893). 'Violante ou la Mondanité', a story written in September 1892 and dedicated to Anatole France (it was collected in *Les Plaisirs et les jours*); and a piece called 'La Conférence parlementaire de la rue Serpente', dedicated to Robert de Flers (reflections on 'high society' and politics).

His friends worried about the tone of the society portraits Proust wrote, and about his lavish compliments. The editorial comment beneath this article ran: 'It must be understood that the opinions expressed in an article are only those of the signatory.' Stung by this, perhaps, Proust did not publish anything in Number 8, in which Robert de Flers dedicated 'La Comtesse de Tripoli' to him.

CHAPTER FIVE

Entering the Adult World

Like all the upper-middle classes of the time, Proust's parents wanted him to enter one of the professions.

In 1893, he had finished his military service and his law studies; his father was pushing him to choose a career. In September, Proust wrote to him: 'I always hoped that in the end I would be able to go on with the literary and philosophical studies to which I believe I am better suited. But since every year now seems to entail increasingly practical disciplines, I would rather choose one of the careers you have offered me straight away. I shall settle down to prepare either for the Foreign Office examinations, or for the School of Palaeography and Librarianship, whichever you choose. As for becoming a solicitor, I'd even rather be a stockbroker – and you can be sure I wouldn't last three days! It isn't that I don't still think that anything I do other than literature and philosophy is time wasted for me; but between several ills there are better and worse alternatives, and even in my blackest moments I have never imagined anything more atrocious than being a solicitor's clerk. By helping me to avoid that fate the Foreign Office will seem a welcome remedy, even if not my vocation.'

In October 1893, Proust spent a fortnight working for a solicitor, Maître Gustave Brunet (1861–1935), the head of a law firm at 95 rue des Petits-Champs. There was then the question of buying into a legal practice.

Proust next exchanged a long series of letters with Charles Grand-jean, the Senate librarian. A career in the museum service seemed to tempt him briefly: 'I can already see myself as director of the Versailles museum.' But he was a little wary of his adviser, who exaggerated the merits of every option: 'you are exactly the opposite of the fairy who changed jewels into toads. Out of the filthy boring jobs on offer you create marvels' (Letter of 12 November 1893). He very soon gave up the idea of the School of Librarianship, against which Grandjean had given him 'some terrible – by which I mean excellent – arguments'.

In 1891, his father (like Professor Surlende in *Jean Santeuil*) had hoped to get him into the Ministry of Foreign Affairs. But in September 1893 Proust, who didn't want to leave Paris, asked the advice of Robert de Billy, who wanted to be a diplomat himself: 'I am in a terrible dilemma because Papa insists that I decide on my career. The Audit Office seems more and more tempting. I have reasoned it out in my mind as follows: if I don't want to work abroad, my professional life in the Ministry of Foreign Affairs in Paris will be as boring as the Audit Office [...] Is the magistrature too disreputable? What else is there, given that I am determined not to be a lawyer, a doctor or a priest [...]?'

In the end, Proust chose literature and freedom. The fate of Mallarmé, a poet subjected to the weary duties of teaching at Condorcet, did not entice him, and he informed his father that he did not want to become equally tied down. His father then allowed him to finish his literature degree in 1894, pledged his financial support and ended his opposition to Proust's literary vocation.

In *Jean Santeuil*, which is strongly autobiographical, Proust makes Madame Santeuil say: 'It is not that we want to go against our son's wishes in any way – he will always be free to choose – as long as his preferences centre on a real career, the Magistrature, the Foreign Office or the Bar.'

In *A l'ombre des jeunes filles en fleurs*, he shows the narrator's father to be influenced by Norpois, as his own father was by Gabriel Hanotaux: 'My father had put up continuous opposition to my pursuing a career in literature, which he judged to be sadly inferior to that of a diplomat, denying it even the status of a career, until the day when M. de Norpois, who did not much care for the new class of diplomats, assured him that as a writer one could attract as much respect, exercise as much influence and retain more independence than in the ambassadorial service.'

In June 1895, probably on the advice of Gabriel Hanotaux, who was then Minister of Foreign Affairs, Proust veered towards librarianship. Anatole France had been the Senate librarian from 1876 to 1890, and fifty years earlier Sainte-Beuve had been librarian at the Mazarine. On 29 May Proust took an examination for a post as unsalaried assistant at the Mazarine, where there were three vacant positions. On 8 June he was chosen for one of the positions (he came third in the examination). He was to work with Paul Marais, the great scholar of incunabula, and Alfred Franklin, the chief librarian of the time. His colleagues appreciated his pleasantness, but not his efficiency. André Maurois later said: 'He was the most detached of attachés and went from one period of leave to another' (A. Maurois, *op. cit.*, p. 70). When he was neither ill nor on holiday, he put in brief appearances to consult a few rare volumes. The dust troubled him, and he armed himself with a eucalyptus vaporiser. On 25 October 1895 he was assigned to the legal department of the Ministry of Public Education. But thanks to pressure from Hanotaux, on 24 December he obtained a year's leave from the Minister of Public Education, Raymond Poincaré.

In 1896 he appeared at the Mazarine only once, to present *Les Plaisirs et les jours* to his colleagues. After that he went to great lengths to renew his year's leave of absence every December, although he did not resign, so his father retained the illusion that he had a job.

In 1899 an official inspector was amazed to discover that Proust had been absent for several years. Finally, after some acerbic comments from Albert Franklin, he was given an ultimatum on 14 February 1900 to return to his post without delay. He failed to do so, and on 1 March the minister officially sacked him and put an end to Proust's phantom career as a librarian.

In September 1903 Constantin de Brancovan, brother of the Comtesse Anna de Noailles, offered him a position as theatre critic for the magazine *Renaissance latine*, then changed his mind in December and took on Gaston Rageot instead. Even if de Brancovan appreciated Proust's genius, he was wary of his punctuality as a salaried employee, and worried about the hyperbolic praise Proust tended towards, which would not always be to the subscribers' taste. A quarrel between the two friends resulted on 11 January 1904.

CHAPTER SIX

Daily Life

Where Proust Lived

Before birth. During Madame Proust's pregnancy, the couple lived at 8 rue Roy, in an apartment rented for 2500 francs a month, a large sum at the time.

Place of birth. 96 rue La Fontaine, in Auteuil, in the house that his great-uncle Louis Weil had bought, fully furnished, from the actress Eugénie de Plunkett, better known under the name of Madame Doche. For 25 years Proust and his parents often went to stay there, in spring and at the beginning of the year. The house had three storeys, the top one of which had mansard roofs. Fake tapestries depicting subjects borrowed from Téniers hung in the dining room of this tasteless house. 'The Weils' park is laid out *à l'anglaise*, with carefully raked paths; a fountain feeds a mossy pool in which fish swim around. The great house is furnished in the style of Louis-Philippe, with heavy drapes at the windows and upholstered armchairs. There are bronzes, porcelain, and pot plants' (C. Francis, *Marcel Proust et les siens*, p. 13). The scene of the goodnight kiss is set in this house. In 1881 the garden was truncated when the avenue Mozart, which runs from Passy to Auteuil, was built through it. In 1897 the house was sold, then demolished. On the site today stands a middle-class block of flats with a plaque to Proust's memory.

From August 1871 to October 1900. At 9 boulevard Malesherbes (see ground plan on p. 376), the Prousts moved into a modern seven-storey block built by Haussmann, which boasted gas lighting, running water, coal-fired central heating and even a lift. There were balconies over-looking the rue de Surène. The Prousts lived on the first floor, at the back, in a large apartment with a 50-foot corridor running from the kitchen to the dining room. They had a bathroom and a lavatory (rare at the time). Madame Proust combed the antique shops for the furnishings, although she installed dull department-store furniture in her sons' bedroom. Fernand Gregh recalls 'a dark interior crammed with heavy furniture, muffled with curtains, suffocated with carpets, all in red and black; a typical apartment of the time, not as far removed as we think from the gloomy bric-à-brac described by Balzac' (F. Gregh, *op. cit.*, p. 154). This apartment still exists; it now houses a travel agent's offices.

Holidays – Until 1881. 4 rue du Saint-Esprit in Illiers, at the house of his Aunt Amiot (see map on p. 375). Proust went there with his parents at Easter and during the summer holidays until his first asthma attack, when he was 9 years old. The house has been restored to its condition at the time, following the description in *Du Côté de chez Swann*: the narrator's bed is hung with high white curtains and covered with embroidered bedspreads, marceline coverlets, a floral-patterned eider-down and cambric pillowcases. On the bedside table stands the blue-patterned glass, the sugar basin and the carafe; on the mantelpiece, the pendulum clock under its glass bell; on the walls, a picture of the Saviour and a portrait of Prince Eugène (a free gift from a biscuit manufacturer). The house has two entrances: one at the front, onto the rue du Saint-Esprit; the other giving onto the place Lemoine, where an iron gate opens into a small courtyard. His aunt never left her bedroom: 'On one side of her bed stood a large yellow chest-of-drawers in lemon-wood, and a table which served both as pharmacy and high altar. There, under a statuette of the Virgin and a bottle of Vichy-Célestins, were prayer-books and doctor's prescriptions' (*Du Côté de chez Swann*). The housekeeper, Ernestine Gallou, was always in the kitchen: 'One caught glimpses of its red-tiled floor, gleaming like porphyry. It seemed less like Françoise's lair than a little Temple of Venus.' This room opened onto a small, partly paved garden with a minuscule lawn and a bed of pansies. In front of the kitchen, a summerhouse with panes of coloured glass projected from the main building; this was the refuge of Uncle Amiot. Out of nostalgia for Algeria, where he had lived, he had decorated it with carved coconuts, photographs of mosques and straw matting on the tiled floor. In *Du Côté de chez Swann*, Proust often juxtaposes the décor at Illiers with that at Auteuil. The house was made into a museum thanks to P.-L. Larcher.

In September 1886 Proust went with his parents for one last stay in Illiers; they had to sort out the estate of his aunt, Françoise Élisabeth Amiot, Adrien Proust's sister. His paternal grandmother still lived in Illiers with old Ernestine Gallou as a companion. During this stay, the young Marcel read a book which proved decisive for his sense of vocation as a writer: *L'Histoire de la conquête de l'Angleterre par les Normands* by Augustin Thierry.

From October 1900 to August 1906. 45 rue de Courcelles (see ground plan on p. 376). This quiet neighbourhood in Monceau reflected the rise in Dr Proust's social and professional status. Living in the same street were Princesse Mathilde (who had a large town house) and, at number 69, the Bibesco family. The Prousts had chosen a seven-storey building with balconies, cornices and balustrades; it was built in 1881 and belonged to the Phénix company (who later caused Proust some difficulties, in 1905, when he wanted to give up the lease). The family moved in on about 15 October, when Proust was away in Venice. The apartment was about 300 square metres in size; the rooms were enormous and richly furnished, decorated with Barbedienne bronzes and pot plants. The drawing room contained the mahogany plush furniture from the boulevard Malesherbes apartment. Proust worked in the dining room 'with severe panelling of gleaming mahogany', at a huge oval table covered with a red cloth. It was lit with a Carcel oil lamp, whose 'fair sweet light' he loved. In Dr Proust's study the portrait Lecomte du Noüy had painted of him in 1885, wearing his scarlet university gown, had pride of place. After Dr Proust's death in 1903, Proust and his mother kept the apartment, but closed off a part of it. When his mother died, in 1905, Proust found the apartment too big and decided to move. The lease expired on 30 September 1906, and his brother took care of the moving arrangements while friends, including Lauris, busied themselves finding Proust a new apartment.

From 6 August to 27 December 1906 Proust installed himself in the Hôtel des Réservoirs, Versailles. Built in the eighteenth century for the

Marquise de Pompadour, the hotel was separated from the north wing of the château only by the reservoirs which feed the fountains in the park, and Proust could look out over the basin of Neptune.

From 27 December 1906 to 27 September 1908 Proust sublet the apartment of his great-uncle Louis Weil at 102 boulevard Haussmann, even though he was, through the latter's will, a co-owner of the building. Proust could have moved into this first-floor apartment on 8 October, but he had some work done which delayed his move until December. He knew the place well, as he had often dined there with his mother. In a letter to Madame Gaston de Caillavet, he wrote: 'It is a very ugly apartment, dusty, overhung by trees, everything I hate, which I have taken because it is the only one I have been able to find that Maman knew.' After he moved in, he had to endure the noise of building work in an adjoining apartment let to Madame Katz: 'after all these months twelve workmen hammering with such frenzy every day ought to have built something as majestic as the pyramid of Cheops, which people who go out must be amazed to see standing between the Printemps and Saint-Augustin. I don't see it myself, but I hear it' (Letter to Madame Straus of April 1907). On 8 November 1907, Madame Georges Weil bought the whole building at auction.

From 27 September to 3 November 1908 Proust once again stayed at the Hôtel des Réservoirs.

From 4 November 1908 to June 1919 he returned to 102 boulevard Haussmann.

Proust's bedroom looked out on the boulevard, but he kept the shutters, as well as the windows with their blue curtains, closed. The room was huge, with a high ceiling. In September 1910 he had the walls lined with cork. These cork panels were never covered with wallpaper or material (which was the original intention); they gradually turned black with dust and gave an overall impression of dirt. A bronze pendulum clock and an unmatched pair of candelabra with blue glass shades stood on the mantelpiece of carved white marble. The only lighting was provided by a bedside lamp with a dark green shade; Proust never used the central chandelier. Like the rest of the apartment, the bedroom was cluttered with furniture. Between two windows stood a mirror-fronted wardrobe of Brazilian rosewood inlaid with bronze, with a decorated pediment, but it was almost concealed by a grand piano. On the left, an oak desk was strewn with books. Two double doors, one of which was blocked by two revolving bookcases, gave onto the main drawing room. In front of these was placed a Boulle work table, with his mother's initials, J.P., on it. To the left of the door that could be opened (the one nearest to the window), Proust kept his silver in a small Chinese chest on which photographs were placed. On a large rosewood chest of drawers topped with white marble stood two white cups framing an infant Jesus crowned with bunches of grapes, and the famous notebooks covered with black moleskin. The drawers contained souvenirs and photographs. A third door gave access to a lavatory. The bed, with its brass bars tarnished from fumigation, was parallel to the windows. It was covered by two blankets and a quilted counterpane with a pattern of apple blossom, yellow on a red background, which Proust had bought from Céline Cottin because of its resemblance to a counterpane of Aunt Amiot's. A fine Chinese screen stood behind the bed. Three tables were grouped within reach. One, made of carved bamboo, had two shelves and was used only for hot-water bottles, handkerchiefs and books. The second, an antique rosewood night table, contained a penholder, a school inkwell, manuscripts, notebooks, his watch, the bedside lamp and, later on, various pairs of spectacles. The third, which was made of walnut, was for the tray of coffee or Évian water. The only seats were the piano stool and, close to the bed, an armchair upholstered in velvet which came from his father's study. An oriental carpet served as the bedside rug. The oak parquet floor was never waxed because of the smell.

Every day of the year, to get rid of the fumes from Proust's medicinal fumigations, the apartment was heated with wood fires, never coal; the central heating was not used. Proust spent his time in his bedroom or in the small sitting room. This contained a large black bookcase which contained the works of Ruskin and of Madame de Sévigné, and autographed books. On the wall hung the portrait of Proust which Jacques-Émile Blanche had painted in his Uncle Weil's house at Auteuil. The picture shows Proust at the age of 20, in evening dress, with an orchid in his buttonhole.

In the hall stood a chest with a red moquette cover, on which there was a silver tray for the post, and for the handkerchiefs and gloves Proust never forgot when he went out. The dining room was closed up and used only as a furniture store.

Dr Gagey lived in the apartment on the ground floor. Dr Williams, the dentist who treated Proust and Madame Straus, lived on the second floor.

In mid-January 1919 Proust's aunt, Emilie Weil, informed him that she had sold the building in the boulevard Haussmann to her banker, M. Varin-Bernier. In February the bank began building work and Proust, unable to sleep, considered leaving for Italy or renting Madame Catusse's villa in Nice. In May, Proust found an apartment on the 5th floor in the rue de Rivoli, near the Ritz, but he did not take it.

From 30 June to 1 October 1919. 8 bis, rue Laurent-Pichat was the town mansion belonging to the actress Réjane, who lived on the second floor; her son, Jacques Porel, lived on the third with his wife. Proust moved into the fourth floor, which Réjane kept for her daughter, who was then in America. The apartment was furnished, but Proust had the furniture from his bedroom moved there. He did not like the house; the noise bothered him. He was troubled by the sounds of bathwater coming from the neighbouring building, where the actor Le Bargy lived. The nearby Bois de Boulogne exacerbated his asthma attacks. From July onwards Proust was anxious to move again, and consulted an estate agent in the place Victor-Hugo. He had made friends, however, with the old concierge Charmel (who was to give his name to one of Charlus's valets). At the end of *Le Temps retrouvé*, when Berma's death is near, Proust describes the atmosphere of this house. When he left, Maurice Martin du Gard took over his apartment. In a letter to Porel, Proust said he was sad to leave the black and white flowers set on a red background in his bathroom; he described them in the narrator's bathroom at Doncières.

From 1 October 1919 until his death on 18 November 1922 Proust lived at 44 rue Hamelin, in a small furnished apartment on the fifth floor. There was a lift. He paid rent of 16,000 francs a year to his landlady, Madame Boulet. Madame Standish lived nearby, in the rue de Belloy. As he wrote to Montesquiou, Proust felt he lived in a 'wretched slum which

barely holds my miserable pallet'. On the ground floor was M.
Montagnon's bakery, where Céleste went to telephone on the night of
Proust's death.

Proust's bedroom had two doors: a set of double doors through which
one entered the room, and a single door which led to the bathroom.
Apart from the piano, the chest of drawers and the mirror-fronted
wardrobe, the bedroom furniture was installed there – the decorated bed
with the screen behind it, the little Chinese chest, the visitor's armchair
and the three small tables. The mantelpiece was covered in books. Long
curtains of blue satin hung from the windows. Opposite, in the passage
next to the bathroom, was a room full of books and silverware. Céleste's
room was off the hall to the right.

The small sitting room retained the glass-fronted bookcase surmounted by two bronze Chinese elephants, but the armchairs had been
replaced by low fireside chairs. Proust had kept the pictures: the pretty
portrait of the Infanta, the portraits of his parents, his own portrait by
Blanche, and the landscape by Paul Helleu. As the fireplaces in the
apartment were small, and drew very badly, Céleste did not make up the
fires. The building has been converted into a hotel, and the apartment,
now divided into small rooms, no longer exists.

Domestic Servants

Proust's Parents' Domestic Servants

COOKS Ernestine Gallou: She was a faithful servant to Proust's grandmother and Aunt Amiot in Illiers, remaining in their service for 33 years.
She appears as Félicie in the preface 'Sur la lecture', and she is an
important model for Françoise in *Du Côté de chez Swann*. Félicie Fitau: An
old servant in a white hat who left Proust in 1907. She was the aunt of
Robert Ulrich, one of Proust's secretaries. An excellent cook, she had a
marvellous way of making *boeuf à la mode*, like Françoise in *A la
Recherche*. Marie: The Prousts' chambermaid, and cook when Félicie was
away. She was very beautiful, and seemed to be falling in love with
Proust when Madame Proust, informed of the situation, sent her away
in March 1905. She was another model for Françoise.

VALETS Arthur: Letters between Madame Proust and her son describe both his loyalty and his ill health. Auguste: Uncle Louis Weil's old valet. In November 1906, Proust gave him his furniture. Baptiste: One of Madame Proust's servants who appears in the letters of 1904. Antoine Bertholhomme: The Breton concierge at 102 boulevard Haussmann. Together with Jean Blanc, he played an active part in Proust's move. He was so devoted that when he saw Proust waiting for a car he would rush out of his lodge to offer him a seat. During the war their relationship deteriorated because of spiteful interference by Céline Cottin. Jean Blanc: Proust's father's valet, whom Proust kept until 1908. It was he who, in February 1900, woke up Léon Yeatman to say: 'Monsieur Marcel has sent me to ask Monsieur what happened to Shelley's heart.' In *Jean Santeuil* he was the model for Augustin, the witness to the hero's quarrel with his parents.

Proust's Domestic Servants

After the death of his parents, Proust kept on Félicie Fitau and Jean Blanc for a time, but was soon thinking of hiring a new servant.

NICOLAS COTTIN (1873–1916): Valet to Proust's parents, then a croupier at the Cercle Interalié. Madame Proust advised her son against taking him back, because he drank and gambled. But Proust engaged him and his wife in 1907, on condition that he took no time off. The usual salary for a married couple was then 150 francs a month; Proust paid them double, but the work was not easy. Cottin was on duty until four in the morning, forced to adopt his master's nocturnal lifestyle. The suffocating heat of Proust's room made him bronchitic. However, he managed to remain charming, devoted, well-trained and attentive. He played dominoes with Proust, and put the sheets of his novel in order in a file. At the beginning of the war he became cook to General Joffre. He died of pleurisy in 1916. To replace him, Frédéric de Madrazo recommended to Proust a young man who was very willing, but very shy. Seeing him arrive at the apartment, Proust said: 'I saw Galloping Consumption walk in. He left me with great regret because he had been "called".'

ERNST FORSSGREN See p. 180.

CÉLINE COTTIN (1879–?): Nicolas Cottin's wife. Her job was no easier than her husband's. Roused at dawn to make coffee, she often did not finish until 9.30 at night. Proust nicknamed her 'the warmonger' because she had said to him one day: 'I'd like to see what war is like.' In November 1913 she fell ill, and was operated on by Robert Proust at the Broca hospital. Her master sent her a copy of *Du Côté de chez Swann* inscribed: 'With best wishes to the patient, who will soon be free of her patient indefinitely.' When she returned she became jealous of Céleste Albaret, who had replaced her, and called her 'the wheedler' and 'the little schemer'. Proust had to send her away. When her husband died in 1916, she held Proust responsible for Nicolas's weak lungs. Since she was a widow and had lost everything, Proust gave her some financial help.

Some of her characteristics can be found in *A la Recherche* (particularly her *boeuf à la mode*, which she cooked as well as Félicie Fitau). According to George D. Painter, it was she who, in January 1909, gave Proust the cup of tea and toast which aroused his involuntary recollections.

JOSSIEN: A driver for the Taximètres de Monaco company. Proust employed him from October 1907 to April 1908. His sister-in-law was Jacques Bizet's maid. His name inspired that of Jupien in *A la Recherche*, and he was to be a model for the coachman Théodore, brother to Madame Putbus's maid.

ODILON ALBARET (1881–1960): A driver for Taximètres de Monaco. In 1907 he entered Proust's service, along with Jossien and Agostinelli, and was regularly employed in Paris. In mid-August 1914, when Odilon was mobilised, he advised Proust to employ his elder brother Edmond, who had been exempted from the army because he was slightly deaf. Odilon came back when he was demobbed in 1918, by then suffering from a lung condition. Proust sent him to spend three months in the military hospital in Vésinet. He did not get back into his old red Renault until the end of 1919. Proust supervised his draconian regime. Odilon, who was known for his excellent financial sense, remained Proust's most trusted servant. He never baulked at getting up in the middle of the night for an errand, and his master was very demanding: 'When he had ordered the car, my husband had to be waiting down below before he went out, and once he had the car out he kept it. Sometimes when he came home he asked Odilon to wait, just in case he went out again. At other times a sudden yen for an iced beer, at two in the morning, meant a trip to the Ritz, which was closed' (C. Albaret, *op. cit.*, p. 254). (The writer Ramon Fernandez had introduced Proust to iced beer at Lipp's, and Proust liked Odilon to bring him some in a little carafe to quench his thirst. The kitchens of the Ritz were closed at that late hour, but Proust's wants were catered for with the help of Olivier Dabescat, the maître d'hôtel.) Odilon used to relate to Proust the cries of the street-sellers which he used in *La Prisonnière*.

CÉLESTE ALBARET, *née* Gineste, (1891–1984): Born in the Lozère, she married Odilon Albaret on 27 March 1913 at Auxillac (in the Commune de la Canourgue, Lozère). Proust sent them a telegram: 'Many congratulations. I will not write to you at any length because I have flu and am feeling tired, but with all my heart I wish you and your families every happiness. Marcel Proust.' In April 1913 the Albarets moved to Levallois; it was the first time Céleste had left her native province. She met Proust and saw him again in September when he had just shaved off his black beard: 'Madame, may I introduce Marcel Proust, badly dressed, unkempt and beardless' (C. Albaret, *op. cit.*, p. 17). In mid-November, when Céline Cottin was ill, he asked Céleste to deliver complimentary copies of *Du Côté de chez Swann*. After the books, it was letters she fetched every day from the boulevard Haussmann. She became the 'messenger girl' of *A la Recherche* before her later incarnation as Françoise. As Céline's illness became protracted, Céleste came to take her place. In the morning she prepared the coffee and croissants, then from two to five in the afternoon she helped in the kitchen. Things turned sour on Céline's return, and Proust had to sack the latter. At the outbreak of war Proust lost Nicolas Cottin and Odilon Albaret, who went off to the front, so Céleste moved in to Nicolas's room in the boulevard Haussmann, and stayed there, in Proust's service, until his death in 1922. She was watchful but discreet, and faithful for many years: she advised Proust on his novels, as well as on those he received; she took care that visitors did not stay too long and tire him out; she even adopted the habit of going to bed as late as he did, and listening attentively to all he had to say – these late hours accentuated the pallor of her complexion. After Proust's

death, Antoine Bibesco claimed that the only two beings in the world
Proust had really loved were his mother and Céleste, and the latter,
without the least pretentiousness, did not contradict this in her memoirs.
In April 1923, the Albarets left the rue Hamelin. Since Proust had left no
will, his brother Robert, Horace Finaly and Madame Straus offered
Céleste some financial help, but she did not accept it. In 1924 she and her
husband bought a hotel of about fifty rooms in the rue des Cannettes, in
Paris, which they later sold. Odilon died in 1960, and for some years
Céleste took care of the Ravel museum in Montfort-l'Amaury. Her
daughter, Odile Gévaudan, fell ill, and she was obliged to sell some of
her souvenirs of Proust: thus the screen, the three small night tables,
the little green lamp, the armchairs, the fireside chairs and the dressing
table were preserved. She never parted with the beautiful opal pin he
had given her. At the age of 82, she finally decided to publish her
memoirs, feeling duty-bound to rescue Proust's reputation from those
who had written about him without first-hand knowledge. Her book
of memoirs was called *Monsieur Proust* – Memoirs collected by
Georges Belmont. Published in 1973, it ran to 455 pages. It had been
preceded, two years earlier, by a book called *Céleste*, written by Jean
Plumyène. At the end of 1981, the Minister of Culture, Jean-Philippe
Lecat, awarded Céleste the insignia of Commandeur des Arts et
Lettres. She died at Méré, near Montfort-l'Amaury, on 25 April 1984.

LÉONTINE: Céleste's sister-in-law. In April 1915 she took Céleste's
place in Proust's household for a short time when Céleste's mother
died. Proust, who was used to his regular housekeeper and disliked
Léontine's talkativeness, thought very little of the arrangement.

MARIE GINESTE: Céleste's unmarried sister. Proust hired her on an
occasional basis in October 1918 to share Céleste's errands. In 1922 she
became a permanent fixture in the rue Hamelin. She would arrive at
lunchtime and leave again in the evenings; she took care of all the
shopping and household duties. It was she who went to fetch the Cross
of the Légion d'honneur which the painter Béraud had had made for
Proust at Cartier's.

YVONNE ALBARET: Céleste's niece. She came to the rue Hamelin in the
spring of 1922 to complete the typing of *La Prisonnière* and *La Fugitive*.

She was depicted in *A la Recherche* in the guise of Françoise's daughter, whose use of slang astonished the narrator.

Meals

BREAKFAST Proust drank two cups of very strong coffee accompanied, one after the other, by a croissant. It was served on a large silver tray with a small silver coffee pot engraved with his initials, a bowl with a gilt edge decorated with the family crest, a porcelain milk jug and a saucer for the croissant. He always drank Corcellet coffee, which was roasted for him in a shop in the rue de Lévis, in the 17th arrondissement. 'One had to stuff the filter with very finely ground coffee, packed tight, and in order to get the brew Monsieur Proust wanted the water had to pass through the filter very slowly, drop by drop, taking a long time, while one kept the pot hot in a *bain marie*, of course' (C. Albaret, *op. cit.*, p. 37). The milk was delivered every morning by a dairy in the district, so that it should be very fresh; even so, Céleste never reheated it, but boiled it from cold for the coffee each time. The croissants came from a baker and pastry-cook in the rue de la Pépinière.

AT NIGHT The silver tray was replaced by a lacquer tray on which was a bottle of Évian water, some lime-flower tea, a small cup and a sugarbowl, in case Proust wanted to make himself a *tisane* with his electric kettle. In fact, Proust never made any, nor did he ever drink a drop of the Évian water. But he often plugged his kettle in by accident, and it was taken to be fixed at Morse, in the rue de la Bienfaisance.

MAIN MEAL Proust ate very little. As he wrote to Dr Linossier in 1904, he had only one meal a day, which consisted of: '(two creamed eggs, a whole wing of roast chicken, three croissants, a plate of fried potatoes, some grapes, some coffee, and a bottle of beer) and throughout the rest of the twenty-four hours the only thing I take is a quarter of a glass of Vichy water, when I go to bed'. Before the war Nicolas or Céline sometimes used to cook him a sole, or – as Proust loathed the smell of cooking – order a dish from Larue's (the restaurant on the corner of the rue Royale and the place de la Madeleine). From there he sometimes ordered 'la petite marmite' (pieces of beef and chicken gizzards simmered for a long time over a low heat), of which he would eat a few mouthfuls, straight out of the pot, before asking for it to be taken away again immediately. In 1913, he at times ate nothing more than two bowls of *café au lait* and two croissants in the course of a day. During the war he gave up the croissants, which Céleste tried in vain to replace with shortbread. After that, he drank almost nothing but coffee, sometimes as much as a litre a day. At the end of his life he relied on the services of the Ritz.

Culinary Tastes

Proust loved good food, especially sweet things. He did not like meat very much, apart from chicken, preferring the fried sole which Céleste bought at Félix Pontin in the place Saint-Augustin. This was in fact the only dish he ever finished. Only once did Céleste see him eat some red mullet from Prunier's. Occasionally he would nibble at some fried smelts. He also liked the Russian salad at Larue's, and well-drained fried potatoes served on a folded napkin. He sometimes enjoyed scrambled eggs.

DESSERTS Each of his likings was associated with a specific supplier which reminded him of his youth and his parents. *Petits fours* had to come from Rebattet (his mother's supplier) and *brioches* from Bourbonneux in the rue de Rome. When he felt like chocolate, Céleste went to get a sweet dessert from Latinville, in the rue de La Boétie, or a pear Bourdaloue from Larue's. She would buy fruit (usually a pear or a bunch of grapes) from Auger in the boulevard Haussmann. As he got older, Proust preferred stewed fruit with very little sugar, or the strawberry or raspberry ices that Odilon brought from the Ritz, to fresh fruit. Once or twice he ordered jams and gooseberry syrup from Tanrade, in the rue de Sèze, but he hardly touched them.

DRINKS Proust never drank wine or spirits; he liked the iced beer that Marie Gineste bought at the Brasserie Lipp in a bottle that was refilled at the pressure pump. After the war Odilon was once ordered in the middle of the night to fetch some from the Ritz, where, thanks to Olivier Dabescat, the maître d'hôtel, he was allowed to help himself in the empty kitchens. From time to time, Proust would also drink cider with his fried potatoes.

Proust and his Guests

GUESTS When he entertained someone for dinner, Proust would settle his guest – usually just one person – at the small table beside his bed, but did not dine with him. The menu, which never changed, consisted of fillets of sole, chicken, and an ice from Poire-Blanche, accompanied by good red or white wines according to the dishes. Before and after the meal Proust would offer Veuve Clicquot champagne or port with *petits fours* from Rebattet's. He himself never touched a thing, claiming he liked to leave his mind unencumbered.

DINNER PARTIES. At first, he gave dinner parties at his mother's house, and presided over them without touching a single dish. Sorbets were often served. Later on he organised dinners at Larue's, at the Crillon or at the Ritz.

Thus Proust was a gourmet, but not an enthusiastic eater. For him, meals took on an intellectual significance which outweighed their sensual role. He preferred the memory of certain dishes to their reality, as with *boeuf à la mode* or fried sole. Meals became a rite which helped him, through their associations of smells and images, to recover the past.

Dress

Proust was only interested in fashion for his novels. For himself, comfortable protective clothing was enough. He often appeared with his collar stuffed with cotton wool. During parties, he always kept his fur coat on. Lord Derby, the British Ambassador, who met Proust after the war at a dinner at the Ritz, wrote: 'Of all the impressions my wife and I took home with us from Paris, Monsieur Proust was the most indelible. Yes, he was the first chap we'd ever seen dining in a fur-coat' (George D. Painter, *Marcel Proust*). Anna de Noailles also used to keep her coat on, and they were called the 'two Laplanders padded with fur'.

When Proust went to Cabourg, Céleste would pile linen, woollens and innumerable items of clothing into a wheeled trunk. Even in summer Proust used to keep thickly covered up, and changed his clothes constantly. He had had made two vicuna overcoats 'for wearing at the sea': one was pale grey lined with mauve, and very light, the other was brown. He wore them with matching hats.

He never went out without gloves, but he never had them cleaned because he disliked the smell of the cleaning fluid. He couldn't bear new handkerchiefs, but liked them well worn (as with shoes). After the war he kept to his early style of dress, wearing clothes of outdated cut and high, stiff shirt collars, which detracted little from his elegance, however. Proust had several overcoats: a mink-lined coat with a black otter collar, a black overcoat lined with black and white check, and one for wearing inside. He had his suits made at the Carnaval de Venise, near the Opéra: the old English tailor came to do fittings at his apartment. 'Apart from his dress suit and his dinner jacket, he had several other jackets which he wore with striped trousers, and a loose black braided jacket. Everything was made to measure, naturally' (C. Albaret, *op. cit.*, p. 110). Proust possessed a collection of plain coloured waistcoats: he had one in red silk, lined with white silk, but he considered it too loud and never wore it. His bow ties were sober – black for his dinner jacket, white for dress clothes, and a garnet-red one which he seldom wore. When he was young, Proust wore ties from Liberty's. He always wore the same pair of black patent buttoned boots from Old England. Céleste later bought him from another shop a pair of top-boots in beige canvas which he liked enormously.

Proust was most attached to the clothes he had worn for a long time, since he used them relatively little. Shopping and trying clothes on seemed to him a waste of time. Besides, since the shops were shut by the time he went out, he had to order everything.

OUTDOOR CLOTHES When he went out, Proust changed completely. Because he suffered from the cold he put on a jersey and long johns made of Rasurel wool, which had just come out of the oven where they had been wrapped in bath towels and warmed. He tied his bow ties himself, but sometimes asked Céleste to help him with the buttons on his boots or his shirt-front. She got ready his gloves and handkerchiefs, helped him on with his overcoat, then held out to him his cane (a present from d'Albufera) and a hat (a bowler, opera hat or homburg) that matched his outfit.

The servants did no washing, but sent everything to the Lavigne laundry – formerly called the Maison Bleue – which Proust's mother had used.

A Typical Day Towards the End of Proust's Life

Proust's day began at about four or five in the afternoon. The previous night he would have fixed a time for his coffee; he would give two rings on the bell when he wished to be served. Céleste would enter without knocking, carrying the silver tray. Proust rang again for his second croissant before starting to read his mail and browse through the newspapers.

He washed meticulously – in memory of his father (who was a specialist in hygiene) – and with great ritual. Proust never allowed anyone into the bathroom. Apart from a disinfectant, he did not use any toilet products like eau de Cologne or creams, because of his allergy to perfumes. He did not even wash with soap, using damp towels instead, because of his delicate skin. He began with the foot-bath (it was white enamel with a gold stripe) and two pots of water heated to 50 degrees in the large kitchen furnace. To wash himself he used about twenty fine linen towels prepared by Céleste; he wiped himself once with each one, then discarded it and went on to the next, fearful that the dampness would chap his skin. Once dressed, he would spend some time cleaning his teeth with a fine white powder prescribed in the past by his father, which he obtained from the pharmacy Leclerc in large cans. He used to spatter it all over his tie, the mirror and the dressing table. Monsieur François, a barber in the boulevard Malesherbes, came every day to shave him.

After dining alone, Proust would get ready to go out. Céleste would call the lift; he would smile at her and say: 'Goodbye, Céleste. Thank you. I'm very tired; I hope it'll pass. I don't know whether I'll be back early or late. Don't forget to telephone the people I've mentioned and to tidy my papers' (C. Albaret, *op. cit.*, p. 151). Odilon, his chauffeur, was waiting in the street. It would be about eleven o'clock in the evening.

Always late, because the time of society dinners (eight or nine o'clock) did not suit him, Proust would arrive full of apologies but never ate anything, since he was too busy talking or watching the other guests. He never arrived at receptions before midnight. Some people avoided him because they were afraid he would keep them talking until two in the morning; in any case, many of the guests had gone home by the time he arrived. Before greeting his hostess, he would ask, through one of the servants, if he could keep his coat on (since he ate so little, he was always cold). Then he would repeat his apologies, or stop to admire a picture. The remaining guests usually formed a circle around him, enthralled by his conversation. Proust was very talkative and a brilliant conversationalist, curious about everything, always wanting to ask about a dinner party, a genealogical detail, a nicety of dress, a name that escaped him. 'The candles went out one by one. The footmen yawned and nodded off. Even the hostess was weary. Marcel Proust went on talking' (Léon Pierre-Quint, *Marcel Proust*, p. 44). He sometimes played host to four or five friends in the middle of the night, in the deserted hall of the Ritz (where he operated the light-switches himself), and he would also pay impromptu visits at unsociable hours. 'Two minutes in the drawing room and he would leave again. But if you saw him out he would dawdle in the hall for half an hour' (L. de Robert, *Comment débuta Marcel Proust*, p. 89).

Proust liked to accompany his friends home. If the weather allowed, he used to walk them home; his car followed behind. Once he got to a friend's house, Proust sometimes insisted that the friend should in turn walk him home; Proust would then ask him up to his flat to chat and argue until dawn. But often he came home alone, usually towards two or three in the morning. Céleste waited up for him, since he had no key; as soon as she heard the lift she used to go out on to the landing to open the door for him. Proust would smile and thank her, and ask her to come into his bedroom. There he would sit down, while she remained standing in front of him, listening. 'Perched on the edge of the bed, he looked like a young prince who had just come in from the ball of life' (C. Albaret, *op. cit.*, p. 153). These 'vigils' could last until seven, or even half past nine in the morning. Proust preferred to live at night, like many asthmatics who find it easier to breathe then than during the day.

Often, on his return home, Proust got into bed (the sheets were changed every day). Rolled around his hot-water bottles he would find his pyjamas and a very thick jumper of Pyrenean wool. He would then work until seven in the morning, or later, if he had already discussed his impressions of the night with Céleste. Sitting up in bed, supported by a pile of jumpers fallen one after the other from his shoulders, he used his knees as a desk; he never made use of the night table-cum-writing desk Horace Finaly had given him. The position he adopted was not at all practical, but Proust seemed indifferent to his health and his comfort when he was working. In a letter to his friend Louis de Robert, he described how exhausted he felt after writing about ten lines, lying in bed propped on one elbow, the paper loose in front of him. He wrote quickly, using pens made by Sergent-Major; a litter of penholders lay on the floor around him, because whenever one fell he didn't pick it up. In his night table he kept about fifteen penholders, two glass inkwells and a cheap watch Céleste had bought for five francs; the things he needed for his inhalations were also within reach. From about 1918 onwards, he used various pairs of spectacles. At daybreak, in bad light, his eyes too tired to go on writing, he would try to sleep. But did he ever really sleep? Céleste always doubted that he did.

History of the Ritz Hotel

César Ritz was born in Switzerland in the little village of Niederwald, son of a peasant family. He began his career in a very modest way, as apprentice wine-waiter in Brigue. Then, moving from the job of waiter to that of maître d'hôtel, he became a hotel manager (notably at the Savoy in London). In 1896, he founded a London company called the Ritz Hotel Syndicate Ltd, with the society lawyer Henry V. Higgins. Ritz's ambition was to open his own hotel, and he bought the former town house of the Duc de Lauzun in the place Vendôme, then the offices of Crédit Mobilier, who were about to vacate the premises. In collaboration with the architect Charles Mewes, Ritz set about creating his ideal hotel, the first in the world to have electricity on every floor. On 1 June 1896, under the eyes of the whole of Paris society, the palace which was quickly to become the rallying point of the upper echelons was opened. In 1902 César Ritz, by then suffering from a depressive illness, left the Parisian scene and his 36-year-old wife, Marie-Louise Ritz, took over and ran the hotel with the help of Olivier Dubescat. In ten years she expanded it three times. After the First World War the Ritz became the haunt of writers such as F. Scott Fitzgerald (when he was in Paris) and Ernest Hemingway. Marie-Louise retained control of the hotel until 1953, when her son Charles became president of the administrative board until his death in 1976. In 1979, Mohamed Al-Fayed, an Egyptian businessman resident in Great Britain, bought the hotel jointly with his two brothers for $30 million. In recognition of the restoration work he carried out, Jacques Chirac awarded him the grande médaille de la ville de Paris in 1985, and the Légion d'honneur in 1986. Since 1985 Al-Fayed has become a major patron of the arts, creating the Ritz Paris Hemingway international literary prize (in 1985) and endowing the Marcel Proust prize with 250,000 francs (in 1986).

Travels

1878. *September?*, Proust family holiday in Illiers, where the incident of 'Robert and the baby goat' recounted in *Contre Sainte-Beuve* took place. 1880. *6 September*, a stay in Dieppe. 1884. *August*, holiday in Houlgate. 1885. *September?*, stay at Salies-de-Béarn. 1885. *Autumn*, to Illiers with his parents to deal with his Aunt Amiot's will. 1889. *September*, a stay at Ostend with the Finalys. *From 15 November 1889 to 14 November 1890*, military service in Orléans. 1890. *September*, on leave in Cabourg.

1891. *September*, to Cabourg. *1 October*, to Trouville, staying with the Baignères at 'Les Frémonts'. Jacques-Émile Blanche does his portrait in pencil.

1892. *August, 7–8*, at Princesse Mathilde's in Saint-Gratien. *14*, departure for Trouville, to the Finalys. *29*, Paul Baignères does a drawing of Proust in an album.

1893. *August*, a three-week stay in St Moritz. He goes up to the Righi by funicular and climbs Alpe Grün on foot. *End August/early September*, a week's stay in Évian. *6 September*, with his mother to Trouville, at the Hôtel des Roches-Noires. He stays until the 28th. *31 December*, to Chartres for New Year's Eve with Pierre Lavallée, who is doing his military service there.

1894. *August, 18*, he sets off for the Château de Réveillon, where he is Madame Lemaire's guest for a month. Reynaldo Hahn joins him on *20 August* and is present at the incident of the rose bush. *September, 14 or 15*, in Trouville, staying at the Hôtel des Roches-Noires with his mother. He sees a lot of the Strauses and the Porto-Riches. *23*, Madame Proust leaves him in Trouville. He returns to Paris on the 25th.

1895. *5 or 6 April*, with his friend Pierre Lavallée at the Château de Segrez (Seine-et-Oise). *July*, in the Prussian Rhinelands, his first stay at

Kreuznach, a spa, where he accompanied his mother for treatment. Robert de Billy and his wife visit them. Some parts of this stay can be found in *Jean Santeuil*. *End July/early August?*, to Champrosay, staying with the Daudets, together with Reynaldo Hahn. *10 August*, to Madame Lemaire's at Dieppe, with Hahn. *August*, to Appeville-le-Petit, during which excursion he admires the beeches on the Rouen road. He later writes 'Sous-bois' for *Les Plaisirs et les jours*. *21 August*, return to Dieppe, where Madame Lemaire introduces him to Saint-Saëns. Returns to Paris on the 30th. *4 September*, he leaves Paris for Belle-Ile-en-Mer to stay with Sarah Bernhardt, together with Reynaldo Hahn. *6 September*, they leave Belle-Ile-en-Mer for Beg-Meil (Finistère) and settle in to the little Hôtel Fermont. They later meet the painter Harrison. *27 October*, return to Paris. *31 October?*, at the Château de Réveillon he writes 'Les Marronniers' for *Les Plaisirs et les jours*.

1896. *8 August*, he and his mother go to Mont-Dore to take a course of treatment, returning to Paris at the end of the month. *19 October*, to Fontainebleau, where he settles down to work on his novel and writes 'Le Téléphonage à sa mère', which evokes his despair on arriving at the hotel. Returns to Paris about *25 October*.

1897. *About mid-August*, he accompanies his mother to Kreuznach. *About 9 September*, returns to Paris. *Autumn*, to Dieppe with Léon Yeatman.

1898. *October*, first trip to the Netherlands; to Amsterdam for the Rembrandt exhibition.

1899. *Early September*, he joins his parents in the Splendide Hôtel in Évian, where he meets Antoine Bibesco and the Brancovans again. *10 September*, to Thonon to stay with Clément de Maugny, and to Geneva on *13 September*. *14 September*, he sees Pierre de Chevilly in Thonon, then goes to Coudrée to stay with the Bartholonis. *21 September*, excursion to Coppet with Constantin Brancovan and Abel Hermant. *1 October*, a tour of Lac Léman. *4 October*, he drives Maugny to Annemasse. He returns to Paris about the *8th*.

1900. *About 28 April*, leaves for Venice with his mother; they book in to the Hôtel Europa. Meets Reynaldo Hahn, Marie Nordlinger and the

Princesse Hélène de Caraman-Chimay, with whom he looks at the St John of Acre columns in front of St Mark's basilica. He makes several trips in a gondola. *End May*, back to Paris. *13 October*, leaves for Venice again, alone. He visits the monastery of the Mechitarist fathers on San Lazzaro island on the *19th*. Back to Paris at the end of the month.

1901. *7 September*, to Amiens, to lunch with Léon Yeatman; spends the afternoon in Abbeville working alone in front of the cathedral. Dinner at the station in Amiens, then returns to Paris the same evening.

1902. *28 March*, visits the Coucy dungeons with the Bibesco brothers, Bertrand de Fénelon, Robert de Billy and Georges de Lauris. *September: 6*, leaves Paris by train with Bertrand de Fénelon, but only he spends the night with the Daudets at Pray. *7*, leaves Pray by car with Lucien Daudet to go to the Château de Fresne to visit Madame de Brantes. Returns to Paris the same evening. *October: 3*, he and Fénelon leave Paris for Bruges in order to see the Flemish primitives exhibition. *9 to 10*, at Anvers. Fénelon leaves him to go to Amsterdam. *11 to 13*, leaves by train for Dordrecht (in the Netherlands). Travels by boat as far as Rotterdam. Visits Delft. *14*, arrives in Amsterdam where he joins Fénelon at the Hôtel de l'Europe. *15*, takes a passenger barge to Vollendam, without Fénelon. *17*, he sees pictures by Frans Hals in Haarlem. *18*, sees Vermeer's *View of Delft* in The Hague. (See p. 337) Returns to Amsterdam the same evening. *19*, back to Paris from Amsterdam.

1903. *10 April* (Good Friday), car trip to Provins, Saint-Loup-de-Naud and Dammarie-les-Lys with the Bibesco brothers, François de Pâris, Georges de Lauris and Lucien Henraux. *21 April*, car trip to Laon, Senlis, Coucy-le-Château and Saint-Leu-d'Esserent with the Bibesco brothers and Georges de Lauris. *16 August*, at Madame Straus's in Trouville. *31 August*, goes to Évian to join his parents. Stops off at Avallon and visits Vézelay. *1 September*, leaves Avalon for Dijon in the morning, seeing Semur on the way. Looks round Dijon and returns to Évian at 11 in the evening. *September*, to Chamonix with Louisa de Mornand. They go up to Montanvers by mule and take a trip across the Sea of Ice. *10 October*, leaves Évian, stopping at Bourg-en-Bresse to see the church at Brou. He makes another stop at Beaune where he visits the hospice before catching the Paris train.

1904. *9 August,* leaves for Le Havre where he goes aboard the yacht *Hélène,* as the guest of Paul Mirabaud and Robert de Billy, with Madame Fortoul and Jacques Faure. They make for Ouistreham, then Cherbourg, Guernsey and Saint-Malo, where they anchor for two days in the roads of Dinard. They are at Dinan by the *13th,* and return to Paris on the *15th.*

1905. *About 6 September,* he arrives at Évian with his mother, who falls seriously ill. Robert comes to get her, but Proust, ill himself, stays on for several days and returns to Paris about the *13th.*

1906. *End July,* he considers renting a villa near Trouville with Louis d'Albufera and his wife, but he stays in Paris throughout this year.

1907. *About 7 August,* leaves for Cabourg. *First fortnight in August,* he takes a trip with Georges de Lauris to Trouville, passing through Houlgate. They go to see the Guiches, at the villa 'Mon Rêve' in Bénerville, and Louisa de Mornand and the Strauses in Trouville. *About mid-August,* a journey by car to Bayeux, Caen, Balleroy and Dives with Sem or Paul Helleu. He looks round the Château Norrey at Bretteville-l'Orgueilleuse. *Towards the end of September,* after leaving Cabourg he spends five days in Évreux, and goes from there to admire the stained-glass in the church at Conches. The day before going back to Paris he pays a visit to the Clermont-Tonnerres at Glisolles.

1908. *18 July,* reaches Cabourg, where he goes to bed with a fever. He then goes on to Trouville, to the Finalys and the Strauses. *August,* he goes to see Louisa de Mornand, Robert Gangnat and Gaston Gallimard in Bénerville. *About 26 September,* leaves Cabourg by taxi for the Hôtel des Réservoirs at Versailles.

1909. *About 14 August,* suddenly leaves for Cabourg. *25 August,* he goes to Villers-sur-Mer to hear *Werther. About the end of September,* returns to Paris.

1910. *3 July?,* he spends an hour in Fontainebleau between trains. *17 July,* a sudden departure for Cabourg (because of the building work in the boulevard Haussmann). His luggage was badly labelled and goes astray. *About the end of September,* returns to Paris by taxi.

1911. 11 July, leaves suddenly for Cabourg, where he stays until *26 September?* He is too ill to go out during his stay.

1912. *Second fortnight in April,* trip to the country in Odilon Albaret's taxi (stopping in Rueil to see the apple trees in blossom). People who see them mistake them for Bonnot and Garnier, the bandits. *7 August,* a sudden departure to Cabourg. *September,* two days before returning home, he pays a visit to Madame Straus in Trouville and takes her to Honfleur by car.

1913. *February,* he wants to take a course of treatment in a sanatorium in Switzerland, and dreams of going on to Florence from there, but he stays in Paris. *26 July,* leaves on the spur of the moment for Cabourg, where he arrives at five o'clock in the morning after a journey full of incident; the car, driven by Agostinelli, had gone off the road. *4 August,* after going to Houlgate with Agostinelli, he suddenly decides to take the train back to Paris. He sends word to Nicolas Cottin, asking him to pack the trunks and to meet them in Paris. *End of October,* he hopes to rent a property outside Paris, but cannot make up his mind to leave.

1914. *3 September,* leaves for Cabourg with Céleste Albaret and Ernst Forssgren. *About 13 October,* returns to Paris. He never leaves the city again.

Material Circumstances

Capital and Income

FAMILY FORTUNES Proust's parents were very rich: his mother had inherited a large fortune from the Weils and his father earned substantial fees. Proust inherited large sums after their deaths, and no real financial worries ever interfered with his life as a writer.

STOCK EXCHANGE INVESTMENTS Proust was very interested in investments, notably in De Beers shares. Horace Finaly, his old friend from Condorcet and later the director of the Banque de Paris et des Pays-Bas, often gave him astute advice. Through extremely precise letters he instructed Albert Nahmias to carry out transactions for him. He was introduced to the Rothschilds by Léon Neuburger. He had an account at

Crédit Industriel, and kept up a large correspondence with his financial adviser, Lionel Hauser. He was obsessed with the idea that he might go bankrupt, and in fact his speculations were often disastrous.

In 1911, Proust had spent 300,000 francs on gold-mining shares; in March 1912 he had to sell out with a loss of 40,000 francs. On 30 April 1913, he suffered another major loss: 'Papa used to say that I'd die on a bed of straw; I think he was right' (C. Albaret, *op. cit.*, p. 256). In May 1914, once again in difficulties because of ill-judged investments, he asked Robert de Flers to take him on as a columnist on *Le Figaro*, even to cover 'dogs that had been run over'.

EXPENDITURE All his life, Proust was very extravagant, on his own behalf, towards his friends – to whom he gave sumptuous presents – and towards servants, whom he tipped lavishly. In 1902, travelling to the Netherlands with Fénelon, he stayed in the most expensive hotels; soon short of money, he pretended to his parents that he had been robbed. At that time his father gave him a fixed allowance, although he never refused to pay his bills. Dinners, orchids, presents and trips in hired cars often ran to hundreds of francs a month. Every summer between 1908 and 1913, a gardener in Houlgate, Lerossignol, used to supply him with immense sheaves of gladioli, phlox and roses for his friends on the coast. In 1914, he bought Agostinelli an aeroplane costing 27,000 francs.

GAMBLING Proust loved playing baccarat at the casino in Cabourg. He lost substantial amounts there in 1911.

DANGER OF DEBTS From time to time Proust felt afraid of running short of money, but his situation never in fact became dire. In November 1917, he sold some of his furniture, and thanks to the Strauses got 10,000 francs for a Louis XVI suite and 4000 francs for some carpets. In 1919, Proust felt overwhelmed when he had to pay three years' rent (about 20,000 francs) to his aunt, the owner of 102 boulevard Haussmann; Guiche covered the debt for him. That year, the Goncourt Prize brought him 5,000 francs which he instantly spent on 'thank-you dinners'. However, in September 1922 he was able to lend 5,000 francs to some 'pestering poor'.

REVENUE FROM HIS WORK 11 March 1913: *contract with Grasset*. This was a contract to publish at the author's expense, which was then much more common than it is now; it was even usual for young writers (André Gide, Roger Martin du Gard, Henri Bergson and others underwrote the cost of launching their first books). Grasset's proposal allowed Proust half the selling price, but Proust only took three-sevenths, and gave the percentages from the de luxe editions over to Grasset entirely. Grasset wanted to sell translation rights for 500 francs, but since Proust only wanted half they finally decided on a first edition of 1200 copies (which in fact rose to 1750) priced at 3F 50 (Grasset had at first suggested 10F) of which Proust received 1F 50 per copy. Proust was in favour of this low price to encourage wider distribution of his work. In 1916, however, he complained that he had seen no money at all, despite the five successive editions of *Du Côté de chez Swann* since April 1914. Grasset's share (60 centimes per copy) only amounted to 720 francs for the whole publication. Proust received nothing from the translation rights because the work was not translated by Grasset. The publisher accorded Proust a 20 per cent share on the rest of the work to be published.

14 April 1916: *contract with Gallimard.* Proust saw little more money from his new publishers. According to Céleste: 'Between the year he went to Nouvelle Revue Française and that of his death, I can only remember two occasions on which money from his publications arrived: one, at the outset, a payment of 10,000 old francs; the other, much later on, almost at the end, was 30,000 francs. If there were others I wasn't aware of them' (C. Albaret, *op. cit.*, p. 349). However she forgot a payment of 7,500 francs made in January 1921 for the rights in *Le Côté de Guermantes.*

PRINT-RUNS AND SELLING PRICES DURING PROUST'S LIFETIME *Les Plaisirs et les jours*, 1896. De luxe quarto edition, only a few copies printed, sold at 13F 50. There were also 30 copies on *papier de Chine* and 20 on *papier Japon.*

Du Côté de chez Swann, 1913. November: 1750 copies at 3F 50; December: 2nd edition. 1919: June 3,300 copies; November: 8,800 copies. 1920: no printing.

A l'ombre des jeunes filles en fleurs, 1919. June: 3,300 copies; November: 6,600 copies. 1920. January: 6,600 copies; de luxe edition of 50 at 300F (in octavo on Bible paper); July: 6,600 copies. At the same time, the print-run of *Croix de Bois* by Roland Dorgelès, his competitor for the Goncourt Prize, reached 85,000 copies.

In the long term, *Du Côté de chez Swann* has sold more than *A l'ombre des jeunes filles en fleurs* (1,263,400 copies against 837,000, up to 1980, counting all editions).

CHAPTER SEVEN

Family*

Ancestors

Marcel Proust's antecedents belonged to two very different social groups, which may explain some aspects of his character and the orientation of his work. His mother was a member of a rich Jewish Parisian family; his father came from the provincial petite-bourgeoisie, originally from Illiers, in Eure-et-Loir.

PATERNAL ANCESTORS The Proust family, whose name is still pronounced 'prou' in the region, has lived for centuries in Illiers, a small town not far from Chartres, between the Beauce and the Perche. It is an old family, but not of the nobility; its social status has fluctuated little through the ages. The Prousts were bailiffs, elected representatives and lawyers. In the sixteenth century, Jehan Proust belonged to the *assemblée des notables*, an urban institution dating from the Middle Ages. Under Louis XIII, Gilles Proust finally became a member of the upper bourgeoisie of Illiers. He was exempted from the poll tax paid by serfs and commoners, and bought the office of bailiff. By letters patent issued at Meaux by the King, Gilles' brother, Robert Proust, was in August 1633 made *receveur de la Seigneurie*. In this capacity he had every year to supply the Marquis d'Illiers with 10,500 *livres tournois* and 'furnish a candle for each year in the church of Nôtre-Dame de Chartres, on the feast-days of Nôtre-Dame de le Chandeleur'. The Marquise d'Illiers was godmother to his son Claude in 1669. The bailiwick stayed in the family: Michel Proust, a university graduate, held it from 1673 until his death in

---

*See also the family trees, pp. 377–381.

1693. Proust's other antecedents were in commerce or attached to the land.

MATERNAL ANCESTORS The Weils, like many Jewish families, took their name from their native town. In the eighteenth century Weil was a free Imperial city, near Stuttgart, in Wurtemberg. At that time Proust's ancestors were china makers, a rising trade. France, like other European countries, needed skilled craftsmen. So, at the demise of the Ancien Régime, the writer's great-grandfather, Baruch Weil (1782–8 April 1828), left for the Niederwiller factory in Alsace, owned by the Comte de Custine. The French Revolution gave French citizenship to all Jews resident on French soil, so Baruch Weil then left Alsace to move to Paris. Under the Consulat, he became head of a porcelain factory in the 10th arrondissement: it was brilliantly successful, for Paris porcelain then rivalled that of Sèvres. He lived at 55 rue du Temple, then at 23 rue Boucherat, which became part of the rue de Turenne.

From his marriage in 1800 to *Hélène Schoubach*, he had seven children, amongst whom were *Godchaux*, born on 16 April 1806, *Benjamin*, born on 21 November 1807, and *Moïse*, born in 1809. He then lived near the Bourse, in the business district which was beginning to be built at the time. Hélène died in Paris on 20 November 1811. Baruch remarried on 2 November 1812; his second wife was *Marguerite Nathan*, daughter of Joseph Nathan (Lunéville, 1754 – Lunéville, 5 January 1813), a street trader, married to Rosette Mayer. He had six children, among them *Nathé Weil*, Proust's grandfather, *Lazard* – who later called himself Louis –, *Abraham*, *Alphonse* and *Adèle*, whose grand-daughter, Louise, was to marry Henri Bergson. After the Empire, the Restoration founded the Weils' fortunes.

In 1827, Baruch published a memoir which included plans for the creation of an exhibition hall. The holder of various offices, decorated with the Légion d'honneur, member of the Schools Committee, chief administrator of the Temple, vice-President of the *Consistoire israélite* of Paris, he died in Paris on 8 April 1828, owner of a solid fortune. He was the first of the Weils to be buried in Père-Lachaise.

Grandparents

Paternal Grandparents

Great-grandfather: RENÉ-FRANÇOIS PROUST (Nogent-le-Rotrou, 1 January 1772 – Illiers, 18 January 1829). Son of Roch Proust (Nogent-le-Rotrou, 16 August 1750 – Argenvilliers, 25 November 1817), labourer and merchant, and of Marguerite-Luce Mondeguerre (Argenvilliers, 13 December 1750 – Argenvilliers, 7 October 1808). François married *Louise Lejeune* in Illiers on 17 April 1792. He set himself up as a grocer and chandler in Illiers, and became deputy mayor. They had seven children, among them *Anne-Monique* (Illiers, 25 January 1797 – Illiers, 3 November 1863), married in Illiers on 20 August 1822 to Jacques-Étienne Cannet (St-Germain-le-Guillard, 20 November 1798 – Chartres, 29 January 1835), a potter in Chartres; *Catherine-Élisabeth* (Illiers, 20 January 1798 – Illiers, 27 October 1857), married in Illiers, on 1 October 1816, to Jacques-André Jacquet (born at La Loupe on 29 November 1789), a milliner; *Louis-François-Valentin; Aimée-Thérèse* (born in Illiers on 15 October 1806), married in Illiers on 12 April 1831 to Arsène-Alexandre Godard (La Ferté-vidame, 27 September 1807 – Illiers, 7 August 1888), tutor.

Great-grandmother: LOUISE-MONIQUE LEJEUNE (Illiers, 4 May 1770 – Illiers, 26 June 1845). Daughter of Louis Charles (born about 1749), master baker, and of Françoise-Marie Buisson (Illiers, 1748 – Illiers, 23 December 1827).

Grandfather: LOUIS FRANÇOIS VALENTIN PROUST (Illiers, 18 April 1801 – Illiers, 2 October 1855). On 25 October 1825, at Cernay in the Eure-et-Loir, he married *Catherine Virginie Torcheux*. In business as a general grocer at 11 place du Marché, opposite the church of Saint-Jacques, he supplied his fellow townspeople with wax, candles or *'chocolat de Santé'*, and manufactured candles for the parish in the back of his shop. He had three children: two girls, *Louise-Virginie* (Illiers, 2 August 1826 – Illiers, 1 September 1832) and *Françoise Élisabeth* (born on 9 August 1828), then, in 1834, a son, *Adrien*, whom he intended for the priesthood. His hopes were dashed, and when he died in Illiers on 2 October 1855 his son had already been studying medicine for some time. Like Marcel Proust's father, he was not to know of his son's brilliant career.

Grandmother: CATHERINE VIRGINIE TORCHEUX (Cernay, 9 June 1808 – Illiers, 19 March 1889). Daughter of Pierre Armand Torcheux (St-Aubin-des-bois, 18 May 1772 – Cernay, 9 August 1808) and Marie Anne Henriette Motte (born at Montigny-le-Chartif on 14 August 1778). After her husband's death in 1885, she ran the family's grocery shop alone. When her son Adrien qualified in 1866 and could provide for her, she moved a few doors down, to 6 place du Marché, into an apartment above a shop. From behind her calico curtains she could observe the comings and goings of the little town.

The ravages of the war of 1870 did not spare the Beauce; the Germans fought the army of the Loire in the country surrounding Illiers. In October 1870 they sacked Châteaudun and occupied Chartres, about twenty kilometres from the Prousts' native town. For several months Adrien Proust had no news of his mother. In December he resorted to the balloon-post, sending an anguished letter to a friend in Tours, a draper called Esnault: 'Has she left Illiers? Is she with you? Is she all right? I beg you to send me answers to all these questions by carrier-pigeon' (University of Illinois Library, Urbana). But soon calm was restored, and Proust's grandmother spent the end of her life peacefully waiting for visits from Adrien and his family at Easter and in the summer holidays. She died of uraemia in the serene provincial surroundings of Illiers on 19 March 1889.

Maternal Grandparents

Grandfather: NATHÉ WEIL (Paris, 19 April 1814 – Paris, 30 June 1896). On 6 December 1845 he married *Adèle Berncastel*, and they had a son, *Georges-Denis* (1847–1906) and a daughter, Jeanne Clémence (1849–1905).

Occupation. A Saint-Simonian like his brother Louis, he turned to business very early in life and set up a company. He financed many projects, including a foreign exchange dealers' office. A conservative, he was a member of the Garde Nationale, the pillar of Louis-Philippe's régime.

Character. His photographs reveal an authoritarian figure with a severe profile and prominent lips. His avarice was legendary in the Weil family. At meals, he served mediocre wines, keeping a bottle of better vintage well *chambrée* at his feet for his personal consumption. His horror of travelling and his stay-at-home habits were also singular: effectively he never left the family home at 40 bis, rue du Faubourg Poissonnière. If he ever had to make a brief excursion to Dieppe, he made sure he could get home the same evening, for fear of having to spend a single night away from Paris. Every day his coachman drove him to Auteuil, to his half-brother Louis's house, but he never failed to drive home again at night: 'for even though he came to dine every night, he insisted on returning to Paris for the night. He never left the place during the eighty-five years of his life (except at the time of the siege of Paris, when he took my grandmother to safety in Étampes). [...] Returning to Paris in the evenings, he used to pass the railway viaduct, and the sight of carriages conveying mad, questing strangers beyond the Point-du-Jour or Boulogne filled him, deep in his coupé, with an intense feeling of "Suave Mari Magno". "And to think," he would cry, watching the train with a mixture of astonishment, pity and horror, "and to think that there are people who like travelling".' (*Contre Sainte-Beuve*, p. 572).

Politics caused many quarrels with his half-brother Louis.

Relationship with Marcel Proust. Like Monsieur Sandré in *Jean Santeuil*, who was based on him, he was sparing both with his affection and with his sense of discipline for the young Marcel, especially when the latter's future seemed uncertain. On the news of his death at home on 30 June 1896, as a result of injuries to his lungs, Proust felt nothing but indifference. After the burial service, however, when he went into the dead man's room, he burst into sobs. This heartfelt grief comforted him greatly, since he had previously considered himself unfeeling. He admired the strength of his mother, who hid her pain beneath an unruffled surface.

Grandmother: ADÈLE BERNCASTEL (Paris, 5 February 1824 – Paris, 2 January 1890). Born at 10 bis, rue de Trévise, she was the daughter of Nathanael Berncastel (Trèves, Germany, 7 October 1791 – Paris, 29 October 1864), a businessman, and of Rose Silny (Metz, 17 September 1794 – Paris, 23 March 1876), whose parents were tradespeople from

Metz. The Berncastels, like the Weils, were powerful and wealthy. They lived in the 7th arrondissement and belonged to the Jewish haute bourgeoisie of Paris, with many links to the bar and the financial institutions. It was this side of the family which first opened the doors of high society for the young Proust.

Character. A gentle and self-sacrificing woman, she was the opposite of her selfish and cantankerous husband. Her daughter took after her in temperament and taste.

Like her mother, Rose Silny, she was well educated. It was traditional in that middle-class Jewish Saint-Simonian world to take trouble over the girls' education, so that they could carry on the brilliant salons of the Age of Enlightenment. With this in mind, she was an assiduous visitor to the salon of her aunt Amélie, whose husband, Adolphe Crémieux, was her tutor. There she met Lamartine, Musset, Rossini, Lamennais, Victor Hugo and George Sand, whose work she loved. Above all other literature of the Grand Siècle she valued Saint-Simon's *Mémoires* and the Letters of Madame de Sévigné. To Proust, his grandmother would always be '*plus Sévigné que Sévigné*'. Her knowledge also extended to music.

She was seen as much in the Comtesse d'Haussonville's liberal salon as in that of Princesse Mathilde. The influence of Saint-Simonian thought and the positivism which held sway there formed her scientific humanism, which in turn she transmitted to Proust's mother. Her literary tastes guided her grandson, who, when young, enjoyed *François le Champi* and the writings of Augustin Thierry, which she also loved.

She used to take him into her reading room to initiate him into the classics in unexpurgated form, because 'she considered idle reading to be as unhealthy as sweets and cakes, never thinking that the great gusts of genius might have an effect on the soul, even the soul of a child, which was more dangerous and less invigorating than the effects of the open air and the wide winds on his body' (*Du Côté de chez Swann*). She had often met the actress Rachel at the Crémieuxs', and she was to instil in Marcel a love of the theatre, especially of tragedy.

Her death affected Marcel and his mother very deeply; the latter followed the dead woman's example and took to re-reading Madame de Sévigné and walking along the Normandy coast in the wind and the rain. In her letters to her son, she constantly remembered her own mother's generosity and goodness: '"I know of another mother who thought nothing of herself, but gave everything to her children." Doesn't that apply perfectly to your grandmother? Only she would never have said it of herself.' As Proust's grandmother had done, she had the difficult job of calming her son's acute sensitivity. She wrote to him: 'Think of her, cherish her memory with me, but don't let yourself spend whole days in fits of tears which fray your nerves and which she would not have wanted. On the contrary, the more you think of her the more you should try to be as she liked you to be, and to behave as she wanted you to behave.' For many years afterwards, the Weil family was in mourning on 2 January, the anniversary of her death, and on 5 January, the day of her funeral. All entertainment and social engagements were cancelled on these dates for some time.

In Proust's work. In *A la Recherche*, the narrator's grandmother loves nature and goes for walks in the wind and rain in the little garden at Combray. In reality, it is unlikely that the Weils ever went to Illiers; if these scenes took place, it is more probable that they were at Auteuil, at Uncle Louis' house. At any rate Proust, who spent his summer holidays on the Normandy coast with her between 1880 and 1889, talked to his mother about 'those years at the sea when grandmother and I, melted together, walked into the wind, talking'. Those summers with his grandmother stayed vividly in his mind. He adapted them for several passages in *A l'ombre des jeunes filles en fleurs*: her knock on the partition that separated their two rooms in the Hôtel des Roches Noires in Trouville echoed in his memory all his life. Her last two weeks of life were overshadowed by the pain of her illness. She was put on a diet of milk products, but refused even to drink milk, 'only agreeing to have some on condition that it did not taste of milk'. In *A la Recherche*, the grandmother's end is directly inspired by that of her daughter, which took place fifteen years later.

Father

ACHILLE ADRIEN PROUST (Illiers, 18 March 1834 – Paris, 26 November 1903).

Education. At the *école communale*, then at college in Chartres, where he successfully prepared for his *baccalauréats* in literature and science subjects. All his life, despite his other grand titles, he liked to recall that: 'My name appears on the roll of honour at the college in Chartres.' His father wanted him to join the priesthood, but even though he did not lose his faith he soon gave up the seminary and turned to medicine. In July 1853 he obtained his certificate of aptitude in the physical sciences and left to study medicine in Paris. He was the first Proust to leave the Beauce. He was awarded his doctorate on 29 December 1862, with a thesis on the 'idiopathic pneumothorax'. He succeeded in everything: he won prizes for hospital work and at the Faculty of Medicine, and took first prize in the École pratique. On 14 March 1866, he got an honourable mention in the *concours d'agrégation*, a competitive examination of teaching posts; his thesis was on 'Different types of softening of the brain'.

Career. He was now qualified to teach in medical faculties. In 1866 there was an outbreak of cholera in France. Adrien Proust was noted for his devotion to his work and his disregard of danger. To stop the spread of the disease through Europe, he borrowed from his teachers Tardieu and Fauvel the effective theory of a 'cordon sanitaire'. His turns of phrase 'à la Norpois' (the diplomat in *A la Recherche*), such as 'questions of international hygiene reach beyond the borders established by politics', brought him to the notice of politicians. Also, a year after his qualification as a teacher, he obtained a brilliant result in the medical examinations for the *Bureau central*, which admitted him to government circles. In 1869 the Ministry of Agriculture and Commerce sent him to Persia on a mission to establish the routes by which cholera spread to Russia. He left for Moscow in a luxurious train, but had to continue his journey to St Petersburg and Astrakhan on horseback, in burning heat. But nothing was too much for his robust constitution. The Shah of Persia presented him with some sumptuous carpets, which Proust later inherited, and the Grand Vizier Ali Pasha gave him a magnificent reception in Constantinople after his visit to Mecca. His wide learning and his perfect command of the sciences were reflected in the conclusions he delivered in *La Défense de l'Europe contre le choléra*, acclaimed by the Institute in 1873. His theory, according to which the plague originated in India, and which he propounded at international conferences on health, earned him opposition in England, whose economic interests dominated that part of the world.

In 1879, he was elected to the Académie de Médicine (of which he was secretary from 1883 to 1888), in place of his teacher, Ambroise Tardieu. In 1884, as successor to Fauvel, he obtained the position of Inspector-General of Sanitary Services, and in 1885 that of Professor of Hygiene in the Faculty of Medicine. Social medicine and work-related illness fascinated him; he was also interested in the brain, in hypnotism and in neurasthenia, which, he believed, was a product of life in society circles. He also oversaw the sanitisation of the French ports he visited. The Mayor of Toulon presented him with the keys to the town. In Marseilles, he gave his name to the quarantine hospital in the port of Frioul. As technical adviser to France at international health conferences, he undertook a mission to Spain, then stricken with cholera, in August 1890. Under a scorching sun, he once again demonstrated his tenacity and efficiency. On his return he simply said: 'Travelling is a wonderful thing, since one is delighted to go and delighted to return.' He also went to Venice, Rome, Dresden, Vienna and Egypt. He was a contemporary of Charcot, whose work he knew well, and he attended Charcot's funeral in 1893.

On 7 June 1903, now world-famous, he inaugurated the Pasteur monument in Chartres: his speech revealed his remarkable knowledge of iconography. On 27 July he presided over the prize-giving at Illiers. Several months later, on 24 November, he suffered a cerebral haemorrhage and died in the rue de Courcelles apartment on 26 November, without having regained consciousness.

Marriage. On 3 September 1870, the eve of the fall of the Second Empire, Adrien Proust married *Jeanne Weil.* They had probably met in the government circles the Weils and the Crémieux frequented. This marriage, a brilliant one for the son of a provincial grocer, gave the seal of approval to the social status his blossoming career had brought him. The couple first lived at 35 rue Joubert. About 15 January 1871 they moved to 8 rue du Roy, near the place Saint-Augustin (the monthly rent of 2,500 francs shows how well-off he was). After the hardships of the siege of Paris, the Prousts had to suffer further at the hands of the Commune. On his way to the Hôpital de la Charité, where he was head of clinical medicine, the doctor was brushed by a stray bullet. Prudently, the couple went into a few months' exile at the home of Uncle Louis at Auteuil (where Marcel Proust was born on 10 July 1871). They then left the rue du Roy for 9 boulevard Malesherbes, where they stayed for almost thirty years.

However, it was at Auteuil, on 24 May 1873, that Madame Proust gave birth to her second child, Robert. For twenty-five years, each spring and early summer, Dr Proust and his family went to spend several weeks in Uncle Weil's peaceful home. This did not prevent him going to the Hôpital de la Charité or to Hôtel-Dieu every morning. He would take the Auteuil-Madeleine omnibus, which his faithful servant Jean Blanc would keep waiting while he kissed his young family goodbye.

When he could free himself from his professional obligations, Adrien Proust would take his family to Illiers, to stay with his sister, Madame Jules Amiot. There, in the rue du Saint-Esprit, every Easter and summer, the doctor relaxed from his bustling life in Paris during holidays lived to the simple rhythm of meals and naps. In 1898, he was worried about his wife's operation for cancer. Like a good husband, he accompanied her to Trouville for her convalescence. The following year they spent their holidays in the Splendide Hôtel in Évian with their son Marcel. In September 1900 the Proust family moved to 45 rue de Courcelles: the neighbourhood in which their new apartment was situated reflected Professor Adrien Proust's social and professional rise. The whole of Paris society were his patients. He was given a drawing by Caran d'Ache and some bronzes by Barbedienne. The President of the Republic, Félix Faure, was an acquaintance. He also kept up his friendship with the brilliant diplomat Gabriel Hanotaux and with Camille Barrère, the French ambassador to Italy. Some great doctors such as Dr Samuel Pozzi were among his circle of friends. The élite of which his father was a member is found in Proust's work, where the medical world occupies a prominent place.

Relationship with his son. Even though Marcel Proust once told the Comtesse de Noailles that he had been 'the black spot' in his father's life, there was a certain intimacy and deep affection between them. The letters Marcel exchanged with him during his military service testify to this. The son confided in his father: 'Just imagine how scandalised the Derbannes were when the Cabourg maids, catching sight of a raw recruit, sent me a thousand kisses'; the father gave him touching practical advice: a soldier must always look after his shoes, saying 'Gaiters, gaiters, gaiters'.

After his return home in 1891, he proved a continual worry to Dr Proust because of his extravagance and his uncertain future; violent quarrels sometimes resulted, as *Jean Santeuil* and *A la Recherche* reveal. But his father, more than his mother, looked the other way and allowed Marcel to follow the path he wanted: 'My father regarded my kind of intelligence with a contempt sufficiently mollified by tenderness so that, overall, his attitude to everything I did was one of blind indulgence' (*A l'ombre des jeunes filles en fleurs*). Besides, his son's state of health, his repeated asthma attacks, affected the doctor deeply. From 1881 onwards he had tried in vain to cure him with a treatment based on strict rules of hygiene.

For a time, politics caused a rift between father and son. Although later Adrien Proust shared his son's view of the injustice of the Combes laws, in 1898, during the Dreyfus affair, he followed the opinions of the members of the government with whom he was friendly. For a whole week he refused to speak to either of his sons, who were both ardent supporters of Dreyfus. He went so far as to throw one of his colleagues, who asked him to sign the *Manifeste des cent-quatre*, out of the house.

Portrait. In 1885, the painter Jules Lecomte du Noüy (1842–1923) – a distant relation by marriage of his wife's – did an austere portrait of him, in the manner of Holbein: 'In his robe of scarlet satin lined with ermine, like that of a Doge ...', he looked severe and imposing. His late photographs show him in black clothes, with a beard like that of Edward VII, and wearing his eternal pince-nez.

Burial. His funeral was at Saint-Philippe du Roule. It was attended by the university Council members, the Faculty, the Academy of Medicine, Méline, Fallières and Barthou. Professor Debove, doyen of the Faculty of Medicine, to whom he had once confided: 'I have been happy all my life', gave the farewell address at Père-Lachaise. Madame Proust commemorated the dates of her husband's attack, of his death and of his funeral first every week, then every month. Marcel also observed them, and always refused invitations for the 26th of the month. In May 1904 he commissioned Marie Nordlinger to make a bronze plaque with his father's portrait for the tomb in Père-Lachaise (the medallion remained on the Proust family grave until April 1966, when it was moved to Illiers, to the house where Adrien Proust was born). Marcel dedicated his translation of *The Bible of Amiens* to his father. The rue du Saint-Esprit in Illiers, where Aunt Amiot's house (now the Marcel Proust museum) stood, was renamed after him.

Distinctions. In August 1870, on his return from Russia, Adrien Proust was named Chevalier de la Légion d'honneur by the Empress Eugénie. In 1892 he was promoted to Commander, but he was never a member of the Académie des sciences morales et politiques.

Works. He left 34 authoritative medical works. His manual entitled *Éléments d'hygiène* (1883) was adopted by the ministry of public instruction, and Albert Camus read his *Défense de l'Europe contre la peste* for background to his novel *La Peste* (1947).

In Proust's work. In *A la Recherche*, the narrator's father, admired by his wife and feared by his son because he made no allowance for other people, took them on unforgettable walks through the two sides of the town, thanks to his perfect sense of direction and his wide knowledge of meteorology. These excursions echo the revitalising outings prescribed by Professor Adrien Proust's theories on health.

Mother

JEANNE CLÉMENCE WEIL (Paris, 21 April 1849 – Paris, 26 September 1905). She was born at 40 bis, rue du Faubourg Poissonnière.

Education. According to the principles of Saint-Simonian thought, she received a solid education which complemented her lively intelligence and the enlightened tastes of her mother. She studied ancient languages, English and German.

Marriage. She was very beautiful, as the painting by Landelle shows, and at the age of 21 she married Dr Adrien Proust, who was fifteen years her senior. The ceremony took place in the Mairie of the 10th arrondissement on 3 September 1870, a day when Paris awaited the surrender of Sedan. Her dowry was 200,000 gold francs, and Adolphe Crémieux, the future Minister of Justice, was her witness at the Mairie. She never converted to Catholicism. She was loyal to her family, and always remained attached to Jewish traditions, even if not to the Jewish religion.

She became pregnant a few weeks after her marriage, and found the privations of the siege of Paris very hard. When the Commune arrived in the spring of 1871, she took refuge with Uncle Louis at Auteuil. On 10 July 1871, after a difficult labour, she gave birth to Marcel, and on 24 May 1873 to her second son, Robert.

Character. Like her mother, she was a very cultured woman. A great reader of the classics, she also enjoyed Loti, George Sand, Tolstoy and Musset. She used to write her favourite passages in a notebook, and followed her sons' reading. She was an accomplished musician; she also chose fine furniture for the family home and liked to delve in antique shops. But she remained very modest. Proust once wrote to Montesquiou: 'You don't know my mother. Her extreme modesty hides her extreme superiority from almost everyone . . . With people she admires – and she admires you enormously – this excessive modesty completely screens the merits that only I and a few friends know to be incomparable. As for the unremitting self-sacrifice that characterises her life, it is the most moving thing in the world.'

Her love of literature, her refined nature and her subtle sense of humour shaped Marcel's mind and tastes: 'She was sure to have an exact notion of the perfect way to cook certain dishes, to play Beethoven sonatas or to entertain amiably, and she could discern how close to this ideal other people came: it was a sort of simplicity in the means to an end, always sober, always charming.'

Health. In July 1898 her health suddenly worsened. Dr Terrier, a colleague of her husband, performed a three-hour operation for cancer. For the two days that followed the operation she hovered between life and death, and then spent two months in a nursing home before going to Trouville with her husband to convalesce. In 1900, she spent the month of August at the Splendide Hôtel in Évian with her husband, as she often did. She followed a course of treatment for excessive weight. Photographs taken at the time show a woman of heavy build whose hair is beginning to go grey. In 1902, a few weeks after the burial of his maternal grandfather (Nathé Weil), Proust went with his mother to Mont-Dore. But he had trouble with his asthma, and he left her to finish her holiday alone in Dieppe. Following her doctor's orders, she bathed regularly and, remembering the example of her own mother, went for long walks in all weathers. But the pain of her illness had dealt her a heavy blow. Proust was distraught: 'Suddenly, over the telephone came this little, broken, ravaged voice, changed forever from the voice I had always known, flawed and cracked; and as I gathered up the shattering and bleeding pieces in the telephone receiver I felt for the first time the atrocious truth of what had broken forever within her.'

Her health deteriorated. In February 1903 she went to her son Robert's wedding in an ambulance. When her husband died, on 26 November of the same year, she slept in a different bedroom for several months, before she could go back into the marital bedroom whose familiar furniture reminded her of her dead husband. Under a serene exterior she was racked with grief. Faithful to her mother's memory, she re-read Madame de Sévigné in the salon of the rue de Courcelles. Beside her stood an easel draped in black supporting the portrait of Adrien Proust painted by Lecomte du Noüy. In September 1904 she set off for Dieppe, alone.

Relationship with her son. She always had a soft spot for her sensitive, nervous eldest child. The passionate love he felt for her inspired the scene of the goodnight kiss (which Proust described in *Du Côté de chez Swann*). When he suffered his first asthma attack in 1881, Madame Proust redoubled her care of him. All her life she was attentive to his every action and gesture. Each year from 1880 to 1890, she (or her mother) took him to the Normandy coast or to Salies-de-Béarn in the Pyrenees. When Marcel did his military service in 1889, she wrote to him every day to keep him amused. Their lives were marked by this close complicity and constant intimacy. During his long periods of insomnia, Marcel would write notes that he left in her antechamber for her to find when she woke up: 'My darling little Mummy, I'm writing this quick word when I can't sleep to tell you that I am thinking of you. I should so much like, and I want so much to be able to get up at the same time as you, and drink my coffee beside you. To feel our sleep and our waking spread out over the same expanse of time would be, will be so wonderful' (coll. Mante-Proust). In May 1900, he went with her to Venice. They stayed at the Hôtel de l'Europe, and went out to drink 'granita' in the Café Florian in St Mark's Square with Reynaldo Hahn and his cousin, Marie Nordlinger. At the time Madame Proust was helping her son to translate Ruskin's *The Bible of Amiens*; she drafted a word-for-word version that filled several yellow, green and red school exercise books. In Paris she attended the 'grand dinners' which Proust sometimes gave, sitting opposite him.

But her son's excessive spending, the extraordinary hours he kept and his still uncertain future gradually cast a shadow over her life, and their great affection suffered. When he was granted some remission from his asthma attacks, his mother tried to correct his strange ways of passing his time by restrictions he considered niggardly. For example, she forbade the servants to serve Proust at night, or to make up a fire for him during his friends' late-night visits (on one nocturnal visit by Bertrand de Salignac-Fénelon in 1902, Marie, the maid, refused to put any wood in the fireplace: 'I daren't,' she confessed, 'or Madame will sack me.').

Proust ascribed his mother's nagging to jealousy of his social activities: 'The truth is that since I have been well, the life that keeps me feeling well exasperates you, and you demolish everything, to the point where I feel ill again [...] It is hard not to be able to have affection and health at the same time.' In November 1903, when her husband died, she pushed him to finish his translation of *The Bible of Amiens*: 'It was the only thing your father wanted. He was waiting day by day for its publication.' But Proust, who was dissatisfied with the brief respite from his asthma and annoyed by his mother's fervent desire to see him working, replied: 'You are absolutely impossible. Instead of being pleased by my virtual resurrection, and loving the thing that made it possible, you insist that I get back to work straight away.'

Madame Proust, who was active until the end of her life, spent her time performing services for her son, and running countless errands all over Paris on his behalf. It helped her to battle with her weight problems. In fact, self-sacrifice was part of her nature (as in her own mother). Two months before her death, she went to Neuilly for Proust in order to get news of Robert de Montesquiou's secretary, Gabriel d'Yturri, who was dying.

Death. In September 1905, just as she arrived in Évian for a restful holiday with Marcel, she was struck down with terrible symptoms of nephritis (headaches, sudden loss of appetite, nausea). 'I shall go back to Paris,' she told him, 'since I am powerless to do anything to help you when you are ill.' Her son Robert begged her to come home without delay; he also telegraphed Marcel to return. In Évian, a friend, Madame

Catusse, helped Madame Proust to board the train. Back in Paris, despite the attentions of Dr Merklen, uraemia overtook her: she refused all food. She bravely hid her pain and continued to get up and dress every morning. To comfort Proust at her bedside, she joined him in playing their old game of amusing quotations. Troubled with aphasia, she pronounced her last words: 'If you are not a Roman, be worthy of being one.' She died on 26 September 1905.

Reynaldo Hahn retained an image of 'Marcel, beside Madame Proust's deathbed, crying and smiling at the corpse through his tears' (R. Hahn, *Journal d'un musicien*, p. 33).

Burial. There was no religious ceremony. The funeral procession, led by Proust and his brother Robert, went directly to Père-Lachaise on the morning of 28 September. The coffin was invisible under all the wreaths, the most beautiful of which was from Louisa de Mornand.

For a whole month Proust stayed in bed, prostrate with grief, unable to sleep. A great emptiness stretched before him. He was 35, and his mother, from whom he had never wanted to be far away, had just left him. He confided to Montesquiou: 'My life has just lost forever its only purpose, its only sweetness, its only love, its only consolation. I have lost the person whose ceaseless vigilance brought me peace and tenderness, the only honey of my existence [...] As the sister who nursed her said, in her eyes I was always four years old.'

Inheritance. Robert and Marcel jointly inherited their mother's share in the building at 102 boulevard Haussmann. Robert took charge of dismantling the family home in the rue de Courcelles. In the face of Marcel's bad temper and unreasonable demands, he behaved in a conciliatory manner, giving Marcel the choice of the furniture: 'Keep what you want, put the rest in store.' But there was further friction between Marcel and his sister-in-law Marthe, who spoke to him on the telephone 'with unnecessary brevity'. It is true, as Proust himself admitted, 'that without realising it, I was disagreeable in the extreme' (Madame A. Catusse, *Marcel Proust. Lettres à Mme C.*, p. 55).

In Proust's work. Jean Santeuil and *A la Recherche* bear witness to the violent altercations that took place between Proust and his parents. During a quarrel in about 1897, he left the room, breaking a glass door and a Venetian glass vase his mother had given him. In her sweet and accommodating way, she put an end to the incident: 'Let's not think about it any more, and let's not talk about it again. The broken glass will be just what it is in the temple – a symbol of indissoluble union.'

Brother

ROBERT PROUST (Paris, 24 May 1873 – Paris, 29 May 1935).

Education. He first went to a private school, Pape-Carpentier, then to the Condorcet lycée. He was athletic, and enjoyed riding and walking. Unlike his elder brother, he was passionately keen on mathematics. At the age of 12 he won first prize for geometry. However, despite an astonishingly good memory and great intellectual ability, he failed his *baccalauréat*. But in September 1890, thanks to lessons from Léon Brunschwicg, he became *bachelier ès lettres et ès sciences*. In 1891 Darlu, his philosophy master, entered him for the Concours général where he achieved a first merit award in philosophy. He then enrolled in a university course to study medicine and literature. He became *licencié ès lettres* in 1893. At the age of 20 he became a hospital intern (he came third in the internship examinations).

Youth. In November 1894 he began his military service in Reims, in the 132nd Infantry Regiment. A womaniser, he had an affair with his captain's mistress, and the latter made life difficult for him: 'I've just had another ten days' punishment inflicted on me, in a way that was quite undeserved.' On his return to Paris he became passionately interested in politics. Even as an adolescent he had followed current events carefully and with irony, as this letter of 1887 showed: 'The proximity of Général Revanche ("Hope" and "Victory") doesn't make itself felt much. People shout "He must come back" in the streets, and "Returning from the Review" is played in the Guignol theatre, but really there's nothing new, especially in Paris. On that note, I'll stop going on about "His" popularity.' But during the Dreyfus affair he was actively involved alongside Marcel, whom he used to meet on the first floor of the Café des Variétés. It was there that they planned their strategy. He was an ardent supporter of Dreyfus's cause, and Proust had to write to his mother in 1899: 'Advise Robert to calm down.'

Appearance. He was, like his father, tall and thick-lipped, with an air of being strict and kindly at the same time. Helped by a fine voice that he used well, the 'handsome Proust', as his medical friends used to call him, followed in the footsteps of Professor Adrien Proust, whose character, erudition and scientific mind he had inherited.

The war. On 2 August 1914, the day of the general mobilisation, Robert took a train from the Gare de l'Est to Verdun. His wife and daughter went to a safe refuge in Pau for a time. Feeling himself somehow to be the new head of the family, Proust wrote regularly to his sister-in-law. In October 1914 Robert's field hospital at Étain, near Verdun, was bombed. Fragments of shell even reached the operating table. Robert was made Captain and awarded the Légion d'honneur. An efficient and practical man, he invented the surgical cars called 'autos-chir', a sort of mobile ambulance which allowed operations to be carried out just behind the firing-line. In mid-November 1917 he left for the Italian front, after the disaster at Caporetto. By means of a safe-conduct she had obtained with her brother-in-law's help, Robert's wife came out to join him and worked beside him as a nurse. In the spring of 1918 they left Italy. Robert was made surgeon to the 10th army, commanded by his friend General Mangin. He often spent his leaves with his parents-in-law, the Dubois-Amiots, where he met up with Marcel. He returned to Paris for good in October 1918, to convalesce after a head injury sustained in an automobile accident.

Career. Surgery became his specialisation under the tutelage of Professor Guyon, a urologist. In 1901 he was the first person in France to carry out a successful ablation of the prostate. His studies on the subject were widely known and much respected. Amongst medical students, prostatectomy was always known as 'proustatectomie'. In 1904 he gained a brilliant result in his *agrégation* with a thesis on 'Surgery of the female genitals'. From 1904 to 1914 he was assistant to Dr Pozzi at the Broca hospital, where in 1910 he successfully performed the first open heart operation followed by a complete recovery. Like Pozzi, he was very interested in hermaphrodism, and had the opportunity to examine the strange Adèle H. Numerous articles on the subject were included in the *Journal de chirugie* which Robert founded at the age of twenty with Hartmann and Cunéo.

By the summer of 1906 Robert was a qualified hospital surgeon. With the encouragement of Dr Pozzi he embarked at Cherbourg on a ship for New York. In North America he travelled to Rochester, Minnesota, to visit the Mayo clinic, then to Trois-Rivières in the province of Quebec to attend the Third Congress of French-speaking Doctors in America. He left Canada in July to return to France.

Robert's brilliant career continued. He became a hospital doctor, in turn head of medical services at Tenon, Beaujon, Laënnec and Broca. He set up the cancer centre that bears his name at the Tenon hospital. He was then involved in treating tumours with radiology, and established a table of radiation called the 'Proust table'. He had many dealings with Marie Curie, who declared: 'Proust is the only person who understands our work, because of his mathematical knowledge' (C. Francis, *Proust et les siens*, p. 157).

Marriage. Robert Proust married *Marthe Dubois-Amiot* (1878–1953) on 2 February 1903, at the church of Saint-Augustin. Marcel, who was witness and best man, took the collection, helped by his cousin Valentine Thomson, daughter of the Minister for the Navy. The young couple were in the midst of moving in to a new apartment at 136 boulevard Saint-Germain when Robert discovered his father lying unconscious at the École de Médicine on 24 November. The next day, while his wife was undergoing a difficult labour and giving birth to their only child, *Adrienne* (who later called herself Suzy), he looked after his dying father. At the end of the war the relationship between Robert and Marthe deteriorated, and they considered divorce. The great affection of her husband for his brother Marcel troubled Marthe (and she was deeply shocked, as were her friends, by the publication of *Sodome et Gomorrhe* in 1921).

Relationship with his brother. Robert's birth was a great shock to Marcel, and this may explain why the latter's love for their mother became more and more exclusive and tyrannical. In letters to each other, Proust and his mother nicknamed Robert 'Dick', 'His Majesty' or 'Proustovitch'. Robert, on the other hand, was intimate with his father. Marcel always affected a protective attitude towards his younger brother, as shown by photographs in which he sometimes appears with his arm round Robert. When in 1888 Madame Proust took Robert alone with her on holiday to Salies-de-Béarn, Marcel dissolved in tears. Even though there was no real intimacy between them, theirs was a solid friendship. When they were children, they planted a young poplar together in the Pré Catelan on Uncle Amiot's property in Illiers. At Auteuil, they played at being savages, stark naked, in front of their flabbergasted family. Robert was possessive about his toys, and only ever lent them to Marcel: 'You're nice; you'd never hurt me. Here, I'll lend you my tip-up truck!' (C. Francis, *op cit.*, p. 138). Madame Gérard Mante-Proust, Robert's daughter, says that one day in anger Robert was reputed to have hit his brother so hard he shattered Marcel's eardrum, but knowing her father's good nature she was doubtful about the story. 'They can't bear to be apart,' their grandmother wrote to Madame Proust.

When Marcel was a schoolboy at Condorcet, Robert used to help him with his weakest subject, mathematics. On the other hand, Robert was in awe of his brother's literary judgement, as he gave his mother to understand in 1899: 'Don't show this letter to my angel of a brother, who is indeed an angel but also a severe critic, and who would infer from my remarks about the Comte d'Eu a snobbery or frivolity which are far from my true feelings.' The two brothers complemented each other perfectly, according to Jean Rostand: 'There was something of the artist in him; besides, wasn't there something clinical and learned about his brother Marcel?' (*Les Nouvelles littéraires*, 8 June 1935).

When his brother married in 1903, Marcel told his friend Madame Catusse: 'Robert's marriage has literally killed me' (Madame A. Catusse, *op. cit.*, p. 20). Robert gave him a beautiful fur coat to distract him from his misery. During the war, Marcel was terrified on his brother's behalf, and poured out his worries to Madame Catusse once again: 'My poor brother has been sleeping in a tent (with dysentery) for more than a year (before that he had a bed), woken up twenty times a night, but is passionately committed to what he is doing. He has earned another very fine citation for bravery and his fourth stripe.'

At Proust's death in 1922, Robert was with him through his last moments. He asked Paul Helleu, Dunoyer de Segonzac and Man Ray to come to the deathbed, to make sketches and portraits of the dead man. In *Hommage à Marcel Proust* in the *Nouvelle Revue Française* in 1923, he declared: 'Towards me he always had the benevolent fraternal feelings of an elder brother, but in addition to that, I felt that our departed loved ones were still alive in him, and until his last day he was more than the guardian of this surviving moral spirit; he was the whole of my past life; the whole of my youth was contained in his individual existence.'

With the help of Jacques Rivière, who spent most of his nights working on them, Robert was actively involved with the publication of

Marcel's posthumous works: *La Prisonnière, Albertine disparue* and *Le Temps retrouvé*. (His copy of *Du Côté de chez Swann* bears this loving dedication: 'For my little brother, a remembrance of things past, recaptured for a moment each time we are together.') Robert encouraged Marcel's old friends to write their memoirs. Reynaldo Hahn, Anna de Noailles and Princesse Bibesco often visited him, and in the preface to his memoir Robert Dreyfus addressed him as follows: 'It was you who encouraged me and helped me make up my mind to gather up my memories, and to collect and annotate the letters I received from your marvellous brother' (R. Dreyfus, *Souvenirs sur Marcel Proust*).

Death. In 1932, when he had become the director of the Broca hospital, where he had begun his career, Robert almost worked himself to death. In 1935, a few weeks after a holiday spent in Illiers with his daughter Suzy retracing his childhood, he suffered a heart attack. He asked to be given extreme unction and died on 29 May 1935. His wife, who died on 21 January 1953, was later buried beside him in Père-Lachaise.

On 17 October 1972, the Robert Proust building at the Tenon hospital was opened in his honour.

Works. He published 250 articles and 27 books. His medical studies, which were as numerous as his father's, are less easily obtainable today. Robert was also editor-in-chief of the *Bulletins de la société anatomique de Paris*.

In Proust's work. Robert appears in *Jean Santeuil*. In *A la Recherche*, the narrator has no brother. However, an incident from Robert's youth is converted into Gilberte's accident in *La Prisonnière*. During the summer of 1894, while he was a hospital intern, he fell off a tandem in Rueil. A coal wagon weighing 3,000 kilos ran over his thigh, luckily without harming him very much. His mother, who came rushing over to look after him, found his mistress at his bedside. She immediately sent Robert to recover at his Uncle Louis' house at Auteuil.

Niece

SUZY MANTE-PROUST (Paris, 25 November 1903 – Paris, 22 February 1986). Although she was christened Adrienne in memory of her grandfather, who died the day after she was born, she disliked the name and, at the beginning of the war in 1914, changed it to Suzy (a name originally chosen by her maternal grandmother).

Childhood. She spent her childhood in an apartment on the ground floor of a building in the avenue Hoche. In summer and on some weekends her parents went to Louveciennes, to the villa they rented in about 1908 from the actress Léonie Yahn. Apart from the unexpected and rather magical visits from her Uncle Marcel, Adrienne lived alone with her parents. Her grandfather, Léon Dubois-Amiot, owed his fortune to an uncle in America, who had left as a cabin-boy bound for New Orleans, and probably become rich dealing in ebony. Her grandmother, Madame Dubois-Amiot (*née* Favier) spent a lot of time with her and often told her spicy family stories. A strange coincidence is that the grandmother, when a child herself, had spent every Sunday playing at the Château de Guermantes, which belonged to her relations, near Saint-Thibault-des-Vignes.

Education. Although the education of girls in the Dubois-Amiot and Favier families was very strict, it was not very deep. Her mother rigorously supervised the company she kept and the books she read, but paid little attention to her studies. Proust worried about this, wanting her to be brought up as his own parents would have done. She was sent to school at Parc Monceau. She preferred literature to mathematics, which she couldn't understand. The Abbé Mugnier, the father-confessor to the Faubourg Saint-Germain who was renowned for his cultural breadth, guided her reading choices. She took piano and singing lessons; she liked Wagner, especially *Tristan*, and also Debussy's *Pelléas*. To her great regret she was not allowed to see the Ballets Russes, because her mother and her uncle considered it improper for her. In 1921, while on holiday in Cannes, she had an attack of malaria, and for the next two years she lived the life of an invalid.

Marriage. On 23 January 1926, in Paris, she married *Gérard Mante* (Marseille, 5 March 1891 – Paris, 28 February 1947), nephew of the writer Edmond Rostand (1868–1918). To mark the occasion the Comtesse de Noailles gave them three of her works, each bearing a charming dedication; one of them evoked the couple's two famous uncles (Proust and Rostand): 'To Gérard Mante and to Her with all the friendly feelings of a heart in which the glorious rays of two beloved haloes cross in faithful memory. Anna de Noailles.'

Suzy had three children: a boy, *Patrice* (Paris, 5 November 1926), who obtained permission from the Conseil d'État to add the surname Proust to that of Mante in a decree dated 26 January 1952, and two daughters, *Dominique* (Paris, 30 November 1929) and *Marie-Claude* (Paris, 11 February 1932). The latter married *Claude Mauriac*, the son of François Mauriac (1885–1970), in Paris on 10 July 1951.

Relationship with her uncle. Whenever Proust paid a visit to his brother, he showered his niece with presents. He didn't give her books, but all the things little girls like: a sewing basket, an English print, and, in 1914, a medallion for her first communion. So concerned was he that his gifts should suit Suzy's tastes that he would send over his housekeeper, Céleste, or even the supplier himself, so that she could choose. One day she asked him for a pink flamingo. He replied: 'You shall have it' (C. Francis, *op. cit.*, p. 137), but her mother vetoed the idea. Proust thought his niece took after Robert, and he told his friend Paul Morand that she had the same goodness of heart. He lavished all his affection on her, and worried about her health. At the age of three she contracted diphtheria. Proust wrote to Madame Catusse: 'It pains me terribly that this child, in whom I like to feel a little of my mother and father lives on, has begun her life so sadly' (Madame A. Catusse, *op. cit.*, p. 80). The following year she had an operation to remove her appendix. A very worried Proust wrote to his friend Antoine Bibesco: 'If you found me a little nervous on the telephone, it was because my niece had just had a very serious operation for appendicitis and I was waiting for a telephone call from my brother.'

Although she enjoyed reading, Suzy didn't even open *A la Recherche* until after her marriage, because, in the opinion of her mother and of Proust himself, it was not suitable for a young girl. In 1919 Suzy congratulated her uncle on winning the Goncourt Prize and received this note in reply: 'Darling Suzy, I've got eight hundred and seventy letters to answer. That's my excuse for telling you in two lines that yours was wonderful, that you have as much wit as you have heart and that nobody loves you more than your uncle, Marcel.' Using his brother as an intermediary, he dedicated a de luxe copy of *A l'ombre des jeunes filles en fleurs* to her with the following words: 'For the darling girl.'

In 1922 her parents gave a ball for her 18th birthday; Proust made a brief appearance, very late. He had sent her flowers; extravagant as ever, he would have covered her with them, but once again his sister-in-law put the brakes on his over-generosity. At this time Proust saw a lot of his English friends, the Schiffs. They were keen to marry off their nephew, and were fond of Suzy, so they invited her to England, but Proust, who had very firm ideas about his niece's marriage and who feared the effects of a journey across the Channel on a young girl in delicate health, put a stop to the idea. That same year, in spite of his perilous state of health, Proust invited the Schiffs, together with his sister-in-law and Suzy, to the rue Hamelin for the last time. Always enthralled by the impassioned discussions she had with her uncle, she was to remember all her life the conversation they had that evening about Vermeer's *View of Delft*. On 19 November 1922, after Proust's death, Suzy and her mother paid a visit to the dead man. She knew how much he had loved her: 'My dear Suzy,' he once wrote, 'you would certainly have a fat volume if you received all the letters I write you in my thoughts every evening.' Profoundly affected by his absence, she went to see the Abbé Mugnier, who said: 'Proust? No one is less dead than he.' After the death of her father in 1935, Suzy and her mother found themselves in possession of an important collection of manuscripts, letters, furniture and objects d'art which Robert had inherited from Marcel.

Death. She died on Saturday, 22 February 1986. In spite of the Parkinson's Disease which had affected her for many months, she had continued to take part in all the major Proustian gatherings. Two days before her death, she was present at the meeting in the Ritz of the Marcel Proust prize jury. At her funeral service at Saint-Philippe-du-Roule on 26 February, the Dominican father Jacques Laval praised her in his address. The only descendant of Robert Proust, she was a grandmother several times over and even a great-grandmother. Gaston Palewski had awarded her the medal of the *ordre nationale du Merite*.

Maternal Great-uncles

MOÏSE BARUCH WEIL (Paris, 9 May 1809 – Beauvais, 26 September 1874). The son of *Baruch Weil's* first marriage to *Hélène Schoubach*. He was an architect in the town of Beauvais. He was socially and politically close to Adolphe Crémieux (1796–1880), and in 1844 he married

Crémieux's niece, *Amélie Berncastel* (Paris, 19 September 1821 – Beauvais, 15 November 1911).

They had four daughters: *Jenny* (1846–1922), who married François Boeuf, a professor in the Faculty of Law in Paris, with whom she had three children: Marie (1870–1907), Henri (1872–1925) and Jeanne (1877–1950). *Hélène* (1847–1925) married Casimir Bessière (1829–92), great-nephew of the maréchal de l'Empire (Duc d'Istrie), director of an insurance company, with whom she had three children: Jacques (1875–1906), Amélie (born in 1877) and Jean-Pierre (1880–1955), a future general. *Claire* (1849–1929) married Léon Neuberger (1840–1932), a director of the Rothschild bank, with whom she had three children: André, Georges and Noémie. Finally, there was *Adèle* (born in 1850).

LOUIS WEIL (Paris, 16 November 1816 – Paris, 10 May 1896). Born Larard (called Louis), son of *Baruch Weil's* second marriage to *Marguerite Nathan*.

Marriage. Although he has been described as a confirmed bachelor, he in fact married *Émilie Oppenheim* (Hamburg, 1821 – Paris, 22 November 1870), the daughter of a rich Hamburg banker, on 29 June 1844 in Hamburg, when he was 28. They had no children.

Career. He was first a lawyer, then President of the Court of Appeal in Paris, but gave up his practice to devote himself to business, like his brother Nathé. Both were Saint-Simonians, and they rallied to the Second Empire, which gave noble status to capitalism. A clever and lucky businessman, an indefatigable traveller, Louis held the much-envied position of council member at the *Comptoir d'escompte* in Paris. He had a button factory at 246 rue de Bercy Saint-Antoine, and he lived first at 33 rue d'Hauteville. His establishment (Trelon, Weldon and Weil) was considered the most substantial in Paris, with its shop at 14 bis, boulevard Poissonnière; in 1867 he was employing 5000 workers in his workshops and almost as many outside. This prosperous enterprise also employed his wife's family. Émilie Oppenheim's brother Wilhelm (who died in London on 28 November 1871) and two of her nephews, Alphonse and Robert, made their careers there. An enormously industrious man, he made his way into the grande bourgeoisie of Paris through wealth and business. Proust spoke of him in his correspondence as 'a slightly less rich Nucingen' (Madame A. Catusse, *op. cit.*, p. 64).

Louis acquired a second house at 96 rue La Fontaine, in Auteuil, and invested in a building at 102 boulevard Haussmann. From then on he lived in a vast apartment on the first floor of 29 rue Bleue. The stables and coach-houses in the courtyard reflected his grand lifestyle.

After his wife died on 22 November 1870, he retired to Auteuil, where he devoted himself to a life of pleasure. He was a man of the world, 'witty and a little caustic', according to Robert de Billy (R. de Billy, *Marcel Proust: Lettres et conversations*, p. 64). He was used to the Parisian salons and he spent a lot of time at the spa towns made fashionable by Napoleon III. His promiscuity displeased the rest of the family. The episode of the 'lady in pink' in *A la Recherche* demonstrated this. Of these easy-going women, 'my uncle knew many, and also many tarts which I could never distinguish from the actresses. He entertained them at his home [...]. Often when the name of an actress came up in conversation, I would hear my father say to my mother, with a smile: 'A friend of your uncle's ...' (*Du Côté de chez Swann*).

Death. At the end of his life, Louis Weil left Auteuil and moved to 102 boulevard Haussmann for good. On 10 May 1896, he died of the aftermath of pneumonia, in the bedroom Proust himself was later to occupy (he died of the same illness in the rue Hamelin). The bedroom was then painted flesh pink with gilded wood, a reflection of the old roué's tastes during his lifetime.

Burial. Louis Weil had wished to be buried without flowers or announcements. However, his mistress, Laure Hayman, sent an impressive wreath by cyclist. To lessen the impact of the incident, Madame Proust had it buried with the coffin at Père-Lachaise. Laure did not come to the ceremony, although Proust had written to her: 'What a ridiculous idea to suppose that you might shock anyone! Your presence could only be touching. It would be that of someone my uncle particularly loved [...] But I am afraid that it might be tiring for you, and there will be very few women there.' He sent her a tie-pin of his uncle's as a keepsake. Later he found in the boulevard Haussmann a collection of signed photographs from actresses, among them one of Marie van Zandt in male dress, which inspired the 'Miss Sacripant' of Elstir, the painter in *A la Recherche*. Apart from Jules Amiot, Louis Weil formed the chief model for Uncle Adolphe in *A la Recherche*.

Titles. He was awarded the Légion d'honneur in 1873. He was also a member of the Académie, and an honorary member of the Customs Commission.

Will. In his will of 30 December 1886, Louis Weil had designated as overall heirs his nephew, the lawyer Georges Weil, and his niece, Madame Adrien Proust: they inherited the house at Auteuil – which was sold by 1896 – and the building at 102 boulevard Haussmann.

ABRAHAM ALPHONSE WEIL (29 June 1822–10 December 1886). Louis' younger brother, born of Baruch Weil's second marriage to Marguerite Nathan. He was captain of an infantry battalion and Chevalier de la Légion d'honneur.

Uncles and Aunts

Paternal uncle: JULES AMIOT (Illiers, 6 June 1816 – Illiers, 23 October 1912). Son of René-André Amiot, a merchant draper, and Catherine-Charlotte Pitou. He went to Algeria at the time of its conquest, hoping to make his fortune in the cloth and wine trades. On his return to Illiers, his home town, he lived on the income from a flourishing draper's shop permeated by a 'smell of holland cloth'. Situated at 14 place du Marché, it was the town's most prestigious store. On 4 May 1847, he married *Élisabeth Proust* in Chartres. The couple settled in the house Jules owned below the square, at 4 rue du Saint-Esprit (since renamed rue du Dr Adrien-Proust; the house is now a museum). From Algeria, which he often visited (his brother had settled there, and later two of his children did the same), he brought back photographs and carpets to decorate an extension attached to the house, where he liked to shut himself away and paint. Very rich and nostalgic for the orientalism he loved, he set up a little hammam within the confines of his family house. He had also created an English-style park, the Pré Catelan, some way out of the town close to the Loir, where the Amiots and the Prousts liked to go for walks. In it he built an octagonal summer house in red brick called the 'Maison des Archers'. A stone from the ruins of the church of Saint-Hilaire, demolished during the Revolution, was set on top of the Pré Catelan's gates. He also tended a vegetable garden in the rue des Lavoirs; Proust nicknamed him 'my gardener uncle'. Politics interested him too. In 1903 he became deputy mayor and, to Marcel's great displeasure, fiercely anti-clerical. He died in 1912, leaving the shop to his son Fernand.

In Proust's work. Jules was one of the models for Uncle Adolphe in *A la Recherche*, and for Monsieur Sureau in *Jean Santeuil*. The character based on him is a secondary one, but none the less vivid.

Paternal aunt: FRANÇOISE ÉLISABETH JOSÉPHINE AMIOT (Illiers, 9 August 1828 – Illiers, 1 June 1886). Born at 11 place du Marché, the eldest daughter of Louis François Valentin Proust and Catherine Virginie Torcheux, grocers. She was 19 when she married *Jules Amiot*, who was twelve years her senior. They had three children: *Mathilde*, the eldest (Illiers, 16 September 1848 – Mustapha, Algeria, 26 February 1882), who was married to André Hamart, a shopkeeper, in Illiers on 27 September 1869, and ended her days in Algeria; *Fernand* (Illiers, 24 February 1853 – Versailles, 28 December 1931) who took over the family shop, married Berthe Ménager (1859–1920) in Magny on 6 October 1879; *André* (Illiers, 13 April 1860 – Versailles, 19 February 1925), an amateur painter like his father, who also lived in Algeria where he had a wine business.

It was to the rue Saint-Esprit that the Proust family came during their holidays in Illiers, to stay with Aunt and Uncle Amiot.

Unlike 'Tante Léonie' in *A la Recherche*, Élisabeth Amiot died at the age of 58, well before her husband, of stomach cancer. The Proust family went to Illiers for the settling of her will.

In Proust's work. From the memories of these summers Proust drew the descriptions which feature in 'Combray', the first part of *Du Côté de chez Swann*. Élisabeth inspired the character of Aunt Léonie, and Ernestine Gallou, the servant who stayed in her service for 33 years, was one of the models for Françoise, Aunt Léonie's cook. The solid family meals Ernestine prepared and Élisabeth Amiot's illness gave rise to some highly charged scenes, but Proust made little use of them in his work.

Maternal uncle: GEORGES-DENIS WEIL (Paris, 26 October 1847 – Paris, 23 August 1906). The son of Nathé Weil and Adèle Berncastel. He married *Amélie Oulman* on 20 April 1891, and they had a daughter, *Adèle*, in 1892. First a lawyer at the Court of Appeal, then a magistrate at the *Tribunal de 1ère instance de la Seine*, he ended up as counsellor to the Paris

Court of Appeal. He published various highly regarded studies, among them *Les Élections législatives depuis 1789, histoire de la législation et des moeurs*, which appeared in 1895. On the death of his uncle Louis Weil in 1896 he inherited the building at 102 boulevard Haussmann with his sister.

His nephews Marcel and Robert, and his sister Jeanne, their mother, liked him for his subtlety, his humour and his extreme pleasantness. When Marcel went for walks with him, he didn't want to let him go and would go to great lengths to make him miss his tram: 'I lured him away for ten minutes so that he would let the tram go by. It worked. Unfortunately, as I spied on it in the last few minutes before it left, I was so pleased I gave myself away a bit. He ran off after it. It's so good to see him.'

But his precarious health worried his sister and his nephew. Marcel confided to Fernand Gregh: 'I have an uncle who has been very ill with stomach trouble for several years, extremely neurasthenic, who would like to try your doctor. But if you're not just neurasthenic, if you have something badly wrong with your stomach and it is not just nervous, will he still treat you?'

His sister Jeanne died before him, in 1905. After her death, Georges stayed very close to Proust, who nicknamed him 'Uncle G.'. He often visited him in the evenings in the rue de Courcelles. But several months later, Georges had to take to his bed with an attack of uraemia. Unlike his sister, he suffered terribly. In August 1906, Proust, who was then living in Versailles, went to see him at his home at 22 place Malesherbes. His uncle could no longer recognise him. He died on 23 August, and was buried on the 26th in the Jewish cemetery at Père-Lachaise, near the gate to the rue du Repos. Proust was very ill and could not be present at his uncle's funeral.

Maternal aunt: AMÉLIE OULMAN (Paris, 27 January 1853 – Paris, 22 January 1920). The daughter of Émile and Simonette Cohen. Amélie's first marriage was to Wilhelm Jacob Hermann. When Georges-Denis Weil, her second husband, died in 1906, she inherited his share of the building at 102 boulevard Haussmann. She was an astute business-woman, and she managed to acquire the whole of the property when the interests of her co-owners were auctioned on 8 November 1907 – she had no trouble in getting the better of her nephews. In 1919 she decided to sell the building, to the great dismay of Proust, who was then her tenant. She preferred, as she wrote to him with some humour, 'the gentler title of aunt to that of landlady [...] Our conversations can always be about literature now, not about the house'. She died in Paris on 22 January 1920.

Cousin: ADÈLE WEIL (Paris, 3 March 1892 – Ravensbruck, Germany, 5 December 1944). Like all the Weils, she often stayed with Uncle Louis at Auteuil. Marcel was very fond of his young cousin Adèle, and he liked to spoil her. In 1906 he asked his friend Reynaldo Hahn to buy her the English edition of Walter Scott. On 27 March 1920, in Paris, she married *Maxime Weil* (Barr, 15 September 1877 – Buchenwald, 30 November 1944), an engineer. They had one daughter, *Annette* (born in Paris on 8 January 1921). All three were arrested by the Gestapo in Toulouse and deported to Buchenwald on 30 July 1944, in Convoy 81. Only Annette ever returned.

On 12 March 1948 she married Claude Heumann (born at Saint-Cloud on 19 March 1917). He was then *maître des requêtes* at the Conseil d'État. They had two children: Danielle, Madame Dominique Brogly, and Guy.

Deaths in Proust's Family

1855. 2 October: his grandfather, Louis François Valentin Proust.

1886. 1 June (Proust was 14): his paternal aunt, Madame Jules Amiot.

1889. 19 March (Proust was 17): his paternal grandmother, Madame Valentin Proust.

1890. 2 January (Proust was 18): his maternal grandmother, Madame Nathé Weil.

1896. 10 May (Proust was 25): his maternal great-uncle, Louis Weil. 30 June: his maternal grandfather, Nathé Weil.

1903. 26 November (Proust was 32): his father, Dr Adrien Proust.

1905. 26 September (Proust was 34): his mother, Madame Adrien Proust.

1906. 23 August (Proust was 35): his maternal uncle, Georges-Denis Weil.

1912. 23 October (Proust was 40): his paternal uncle, Jules Amiot.

On his death in 1922, Proust left no antecedents or descendants, apart from his brother Robert (who died in 1935), the father of one daughter, Suzy Mante-Proust (who died in 1986) and some more distant relations.

On the Weil side: His aunt Amélie Weil (who died in 1920) and her daughter Adèle (who died in a concentration camp in 1944).

On the Proust side: Two first cousins: André Amiot (died 1925), father of one daughter (who died in 1942), and Fernand Amiot (who died in 1931). The latter had three children: a son who died at an early age, another who was killed at Ermenonville in 1916, and Germaine Amiot who died in 1977.

CHAPTER EIGHT

Love Life

Male Liaisons*

In the absence of documents and letters which were unfortunately destroyed, the mystery surrounding Proust's homosexual life is impenetrable. At the time when he was at the Condorcet lycée – already an elegant dresser, he sported silk ties and a frock coat to the first salons he visited – it would be more accurate to describe his relationships with, for example, Daniel Halévy or Jacques Bizet as loving friendships.

After these special friendships, Proust made relationships with young people from his own milieu, often aspiring artists or writers at the start of their careers. This was the case with Willie Heath, Robert de Flers, Reynaldo Hahn and Lucien Daudet. He also pursued his dream of happiness in the company of young noblemen from the Faubourg Saint-Germain (who later became the models for the character of Saint-Loup in *A la Recherche*). Among these were Prince Antoine Bibesco and Comte Bertrand de Salignac-Fénelon. About 1902, Proust formed new aristocratic friendships with Prince Léon Radziwill, Duc Armand de Guiche, Marquis Louis d'Albufera and, later, the Marquis Illan de Casa-Fuerte.

With Illan de Casa-Fuerte the period of friendship with the 'young Dukes' came to an end. From that time onwards, until his death, Proust was to spend his time with young people of modest origins who became his secretaries, valets or protégés. By 1899 he had met the son of a

---

* Biographical details of the people mentioned here can be found in alphabetical order in the chapter entitled 'Dictionary of Proust's Acquaintances'.

roofer, the young Poupetière, to whom he gave money and patronage. Proust was disappointed in his aristocratic friendships, and, since his mother's death had lifted the obligation to hide his homosexuality – which was, in theory, a secret – he turned to new relationships. In August 1906, at the Hôtel des Réservoirs where he was living, he formed an attachment to a young servant, a protégé of Reynaldo Hahn's called Léon, whose devotion he rewarded generously. In November 1906 he asked Robert de Billy to find a job in his father-in-law's bank for an anonymous 'young man of twenty-five, very distinguished and fine-looking, quite compatible, very nicely-mannered, very responsible, who can write well enough but has no education beyond that'.

He also saw a great deal of Robert Ulrich, who acted as his secretary; Albert Nahmias, another secretary who also helped with his speculations on the stock market. Alfred Agostinelli, who was employed as his secretary and chauffeur in 1913, occupied a significant place in his life until the tragic end of their liaison caused by Agostinelli's death by drowning in May 1914. Next came the Swedish valet, Ernst Forssgren, whom Proust saw for the last time in the month he died.

Henri Rochat was the last secretary with whom Proust had an intimate relationship, beginning in 1919. But, on 4 June 1921, Rochat embarked for Argentina. Finally, Comte Louis Gautier-Vignal claimed, towards the end of his life, to have been one of Proust's last 'friends', although he was always very discreet about the precise nature of their relationship.

The Boy in 'Marcel Jouhandeau's Notebook'

A young inmate of Albert Le Cuziat's brothel in the Hôtel Marigny at 11 rue de l'Arcade, Jouhandeau confided his story to a notebook (which Henri Bonnet discusses in *Les Amours et le sexualité de Marcel Proust*). In the spring of 1917, 'Marcel came to Le Cuziat's and looked through a glass pane into a room where a game of cards was in progress. He chose his partner and went upstairs. A quarter of an hour later,' said the boy, 'I knocked on the door, went in, and found Marcel already in bed with the sheet drawn up to his chin. He smiled at me. My instructions were to take all my clothes off and remain standing by the closed door while I satisfied myself under the anxious gaze of Marcel, who was doing the same [...] If he didn't reach the desired conclusion, he would make a gesture for me to leave and Albert would bring the cages.' These cages contained hungry rats which Le Cuziat would encourage to eat each other for Proust's enjoyment. Gide confirmed this episode: 'During a memorable night-time conversation [...] Proust explained his pre-occupation with bundling together the most diverse sensations and emotions in order to achieve orgasm. That was the justification for his interest in rats, among other things; in any case, Proust wanted me to see it as such. Above all, I saw it as the admission of some sort of psychological inadequacy' (A. Gide, *Ainsi soit-il*, p. 151). Céleste Albaret protested against these slanders.

Close Relationships with Women*

Proust's relationships with women are difficult to define if one takes into account the opinion of André Gide. When Gide visited Proust on May 1921, Proust confided to him that he had 'never loved women in any way other than spiritually, and never known love except with men'. Thus, Gide held him to be a 'grand master of pretence' (A. Gide, *Journal 1889–1939*, pp. 692 and 848).

To begin with, there were childhood friends such as the sisters Marie and Nelly Bénardaky (with whom Proust often used to play in the Champs-Élysées), and the pretty Jeanne Pouquet, whom he courted ardently despite her engagement to Gaston Arman de Caillavet. Later, about 1890, he began to form relationships with older women, spending a fortune on presents for them. He was 17 when he met his great-uncle Louis' mistress, Laure Hayman (who was then 37). His friend Jacques Bizet's mother, Madame Émile Straus (*née* Geneviève Halévy), to whose salon he was a regular visitor, remained a very devoted friend to the end of her life. In 1892 he was attracted to the Comtesse de Chevigné, and used to lie in wait for her on her morning outings. This was once again the beginning of a friendship that lasted more than twenty-five years. The following year it was the Comtesse Greffulhe that he eagerly went to the Opéra to see.

Insofar as real liaisons between Proust and women are concerned,

---

* Biographical details of the people mentioned here can be found in alphabetical order in the chapter entitled 'Dictionary of Proust's Acquaintances'.

opinions are divided. According to George D. Painter, Proust's hetero-
sexual relationships were authentic. In Henri Bonnet's view, it was more
a matter of schoolboy bravado, or, later on, of disguising his real
sexuality. This was probably the case, about 1888, when he fell in love –
or made people think he had fallen in love – with Laure Hayman,
Madame Chirade or the '*jolie Viennoise*'.

Proust talked about the '*jolie Viennoise*' to his friend Robert Dreyfus in
a letter of 25 September 1888. He described 'a very uncomplicated
intrigue which led smoothly to the inevitable conclusion and which
began an absorbing liaison that looked as if it would last at least a year,
to the great benefit of café-concerts and that sort of place, where one
goes with that sort of person' (R. Dreyfus, *Souvenirs sur Marcel Proust*,
1926). Proust had met this young lady at the Perrin school of dance in
the rue de la Victoire. In Philip Kolb's opinion, the cynicism of the letter
leads one to think that once again this liaison was perhaps less absorbing
than he would like people to think.

As for the actress Louisa de Mornand, whom Proust met in 1903 at the
same time as Louis d'Albufera, she became more attached to him than he
really wanted: evidence for this is the correspondence they exchanged
(simple replies from Proust to the pressing notes she addressed to him)
and particularly the revelations she made to the press in 1928, describing Proust's 'keen passion finely balanced between affection and
desire'.

Marriage Plans

In 1892, the year when he met Mary Finaly, the 21-year-old Proust had
'tender feelings' for his cousin Amélie Bessière, whom he often saw at
Auteuil, staying with his great-uncle Louis Weil, and he thought of
marrying her. Seven years later, in the autumn of 1899, he felt little
enthusiasm for the idea of marrying Suzanne Thibault (1881–1918), the
only daughter of Anatole France, who was keen on the match. During a
stay in Cabourg in 1908, he met a mysterious young lady whom he saw
from time to time in Paris. Antoine Bibesco, who knew her, would never
reveal her name. She was one of the chief models for Albertine. The
following year, 1909, Proust considered marrying her, as he hinted in a
letter to his friend Lauris: 'Georges, if I leave Paris, it may be with a
wife'. According to Henri Bonnet: 'It was certainly a ruse [...] But to

proclaim it to his friends who did not know about his inclinations, or only suspected what they were, that was cunning, and likely to be convincing!' (H. Bonnet, *op. cit.*, p. 40).

CHAPTER NINE

Dictionary of
Proust's Acquaintances*

AGOSTINELLI, Alfred (Monaco, 30 May 1888 – Antibes, 11 October 1914). A chauffeur-mechanic from Monaco working for the Taximètres-Unic company (directed by Jacques Bizet) at a time when this was an unusual occupation which attracted sporting young men. In 1907 and 1908 he and Proust made numerous excursions, inspiring the 'Impressions de route en automobile' which appeared in *Le Figaro*. Proust took him to Versailles, and later dismissed him. It was in 1913, when Proust re-employed him as a secretary to type his novel, that their relationship began. Alfred, who was passionately keen on flying, left him in December to enroll in the brothers Garbero's school of aviation in Antibes, using the pseudonym 'Marcel Swann'. On 30 May 1914, at about five o'clock in the afternoon, while Proust was writing to him to tell him that he had bought him an aeroplane (at a cost of 27,000 francs) – on which he had had Mallarmé's sonnet 'The Swan' engraved, as the narrator does on Albertine's Rolls-Royce – Agostinelli's monoplane crashed into the Mediterranean near Biot. The 26-year-old Agostinelli had just obtained his pilot's licence and was making his second solo flight; he had just communicated the news to Proust in a long letter of gratitude which arrived too late. On 2 June, Agostinelli's brother asked Proust to 'have divers sent down to recover the body of his brother, who had all his belongings on him' (this referred to the money which Proust

---

*In the biographies in this chapter, complete lists of publications are not given for well-known authors whose works are numerous.

generously gave his chauffeur). A week after the accident, on 7 June, fishermen found Agostinelli's body near Cagnes, about a dozen kilometres north-east of where the accident happened. On hearing the news of his death, Proust compared his feeling to the grief he had felt at his mother's death. His sorrow was compounded by remorse that he had indirectly encouraged Agostinelli in his new venture. He even contemplated suicide: 'I knew what it was like to hope with all my heart, every time I got into a taxi, that the next bus would run me over.' He went to great lengths to help the dead man's family, and he welcomed Anna, Agostinelli's companion, to the boulevard Haussmann. In June Proust wrote to Gide: 'The last straw has been the death of a young man I must have loved more than any of my friends, since his death is making me so miserable.' Agostinelli, who was intelligent and sensitive, was the main inspiration for Albertine. Proust paid tribute to him by using part of his last letter in Albertine's.

ALBUFERA, Louis, Comte Suchet, 4th Duc d' (Paris, 4 May 1877 – Ville d'Avray, 15 June 1953). His nickname was 'Albu'. Proust met him in December 1902, at the same time as the Duc de Guiche. He was 25, and loved cars and travelling. He was the only one of the 'young Dukes' who was not an intellectual and pro-Dreyfus. On 10 October 1904 he married Anna Masséna d'Essling (1884–1967) in Paris. His mistress was Louisa de Mornand, an actress (like Saint-Loup's mistress in *A la Recherche*). Proust soon became the couple's confidant. When *Sodome et Gomorrhe* appeared in 1922, d'Albufera, who thought he recognised himself in the portrayal of Saint-Loup in love with Rachel, quarrelled with Proust. Marcel wrote to him in hope of a reconciliation, but without success.

ALTON, Charles, Vicomte d' (Giraumont, 20 September 1857 – Paris, 8 March 1931). He met Proust in 1908. They corresponded frequently. He was the father of Colette d'Alton, one of the models for Albertine, to whom Proust gave a golden dressing-case, as the narrator did to his mistress.

ARMAN DE CAILLAVET, Madame Albert, *née* Léontine Lippmann (1844 –1910) Anatole France's new patroness in 1886, she was at home every Sunday in her apartment at 12 avenue Hoche. Proust was a regular visitor to her salon and became close to her son Gaston in 1890. She was one of the models for Madame Verdurin.

ARMAN DE CAILLAVET, Gaston (Paris, 13 March 1869 – Essendiéras, 14 January 1915). He was a journalist and playwright whom Proust met at his mother's house during his military service in 1890. On 11 April 1893, Gaston married Jeanne Pouquet (1874–1961) (see p. 214), but was never faithful to her. By a decree awarded on 19 June 1893 he added the name Caillavet to his surname Arman; later he included the particle *de*, to which he had no legal right. After a career as editor of *Le Figaro* and as a playwright, he was killed in the war in 1915, leaving one daughter, Simone (1894–1968) whose second husband was André Maurois. Proust asked to see Simone one evening in April 1909; she became the inspiration for the character of Mademoiselle de Saint-Loup.

Works: A comedy in collaboration with P. Grünebaum: *Noblesse oblige*, 1891. Comedies in collaboration with Robert de Flers: *Miquette et sa mère* (1906), *L'Amour veille* (1907), *Le Roi* (1908), *L'Ane de Buridan* (1909), *Le Bois sacré* (1910), *Primerose* (1911), *L'Habit vert* (1913), *La Belle Aventure* (1913), *Monsieur Bretonneau* (1914).

AUBERNON, Madame, *née* Lydie Lemercier de Nerville (1825–99). Even though the Faubourg Saint-Germain did not attend it, her literary and artistic salon had great prestige. Plump and vivacious, 'she looked like Queen Pomaré on the lavatory', as Montesquiou said of her. She was at home on Wednesdays, and she would determine the subject of conversation. If attention wandered from the topic, she used to ring a little bell. Proust was introduced there about 1892 and often went with Jacques-Émile Blanche and later with Reynaldo Hahn. She also owned a house called Coeur-Volant in Louveciennes, where her regular circle of guests went by train in summer. She was another of the models for Madame Verdurin.

BAIGNÈRES, Arthur (1834–1913). One of the wittiest men of his day; the grandson of the famous politician and financier Jacques Lafitte. He published two collections of stories, *Histoires modernes* and *Histoires anciennes*, written in an outmoded style that Proust compared to Sainte-Beuve. He and his wife, *née* Charlotte Borel, lived at 4 rue du Général-

Foy. Proust was friendly with their son Paul (1869–1936) and spent holidays with them at Les Frémonts, in Trouville, where Paul Baignères painted his portrait in 1892.

BAIGNÈRES, Madame Henri, née Laure Boilay (1844–1918). Arthur Baignères' sister-in-law. She owned a town house at 40 rue du Général-Foy. She was a regular guest at Madame Aubernon's salon; Proust also frequented hers. She had a house near Geneva, the Villa Quatorze, which Proust knew well. He was a friend of her son Jacques, an old classmate from Condorcet who, after Le Banquet, wrote for La Revue blanche. The character of Madame Leroi was based on Madame Baignères.

BARDAC, Henri. Son of Noël Bardac and a close friend of Reynaldo Hahn, with whom he went to Cabourg. Proust met him in 1906 and called him 'the pink coral guinea-pig'. Bardac was seriously wounded in the head at the battle of the Marne in 1914, then sent as an attaché to the London embassy, where he sang the praises of Swann. On leave in Paris in 1915, he visited Proust assiduously. The scar on his forehead inspired that of Saint-Loup. An acquaintance of Montesquiou's as well, he published an article entitled 'Proust et Montesquiou' in La Revue de Paris of September 1948.

BARRÈRE, Camille (La Charité-sur-Loire, 23 October 1851 – Paris, 23 October 1940). A diplomat who was a friend of Dr Proust's and who supported him in his fight against cholera despite opposition from England. He came to dinner at the Prousts' every week. He was French ambassador to Italy from 1897–1924. Barrère recognised himself in the character of Norpois.

BARRÈS, Maurice (Charmes, 19 August 1862 – Neuilly, 4 December 1923). A politician and writer born to a well-to-do bourgeois family and brought up in Nancy, he came to Paris in 1883 to study law, and was 29 when Proust first met him. As well as being a friend of Princesse Mathilde's and of Montesquiou's, and member of parliament for Nancy from 1889, he was also a respected author known as 'the prince of youth'. Although Proust admired this individualist writer's musical turn of phrase and shared many of his ideas, he differed from him in his nationalist political opinions. Barrès, who supplied one of the models for Bergotte, attended Proust's funeral; turning to Mauriac, he said: *'Enfin ouais, c'était notre jeune homme!'*

Works: *Huit Jours chez M. Renan* (1888), *Sous l'œil des barbares* (1888), *Un homme libre* (1889), *L'Ennemi des lois* (1893), *Du sang, de la volupté et de la mort* (1893–1904), *Les Déracinés* (1897), *L'Appel au soldat* (1900), *Leurs figures* (1901), *Au service de l'Allemagne* (1905), *Le Voyage de Sparte* (1905), *Colette Baudoche* (1909), *Gréco ou le secret de Tolède* (1911), *La Colline inspirée* (1913), *La Grande Pitié des églises de France* (1914), *Amori et Dolori sacrum* (1921), *Un Jardin sur l'Oronte* (1922), *Mes Cahiers 1896–1923* (1929–57).

BARTHOLONI, Madame Anatole, *née* Marie Frasier-Frisell. Lady of honour at the court of the Empress Eugénie, famous for her beauty and wit. The Bartholonis lived at the Château de Coudrée near Thonon on Lake Leman. During his holidays in Évian, Proust made friends with their daughter, nicknamed Kiki, and corresponded with her from July 1897 onwards.

BEAULAINCOURT, Comtesse de, *née* Sophie de Castellane (1818–1904). Daughter of the Maréchal de Castellane and of Cordélia Greffulhe – who had been a mistress of Chateaubriand and of Molé; the great-aunt of Boni de Castellane. She was cultured, elegant and worldly. Her first marriage was to the Marquis de Contades (died 1858) and she had several lovers. Under the Second Empire, these included the Comte de Fleury, French ambassador to St Petersburg (and one of the models for Norpois), then the Comte de Coislin with whom she had a son. After Contades died in 1858 she married the Comte de Beaulaincourt. Proust was invited to visit her on 13 May 1897. In a letter to Montesquiou of April 1921, he described her as being the chief inspiration for Madame de Villeparisis. In *A la Recherche* Proust explained why, like her character, she did not receive as her guests the whole of Faubourg Saint-Germain society, whom she regularly made fun of. She ended her days more modestly, dividing her time between Paris and her Château d'Acosta, in the Yvelines.

BEAUMONT, Comte Étienne de (Paris, 1883 – Paris 1956) and Comtesse de, *née* Edith Taisne de Raimonval. They were friends of Paul Morand's who lived in a town house in the rue Masseran in the 7th arrondissement and entertained frequently. They attended the dinners Proust gave at the Ritz with the Princesse Soutzo and Paul Morand. At one dinner, on 27 July 1917, the Comte fell asleep under hypnosis in Proust's presence. They were also close to the Abbé Mugnier. Proust spent his last New Year's Eve with them at the ball they gave on 31 December 1921, and paid his last social call on them at the beginning of October 1922.

BÉNARDAKY, Madame Nicolas, *née* Lebrock. Married to a Polish nobleman who had made a fortune in tea and then become master of ceremonies at the Russian Tsar's court. She lived in a town house at 65 rue de Chaillot. The mother of Marie and Nelly, Proust's friends in the Champs-Élysées, and of a very handsome boy who died at the age of 18. It was said she was not interested in anything but champagne and love. Paul Nadar photographed her several times in sumptuous disguises, notably as a Valkyrie in a dress by the couturier Worth which emphasised her statuesque beauty. In *Jean Santeuil*, she and her husband became Monsieur et Madame Kossicheff; she was one of the originals of Odette de Crécy in *A la Recherche*.

BÉNARDAKY, Marie (born in Russia about 1875). Daughter of the above and Nicolas Bénardaky. Proust met her and her sister Nelly for the first time during the summer of 1886. They lived close to the Champs-Élysées where Proust played with them. On 21 August 1898 Marie married Prince Michel Radziwill in St Petersburg. They divorced in 1915 after having one daughter, Léontine. Proust described her as 'one of the two great loves of my life'. This childhood friend was one of the chief models for Gilberte.

BÉRAUD, Jean (St Petersburg, 1849 – Paris, 1935). A French painter, friend of the Impressionists, very worldly, famous for his many depictions of bourgeois life in Paris – *Le Dimanche près de Saint-Philippe-du-Roule* (1877), *Sortie de l'Opéra* (1883), *Place de la Concorde, Promenade aux Champs-Élysées, Sortie de Condorcet, rue Caumartin* (about 1890) – he was a regular guest at the salons of Comtesse Potocka and Madame Lemaire, where Proust met him in 1896. On 6 February 1897, together with Gustave de Borda, he was Proust's second in his duel with the writer Jean Lorrain. In 1920 he gave Proust his Légion d'honneur cross. He was one of the originals of Elstir in *A la Recherche*.

BERL, Emmanuel (1892–1976). Writer. Cousin of the poet Henri Franck, related by marriage to the philosopher Henri Bergson. During the war, Berl had written a letter from the trenches which had moved Proust deeply. Invalided out of the army, he visited Proust enthusiastically. On one of his visits, Berl claimed that happy love was possible; Proust threw him out, hurling slippers at his head. They never had the same view of love, and Berl justified his position in his work (*A venir, Regain au pays d'Auge*).

BERNHARDT, Henriette Rosine Bernard, known as Sarah (Paris, 1844 – Paris, 1923). Actress. Second prize winner at the Conservatoire, she went into the Comédie-Française in 1862. Her personality and her talent as a tragic actress were the subject of conversation for the young Proust even in the Champs-Élysées. The journey he made to Brittany in 1895 with Reynaldo Hahn was also, as he wrote, 'a pilgrimage to the places illuminated by Sarah Bernhardt' (Belle-Ile was the summer residence of 'the Divine Sarah'). Berma's performance in *Phèdre* was based on her; Nadar photographed her in the part, which she played again in 1893, the year she became director of the Théâtre de la Renaissance.

BERRY, Walter V. R. (Paris, 29 July 1859 – Paris, 1927). He was President of the American Chamber of Commerce in Paris from 1916 to 1923, an expert in international law and an ardent advocate of America's entry into the war. Paul Morand described him as 'the American of Henry James's novels'. Berry became friendly with Proust in 1916 and sent him, in May, a book printed in 1709 with the crest of Paulin Prondre de Guermantes on the cover. In November 1917 and November 1918, Proust asked his help with the sale of his furniture. In 1920 he acquired three de luxe copies of *A l'ombre des jeunes filles en fleurs*. A regular of the Ritz dinners, he was to prove one of Proust's most loyal friends.

BIBESCO, Princesse Alexandre, *née* Hélène Costaki Epurano (1849 – Bucharest, 31 October 1902). Daughter of Kostaki Epurano, President of the Council of Romania in 1879. She was a brilliant pianist and knew Liszt, Wagner and Gounod. In her salon at 69 rue de Courcelles she received musicians (Fauré, Debussy, Saint-Saëns), painters (Bonnard, Puvis de Chavanne, Vuillard, Odilon Redon) and writers (Loti, Anatole

France, Porto-Riche, Jules Lemaitre). Proust, who then lived with his parents at 45 rue de Courcelles, was very friendly with her two sons, Antoine and Emmanuel; they visited each other's houses frequently. She died of illness in Romania, on the family estate at Corcova.

BIBESCO, Antoine, Prince (1878 – Paris, 2 September 1951). Son of the above and Prince Alexandre Bibesco. Proust met him and his brother Emmanuel in June 1899 through Anna de Noailles, their mother Hélène's niece. Shortly afterwards, Antoine left to do his military service in Romania. He returned to Paris in the autumn of 1901 and became much closer to Proust. He and his brother and Bertrand de Salignac-Fénelon had formed a secret society to which they admitted Proust. Antoine's nickname was 'Téléphas' (in Greek, the one who speaks from afar; Proust christened him this because Antoine talked to him on the telephone so much); Proust was 'Lecram' (an anagram of Marcel) or 'le Flagorneur' ('the toady' or 'the flatterer'). When the two brothers were together, they were 'Ocsebib'. In 1902, to comfort him after his mother's death, Proust suggested that he accompany him to Romania, but on condition that there were no flowers on the family estate which might bring on his asthma. Antoine remained a faithful and devoted friend until Proust's death. Proust once said to Céleste: 'you should read Dostoyevsky's novel, *The Brothers Karamazov*, because you'll see: they are the Bibescos' (C. Albaret, *op. cit.*, p. 270). In March 1919, Proust attended his engagement to Elizabeth Asquith, daughter of the former English Prime Minister Herbert Henry Asquith. Antoine and Elizabeth's marriage produced a daughter, Priscilla.

Works: *Aux Enfers avec Marcel Proust* (1948), 'The Heartlessness of Marcel Proust' in *Cornhill Magazine* (Summer 1950).

BIBESCO, Emmanuel (1875 – 22 August 1917). Brother of the above. He took part in the excursions by car; he knew all the Gothic churches in France and visited them regularly. In the spring of 1914, Emmanuel returned from a journey to Japan, already bearing the traces of the paralysis which later deformed the whole of his left side. On 12 April 1917 he went to see Proust for the last time, but huddled deep inside the car so that no one could see how ugly he had become. Mornand and Proust sat on the folding seats behind, and Emmanuel shouted: 'Let the driver go backwards, so that Paul Morand and Marcel Proust are in front!' After two suicide attempts he killed himself at his house in Grosvenor Square, London, out of despair at the illness which threatened to paralyse him completely. He was a bachelor.

BIBESCO, Princesse Georges, *née* Marthe Lahovary (Bucharest, 28 January 1886 – Paris, 28 November 1973). A member of an illustrious Romanian family and the first cousin of the Bibesco brothers and Anna de Noailles. She was also related to the Guiches, the Greffulhes and the Montesquious. She married her cousin, Prince Georges Bibesco, in 1905. In May 1911, Proust met her at the *Intransigeant* ball, but she tried to avoid him. Her first book, *Les Huit Paradis*, earned praise from Proust, who wrote to Emmanuel Bibesco: 'Please tell the Princess she is both beautiful and delightful'. During the war their common friendship with the Abbé Mugnier brought them closer. They dined together with Walter Berry in 1920. In June 1922, she came to see Proust at 44 rue Hamelin with her cousin Antoine Bibesco and his wife Elizabeth for the last time. But Céleste refused to let her into his bedroom, claiming that: 'Monsieur is afraid of princesses' perfume.'

Works: She published more than thirty books, including six historical novels, her correspondence with the Abbé Mugnier, published in three volumes in 1951 under the title *La Vie d'une amitié*, and some collected memoirs: *Catherine-Paris* (1927), *Images d'Épinal* (1937), *Feuilles de Calendrier* (1939), *La Nymphe Europe* (1960). She wrote three excellent reminiscences of Proust: *Au bal avec Marcel Proust* (1928), *Le Voyageur voilé* (1947) and *Le Confesseur et les poètes* (1970).

BILLY, Robert de (27 June 1869 – May 1953). In February 1890, Proust, who was doing his military service in Orléans, met Billy for the first time at dinner with the Préfet of the Loiret, Monsieur Boegner. Billy was then in the 30th artillery regiment. He was to become one of Proust's closest friends, and keep up an intimate correspondence with him. They met again in November 1890 at the École libre des sciences politiques. Billy advised Proust to aim for the Foreign Service; he himself was appointed to Berlin on 27 December 1892 as a trainee, and later became French ambassador to Bulgaria, Greece and Japan. In 1895 Billy and his wife went to see Proust in Kreuznach where he was on holiday with his mother; they visited the cathedral in Mayence together. In August 1904, he and Proust went on a cruise along the Normandy and Brittany coast aboard the steam yacht *Hélène* which belonged to Monsieur Mirabaud, Robert de Billy's father-in-law. Billy was intelligent and highly cultured. He helped Proust to translate Ruskin and was rewarded with the gift of a Japanese sword-hilt (he collected them) inlaid with gold. He learnt of Proust's death in a letter from Reynaldo Hahn. In 1930 Billy published *Marcel Proust. Lettres et conversations.*

BIZET, Jacques (1872–1922). A cousin of Daniel Halévy's, the son of Madame Straus's first marriage to the composer Georges Bizet (1838–75). Proust nicknamed him 'Carmen's son'. They met at the Pape-Carpentier school; then, at Condorcet, Daniel Halévy, Robert Dreyfus and he formed the trio of the 'three most intelligent boys in the class' (*Jean Santeuil*). In 1887, when they were in 'rhétorique' (the top class), he became an intimate friend of Proust's. In 1888, like his cousin Halévy, he rejected the advances Proust made in an impassioned letter. His mother admitted the young Proust to her salon; he invited them both to the première of Edmond de Goncourt's *Germinie Lacerteux* at the Odéon on 15 December. After Condorcet, Bizet studied medicine. He also took part in the production of *Le Banquet*. From 18 to 20 March 1897, when Proust had published *Les Plaisirs et les jours*, Bizet (who was then living in a flat on the Quai Bourbon) produced *Les lauriers sont coupés*, a satirical review which made fun of the high-society nature of Proust's work. (The sets were designed by Jacques-Émile Blanche, Paul Baignères, Amédée and Charles Rouquès, and Léon Yeatman, not without some reluctance, took on the job of imitating Proust's voice.) In 1898 he was a keen supporter of Dreyfus, and signed the '*Manifeste des cent-quatre*'. His mother's salon had become a headquarters of Dreyfusism. In 1907, when he was the director of a car hire company, Taximètres Unic de Monaco, he hired a car for Proust and recommended three chauffeurs: Jossien, Odilon Albaret and Alfred Agostinelli. In 1922, sunk in alcohol and morphine addiction, persecuted by his mistress, he fired a bullet into his head, a fortnight before Proust's death. Proust is said to have exclaimed to Céleste: 'I am horrified when I think about it. Yes, I could have become a human wreck like one of my friends, who turned into a good-for-nothing' (C. Albaret, *op. cit.*, p. 73).

BLANCHE, Jacques-Émile (Paris, 1 February 1861 – Offranville, 1942). A society painter, friend of Maurice Barrès, Henry James and Montesquiou. He was the son of the famous psychiatrist Antoine-Émile Blanche (1820–93), and his parents kept up a fashionable salon where Berlioz and George Sand were among the guests. Like Proust, he was educated at Condorcet. The two met in 1891 in the salons of Madame Straus, the Princesse Mathilde and Madame Baignères. On 1 October Blanche did a pencil portrait of Proust at Les Frémonts; he used it as a sketch for a second portrait in oils which he painted at Auteuil in the spring of 1892. He exhibited it on 8 May 1893 at the Champ-de-Mars salon. Proust's description of the portrait in *Jean Santeuil* showed that he was pleased with it; in May 1920, the de luxe edition of *A l'ombre des jeunes filles en fleurs* contained a reproduction of it. On 15 April 1914, Blanche wrote of *Du Côté de chez Swann* in *L'Écho de Paris*: 'The book of insomnia, of the thoughts that watch through silence and darkness.' In June 1916 Proust went to see him in his studio; Blanche offered him a cup of tea, a delicate allusion to *A la Recherche*. On 10 April 1918, Blanche asked if he could dedicate the first volume of *Propos de peintre*, a collection of essays on the Impressionists entitled *De David à Degas*, to him; in return, he asked him to write a preface. In May Proust wrote the text, but it led to months of argument between the two friends. The volume, with Proust's preface, appeared in March 1919. At the beginning of January 1921, Blanche's long dedication in the second volume, entitled *Dates*, addressed the controversies left unresolved, in the first. Blanche also painted portraits of Mallarmé, Gide, Cocteau, Stravinsky and James Joyce. He described Proust at length in *Mes modèles*, published in 1928.

BLUM, Léon (Paris, 9 April 1872 – Jouy-en-Josas, 30 March 1950). Politician. In June 1892, in a letter to Fernand Gregh, Proust expressed his bitter opposition to an article by Blum, a former pupil at the École normale supérieure, then a member of the readers' committee of *Le Banquet*: 'Are you all stupid enough to have taken "Méditation sur le suicide d'un de mes amis" by Monsieur I don't know what!' Léon Blum was later a member, like Proust, of the Academy organised by Marie de Hérédia, then became a critic on *La Revue blanche*, but Proust's opposition to him never weakened. The antipathy lasted until 1919, when Proust discovered that this hated person was making every effort to get him awarded the Cross of the Légion d'honneur; they were both awarded the decoration on 23 September 1923. Léon Blum's political career reached its peak with the victory of the Front populaire, when he became President of the *Conseil* from June 1936 to June 1937.

BLUM, René (Paris, 1878 – Auschwitz, 1942). A man of letters, brother of the above. Nicknamed 'le Blumet', he began as editorial secretary of *Gil Blas*. In February 1913 Proust, who knew him to be very friendly with Bernard Grasset, wrote asking him to recommend his novel to Grasset; a correspondence followed. Blum published a long extract from 'Soirée chez Madame de Saint-Euverte' in *Gil Blas* on 18 November. In 1916, during the war, he again acted as intermediary between Proust and Grasset, but this time for the cancellation of the contract. In 1924, as artistic director of the Théâtre Monte-Carlo, he founded the Compagnie des ballets de Monte-Carlo; in 1930 he published *Comment paru 'Du Côté de chez Swann'*. He died in the concentration camp at Auschwitz. He seems to have been one of the models for Bloch in *A la Recherche*.

BORDA, Gustave de (died 1907). A friend of the painter Jean Béraud, nicknamed 'Borda Coup d'épée' ('Borda Sword-thrust'). He acted as Proust's second during his duel with Jean Lorrain in February 1897. On 26 December 1907, Proust wrote his obituary for *Le Figaro*, signed 'D.'

BOURGET, Paul (Amiens, 2 September 1852 – Paris, 25 December 1935). Writer. Son of the mathematician Justin Bourget, pupil at the École des Hautes Études, he was first attracted by literary criticism and poetry, and published several collections – *Vie inquiète* (1874), *Edel* (1878), *Les Aveux* (1882). In the end he devoted himself to writing novels. He was a regular guest at the salons of Madame Straus, the Princesse Mathilde and the Comtesse Potocka, and an especially eager visitor to that of Laure Hayman: he was her lover. In December 1888, Proust met him at her house, and in a letter to his mistress on 26 December Bourget wasted no time in calling Proust: 'Your psychological Saxon, young Marcel [...] quite simply exquisite.' Proust's first articles, as well as *Les Plaisirs et les jours*, owed their novel-like qualities and their style to the influence of Bourget and of Anatole France, two of the models for Bergotte. In 1920, Bourget declared that he was ready to put Proust up for membership of the Académie Française, of which he himself had been a member since 1894. He also presided over the jury of the Balzac prize, for which Proust unsuccessfully supported Jacques Rivière in 1922.

Bourget was a master of the psychological novel, and published, among others: *Cosmopolis* (1893), *Le Démon de midi* (1914), *Le sens de la mort* (1915), *Némésis* (1918).

BRACH, Paul (born at Saint-Cloud on 27 May 1893). In June 1922, this friend of Proust's sent him a reproduction which had appeared in *L'Illustration* of Tissot's painting of the Cercle de la rue Royale showing Charles Haas, the chief inspiration for Swann. On 15 July, Proust went with Paul Brach and Edmond Jaloux to the 'Boeuf sur le toit' in the rue Boissy-d'Anglas (a cabaret set up by Jean Cocteau and named after one of his pantomimes).

BRANCOVAN, Prince Constantin Bassaraba de (born at Amphéron on 1 October 1875). Brother of Anna, later Comtesse de Noailles, and of Hélène, later Princesse de Caraman-Chimay. When Proust spent holidays in Évian with his parents, he saw the Brancovans at their villa Bassaraba in Amphion. In Constantin's room, before dinner, Proust used his asthma inhalers. Brancovan and his friend Abel Hermant came to a large dinner party Proust gave in the rue de Courcelles on 19 June 1901. It may have been through him that Proust met the Bibesco brothers, at the house of the Princesse Hélène de Brancovan, his aunt. After launching a new review, *La Renaissance latine* (which Montesquiou called 'the Brancovans' chamber pot, used by the whole family'), he published an abbreviated version of *La Bible d'Amiens* in the issues of 15 February and 15 March 1903. But when he took on Gaston Rageot as a critic instead of Proust (whose health he considered too delicate), Brancovan quarrelled briefly with Marcel. Anna de Noailles supported her brother. Their relationship was restored to normal in 1905, when Brancovan published 'Sur la lecture' on 13 June.

BRANCOVAN, Princesse Bassaraba de, *née* Rachel Rallouka Musurus. She was from a family of intellectuals of Cretan origin. The mother of Constantin, Hélène (the future Princesse de Caraman-Chimay) and Anna (the future Comtesse de Noailles). From 1893 Proust was a regular guest at her villa, Bassaraba, in Amphion on the shores of Lake Leman. She was a delicate pianist and brilliant interpreter of Chopin; her patronage extended to Paderewski, Fauré and Enesco. In her house in Paris Proust heard Delafosse, Montesquiou's pianist protégé. She was the model for the dowager Marquise de Cambremer.

BRANTES, Madame Sauvage de, *née* Louise Lacuée de Cessac (1842–1914). A likeable but malicious hostess whom Proust took Reynaldo Hahn to visit at the beginning of their friendship in 1895. Her nephew, Robert de Montesquiou, said of her: 'Madame de Brantes in herself is worth the whole of the Council of Trente.' Proust enjoyed her company very much and often invited her to grand dinners at his apartment or at the Ritz.

BRUNSCHWICG, Léon (Paris, 10 November 1869 – Paris, 18 February 1944). Philosopher and ex-pupil at Condorcet (he was a class below Proust, and like him had Alphonse Darlu as philosophy master). He went to the École normale supérieure and came first in the philosophy examinations in 1891. During the summer of 1889 he gave private lessons to Robert Proust. He provided one model for Bloch.

CAILLAVET. See ARMAN DE CAILLAVET.

CALMETTE, Gaston (Montpellier, 30 July 1858 – Paris, 16 March 1914). Journalist on *Le Figaro*, then its editor. He published a large number of articles by Proust in the paper, and Proust thanked him by asking him to dinner at the Ritz on 1 July 1907 (the first dinner Proust gave in the hotel). Thereafter, Proust often repeated his invitations and gave Calmette expensive presents; the official dedication of *Du Côté de chez Swann* in 1913 was: 'To Monsieur Gaston Calmette, as evidence of my profound and affectionate gratitude.' He also wrote on Calmette's personal copy: 'I have often felt that you did not really like what I wrote. If ever you have time to read a little bit of this work, especially the second part, I believe you will finally get to know me.' Calmette, who from January 1914 had waged a campaign against Joseph Caillaux (then Minister of Finance), was shot with a revolver by Madame Caillaux on 16 March 1914.

CAMBON, Jules (Paris, 5 April 1845 – Vevey, 1935). Diplomat. Proust met him with Madame d'Arnoux, Henri Bardac's aunt, at the Hôtel des Réservoirs in Versailles.

CARAMAN-CHIMAY, Princesse Alexandre de, *née* Hélène de Brancovan (1878–1929). Daughter of the Princesse Bassaraba de Brancovan, sister of Constantin and Anna, later Comtesse de Noailles. When Proust met the two sisters, he was initially more attracted by Hélène's quiet charm than by Anna's intelligence. In 1898, Hélène married Prince Alexandre de Chimay, the Comtesse Greffulhe's brother. The Prince was anti-Dreyfus. They spent time at the villa Bassaraba (Hélène's mother's property) where Proust often saw them. Proust, who was himself deeply fond of Hélène, dedicated the preface of *Sesame and Lilies* to her in 1906. According to Le Cuziat, her photograph was abused at the brothel in the Hôtel Marigny in 1917.

CARDANE, Jules Cardon, known as Cardane (died 10 May 1908). Secretary at *Le Figaro*, where he later became editor-in-chief. In March 1903 Proust gave a dinner in his honour. In 1907, Cardane decided that the conclusion of an article Proust had written for *Le Figaro* on 1 February, 'Sentiments filiaux d'un parricide', was immoral, and described it as a 'veritable apology for matricide' before cutting it.

CASA-FUERTE, Illan, Marquis de. Son of the captivating Flavie Lefebre de Balsorano, the Empress Eugénie's niece. André Dorian considered him 'the incarnation of Dorian Gray'. Proust met him one evening in 1899 at the Grand-Guignol where Lucien Daudet introduced them. The asthma from which they both suffered made a bond between them. In 1907 Proust felt the 'sharp, sweet march' of his 'affection' for him. The Italian writer Gabriele D'Annunzio (1863–1938) used him as a basis for the shadowy Aldo in his novel *Forse che si, forse che no* (1910).

CASTELLANE, Marquis Boni de (Paris, 14 February 1867 – Paris, 20 October 1932). He and Robert de Montesquiou were two of the most brilliant dandies of the Belle Époque. After a gilded youth and numerous journeys around Europe, the young aristocrat married the richest heiress in the USA, Miss Anna Gould, daughter of the railway king, on 4 March 1895. Her fortune enabled him to build the Palais Rose (at the corner of avenue Malakoff and avenue du Bois), where he gave sumptuous receptions for the assembled aristocracy of Europe. Before her inheritance was completely swallowed up, Anna Gould – whom her husband called 'the reverse side of the coin' – got a divorce, on 5 November 1906, and married one of Boni's cousins, Hélie de Talleyrand-Périgord, Prince de Sagan. Boni was left penniless, and had to learn a profession at the age of 39. Since he was a connoisseur of objets d'art, he became an antique dealer and adapted to his new position. He died in Paris as the result of encephalitis, after writing his memoirs – *Comment j'ai découvert l'Amerique* (1924) and *L'Art d'être pauvre* (1925). His elegance and his 'blond' skin, with his hair 'as golden as if it had absorbed all the rays of the sun' formed the basis for Saint-Loup's appearance in *A la Recherche.*

CATUSSE, Madame Anatole, *née* Marie-Marguerite Bertrin (1858–1928). An old friend of Proust's mother. She was Proust's most intimate confidante, apart from Reynaldo Hahn. He ran to her for advice whenever he had to make a purchase or take a decision about practical matters. She was actively involved in his move to the boulevard Haussmann in 1906, and in the sale of his furniture in November 1917. Proust thought several times of spending a holiday at her house in Nice. It was she who took a wreath to Agostinelli's grave on 30 May 1915, the first anniversary of his death. She left a large correspondence, published in 1946.

CHEVIGNÉ, Comtesse Adhéaume de, *née* Laure de Sade (1860 – 15 October 1936). She was very proud of being a relation of the 'divine Marquis' (1740–1814). She had lived in Austria for a long time and was much in demand in her youth. She was the first to wear the 'suit costume' from Creed, a fashion she launched at Longchamps. Her salon was known to be one of the most exclusive of the Faubourg Saint-Germain. Proust had seen her at Madame Straus's and Madame Lemaire's since 1891. 'I had a heart attack every time I encountered you,' he later told her, recalling the spring of 1892 when he used to lie in wait for her during her morning outings. At the time he was enchanted by her bird-like profile. In a story he wrote for *Le Banquet*, he gave her the features of Hippolyta, whose beauty made her look like a bird-goddess. Their friendship lasted twenty-eight years, until Laure de Chevigné was hurt by the portrayal of her in the Duchesse de Guermantes. Proust complained about it to Cocteau: 'When I was twenty, she refused to love me. Now that I'm forty and I've put her into the best of the Duchesse de Guermantes, must she refuse to read me?' Her daughter Marie-Thérèse married Francis de Croisset.

CHEVILLY, Marie de. Sister of Pierre de Chevilly, Proust's friend and an ardent supporter of Dreyfus. Proust met her during a trip in the car, when he was going to visit the Bartholonis at the Château de Coudrée. He recited 'La Maison du berger' to her (in *Sodome et Gomorrhe*, the narrator recites the same lines to Abertine).

CHIMAY, Princesse de. See CARAMAN-CHIMAY.

CHIRADE, Madame. The 'beautiful dairymaid' in the rue Fontaine-Saint-Georges who had turned Daniel Halévy's head in his youth. After asking his friend: 'Do you think one could sleep with her?', Proust gave her flowers: 'I saw Proust confront Madame Chirade. Did he say something, stammer a phrase? I don't know, I only remember that I saw a smile pass over her beautiful face, and at the same time as the smile came a shake of the head meaning no' (D. Halévy, *Paysages parisiens*, p. 127).

CLERMONT-TONNERRE, Marquise then Duchesse Philibert de, *née* Élisabeth de Gramont (Nancy, 1875–1954). A friend and relation of Robert de Montesquiou's who became an intimate friend of Proust's after meeting him in 1903. As the half-sister of Armand, Duc de Guiche, she received reports of their parties in the rue de Courcelles. She and her husband were guests at the large dinner Proust gave at the Ritz on 1 July 1907. In September 1907, Proust went to see them at the Château de Glisolles (where Agostinelli lit up the rose bushes with the taxi's headlights). After the war she became close to Nathalie Barney, Lucie Delarue-Mardus and Renée Vivien. She attended Montesquiou's funeral in December 1921, and received Proust's last letters about him. She had inside knowledge of the two men's friendship and in 1925 she published *Robert de Montesquiou et Marcel Proust* and, in 1948, *Marcel Proust*.

COCTEAU, Jean (Maisons-Lafitte, 5 July 1889 – Milly-la-Fôret, 11 October 1963). Writer. A former pupil at Condorcet, Cocteau was already famous at the age of 19, when he recited his poems at the Fémina theatre in April 1908. Lucien Daudet, Anna de Noailles and Maurice Rostand were among his friends. Proust discovered him at the same time as the Ballets Russes, in 1910. Cocteau had in fact helped with the scenario for Reynaldo Hahn's ballet, *Le Diable bleu*. During a supper at Larue's with Diaghilev and Nijinsky, he vaulted over the benches – Bertrand de Salignac-Fénelon had done the same – to pick up Proust's fur coat. On 23 November 1913 he wrote warmly about *Swann* in *Excelsior*. In 1916, Proust visited him at 10 rue d'Anjou at the same time as visiting Madame de Chevigné (she lived in an apartment on the ground floor of the same building; Cocteau lived on the fifth). Cocteau was a regular attender of the dinners given by the Princesse Soutzo at the Ritz. In 1921, Proust complained to him about Madame de Chevigné, who, having recognised herself in *A la Recherche*, refused to read the book. Cocteau replied: 'Fabre wrote a book about insects, but he didn't ask the insects to read it!' At Proust's bedside the day after his death, Cocteau looked at the manuscripts piled up on the mantelpiece and said that they would go on living 'like the wristwatch on a dead soldier'. Octave, the young Balbec dandy turned genial man of letters, was partly based on Cocteau.

COLETTE, Gabrielle Sidonie Colette, known as Colette (Saint-Saveur-en-Puisaye, 28 January 1873 – Paris, 3 August 1954). Woman of letters, the daughter of Jules Colette, an officer, and Sidonie Landoy. In 1896, like Proust, she frequented the salon of Madame Arman de Caillavet, with whom she and Willy, her first husband (they married in 1893), soon quarrelled. In 1913 Louis de Robert suggested that Proust should send Colette a copy of *Swann*, but Proust, who had not seen her since the quarrel with Madame Arman de Caillavet, refused. On 25 September 1920 they both received the Cross of the Légion d'honneur. Later Colette became a member of the Académie Goncourt, in 1944, and a Grand Officer of the Légion d'honneur, in 1953. When she died in 1954, the French government organised an official civilian funeral at the Palais-Royal.

CROISSET, Francis de, pseudonym of Franz Wiener (Brussels, 28 January 1877 – Neuilly, 8 November 1937). A French playwright of Belgian origin; his mother was English, his father a financier. Launched by Mirbeau and Clemenceau, trusting to the pseudonym he borrowed from the name of Flaubert's country house, he made a swift conquest of Parisian literary and society circles. After the death of Gaston Arman de Caillavet, he took his place in collaborating with Robert de Flers on successful light comedies (*Les Vignes du Seigneur*, 1923; *Les Nouveaux Messieurs*, 1925; *Le Docteur Miracle*, 1926). In 1921, Proust involved him in the quarrel with Madame de Chevigné which he had started in 1910:

'As for my books,' he wrote to Guiche, 'I don't send them to her, because since she met Croisset through me and he became her son-in-law I think she has an adequate source of literature in him.' It was probably at this time that Proust used him as a model for Bloch, in his final incarnation as Jacques de Rozier. By becoming anglophile, in memory of his mother, and adopting an air of distant reserve, he had acquired the 'English chic' that transformed Bloch completely.

DABESCAT, Olivier. The first *maître d'hôtel* of the Ritz in the Place Vendôme. Of Basque origin, he had been trained by César Ritz at Le Paillard before the opening of his hotel in June 1898. For ten years, beginning in 1902, Olivier managed the famous establishment with Marie-Louise Ritz (who had taken over the business when her husband retired with a depressive illness). When Proust came to have dinner alone he never arrived before ten o'clock; Olivier waited for him and served him in person in a private room where he had taken care to have a fire lit, whatever the season, for the sake of Proust's health. After he had served dinner, he often went home with Proust. The Duchesse de Clermont-Tonnerre frequently saw him talking to Proust for two hours at a stretch, or walking with him in the Bois de Boulogne. Like Montesquiou, he was one of Proust's sources of society gossip. Dabescat knew everyone in Paris, and would reserve 'the best table' for one guest or another, to the point where a person's social standing could be determined by the table allocated by Dabescat. In a letter to the Princesse Soutzo in August 1918 Proust wrote that the Ritz, 'without Olivier, who has gone on holiday, has lost its keynote'. Dabescat was a dignified and reserved man who never made a public display of his relationship with Proust, even after the latter's death. He was one of the models for Aimé, the *maître d'hôtel* of the Grand Hôtel in Balbec (whom the narrator asks to find out about Albertine's morals), and he also appears in the pastiche of Saint-Simon, revised in 1918, as 'the first *maître d'hôtel* at Le Roi, always respectful and loved by everyone'.

DAUDET, Alphonse (Nîmes, 13 May 1840 – Paris, 15 December 1897). Well known as a writer since the publication of *Lettres de mon Moulin* in 1866. Even when he was young, in Illiers, Proust loved reading his books, as he wrote in a letter to Daudet of 22 February 1895: 'The most beautiful of my childhood dreams promised nothing as unlikely or as delicious as to be so graciously welcomed one day by the Master who already inspired me with passionate admiration and respect.' Proust was introduced to the Daudets by Reynaldo Hahn in the winter of 1894. Bergotte, in *A la Recherche*, was partly based on Alphonse Daudet.

DAUDET, Madame Alphonse, *née* Julia Allard (1847–1940). Alphonse Daudet's wife and secretary. When she had Proust to dinner for the first time, in December 1894, she told her son Lucien that she had met 'a charming boy, unusually amiable . . .'. Proust was regularly invited to her famous Thursdays. It was she who, during a tea party, innocently made an unfortunate comment about Montesquiou: 'Quelle tapette il a! Quelle tapette!' The word means both 'chatter-box' and 'homosexual'. Proust later put the remark into the mouth of Madame Verdurin.

DAUDET, Léon (Paris, 16 November 1867 – Saint-Rémy-de-Provence, 30 June 1942). Son of the above couple. Known for his anti-Semitism, a friend of Charles Maurras from 1904 onwards, co-founder (with Maurras) of the daily *L'Action Française* in March 1908, he was always a loyal friend to Proust. In October 1896 they spent a week together at Fontainebleau, at the Hôtel de France et d'Angleterre, which contributed to the atmosphere of Doncières. Proust enjoyed Daudet's articles enormously, at the same time deploring his excesses and eccentricities. Léon had no time for Proust's friend Montesquiou, whom he nicknamed 'Hortensiou'. It was probably Léon Daudet who introduced Proust to Calmette, the editor of *Le Figaro*, in 1900. In April, Proust dedicated 'Ruskin à Notre-Dame d'Amiens' to him. In 1919, Daudet managed to secure him the Goncourt Prize, and went to wake him up on the afternoon of 10 December to tell him the news. After Proust's death, he paid tribute to him as a writer: '[he] has advanced the state of introspection, the consciousness that man has of himself, as much as the greatest moralists of all time.'

Works: Many volumes of *Souvenirs*, including: *Fantômes et vivants* (1914), *L'Entre-deux-guerres* (1915), *Salons et Journaux* (1917), *Au temps de Judas* (1920), *Vers le Roi* (1921), *L'Hécatombe* (1923), *Moloch et Minerve* (1929), *Vingt-neuf mois d'exil* (1930), *La Pluie de sang* (1932), *Député de Paris* (1935), *Magistrats et policiers* (1935), *Quand vivait mon père* (1940), *Sauveteurs et incendiaires* (1941); novels and essays: *Les Morticoles* (1894), *L'Hérédo* (1917), *Courrier des Pays-Bas* (1928), *Paris vécu* (1929), *Le*

Voyage de Shakespeare (1896), *Devant la douleur* (1932), *Bréviaire du journalisme* (1936), *Panorama de la IIIe République (1870–1936)* (1936).

DAUDET, Lucien (1878–1946). Son of Alphonse; Léon's brother. Despite his talents as a painter and writer, Lucien suffered all his life from the strong personalities of his father and his brother. Proust, who was seven years older than him, met him for the first time in December 1894 in his parents' salon, where Reynaldo Hahn had introduced him. In his *Journal*, Jules Renard described him as: 'A pretty boy, curled, pomaded, painted and powdered, who spoke in a low voice.' After Proust's passionate friendship with Reynaldo Hahn, he turned to Lucien. In 1895, when Proust was made librarian at the Mazarine, Lucien went to collect him from Quai Conti every day. On 31 December of the same year, Proust gave him a New Year present of a seventeenth-century ivory coffer with an allegory of friendship on it. They had in common a taste for jokes and an acute sense of the ridiculous about clichés and ready-made expressions, which they called *louchonneries*. Their attachment did not pass unnoticed, and on 3 February 1897 Jean Lorrain made a reference to it in his article in the *Journal* criticising *Les Plaisirs et les jours*. Proust challenged him to a duel. Lucien was the second person, after Louis de Robert, to read the whole of *Swann* before its publication; he was so impressed that he suggested to Proust that he should review it. Because of the intervention of the Empress Eugénie (whom he had met through Robert de Montesquiou, and whose companion in her exile in Farnborough and Cap-Martin he was to be) his review appeared in *Le Figaro* on 27 November 1913. In June 1922, Lucien paid Proust a final visit. 'I found him rather odd this evening, Céleste. Yes, he was distinctly peculiar. He wasn't very talkative; he seemed shy and depressed. When he was about to leave, he asked if he could kiss me,' Proust said to Céleste. 'Monsieur Proust,' Céleste herself reported, 'preferred him to his brother Léon, the politician. He was extremely sensitive and he put his whole heart into his devotion and admiration for Monsieur Proust. He may have been one of the few people Monsieur Proust loved for himself, without thinking of his usefulness for a character in his book. Or perhaps he didn't constitute an obvious enough type' (C. Albaret, *op. cit.*, p. 270). Lucien died on 16 November 1946, his brother Léon's birthday.

Works: *Autour de soixante lettres de Marcel Proust* (1929), *Dans l'ombre de l'impératrice Eugénie (Lettres intimes adressées à Madame Alphonse Daudet)* (1935), *Vie d'Alphonse Daudet* (1941).

DEACON, Gladys Mary (Boston, 1881–1977). Daughter of Edward Parker Deacon and Florence Baldwin. A renowned beauty of the day. In August 1906, Proust met her at the Hôtel des Réservoirs in Versailles where she had the room below his own. Montesquiou said she 'looked like an archangel' and Madame de Clerment-Tonnerre thought she was like 'a young Greek warrior with a perfect face'. In 1910 the Marquise, using Proust as an intermediary, tried to get her to marry Léon Radziwill, who was then divorced. In fact she married the Duke of Marlborough in 1921, and on 16 June Proust attended a dinner given by Mrs Hennessy to celebrate their engagement. She was the original of Miss Forster in *A la Recherche*.

DELAFOSSE, Léon (1874–1951). Pianist and composer. A very young virtuoso, he won first prize at the Conservatoire at the age of 13. Proust met him in 1894 with the Comte de Saussine. On 15 March he introduced him to Montesquiou, who was bowled over and decided to take him under his wing. On 30 May 1894 Montesquiou gave a party at Versailles in honour of the boy, whom he always called 'the angel'. But three years later, in 1897, Montesquiou, who was very quarrelsome, fell out with him. During the Dreyfus affair, Proust tried to please Montesquiou by claiming that 'that devil D.' referred to in the 'Alexandrine' letter was none other than Delafosse. The pianist's career was not shattered, however. He played at Princesse Rachel de Branco-van's house in Paris, where Proust met him regularly, and in London and Vienna. But he died in obscurity. Certain features of Charles Morel were taken from Delafosse.

DESJARDINS, Paul (Paris, 1859 – Pontigny, 1940). Philosopher. Son of the historian Ernest Desjardins (1823–86). Proust took lessons with him when he was studying law; it was thanks to Desjardins that he discovered Ruskin. In 1892 he founded the *Union pour l'action morale* and, in 1906, the *Union pour la verité*. He began the 'Décades' in the Abbaye de Pontigny when writers and philosophers gather for ten days every year to debate questions of philosophical order and practical morality. Proust planned to attend. These Décades were continued by Desjardins' daughter, Anne Heurgon, at the Château de Cerisy; the 1962 event was dedicated to Proust.

Works: *Esquisses et impressions* (1888). *Le Devoir présent* (1892), *Catholicisme et critique: réflexions d'un profane sur l'affaire Loisy* (1905).

DOÄZAN, Baron Albert-Agapit, known as Jacques (1840–1907). Baron of the Empire. He was a fat man with a bloated face and a moustache dyed black. People said that Madame Aubernon de Nerville, his cousin, paid for his lotions and perfumes. Doäzan had bankrupted himself for a Polish violinist (the first incarnation of Morel in *A la Recherche*). Proust met him in 1892 in his cousin Aubernon's salon. Baron Doäzan loathed Montesquiou, who had taken his 'secretary', Gabriel d'Yturri, away from him. According to Gide and to Proust himself, he was the chief model for Charlus.

DREYFUS, Robert (Paris, 13 March 1873 – Paris, 17 June 1939). A former Condorcet pupil, he was on the editorial committee of *Le Banquet* in 1892 with Proust and Halévy. As a journalist on *Le Figaro*, he published eulogistic articles signed 'Bartolo' about *Du Côté de chez Swann*, on 16 November 1913, and on 7 July 1919, about *A l'ombre des jeunes filles en fleurs* (of which his own copy carried the dedication: 'To Robert Dreyfus, in memory of the young girls of the Champs-Élysées and the balls …'). He began a correspondence with Proust in 1888, and remained an intimate friend and privileged witness of the genesis of his work. Madame Mante-Proust, who inherited his correspondence, gave it to the Bibliothèque Nationale in 1962 with an instruction for it to remain closed for fifty years, in accordance with Robert Dreyfus's wishes. He himself published *Souvenirs sur Marcel Proust* (1926) in the 'Cahiers verts' series then edited by Halévy and named after *La Revue verte*. Henri, his elder brother, became well known in the theatre, specialising in monologues under the pseudonym 'Fursy'.

EDWARDS, Madame Alfred. See GODEBSKA, Misia.

EPHRUSSI, Charles (1849–1905). Jewish, of Polish origin, he was director of *La Gazette des beaux-arts*. Fat and ugly, he was nicknamed 'Matame' because of his horrible way of pronouncing the word 'Madame' (like the Prince von Faffenheim in *A la Recherche*). He was a regular guest at Princesse Mathilde's salon, like Proust. Intellectually he resembled Charles Swann, and wrote an essay on Albrecht Dürer.

FAURÉ, Gabriel (Pamiers, 12 May 1845 – Paris, 4 November 1924). Composer. His teacher was the young Saint-Saëns. It was probably at the Comte de Saussine's in 1893 that Proust met him; Fauré was already famous, and had been appointed *directeur des beaux-arts* a year before. Proust was deeply devoted to his music: 'Monsieur, I don't just like, or admire, or adore your music; I was, and I still am, in love with it.' Proust borrowed certain themes from Fauré's sonata for piano and violin for the sonata by Vinteuil.

FAURE, Lucie (1866–1917). Eldest daughter of President Félix Faure and Madame Faure who received a small circle of friends every Saturday, amongst whom were Madame Proust and the young Marcel. A marriage between him and Antoinette, Lucie's younger sister, was considered by the families. Although sharp-tongued and caustic, Lucie remained a loyal friend of Proust's all her life. An ardent Catholic and a Dante specialist, Madame Félix-Faure-Goyau is supposed (according to Georges de Lauris) to have had a conversation with Proust on religious philosophy while he was translating *The Bible of Amiens*. Proust was buried with the rosary she brought him from Jerusalem.

FÉNELON. See SALIGNAC-FÉNELON.

FINALY, Horace. (Budapest, 1871 – New York, 1945). He was a financier, son of a rich Jewish banker, whom Proust met at Condorcet (where they were together in the philosophy class). In 1889 the Finalys entertained Proust at Ostend; in 1892 he encouraged their uncle, Baron Horace de Landau, to acquire Les Frémonts – the property that had belonged to the Baignères family, near Trouville. Proust was attracted to Horace's sister, Mary Finaly (1873–1918). Horace was deeply cultured (he read the Greek authors in the original) and he pursued a brilliant career as director of the Banque de Paris et des Pays-Bas. Proust followed his advice about investments and, in 1921, asked him to find a job for his secretary Henri Rochat, which Horace did, sending him to work in a bank in Buenos Aires. The character of Albert Bloch in *A la Recherche* is partly based on Horace Finaly.

FINALY, Madame Hugo, *née* Eugénie Ellenberger (Budapest, 31 December 1850 – Neuilly, 24 October 1938). Mother of the above. She obtained Les Frémonts from her uncle, the rich Baron de Landau, in settlement of a bet: 'That's what you call the Great Tease (*Taquin le Superbe*),' exclaimed Arthur Baignères. Proust remembered the expression for *A la Recherche* and used it for the gift of the Château de Brézé that Charlus gives his sister Madame de Marsantes. Madame Finaly entertained Proust of Les Frémonts and toured the countryside with him in an estate car, like Madame de Villeparisis and the narrator in *Jeunes Filles*.

FINALY, Mary (20 August 1873 – October 1918). Sister of Horace Finaly, one of Proust's collaborators on *Le Banquet*. Proust fell in love with her during a stay at Les Frémonts. Their love was linked to their love of music. Proust used to hum her Baudelaire's 'Chant d'automne' (set to music by Fauré), a line of which he quotes in 'A propos de Baudelaire', published in 1921. On 21 June 1897 she married Thomas de Barbarin. She died in October 1918 of Spanish flu, which she caught while caring for wounded soldiers as a voluntary nurse. She inspired Proust to write 'Sonate clair de lune' in *Les Plaisirs et les jours*, whose pale heroine's name is Assunta. She was one of the first models for Albertine in *A la Recherche*.

FITZ-JAMES, Comtesse Robert de, *née* Rosalie de Gutmann. (Vienna, 19 February 1863–1923). She came from a family of Jewish financiers ennobled by the Emperor Franz-Josef. Because of her husband's infidelities, Faubourg Saint-Germain society nicknamed her 'Rosa Malheur', a reference to the painter Rosa Bonheur. She used to keep in her desk a list of all the Jewish marriages contracted by the aristocratic families of Europe. She was at the party at the Pavillon Montesquiou on 30 May 1894, when the Marquise de Brantes introduced her to Proust; in her salon Proust met Charles Haas.

FLERS, Robert, Marquis de (Pont-l'Évêque, 25 November 1872 – Vittel, 30 July 1927). Writer. Like Proust, he was educated at Condorcet, then studied law and literature. In 1892 when *Le Banquet* was founded, he became a close friend of Proust, who wrote to Robert de Billy on 10 January 1893: 'Nothing has changed very much in my emotional life, except that I have found a friend, someone who is for me what I could have been for Cachard [Edward B. Cachard, son of an American lawyer], perhaps, if he hadn't been so cold. It is the young, and charming, and intelligent, and good, and sweet, Robert de Flers.' He and Proust became intimate friends. A photograph of about 1894 shows him standing beside Lucien Daudet, with Proust sitting in front of them. Madame Proust considered that the photograph might throw doubts on the purity of their friendship, and forbade her son to show it to anyone. In 1898, Robert de Flers was one of the first to sign the petition in support of Dreyfus. The same year, Proust published an article called 'Robert de Flers' in *La Revue d'art dramatique*. On 19 September and 12 October 1899, *La Presse* brought out 'Lettres de Perse et d'ailleurs', in which Robert was Françoise de Breyves. He had a brilliant journalistic career, first at *Le Soleil* then, in 1902, at *Le Figaro*, of which he was literary editor. On 23 July 1907, *Le Figaro* published 'La Vie de Paris: une grand'mère', an obituary by Proust of Madame de Rozières, Flers' grandmother. During the Great War, Flers volunteered. In 1915, having lost his collaborator Arman de Caillavet, whose passion for the theatre he shared, he teamed up with Francis de Croisset to write new plays. He was made a member of the Académie Française in 1920.

Works: Travel writing: *Vers l'Orient*. Novels: *La Courtisane Taia et son singe vert* (1896). Comic operettas: *Le Sire de Vergy, Monsieur de la Palice, Ciboulette* (1922). Plays: in collaboration with Gaston Arman de Caillavet: *Miquette et sa mère* (1906), *L'Amour veille* (1907), *Le Roi* (1908), *L'Ane de Buridan* (1909), *Le Bois sacré* (1910), *Primerose* (1911), *L'Habit vert* (1913), *La Belle Aventure* (1913), *Monsieur Bretonneau* (1914); in collaboration with Francis de Croisset: *Les Vignes du Seigneur* (1923), *Les Nouveaux Messieurs* (1925), *Le Docteur Miracle* (1926).

FORAIN, Jean-Louis (Reims, 23 October 1852 – Paris, 12 July 1931). Painter of scenes from Parisian life, from 1887 onwards he specialised in caricature (in *Le Courrier Français, L'Écho de Paris, Le Figaro, L'Assiette au beurre*, etc) which earned him the nickname 'Juvenal of the pencil'. Proust met him in Madame Straus's salon. Although Montesquiou admired him, Forain nicknamed him 'Grotesquiou'. In March 1897, he took part in the evenings organised by Jacques Bizet to parody *Les Plaisirs et les jours*, helping Jacques-Émile Blanche to cut paper silhouettes for the show. During the Dreyfus affair he gave up going to

Madame Straus's salon and founded the anti-Semitic review *Psst'* with Caran d'Ache in 1898. He was a member of the Ligue de la Patrie Française founded by Charles Maurras and remained a close friend of Léon Daudet. From 1925 to 1931 he held the presidency of the Société nationale des beaux-arts.

FORSSGREN, Ernst, called Ernest. Swedish valet. He came into Proust's service in 1914, on the eve of his departure for Cabourg. He travelled with him, and settled in to the Grand Hôtel with Proust and Céleste. Much later, he claimed that Proust had said to him: 'Ernest, in all my life I have never known anyone I loved as much as I love you' (*Études Proustiennes II*). In October, after their return to Paris, he left Proust to go and work in New York. In November 1922 he came back to Paris for a brief stay. Despite his acute illness, Proust went to the Riviera Hôtel and waited for him from eleven in the evening until three in the morning, hastening his demise in the process. Ernst later went to find him but Robert Proust forbade him to go into the bedroom.

FRANCE, Anatole, pseudonym of François-Anatole Thibault (Paris, 16 April 1844 – Saint-Cyr-sur-Loire, 12 October 1924). Writer. In 1899, Proust was introduced to him in the salon of Madame Arman de Caillavet, Anatole France's new patroness, with whom he had had a liaison for the past year. Proust had nursed a passionate admiration for France since his days at Condorcet; he had even written him a message of heartfelt sympathy to 'comfort' him after Monsieur Chantavoine had criticised him severly in an article in *Le Temps*. In 1896, out of friendship for Proust, and despite the fact that he was not one of Proust's most fervent admirers, France wrote the preface to *Les Plaisirs et les jours*, whose style shows his main influence still to be Loti. In the autumn of 1899 he expressed a wish that Proust would marry his only daughter Suzanne, then 27, but the plan came to nothing. In 1921, three years before he died, Anatole France received the Nobel Prize for literature. He was one of the models for Bergotte, who shows a number of his characteristics.

GALLIFFET, Gaston Alexandre, Marquis de (Paris, 23 January 1830 – Paris, 9 July 1909). French general. He was a member of the Greffulhe circle and a close friend of Charles Haas; he distinguished himself in the

Mexican war (he had a silver plate in his stomach from a serious wound he received at the battle of Puebla). In 1870 he was promoted to general and commanded the Chasseurs d'Afrique at Sedan. He also became known for his fierce repressions during the Commune. Following the Dreyfus affair, he was appointed Minister of War in Waldeck-Rousseau's cabinet in 1899. In Tissot's painting *Le Cercle de la rue Royale* he appears beside Charles Haas. Proust often saw Madame de Galliffet in 1891 after her separation from her husband; she lived at the Manoir des Roches in Trouville. Proust mentioned her twice in his novel. As for the general, Proust was probably thinking of him when he compared Froberville's monocle to 'a hideous wound that was glorious to have received, but indecent to display'.

GALLIMARD, Gaston (Paris, 18 January 1881 – Paris, 25 December 1975). Editor. He began as Robert de Flers' secretary. Proust met him in Normandy in August 1908, when Flers was staying with his mother at the Manoir de Bénerville. Proust was then with Louisa de Mornand and Robert Gangnat. They all dined together at the Grand Hôtel in Cabourg. Gallimard became the administrator of the Nouvelle Revue Française publishing company on its foundation in 1911. On 2 November 1912, on the advice of Copeau, Proust wrote directly to him about the publication of his novel and shortly afterwards sent the second typed copy of *Le Temps perdu*. Gallimard gave him a favourable reply, and agreed to publish it the following 15 February if it could be arranged with Fasquelle. He then changed his mind and passed the matter to Copeau, who rejected the book in December. Proust was thus published by Grasset. In 1916, Gallimard and Copeau went to see Proust to negotiate his transfer from Grasset to the N.R.F. On 10 December 1919, he and Tronche, his commercial director, came to congratulate him on the Goncourt prize. According to Céleste this was one of very few meetings Proust granted him, because his opinion of Gallimard was low. Gallimard, however, retained excellent memories of Proust: 'He was very nice, Marcel Proust! He never asked me for any money in advance! Never! And no publicity either!' (Interview with Gaston Gallimard by Madeleine Chapsal in *L'Express*, 5 January 1976).

GANGNAT, Robert (1867–29 October 1910). Lawyer, agent for the Société des auteurs dramatiques. Louisa de Mornand was kept by him from February 1906 onwards, even though she was getting a sizeable pension from d'Albufera without Gangnat's knowledge. Gangnat wanted to break off his relationship with her from about November, because of her flighty behaviour; Proust made constant efforts to reconcile them. In 1908 Gangnat rented the Chalet Russe at Bénerville where Proust met them with Gallimard.

GAUTIER-VIGNAL, Louis, Comte (1888–1982). Writer. Son of Comte Albert Gautier, sportsman and Romanian consul general in Nice who had been ennobled by the Pope, and the Comtesse, *née* Marie Bouteau. They were very rich, and apart from a yacht and a car they owned the Château du Vignal, two kilometres from Contes in the Alpes-Maritimes, the Château Carabacel in Nice, and the Chalet des Traverses in Saint-Martin-Vésubie (Alpes-Maritimes). Louis Gautier-Vignal met Proust for the first time through Lucien Daudet, between 10 and 15 June 1915. Having taken lessons with Roland Garros, it was probably he who told Proust about the avaitor's young pupils practising gliding (Proust used the image in *La Fugitive* when describing Giotto's angels in the Arena chapel in Padua). According to Céleste Albaret, he tried to find Proust a new servant after Nicolas Cottin's departure. A member of the artistic and literary world, he was to be seen with André Gide and Jacques de Lacretelle. He claimed to have explained Kant's philosophy to Proust. Like Florence Gould, the great art patron of the Côte d'Azur, he was very generous. A courteous man, he was always discreet about the nature of his relationship with Proust, but towards the end of his life admitted that he had been one of Proust's last 'friends'. He was president of the Société des Amis de la ville de Nice and President of the Société des Amis du Centre universitaire méditerranéen de Nice founded by Paul Valéry. He was a specialist in Italian literature, among other things (he spent a long time in Italy), and he wrote a large number of books, including a study of Proust.

Works: *Érasme, 1469–1536* (1936), *Pic de la Mirandole* (1937) (the publication of his thesis presented at Fribourg on 11 December 1937), *Arion, Orphée, Amphion, La Flûte et la lyre* (1946), *Lettre aux Italiens* (1947), *Le Chemin de Mazargues* (1948), *Tyrannie de la parole* (1949), *L'Enfer des villes (Problèmes d'urbanisme et solutions)* (1964), *Machiavel* (1969), *Proust connu et inconnu* (1976).

GIDE, André (Paris, 22 November 1869 – Paris, 19 February 1951). Writer. Proust probably met him at Gabriel Trarieux's on 1 May 1891. Two years later he began to write for *La Revue blanche*, an avant-garde literary review founded in 1891, a young contributor among famous writers: Verlaine, Mallarmé, José-Maria de Hérédia, Barrès and Pierre Louÿs. During the Dreyfus affair Gide signed the *Manifeste des cent-quatre* which Proust had organised. After 1911, he was co-director of N.R.F. with Jacques Copeau and Jean Schlumberger. In October 1912, Proust thought of them for the publication of his novel and sent his manuscript to Gide through the Bibesco brothers. On 23 December the N.R.F. declined to published Proust. In fact, Gide then believed Proust to be '*du côté de chez Verdurin*' and considered only the aspect that his pieces for *Le Figaro* showed: 'a snob, a society amateur' (Letter from Gide dated 11 January 1914). Opening the manuscript of *Du Côté de chez Swann*, Gide had come across the passage where Aunt Léonie had 'vertebrae showing through her forehead' and read no further. Céleste Albaret claimed that the package meticulously wrapped by Nicolas Cottin had not even been opened, because the knot was intact. Proust claimed the same thing, to save face, for the episode from *Illusions perdues* in which Lucien de Rubempré receives back the sonnets he sent to Dauriat with the string and seals untouched. After *Du Côté de chez Swann*'s publication by Grasset in November 1913, Gide was brave enough to take responsibility for the blunder, admitting his mistake in the letter of 11 January 1914: 'Rejecting this book will always be the N.R.F.'s gravest error and (since I am ashamed to say I was largely responsible) one of the things in my life I regret most bitterly.'

He told the American novelist Frederic Prokosch (who reported the conversation in his memoirs): 'when people keep saying I refused *Swann* for Gallimard, they forget that one is busy, one can't read absolutely everything, and Proust had a reputation as a faded social butterfly! But after I'd made up my mind to read that little masterpiece, my admiration for Proust has never wavered for a second. I admit I was perplexed by the man himself. To begin with I thought he had no deep strength. I was wrong. He had immense deep strengths. [. . .] It is wrong to consider Proust an innovator. He did what had often been done before, but he did it with infinite care and inexhaustible astuteness. That is what matters: precision and skill, not bravado and bragging. In Proust one often hears echoes of Benjamin Constant and Saint-Simon, even a trace of Rousseau's *Confessions* . . .'

On 20 March 1914, he conveyed to Proust that N.R.F. was prepared to publish the sequel to *Swann* at its own expense. The two writers began to correspond, and Proust talked of Gide to Alfred Agostinelli in affectionate terms. On 24 February 1916, Gide – who hadn't seen Proust since 1892 – paid him a visit to repeat N.R.F.'s offer; this time Proust accepted. Using Odilon Albaret's taxi for the journeys, Gide saw him several times in 1921, and discussed the way he had approached homosexuality in his book. For Gide, Proust was a 'master of pretence'. In 1922 he allocated one of his protégés, Georges Gabory, the task of correcting the proofs of *Sodome et Gomorrhe II*. In fact, Proust had a low opinion of Gide, according to Céleste Albaret, and in his *Journal* Gide himself expressed increasing reservations about Proust as the date of his death receded into the past.

GIRAUDOUX, Jean (Bellac, 29 October 1882 – Paris, 31 January 1944). Writer and diplomat. Former student at the École normale supérieure (1903–04) who went into the foreign service in 1910. Giraudoux met Proust in 1919 when his friend Paul Morand brought him to Proust's apartment. The same year he dedicated *Elpénor* to him affectionately. In June 1919 Giraudoux summarised 'Un amour de Swann' in the first issue of the review *Feuillets d'Art*, but Proust thought very little of the article and said: 'It was wonderful, bursting with wit, and I found it so disappointing!' Proust pastiched his style in *Le Côté de Guermantes*, but praised him in his preface to Morand's *Tendres Stocks* in 1921.

GODEBSKA, Misia (1872–1950). A Polish girl whose wit and beauty gained her an exciting life in high society circles. Her first marriage was to Thadée Natanson, director of *La Revue blanche*; her second, in 1904, was to Alfred Edwards (1857–1914), the co-founder (with Bunau-Varilla) of *Matin* and its director. In 1907 Proust was curious about them when he saw them in the Grand Hôtel in Cabourg. Edwards had with him his mistress, the lesbian actress Lantelme, who became a model for Léa and Rachel. Soon separated from her second husband, Misia set up house in an apartment on the Quai Voltaire where she entertained a large number of artists: Maurice Ravel, Stravinsky, Diaghilev and Coco Chanel, whom she introduced to Paris society. In May 1913, Proust was in her box, together with Rodin and Renoir, to watch *Prélude à l'après-midi d'un faune*. In 1914 she married the Spanish painter José-Maria Sert and they lived a life of luxury. 'The ravishing Princesse Yourbélétieff ... with her enormous, provocative plume of feathers' was based on her.

GRAMONT, Agénor, Duc de (22 September 1850–1925). A regular visitor to Princesse Mathilde's salon. His first marriage was to Princesse Isabelle de Beauvau-Craon, who died in 1875 giving birth to a daughter, Élisabeth (the future Marquise then Duchesse de Clermont-Tonnerre). In 1878 he married Marguerite de Rothschild, by whom he had a son, Armand, Duc de Guiche, Proust's friend. Thanks to his second wife's fortune, he was able to build the huge Château de Vallière at Mortefontaine, where he entertained Proust on 14 July 1904 at the dinner to celebrate his son's engagement. When Proust hesitated over the visitors' book, he called out, like the Duc de Guermantes, who was based on him: 'Your name, Monsieur Proust, but no passing thoughts!'

GRAMONT, Duchesse Agénor de, *née* Marguerite de Rothschild (1855–1905). Proust had known her since December 1893, when he received an invitation from her. Thus she and her sister Berthe, Princesse de Wagram, were the first to open the doors of Faubourg Saint-Germain society to Proust. On 28 July 1905 he attended her funeral at Saint-Pierre-de-Chaillot.

GRASSET, Bernard (Chambéry, 6 March 1881 – Paris, 20 October 1955). Publisher. He founded his publishing company in 1907. On about 20 February 1913 Proust asked René Blum to ask this young publisher if he would publish his work at the author's expense. On 24 February, he wrote to Grasset to say that he had sent him the manuscript of his first volume. On 11 March the contract was signed. On 19 April, Proust voluntarily offered to pay Grasset extra to cover the excessive number of corrections he made on his proofs. *Du Côté de chez Swann* came out on 14 November and sold well. At the beginning of December Grasset decided to bring out a second edition and was already thinking about the Goncourt and Fémina prizes. On 20 March 1914, N.R.F. informed Proust that it was prepared to buy back the rights from Grasset. Proust sent his contract to a specialist, Émile Straus, and gave Reynaldo Hahn the task of sounding out Grasset through the intermediary of a common friend, the Princesse de Polignac. On 28 March, Proust wrote to Grasset to tell him of N.R.F.'s offer. Early in April, Grasset made the mistake of trying to hold the writer to his commitments instead of displaying generosity; then he behaved more wisely, and gave Proust absolute freedom. Won over by his better nature, Proust regretfully wrote to Gide on 7 April saying that he had decided to stay with Grasset and that N.R.F. could only have 'fragments' of his work. But Grasset's company closed on the outbreak of war and the second volume, planned for October 1914, was delayed until the hostilities were over. On 14 April 1916, N.R.F. renewed their offer. This time Proust accepted, and once again asked Blum to be his intermediary with Grasset. At first, Grasset proved impossible to trace: he had been seriously ill with typhoid in 1915, and he was in a nursing home in Neuchâtel, in Switzerland. The negotiations were long and difficult. Grasset eventually gave in: 'Obviously I would not give up an author I value highly without making my distress clear to him, and there is certainly nothing in that for you to be upset about, but I don't want to add to your troubles and your pain by my actions. So, whatever it costs me to do so, I give up the publication rights to the second volume of *A la Recherche du temps perdu*. Grasset behaved well; Proust much less well. He did however continue to correspond with his publisher, reverting to the formula 'Dear Friend' which he had dropped in favour of 'Dear Sir' during their bitter negotiations.

GREFFULHE, Henry Charles, Comte (Paris, 25 December 1845 – Paris, 31 March 1932). Very rich, heir to a Belgian banking family, friend of the Prince of Wales. In 1878 he married Élisabeth de Caraman-Chimay and together they lived a high-society life divided between their town house in the rue d'Astorg and their château in Bois-Boudran. Jacques-Émile Blanche likened Greffulhe, who was tall and had a blond beard, to a king on a playing-card. The Duc de Guermantes was based on him; like the character, he was an unfaithful and jealous husband.

GREFFULHE, Comtesse Henry, *née* Élisabeth Riquet, Comtesse de Caraman-Chimay (1860–1952). Daughter of Prince de Chimay, wife of Comte Henry Greffulhe, cousin of Robert de Montesquiou, the Faubourg Saint-Germain set considered her the greatest beauty of the day. She was exceedingly worldly. She launched a fashion for greyhound racing in France, she was a patron of Diaghilev's Ballets Russes, she presided over the association of 'Grandes Auditions de France' and entertained regularly in her famous salon in the rue d'Astorg. When Proust saw her for the first time in 1893 he was instantly smitten: 'She wore a hairstyle of Polynesian grace, with mauve orchids falling to the nape of her neck [...]. I had never seen such a beautiful woman' (Letter to Robert de Montesquiou of 2 July 1893). After that Proust used to go to the Opéra just for the pleasure of seeing her descending the great staircase. He was at last introduced to her at the party at the Pavillon Montesquiou on 30 May 1894. Proust's idolatry of Madame Greffulhe lasted many years; later, he described her salon for *Le Figaro*, but the sketch was never published. In *A la Recherche*, her behaviour and elegance were models for the Duchesse de Guermantes, and her unique position in society was the basis for the Princesse de Guermantes.

GREGH Fernand (Paris, 14 October 1873 – Paris, 5 January 1960). Poet. Son of the composer Louis Gregh, he was educated at Condorcet and in 1890 won the first prize for French composition in the Concours Général. He graduated in philosophy and became director of *Le Banquet* after the publication of the second issue. At that time he and his friends on the review invented the verb 'proustify', which meant 'simper' or 'mince', after their young and graceful friend Proust. Gregh was also a member of the Académie canaque presided over by Proust's friend Marie de Hérédia. In 1894 he did his military service in Reims with Robert Proust. He became a regular guest at the salons of Madames Aubernon, Straus and Arman de Caillavet. Gregh carried out the musical accompaniment to the parody of *Les Plaisirs et les jours* at Jacques Bizet's in March 1897. During the Dreyfus affair, he and Proust persuaded Anatole France to sign the *'Manifeste des intellectuels'*. In 1902, *Le Figaro* published his manifesto on poetry, extolling 'humanism', a sort of return to nature, as a protest against symbolism. During the 1914 war he was called up with Reynaldo Hahn and Robert Dreyfus to a regimental depot in Albi. On 18 November 1922, he watched over the body of his friend Proust. At the funeral he lost his little dog, Flipot, who had taken refuge under the hearse before disappearing into the crowd. Gregh was elected to the Académie Française in 1953.

Works: Poetry: *La Maison de l'enfance* (1896), *La Beauté de vivre* (1900), *Les Clartés humaines* (1904), *L'Or des minutes* (1905), *Prélude féerique* (1908), *La Chaîne éternelle* (1910), *La Couronne douloureuse* (1917), *Couleur de la vie* (1927), *La Gloire du cœur* (1932), *Le Mot du monde* (1957).

Critical works: *La Fenêtre ouverte* (1901), *Études sur Hugo* (1904), *L'Œuvre de Victor Hugo* (1933), *Portrait de la poésie française* (1936–1938).

Memoirs: *L'Age d'or* (1948), *L'Age d'airain* (1951).

GUERNE, Comtesse de, *née* Marie-Thérèse de Ségur (died 11 March 1933). This brilliant hostess of the Faubourg Saint-Germain sang duets with Reynaldo Hahn during a tea-party Proust gave in the rue de Courcelles on 6 March 1905. Proust thanked her in a eulogistic piece in *Le Figaro* on 7 May, signed 'Écho': 'La Vie de Paris: la comtesse de Guerne.' Hahn later played his *Choeurs d'Esther* for the first time at her house in the avenue Bosquet.

GUICHE, Armand, Duc de (Paris, 29 September 1879 – Mortefontaine, 2 August 1962). Proust met him on 23 December 1902 during a dinner at Anna de Noailles' house. Like Proust he was half Jewish, through his mother, the Duchesse de Gramont, *née* Rothschild. The two often met at the Café Weber or at Larue's restaurant. Cultured and curious about everything, Armand loved art, and he himself painted when the mood took him. He was a fine polo player as well as a brilliant physician, and his research into aerodynamics and optics brought him international renown. He founded the Institut d'optique in Paris and became a member of the Académie des sciences. On 14 November 1904 he married Élaine (1882–1958), daughter of the Comte and Comtesse de Greffulhe. On his father's death in 1925 he became Duc de Gramont.

HAAS, Charles (Paris, 1832 – Paris, 12 July 1902). Son of a director of the Rothschild bank, this young Jewish man was a brilliant dandy and one of the personalities of the Jockey Club, of which he was made a member on 21 January 1871. His membership was sponsored by the Comte de Saint-Priest and the Comte Albéric de Bernis: he had been refused four times before he was eventually admitted to the club. He was erudite and a great connoisseur of Italian painting; in 1868 he was appointed general inspector of historical monuments, thanks to Mérimée. Boni de Castellane described him as having 'marvellous intuition, finesse and intelligence'. He was a leading member of the rue d'Astorg set, the most sophisticated in Paris. Proust met him for the first time a little before 1890, in Madame Straus's salon. Although he never became an intimate friend of Proust's, he was nevertheless the chief model for Swann; Madame Straus ended up calling him 'Swann-Haas'. At the age of 35 he posed for the picture *Le Cercle de la rue Royale*, which its members had commissioned Tissot to paint. In *La Prisonnière* Proust addresses him about the painting: 'In Tissot's picture showing the balcony of the Cercle de la rue Royale, where you are between Galliffet, Edmond de Polignac and Saint-Maurice, you are talked about so much because people see that there are some features of yours in the character of Swann.' When Charles Haas died, on 12 July 1902, Parisian high society attended his funeral: the Marquis du Lau, the Comte d'Haussonville, the Comte Greffulhe, the Ducs de Montmorency and de la Trémoïlle. He was buried at Père-Lachaise on 29 October 1902.

HAHN, Maria (1865–1948). Reynaldo Hahn's sister. Proust met her in 1895 and spent a fortnight with her and her brother in the forest of Saint-Germain-en-Laye in the Pavillon Louis XIV, which belonged to another sister of Reynaldo's, Clarita Seminaris. Proust then wrote her, from Dieppe, a series of impassioned litanies: 'On my sister Maria, confidante of my thoughts, guiding light of my wandering sadness'. In June 1899 she married the painter Raymond de Madrazo, father of 'Coco'. She remained a loyal and devoted friend, and attended Proust's funeral with Diaghilev.

HAHN, Reynaldo (Caracas, Venezuela, 9 August 1875 – Paris, 28 January 1947). Jewish of Venezuelan origin, he lived in Paris with his parents (his father was a businessman) and his many sisters. From 1886 he studied at the Conservatoire under various masters: Grandjany for musical theory, Decombes for piano, Théodore Dubois and Lavignac for harmony, Massenet (whom he always admired) for composition. When Proust met him on 22 May 1894, Hahn was 19. The meeting took place at one of Madame Lemaire's Tuesdays, where Reynaldo Hahn was in the habit of singing his *Chansons grises*, based on poems by Verlaine, accompanying himself on the piano (he knew by heart dozens of tunes by Schubert, Schumann and Gounod, as well as those he wrote himself). He was sensitive, refined, and a dazzling talker. He and Proust became deeply attached to each other during the two years of their passionate relationship; this in turn became a deep friendship that lasted until Proust's death. Proust called him 'my child', 'Master', or 'Buchnibuls'. He gave Hahn his portrait (drawn by Jacques-Émile Blanche on 1 October 1891), and Hahn kept it in his bedroom all his life. In September 1895, returning from a stay in Brittany with his friend, Proust set to work on his first novel, *Jean Santeuil*: 'I want you to be in it all the time, but like a God in disguise, unrecognisable to any mortal', he wrote to Hahn. In 1900 they visited Venice together, accompanied by Marie Nordlinger, Hahn's English cousin. Proust kept him up to date with his work and read him *Du Côté de chez Swann* for the first time. Hahn's tastes were classical, and he didn't understand Proust's enthusiasm for Wagner and Debussy, but he introduced him to the work of Camille Saint-Saëns (1835–1921) whose pupil he was. Proust heard Saint-Saëns' sonata in D minor for violin and piano for the first time at Madame Lemaire's. 'The little phrase' from this piece became the *leitmotif* of their love, as the phrase from Vinteuil's sonata was for Swann and Odette. After Proust's death, Hahn pursued his career as a composer and music critic on *Le Figaro*. Between the wars he was director of the Théâtre du Casino in Cannes. He spent the Second World War in Monaco before returning to Paris in 1945, where he was appointed director of the Opéra.

Works: *L'Isle du rêve* (first musical drama, 1898), *Nuit d'amour bergamasque* (first symphonic poem), *La Carmélite* (to a libretto by Catulle Mendès), *Le Bal de Béatrice d'Este* (ballet, 1909), *La Fête chez Thérèse* (ballet, 1910), *Le Dieu bleu* (ballet, 1911), *Nausicaa* (comic opera, 1919), *La Colombe de Bouddha* (ballet, 1921), *Ciboulette* (operetta with libretto by Flers and Croisset, 1923), *Mozart* (stage music for a play by Sacha Guitry, 1925), *Le Bois sacré* (stage music for a play by Flers and Caillavet), *Brummel* (operetta with words by Rip and Dieudonné, 1931), *Malvina* (operetta with libretto by Maurice Donnay and Henri Duvernoy, 1939), *Le Marchand de Venise* (opera, 1936), *Prométhée* (lyric ode for soloists, choir and orchestra), *Mélodies* ('L'Heure exquise', 'Offrande', 'Cimitière de campagne', 'Paysage', 'Rondels de Charles d'Orléans', 'Études latines', 'La Barcheta', 'Chansons grises', 'Chansons espagnoles'), *Le Oui des jeunes filles* (unfinished comic opera).

Publications: *La Grande Sarah* (1930), recollections of his great friend

Sarah Bernhardt, *Le Journal d'un musicien* (1933), *L'Oreille au guet.* In 1956, Philip Kolb undertook the edition of his correspondence with Proust.

HALÉVY, Daniel (Paris, 12 December 1872 – Paris, 4 February 1962). Son of Ludovic Halévy, Meilhac's collaborator; nephew of Madame Straus. He made friends with Proust at school at Condorcet when he repeated Class 2 in October 1886. Together they founded various reviews, including *Le Banquet* in 1892. In August 1893 he and Proust, Fernand Gregh and Louis de la Salle had the idea of a 'roman à quatre' in the form of letters; Proust was to be the wife, la Salle the lover, Gregh the poet and Halévy the Abbé. But then la Salle and he left to do their military service in Fontainebleau. Proust paid them a visit, and in 1896 used his stay as the inspiration for 'Une petite ville de province' in *Jean Santeuil*. In January 1898, Halévy signed the pro-Dreyfus *Manifeste des cent-quatre* with Proust. The same year he collaborated with Charles Péguy (of whom Proust had a low opinion) on *Cahiers de la Quinzaine.* Until the end he remained a friend and a writer Proust respected. In 1936 he published the letters of his aunt, Madame Straus, which were in his possession.

HANOTAUX, Gabriel (Beaurevoir, 19 November 1853 – Paris, 11 April 1944). Politician. He was head of the Foreign Office under the ministries of Ferry and Gambetta. He was a friend of Dr Adrien Proust. It was through his recommendation that Proust got the post of librarian at the Mazarine in 1895, as well as the long periods of leave he subsequently requested. Hanotaux was Minister of Foreign Affairs from May 1894 to June 1898, then ambassador to Rome in 1920. He also devoted his time to various historical projects. His diplomatic language was Proust's inspiration for that of Norpois.

HARRISON, Alexander (Philadelphia, 17 January 1853 – Paris, 23 October 1930). American painter. Proust and Reynaldo Hahn made his acquaintance in September or October 1895, during a stay at the Fermont hotel in Beg-Meil. In December 1896 Proust and Marie Nordlinger went to have tea in his studio in the rue Campagne-Première, as the narrator and Albertine do at Elstir's studio in *A l'ombre des jeunes filles en fleurs*. He was one of the models for Elstir.

HAUSER, Lionel (1868–1958). Financial adviser. It was at Louis Weil's house in Auteuil that Lionel Hauser, who had been introduced by his uncle Gustave Neuburger, encountered Proust for the first time in 1882. With good references from abroad, Lionel Hauser set himself up in Paris in 1907 (near the Observatoire) as representative of Warburg and of Kuhn-Loeb of New York. Proust came to know him very well: he placed great trust in him in the handling of his financial affairs, and called him '*tu*' in their very full correspondence.

HAUSSONVILLE, Othenin, Comte d' (Gurcy-le-Châtel, 21 September 1843 – Paris, 1 September 1924). Grandson of Albertine, Madame de Staël's daughter. Head of the Orléaniste faction, he achieved unity with the Légitimistes in 1883 after the Comte de Chambord died. Elected to the Académie Française in 1888, he published a number of works devoted to literary history, and enjoyed repeating: 'I shall always be a distinguished man and a mediocre one.' Proust met him in the salons of Madame Straus and Madame Lemaire. D'Haussonville never lost sight of the importance of his social position; with 'harmonious gymnastics', as Proust described it, he would accord his guests the reverence characteristic of the Guermantes. During the Dreyfus affair he gave Madame Straus's name its 'Germanic' pronounciation (as the Duc de Guermantes did to Bloch). On 4 May 1920 Proust saw him, sitting not far away, at a Ballets Russes gala at the Opéra. His age made him seem even more majestic (as is true of Basin at the end of *A la Recherche*. He was one of the models for the Duc de Guermantes.

HAUSSONVILLE, Comtesse d', *née* Pauline d'Harcourt (Paris, 4 March 1846 – Paris, 6 November 1922). Wife of the above. Proust frequented her aristocratic salon in the rue Saint-Dominique, in which hung a painting of one of her husband's ancestors, Béatrix de Lillebonne, abbess of Remiremont under Louis XIV; the Marquise de Villeparisis talks about it to Bloch. Irreverently, Proust called this implacable anti-Dreyfusard 'Pauline'. The d'Haussonvilles spent their holidays in Coppet where Proust met them when he accompanied his parents to Évian. *Le Figaro* of 4 January 1904 published a piece by him called 'Le Salon de la comtesse d'Haussonville' and signed 'Horatio'.

HAYMAN, Laure (1851–1932). A descendent of the painter Francis

Hayman, Gainsborough's teacher. Born on a ranch in the Andean cordillero, the daughter of an engineer, she lost her father very young and her mother decided to make her a courtesan. Among her lovers she numbered the Duc d'Orléans, the King of Greece and Karageorgevitch, pretender to the throne of Serbia, whom she really loved. Like Odette de Crécy in *A la Recherche* she lived in a small town house at 4 rue la Pérouse. Proust met her in the early autumn of 1888; she was 37 and he was 18. He went to see her in Uncle Louis' house at Auteuil; she was Louis' mistress. She was blonde with black eyes, plump but very elegant and witty, and she held a literary salon eagerly attended by her great admirer (and lover) Paul Bourget, who based the heroine of his novel *Gladys Harvey* on her. In October 1888 Laure gave Proust a copy of the book bound in the silk of one of her skirts. She had a collection of porcelain (like Odette) and nicknamed Proust 'My little psychological Saxon'. Proust spent a fortune on flowers for her, always giving her the chrysanthemums she loved. Jacques-Émile Blanche (who was a friend of both of them) insinuated that there was more than friendship between them, but he had no evidence. Robert Dreyfus, however, described the relationship differently: 'A platonic passion for a famous courtesan which ended in an exchange of photos and letters' (R. Dreyfus, *op. cit.*, p. 50). In about 1900, after an unhappy love affair, she began a successful career as a sculptor. A few months before he died Proust almost quarrelled with her irreconcilably. When she recognised herself in the character of Odette de Crécy, for which she was one of the chief models, she sent him a stinging letter calling him a 'monster'; but he went to see her and they made it up. She died in poverty. Laure Hayman also appeared in *Jean Santeuil* in the character of Françoise S. with whom Jean is smitten. In *Les Plaisirs et les jours*, the courtesan Heldémonde was based on her.

HEATH, Willie. A Protestant Englishman who converted to Catholicism at the age of 12. He resembled Edgar Aubert, a young Swiss friend of Robert de Billy's who died of appendicitis in 1892. Proust and Heath met in the spring of 1893, in the Bois de Boulogne, and formed 'a dream, almost a plan, to live together more and more, surrounded by carefully chosen, good-hearted men and women, far away from stupidity, vice and malice' (dedication in *Les Plaisirs et les jours*). On 6 June 1893 Proust gave a grand dinner for his ten best friends: Heath was seated on Madame Proust's left. He died of typhoid fever on 3 October 1893, and in July 1894 Proust dedicated *Les Plaisirs et les jours* to him.

HELLEU, Paul (Vannes, 17 December 1859 – Paris, 23 March 1927). Painter and engraver. Montesquiou, who was his patron, introduced him to Proust in the 1890s. In 1907 Helleu took Proust to see the Château de Balleroy and its tapestries, near Bayeux. They sometimes dined at Dives, at the Auberge de Guillaume le Conquérant. Proust had great respect for his talent and Helleu gave him a picture Proust had admired in his studio, *Automne à Versailles*. In 1922 Helleu made a dry-point etching (he completed 1,700 in the course of his life) of Proust on his deathbed in a two-hour session. Elstir was principally based on him. According to Jacques-Émile Blanche, the Elstirs that the narrator sees on his first visit to the Guermantes' house were Helleus (Helleu, like Elstir, painted flowers and seascapes). On the other hand Degas, who didn't like him, nicknamed him 'a steam Watteau'; Saniette, in *A la Recherche*, takes up the phrase and applies it to Elstir.

HENNESSY, Madame Jean, *née* Marguerite de Mun (1877–1970). Daughter of Albert, the Catholic socialist leader. On 16 June 1921 Proust went to the dinner she gave to celebrate the engagement between the Duke of Marlborough and Gladys Deacon. It was at her house that Proust met his great friend Jeanne Pouquet for the last time in 1922.

HÉRÉDIA, Marie de (1875–1963). In about 1893 Proust used to go to the Saturday at-homes of the great Parnassian poet José-Maria de Hérédia (1842–1905), who entertained guests surrounded by his three ravishing daughters. The eldest, Marie, organised a group of friends, 'L'Académie canaque', which included Pierre Louÿs, Paul Valéry, Fernand Gregh, Léon Blum and the poet Henri de Régnier, whom she married in 1895. Marie was 'queen of the Academy' and Proust 'perpetual secretary'. She wrote novels under the name Gérard d'Houville.

Works: *Le temps d'aimer* (1908), *Tant pis pour toi!* (1921), *L'Enfant* (1925), *Esclave amoureuse* (1927), *Enfantines et amoureuses* (1946).

HERMANT, Abel (Paris, 8 February 1862 – Chantilly, 22 September 1950). Writer. Satirist and drama critic on *Gil Blas* and *Le Figaro*, he was very friendly with the children of Princesse Rachel de Brancovan. He and Proust often encountered each other in the Parisian salons and at Amphion, on Lake Leman, where the Princesse entertained in her villa Bassaraba. A model for Bloch.

Works: *La Carrière* (1894), *Les Transatlantiques* (1897), *Les Souvenirs du vicomte de Courpière* (1901), *Les Trains de luxe* (1908), *Le Caravansérail* (1917), *Les Épaves* (1927), *La Dernière incarnation de M. de Courpière* (1937).

HERVEY DE SAINT-DENYS, Marquise d', *née* Baronne de Ward. Proust met her at the great party at the Pavillon Montesquiou on 30 May 1894. Her husband, a noted sinologist, is mentioned in *A la Recherche* under his real name concerning a Chinese vase that he was to give Charlus. Like the Princesse d'Orvillers, Madame d'Hervey was the natural daughter of the last reigning Prince of Parma. On the death of her husband, who was very rich, she married Madame de Chevigné's nephew, Jacques de Waru, one of the two brothers Proust had tried to befriend in order to be introduced to their aunt.

HERVIEU, Paul (Neuilly, 2 September 1857 – Paris, 25 October 1915). Writer. He published a large number of novels before pursuing his career as the 'modern tragedist' at the Comédie-Française. A friend of Proust's, he paraded through the society salons, like Swann, with icy elegance and an air of melancholy distinction. Proust recalled with regret that Hervieu had never forgiven him for voting against his novel for the Académie Française Prize in June 1914. He was among the models for Bergotte.

Works: Novels: *L'Inconnu* (1886), *Flirt* (1890), *Peints par eux-mêmes* (1893), *L'Armature* (1893); Plays: *Les Paroles restent* (1892), *Les Tenailles* (1895), *La Loi de l'homme* (1897), *La Course du flambeau* (1901), *Théroigne de Méricourt* (1902), *Le Dédale* (1903), *Le Réveil* (1905), *Connais-toi* (1909), *Bagatelles* (1912), *Le Destin est maître* (1914).

HINNISDAL, Thérèse d', Marquise de Lévis. At the Ritz ball on 15 January 1922, Proust asked her to show him the steps of the latest fashionable dance. He remarked: 'She could abandon herself to the most 1922 dances while remaining a heraldic shield, a coat-of-arms unicorn.' He saw her again on 12 June at Madame Hennessy's party.

HOWLAND, Madame Meredith, *née* Torrance. A much sought-after personality of the Faubourg Saint-Germain. Proust met her in St Moritz in August 1893, and dedicated 'Mélancolique Villégiature de Madame de Breyves' in *La Revue blanche* of 15 September 1893 to her. She was a particular friend of Montesquiou's, and was also close to Charles Haas and Edgar Degas.

HUMIÈRES, Robert, Vicomte d' (1868–1915). Translator of Kipling and Conrad who helped Proust with his work on Ruskin and brought out an article on *La Bible d'Amiens* in *Chronique des arts et de la curiosité*. Threatened by a scandal, he got himself posted to a Zouave regiment at the front, where he was killed in 1915: 'I cry day and night for Fénelon and d'Humières, as if I'd only left them yesterday', Proust wrote to Madame Catusse on 27 May 1915. In his final role as war hero and unmasked homosexual, d'Humières lent several characteristics to Saint-Loup.

INDY, Vincent d' (Paris, 2 December 1851 – Paris, 27 March 1931). A Wagnerian disciple of César Franck. Proust met him through the Comte de Saussine. His first name echoes that of Vinteuil in *A la Recherche*. Proust used his work *César Franck* a great deal as inspiration for the creation of Vinteuil.

JALOUX, Edmond (Marseille, 19 June 1878 – Lutry, Switzerland, 15 August 1949). A friend of Jean-Louis Vaudroyer and Georges de Lauris who met Proust at the time of the Ballets Russes in 1910. Like Proust, he was a member of the committee which awarded the Blumenthal Prize. In September 1920 he witnessed the memorable discussion between Proust and Bergson on insomnia and soporifics. On 15 July 1922 Proust went to the 'Boeuf sur le toit' with Jaloux and Paul Brach. Jaloux remained an attentive correspondent on Proust's state of health. He left a book of memoirs: *Avec Marcel Proust* (1953).

JONCIÈRES, Léonce de (Dompierre, 14 February 1871–1952). Genre painter. Proust met him in August 1907 in Cabourg. 'I was greeted here on my arrival at the Tapirs – guess – by that lovable leading boy (Leander or Octavius at a stretch) called Léonce de Joncières' (letter to Reynaldo Hahn of 6 August 1907). He was a model for Octave.

JOYCE, James (Dublin, 2 February 1882 – Zurich, 13 January 1941). Irish writer. Proust met him on 18 May 1922 at the dinner given by the Schiffs in honour of the two writers, Diaghilev, Picasso and Stravinsky. Joyce arrived at midnight, in a bad mood. In October 1920 he had written of Proust: 'I've read a few pages of his. I didn't find that he was particularly talented, but I am a bad critic.' After the dinner at the Ritz, the two writers left together in Odilon Albaret's taxi. Joyce complained about his eyes, Proust about his stomach; the exchange of social banalities continued. Later, Joyce regretted it: 'If only we had had the chance to meet properly and have a conversation somewhere.' His masterpiece *Ulysses* (1922), was in some sense a forerunner to *A la Recherche* (although the latter goes well beyond the limits of interior monologue). In *Finnegans Wake* (1939) Joyce alludes to Proust's name, as well as the titles of his books.

LA BÉRAUDIÈRE, Comtesse de, *née* Marie-Thérèse Trinidad Brocheton (1872–1958). The Comte Greffulhe's mistress. Proust visited the couple in June 1913 and July 1915. She was the model for Odette when the latter became the Duc de Guermantes' mistress.

LACRETELLE, Jacques de (Cormatin, 14 July 1888 – Paris, 2 January 1985). Writer. Son of a diplomat, he studied at the lycée Jeanson-de-Saily then at Cambridge. Proust saw him often in 1917. Even at his first visit, in December 1914, Lacretelle had questioned Proust about the models for *A la Recherche*. But in 1918 Proust wrote him a long dedication in the form of a letter in a copy of *Swann*: 'Dear friend, there are no keys to the characters in this book, or else there are eight or ten for each one'. Lacretelle published a large number of novels, including: *La vie inquiète de Jean Hermelin* (1920), *Silbermann* (Prix Fémina 1922), *La Bonifas* (1925), *L'Amour nuptial* (Grand Prix of the Académie Française 1930), *Le Retour de Silbermann* (1930), *Les Hauts Ponts* (1932–1935). After 1945 he devoted his energies to travel books – *La Grèce que j'aime* (1960) – and to critical works on literary history – *Portraits d'autrefois, figures d'aujourd'hui* (1973).

LA GANDARA, Antonio de (Paris, 16 December 1862 – Paris, 1917). Society painter. Son of a Spanish father and an English mother, he was one of the artists first patronised then rejected by Montesquiou, whose portrait he had painted. He was a friend of Alphonse Daudet, and made a sketch of him on his deathbed in December 1897. He painted portraits of the Princesse de Caraman-Chimay, the Comtesse Greffulhe, the Vicomte Jules de Noailles and others. In *Jean Santeuil*, the portrait of the young hero is executed by him.

LAGRENÉE, Edmond, Marquis de (16 February 1842 – 12 February 1909). Former consul general in La Paz; attached to the diplomatic service, famous for his duels. In 1902, he heckled a friend in the Café Weber: 'Hey there, Dreyfusard!' Proust took the remark to be aimed at him, and sent Léon Daudet and Robert de Flers to demand satisfaction. The duel was avoided: 'Gentlemen, Monsieur de Lagrenée said to us, I declare on my honour that I never had the slightest intention of insulting Monsieur Proust, whom in any case I do not know' (L. Daudet, *Salons et journaux*, 1917).

LA ROCHEFOUCAULD, Aimery, Comte de (3 September 1843–1928) Robert de Montesquiou's cousin. He was renowned for his aristocratic arrogance: his obsessive attention to questions of precedence earned him the nickname 'Place-at-table'. He was told of the death of his brother Gontran when he was on his way to a masked ball. He cut short the news with the reply: 'It's a great exaggeration, a great exaggeration.' Proust remembered this for the Duc de Guermantes. The Prince de Guermantes was based on La Rochefoucauld.

LA ROCHEFOUCAULD, Gabriel, Comte de (Paris, 13 September 1875 – Paris, 18 April 1972). Son of the above. Childhood friend of Élisabeth de Gramont. He had recently made friends with Proust when he attended her tea party in the rue de Courcelles on 19 June 1901. Like Saint-Loup, he aspired to the life of the mind and had committed himself to the Dreyfusard cause. He despised his father's aristocratic prejudices. Since he loved women and nightlife, he was given the nickname 'the La Rochefoucauld of Maxim's' – an allusion to the *Maximes* of his ancestor. Just as Saint-Loup was sent to North Africa to separate him from Rachel, Gabriel went to Constantinople in August 1904 with Pierre Loti to forget an unhappy love affair with a married woman, the Comtesse de Garets, who later committed suicide. The following year there was a rumour that Proust was the author of *L'Amant et le Médecin*, a novel which told the story of this affair. On 19 February 1904 Gabriel married a half-Jewish, half-aristocratic girl, Odile de Richelieu, the daughter of Alice Heine (1858–1925) who had in turn married the Duc de Richelieu and, after she was widowed, Prince Albert de Monaco. She was the model for the Princesse de Luxembourg in *A la Recherche*.

LA SALLE, Louis-Georges Séguin, Comte de (1872–1915). Poet. Former pupil at Condorcet, like Proust. He took part in the production of *Le Banquet*, then in 1893 did his military service with Halévy at Fontainebleau, where Proust visited them (Doncières is reminiscent of this small garrison town). In 1898 he signed the 'Manifeste des intellectuels' with his old school friends. Later he was converted to the nationalist cause, and frequented the Café Weber with Léon Daudet at the turn of the century. In 1910, Georges de Lauris married Madeleine de Pierrebourg, La Salle's ex-wife. La Salle was killed in the war. He had published his first collection of poetry, *Le Joueur des songes*, in 1895, and a novel, *Le Réactionnaire*.

LAURENT, Méry, *née* Marie Louviot (1849–1905). Proust was introduced to her salon in 1897 by Reynaldo Hahn, who often went there with Marie Nordlinger. Méry Laurent, who had played walk-on parts at Le Châtelet, was the mistress of the generous and open-minded Dr Evans, Napoleon III's famous American dentist. She entertained poets and artists. She was Manet's model, and his mistress, before becoming Mallarmé's mistress in 1883. She provided several characteristics for Odette de Crécy, especially her taste for the Japanese art which decorated her villa, Les Talus, at 9 boulevard Lannes, near the Bois de Boulogne.

LAURIS, Georges, Comte then Marquis de (1876–1963). A friend of Bertrand de Salignac-Fénelon. Proust met him in about May 1902, at a dinner given by Madame Léon Fould (1851–1911), during the time when he so assiduously courted the 'young Dukes'. De Lauris was one of the members of the Good Friday expedition on 10 April 1903 with the Bibescos, Proust, François de Pâris and Robert de Billy. On 6 December Fénelon and Georges de Lauris paid Proust a visit; when Fénelon made an unpleasant remark, Proust leapt on him and Lauris had to restrain him. Together with the 'young Dukes', Lauris spent whole evenings in Proust's room drinking cider or beer. He remained an intimate friend of

Proust's through a frequent exchange of letters: thus he was aware of the genesis of *A la Recherche* (Proust questioned him in 1909 about the origin of the name Guermantes). He was a model for Saint-Loup.

LAVALLÉE, Pierre (Paris, 9 February 1872 – Villars Fontaine, 17 December 1946). Curator of the library at the École des beaux-arts. A friend from Condorcet days, he began to visit the Daudet, Lemaire, Baignères and Arman de Caillavet salons with Proust. His mother, who was worried about him leading this society existence in Proust's wake, wrote to him on 2 August 1894: 'Marcel Proust once said something which made me frightened. He said, "I want Pierre to go everywhere that I go!" I found him very nice, but I confess I would be unhappy to see you leading the life he leads.' It was with Pierre Lavallée that Proust met the Abbé Vignot, whose sermons he admired. At the Jardin des Plantes in the spring of 1895 Proust, Reynaldo Hahn and their friend Pierre gazed at the 'colombes poignardées', the 'stabbed doves' (red-breasted pigeons) in the trance-like state Hahn had entered during the episode of the Bengal rose bushes at the Château de Réveillon. (In about 1913 Proust thought of giving the title *Les Colombes poignardées* to one of the volumes of *A la Recherche*.) In April 1895 Proust visited Lavallée at the Château de Segrez in Saint-Sulpice-de-Favières, which had belonged to the Lavallée family since 1856. But he had an asthma attack and had to leave the next morning. Although he never went back, he none the less described Segrez in 'La Promenade' in *Les Plaisirs et les jours*. Lavallée began his career at the library of the École des beaux-arts in 1896, and became its curator in 1910. On 30 November 1899 Proust wrote to him asking to borrow Ruskin's *The Queen of the Air*. Lavallée married in 1900, and his relationship with Proust began to fade, ending altogether in 1906. He attended Proust's funeral with Princesse Murat. In 1938 Lavallée was appointed president of the Société de l'histoire de l'art français, then put in charge of the department of drawings at the Louvre.

Works: *Dessins de maîtres anciens* (1927), *Dessins français du XVIIIe siècle à l'École des beaux-arts* (1928), *Le Dessin français du XIIIe au XVIe siècle* (1930), in the collection *Dessins du Louvre et des musées de France*, books on: Fragonard, Delacroix, Watteau, Jean Baptiste Oudry (after 1936), *Les Techniques du dessin* (1943), *Le Dessin français* (in collaboration with his daughter, Monique Lavallée (1948).

LE CUZIAT, Albert (born in Tréguier on 30 May 1881). A native of Brittany. He became head footman to Prince Constantin de Radziwill, who was known for his homosexuality, then in turn entered the service of Prince d'Essling, Comtesse Greffulhe, Comte Orloff and the Duc de Rohan. Proust met him in 1911 at Comte Orloff's house. He invited him to the boulevard Haussmann several times; he valued his knowledge of etiquette and genealogy, and liked to have short conversations with him late in the afternoons. He called him 'my walking *Gotha*' (the French guide to the aristocracy). In about 1913 Le Cuziat set himself up as a hotelier near the Bourse. Next he managed a bath-house in the rue Godot-de-Mauroy, before opening a brothel in the Hôtel Marigny at 11 rue de l'Arcade, in 1916. Proust furnished his room and the entrance hall with some of his parents' furniture (just as the narrator in *A la Recherche* gives Aunt Léonie's large sofa to a brothel Bloch frequents). Proust sometimes visited Le Cuziat's establishment for his own pleasure, or to obtain, for a large tip, society gossip and information about various people's habits. Céleste Albaret met Le Cuziat in the boulevard Hauss-mann, and described him in her memoirs as 'a great clumsy blond Breton beanpole, with blue eyes as cold as a fish'. Proust presented him with an inscribed copy of *Sésame et les lys*. Jupien in *A la Recherche* was based on him.

LEGRAND, Madame Gaston, *née* Clothilde de Fournès (died 1944). Known in the Faubourg Saint-Germain as 'Cloton', she had married a rich coal-mine owner, (Madame Leroi in *A la Recherche* is the daughter of a timber merchant). Montesquiou owned a picture of *Madame Legrand Coming Home from the Races* by Romaine Brooks. She was invited to the tea party Proust gave in the rue de Courcelles on 6 March 1905.

LEMAIRE, Madame, *née* Jeanne-Magdeleine Coll (Les Arcs, 24 May 1845–Paris, 1928). A tall, energetic woman with neither good looks nor vanity whose glittering salon included many artists and some of the Faubourg Saint-Germain. She entertained on Tuesdays in the studio of her tiny house in the rue de Monceau. She never tired of painting roses on fans; Proust, who went to her salon from 1892 onwards, called it 'the lilac court and the rose studio' and dedicated an article in *Le Figaro* to describing it. On 13 April 1893 he met Robert de Montesquiou there. Together with Reynaldo Hahn, he went to see her at the Château de

Réveillon in the Marne, as described in *Jean Santeuil*, and at her villa in Dieppe. Madame Lemaire illustrated *Les Plaisirs et les jours*, which appeared in 1896. She was one of the originals of Madame Verdurin and Madame de Villeparisis. Proust was equally friendly with her daughter Suzette.

LEMAITRE, Jules (Vennecy, 27 August 1853 – Tavers, 5 August 1914). Writer. He was a literary critic on *La Revue bleue* and *La Revue des Deux Mondes*. A habitué of Madame Aubernon's salon, he also went to Madame Arman de Caillavet's, where he might have met Proust. During the Dreyfus affair he was a fierce nationalist, and he abandoned Madame Straus's salon for his mistress, Madame de Loynes'. He was head of the Ligue de la Patrie Française from 1898 to 1904, then embraced the doctrines of l'Action Française. At the Daudets' house in February 1909 he urged Proust to write pastiches of Voltaire and Mérimée. He was a model for Bergotte.

Works: Poetry: *Les Médaillons* (1880), *Petites Orientales* (1883). Plays: *Le Député Leveau* (1890), *Le Mariage blanc* (1891), *Flipote* (1893), *La Bonne Hélène* (1896), *La Massière* (1905), *Le Mariage de Télémaque* (1910). Stories: *Sérénus, histoire d'un martyr* (1886), *En marge des vieux livres* (1907), *La Vieillesse d'Hélène* (1914).

LORRAIN, Jean, pseudonym of Paul Duval (Fécamp, 9 August 1855 – Paris, 30 June 1906). Society author and one of the contributors to *La Revue blanche*. In *Le Journal* of 3 February 1897, under the name 'Raitif de la Bretonne', he published an attack on *Les Plaisirs et les jours* which contained references to Proust's ambiguous relationship with Lucien Daudet. Proust took this as a slander and challenged him to a duel; he asked Gustave de Borda and Jean Béraud to be his seconds. The duel with pistols took place on 6 February 1897 in the Bois de Meudon at Tour de Villebon. Two shots were fired, harmlessly. Lorrain blamed Montesquiou, but was later reconciled with him. In 1921, André Gide described Proust, fat and bloated by then, as looking rather like Jean Lorrain, who provided some material for Charlus in *A la Recherche*.

LOYNES, Comtesse de, *née* Jeanne Detourbay (died January 1908). Jules Lemaitre's mistress. She held a nationalist salon during the Dreyfus affair, at which Maurice Barrès, Jean Louis Forain and the Comtesse de

Martel were among the guests. Madame Swann's salon at the time of the Dreyfus affair was based on this one. They bore other resemblances to each other: she had been a 'cocotte' during the Second Empire and was always at home to guests at teatime. When she died in 1908, Adrien Hébrard, editor of *Le Temps*, made a cruel remark about Lemaitre and his mistress: 'Poor thing, he will meet her again in a better demi-monde.'

MADRAZO, Frédéric de (1878–1938). Son of the painter Raymond de Madrazo, he married Maria, Reynaldo Hahn's elder sister, in 1899. Frédéric, whom his friends called 'Coco', was a regular at Madame Lemaire's salon, where he was known for his talents as a painter, singer, composer and writer. He was a devoted friend to Proust, who was always grateful for the way Madrazo had talked to him about painting when he was going to Venice with his mother and Reynaldo Hahn in 1900. Madrazo was one of the models for Ski in *A la Recherche*.

MAILLÉ DE LA TOUR LANDRY, Duchesse de, *née* d'Osmond. A relation of Robert de Montesquiou and niece of Madame de Boigne; author of *Mémoires*. She was very old when the young Proust encountered her at balls in the 1890s.

MÂLE, Émile (Commentry, 2 June 1862 – Chalis, 6 October 1954). Historian. Proust read and re-read his book *Art religieux du XIIIe siècle en France*, lent to him by Robert de Billy in 1899. In 1907 he wrote to Mâle from Cabourg to find out about places of artistic interest in the area. Mâle was in charge of the course in Christian art history at the Sorbonne from 1906.

MARTEL, Sibylle de Riqueti de Mirabeau, Comtesse de (Château de Koëtsal, Morbihan, 15 August 1850 – Neuilly-sur-Seine, 29 June 1932). Mirabeau's great-great-niece and a friend of Proust's mother, better known under her pen-name 'Gyp'. She came across the young Proust in the Champs-Élysées playing with Antoinette Faure. A few days later she was amazed to see the precocious child in Calmann-Lévy's book-shop buying the complete works of Molière and Lamartine.

MARTIN DU GARD, Maurice (Nancy, 7 December 1896–1970). Writer and journalist. He was the editor of *Écrits nouveaux*, and in July 1921 he published an unfavourable review of *Le Côté de Guermantes* by André

Germain. In November Jacques Rivière complained bitterly to du Gard about the article, and Proust was determined to fight a duel. Du Gard justified himself by saying that he didn't share his contributor's opinion: the duel was avoided and Proust invited him to dinner on 7 February 1922 with the Princesse Soutzo. At the time Martin du Gard lived in Réjane's town house, where Proust himself had lived. He was editor of *Nouvelles littéraires* from 1923 to 1936.

MATHILDE, Princesse (Trieste, 1820 – Paris, 1904). Niece of Napoleon I. As well as the nobility, she entertained members of the Faubourg Saint-Germain set, including the Strauses, the Pozzis, the Haas and Porto-Riches. Under Napoleon III she had been a glittering hostess, and she still dressed in Second Empire style. Proust visited her salon from 1891 onwards: she had a high regard for him, and her close friends nicknamed him 'Popelin Junior' after her last lover, Claudius Popelin. Proust described her in *A l'ombre des jeunes filles en fleurs* when the narrator is introduced to her by Swann in the zoological gardens. Some of her characteristics might have been used for the Princesse de Parme and Madame de Villeparisis, and perhaps for Madame Verdurin in the *Temps retrouvé* pastiche.

MAUPASSANT, Guy de (Château de Miromesnil, 5 August 1850 – Paris, 6 July 1893). Writer. Proust met him several times at the house of the Princesse Potocka, who was his mistress, and at Madame Straus's. The latter was the model for his heroine in *Fort comme la mort*. Proust also saw him in 1892 when he was sitting for his portrait at Dr Blanche's house in Auteuil, where Maupassant was a lodger. Maupassant became the novelist C. in *Jean Santeuil*.

MAURIAC, François (Bordeaux, 11 October 1885 – Paris, 1 September 1970). Writer. After the publication of *A l'ombre des jeunes filles en fleurs* in June 1919, Mauriac reviewed it in *La Revue des jeunes* on 25 August. He dined with Proust in the rue Hamelin in March 1921 and was surprised by the change in his physical appearance: 'That wax mask [...] in which only the hair seems alive' (F. Mauriac, *Du Côté de chez Proust*, 1947). He attended Proust's funeral with Maurice Barrès. In 1951 his son Claude married Marie-Claire, Suzy Mante-Proust's daughter.

MIRABAUD, Paul (died 12 May 1908). Director of the Banque de France.

He was the father-in-law of Robert de Billy, who married his daughter Jeanne. In August 1914 Proust went with them on a cruise along the Normandy coast aboard his yacht *Hélène*. 'Monsieur Mirabaud is magnificent, a huge strong Saxon god' (letter from Proust to his mother dated 11 August). He had a weak heart, and like Proust was a patient of Dr Merklen's. At the sale of his books after his death in 1908 Proust bought two erotic works by Verlaine, *Femmes* and *Hombres*.

MONACO, Princesse Albert de, *née* Alice Furtado-Heine (1858–1925). After the death of her husband, the Duc de Richlieu (1847–80), she married Prince Albert of Monaco in 1889 and separated from him in 1902. In *A la Recherche* she is one of the originals of the Princesse de Luxembourg. About 1894 Proust met her at Cabourg, where the character also stayed.

MONTEBELLO, Comtesse Jean Lannes de, *née* Albertine de Briey (born 1855). Proust was her guest in the Faubourg Saint-Germain. She gave her first name to the narrator's mistress.

MONTESQUIOU-FEZENSAC, Robert, Comte de (Paris, 19 March 1855 – Menton, 11 December 1921). Son of Thierry de Montesquiou and Pauline du Roux (1823–64) who had two other sons, Gontran (1847–83) and Aimery (1853–73), he was one of the most extraordinary figures of the age. He was of very high birth (marshals and prelates were among his ancestors), very handsome (tall and dark, with artificially curled hair) and elegant in a rather showy way. Brilliantly intelligent and as cultured as he was pretentious, he was to be seen in the most exclusive Parisian salons. He wrote many symbolist poems and was a friend of Mallarmé, Verlaine, Fauré, Whistler and Émile Gallé. Proust met him for the first time on 13 April 1893 at a reception at Madame Lemaire's. Proust was 22; Montesquiou was 38. He lived in the 'Palais des Muses', his house in Neuilly (95 rue Charles-Laffitte) but also owned a residence in Paris. Proust was immediately fascinated by this famous society poet; the aestheticism he made fashionable influenced Proust strongly. In August 1905 Proust published a laudatory review of Montesquiou's *Professionelles Beautés* in *Les arts de la vie* under the title 'Un professeur de beauté'. As the years went by, they felt a mutual admiration mixed with dislike. When *A la Recherche* came out in 1913, Montesquiou was not flattered to recognise himself – and the whole of Paris saw it too – in the character of Baron de Charlus. Hypocritically, Proust wrote to him saying that the character was not based on him, but on Baron Doäzan. Their lives and their relationship were marked by quarrels like this, but Montesquiou was in the habit of breaking off friendships with people who had once worshipped him. Robert de Montesquiou died at the age of 66 from an attack of uraemia. After his death he fell into an obscurity as complete as his life had been brilliant, but in 1965 Philippe Julien brought out a book, *Robert de Montesquiou, un prince 1900*, which paid tribute to him. Several people – François Mauriac and Jacques-Émile Blanche among them – have said that Proust's character and work would not have been what they were but for Montesquiou.

Works: Collections of poetry: *Les Chauves-souris* ('Clairs-Obscurs', 1892), *Le Chef des odeurs suaves* (1893), *Le Parcours du rêve au souvenir* (1895), *Les Hortensias bleus* (1896), *Les Roseaux pensants* (1897), *Le Pays des aromates* (1900), *Les Paons* (1901), *Professionnelles Beautés* (1905). Essays: *Félicité* (1894), *Le Domaine du choix*. Novel: *La Petite Mademoiselle*. Memoirs: *Les Pas effacés* (1923).

MORAND, Paul (Paris, 13 March 1888 – Paris, 23 July 1976). Writer and diplomat. Son of the author and painter Eugène Morand, Paul Morand had Jean Giraudoux as a tutor in 1905. In August 1915 Proust visited the young Morand, then on leave from the army, in the rue Galilée; Morand compared him to Flaubert. The following year, when Morand was a young embassy attaché at the Quai d'Orsay and a friend of Henri Bardac's, he visited the boulevard Haussmann regularly. In 1917 Proust, Morand and his future wife, the Princesse Soutzo, often had dinner together at the Ritz, where the Princesse had an apartment. Early in 1920 Morand published a collection of free verse, *Lampes à arc*, which included the 'Ode à Marcel Proust'. Morand and Proust had a long correspondence which was both intimate and worldly; Morand was among those who used their influence to gain Proust the Cross of the Légion d'honneur, in September 1920. In March 1921 Gallimard published his book *Tendres Stocks*, with a preface by Proust. (Benjamin Crémieux's article on the book in the *Nouvelle Revue Française* did not even mention the preface, whereas other reviews both in France and abroad concentrated more on the preface than on Morand's text.) In

November of that year he introduced Proust to Natalie Barney. In 1949, Éditions Palatine in Geneva published Morand's *Le Visiteur du soir*, in which he discussed Proust a great deal. After successive postings to London, Rome, Bucharest and Berne and journeys to Spain and Tangiers, he was made a member of the Académie Française in 1969. In *A la Recherche* Charlus alludes, during the war, to the 'charming Morand, the delightful author of Clarisse', the first of the three stories that make up *Tendres Stocks*.

MORNAND, Louisa de, pseudonym of Louise Montaud (Lyon, 24 December 1884 – Paris, March 1963). Actress. Proust met her in 1903 at the same time as Louis d'Albufera, her lover. She was very charming, but had little talent as an actress: she acted in some twenty minor plays between 1903 and 1910, but only appeared occasionally after that. In 1904 Proust sent her a copy of *La Bible d'Amiens* with the couplet: 'Whoever cannot have Louisa de Mornand/Will have to resort to the sin of Onan.' After she broke up with d'Albufera in the spring of 1906, other liaisons followed, notably with Robert Gangnat, then with the actor Jean Signoret, Jean Périer and Félix Juvens, the editor of *Rire* and *Fantasio*.

Louisa remained friendly with Proust almost until the end of his life. Her correspondence from him amounted to about fifty letters, mostly unimportant, simple replies to the notes and cards she sent him regularly. After Proust's death she brought out *Lettres et Vers à Mesdames Laure Hayman et Louisa de Mornand* in 1928, collected and annotated by Georges Andrieux, with prefaces by Robert Proust and Fernand Nozière. The book's first printing was 1190 copies, illustrated with four photographs of Louisa by Ph. Reutlinger, the picture by A. de la Gandara and a photographic portrait by Ph. Manuel. The book went on sale on 20 November 1928. Louisa told the press: 'We had a loving relationship which was neither an idle flirtation nor an exclusive liaison, but, on Proust's side, a keen passion balanced between affection and desire, and on mine a deeply felt attachment which was more than friendship' (*Candide*, 1 November 1928). She was suspected of taking advantage of Proust's celebrity to boost her own much slighter fame.

In the 1930s she devoted herself for a time to working in the cinema (she had parts in Henri Roussell's *Violettes impériales* in 1932, then in

Fanatisme et Chanson de Paris; in *Le Rosaire* by Gaston Ravel and Tony Lekain (1934); and in Charles Barois' *Aux portes de Paris* (1935). This rounded off her modest career as an actress. She ended her life in poverty and obscurity, despite the pension which the d'Albufera family gave her. She died in hospital following a fracture of the femur. In *A la Recherche* the character of Rachel, the actress who was Saint-Loup's mistress, was based on her (Rachel was the name of one of her servants).

MUGNIER, Abbé Arthur (Lubersac, 1853 – Paris, 1944). Father-confessor to the Faubourg Saint-Germain who converted Joris-Karl Huysmans (1848–1907) in 1892. He was the vicar of Sainte-Clothilde, an aristocratic parish. From 1896 onwards he began to attend society dinners which he described in his *Journal*. He kept up energetic correspondences with Princesse Bibesco, Cocteau, Montesquiou, Bergson, Barrès, Henri de Montherlant, Mauriac and Proust himself. In 1907 he often saw Proust at the Ritz at the Princesse Soutzo's dinners. He described Proust as 'a bee buzzing round heraldic flowers'. Proust told Jacques-Émile Blanche that the Abbé had tried to get him to think about the state of his soul, but Proust's retort was: 'Tell me about Comte Aimery de La Rochefoucauld instead' (J.-É. Blanche, *Mes modèles*, p. 138). Illness prevented him from being at Proust's deathbed, as the latter had wanted, but for many years afterwards he celebrated an anniversary mass at Saint-Pierre-de-Chaillot.

MURAT, Princesse Lucien, *née* Marie de Rohan-Chabot (1876–1951). On 29 May 1891 her mother threw the famous 'Princesse de Léon's ball'. Proust went to a party given by the Princesse Murat on 22 June 1908 where he took revenge on his enemy Gustave Schlumberger. He also attended her Christmas Eve party at the Ritz in 1917. Proust then included her in his pastiche of Saint-Simon, which he was in the process of revising.

NAHMIAS, Albert (Paris, 1886–1979). His real name was Ben Nahmias. He was the son of a financier (born in Constantinople in 1854) and financial correspondent of *Le Gaulois*. Proust met him in 1909 through a mutual acquaintance, Constantin Ullmann. During his stay in Cabourg in the summer of 1911, Proust invited Nahmias to join him as his secretary. Nahmias mostly helped Proust with his financial affairs, but he also took charge of the typing of *A la Recherche* and employed Miss Hayward for the task. The correspondence between Nahmias and Proust reveals the closeness of their friendship. Proust began his letters: 'Mon petit Albert'. In August 1912 Nahmias set off for Cabourg with his two sisters, Anita and Estie. According to Antoine Bibesco, all three were models for Albertine; when Nahmias was asked whether Albertine was based on him, he replied: 'There were several of us.' On 11 August 1912 Albert ran over a little girl on the road to Caen. Proust, who hadn't heard about the accident, was waiting for him on the sea-wall: since he didn't turn up, Proust wrote him a letter breaking off the friendship. But they were reconciled shortly afterwards. Albert was his confidant. When the relationship with Agostinelli reached a crisis, Proust wrote to Albert on 11 August 1913: 'I'll tell you how I left and you'll understand [...] Don't mention my secretary (ex-chauffeur). People are so stupid that they think (as they did with our friendship) there is something pederastic going on.' In December, when Agostinelli left Proust, Nahmias was sent to try to persuade him to come back.

NISARD, Armand (13 May 1841 – 1925). Marie Bénardaky's uncle by marriage. He was head of political affairs at the Quai d'Orsay, then French ambassador to the Vatican from 1898 to 1904. He spent his holidays in Évian in 1900 at the same time as the Prousts. Although he was an acquaintance of Dr Adrien Proust's, he did little to support his candidature for the Académie des sciences morales et politiques. (In *A la Recherche* Norpois displays the same inefficiency towards the narrator's father.)

NOAILLES, Comtesse Mathieu de, *née* Anna-Élisabeth de Brancovan (Paris, 15 November 1876 – Paris, 30 April 1933). Poet. Proust probably first met her in Amphion in 1893, at her mother the Princesse de Brancovan's house. She married Comte Mathieu de Noailles on 18 August 1897 in Publier (Haute-Savoie), and became a cousin of Montesquiou's by marriage. On 24 April 1899 Proust gave a large dinner at his apartment for her, Robert de Montesquiou and Anatole France; Cora Laparcerie recited Anna de Noailles' first poems. All his life Proust was a deep admirer, and on 15 June 1907 he wrote a highly flattering review for *Le Figaro*'s literary supplement on *Les Éblouissements*, the collection of poems she had just published with Calmann-Lévy. He was the only person she ever allowed to alter a line or a verse of her poems: she always trusted his judgement. Through their letters to each other Anna was party to the genesis of *Contre Sainte-Beuve* and *A la Recherche* (her son later gave all his mother's correspondence with Proust to the Bibliothèque nationale). Early in 1913, when Proust was in a distressed emotional state, he asked if he could come to Florence with her. They both received the Cross of the Légion d'honneur on 25 September 1920 (at the same time as Colette); Anna was later the first woman to be awarded the insignia of Commander of the Légion d'honneur. The Vicomtesse Gaspard de Réveillon, in *Jean Santeuil*, was based on Anna de Noailles.

Works: Le Coeur innombrable (1901), *L'Ombre des jours* (1902), *Le Visage émerveillé* (1904), *Les Éblouissements* (1907), *Les Vivants et les morts* (1913), *L'Honneur de souffrir* (1927).

NORDLINGER, Marie (Manchester, 1876 – Manchester, 25 October 1961). Of German-Italian origin, a student of Fine Arts in Manchester, she came to Paris to pursue her studies in painting and sculpture; in 1902 she joined the collector Siegfried Bing's studio, where she became an engraver. Proust met her in December 1896 in her cousin Reynaldo Hahn's mother's salon; their friendship began from that time. Together they were regular guests at Méry Laurent's salon. In May 1900 she went to Venice with Reynaldo Hahn, Proust and his mother; she helped him correct his translation of Ruskin's *The Bible of Amiens*. From 1899 Proust had adopted the habit of writing to her whenever she was away in England or America to ask her detailed literary questions about his translations, and their correspondence, which became increasingly friendly, lasted until October 1908 (it amounts to 41 letters).

In December 1903, after Dr Proust's death, Marie was an attentive visitor to the rue de Courcelles (as Albertine is to the narrator), and she corrected the proofs of the Ruskin book. Proust gave her Whistler's *The Gentle Art of Making Enemies* (which Montesquiou had given him), and she gave him in return a small watercolour she had done in Senlis in 1898. At the beginning of January 1904, they began the translation of *Sesame and Lilies*. In April, Marie (who knew that Proust couldn't have flowers because of his asthma) gave him some Japanese tablets made of coloured marrow which expanded into flowers when dropped in water.

The following month she started work on the brass plaque engraved with Dr Proust's portrait for his tomb in Père-Lachaise. This sculpture, which neither Proust nor his mother liked, was placed in the cemetery on 26 November 1904. Marie was in the United States at the time, and she only saw Proust twice more: in June 1905 and in 1908.

In 1942, when she was 66, she decided to publish her correspondence with Proust, and Calame Press in Manchester brought out the very successful *Letters to a Friend.* Ten years later, in 1952, she gave the letters to the Bibliothèque nationale (the first Proust correspondence to be deposited there). She continued to present her memoirs in several articles and at various conferences, taking an active part in setting up two exhibitions: 'Marcel Proust and his Time' at the Wildenstein Gallery in London in 1955 (organised by the department of cultural relations at the French embassy), and an exhibition organised by the Whitworth Gallery and the French embassy in Manchester in 1956. In 1957 she was awarded the Cross of Chevalier de la Légion d'honneur by the French government.

PÂRIS, François, Marquis de (1875–1958). A member of the Good Friday expedition in 1903. On 23 May 1909 Proust asked Lauris if the name Guermantes belonged to the Pâris family, because the Baronne de Lareinty, François de Pâris's grandmother, owned the Château de Guermantes.

PÉTER, René (1872–1947). Playwright. His father, Michel Péter (1824–93) had been a colleague of Professor Proust's at the Académie de Médicine and was a cousin of Louis Pasteur's. René Péter, who was a friend of Hahn's and Debussy's, often visited Proust at the Hôtel des Réservoirs because he lived in Versailles himself. They wrote a fairytale play together and planned another on the subject of sadism. Péter left a long correspondence with Proust.

PIERREBOURG, Baronne Aimery Harty de, *née* Marguerite Thomas-Galline (1856–1943). Under the pseudonym 'Claude Ferval', she published *L'Autre Amour* and *Le Plus Fort.* Paul Hervieu met this beautiful and talented woman at Madame Aubernon's house and fell in love with her. She lived apart from her husband, as Odette de Pierre lived apart from Verjus, Comte de Crécy. Like Odette, she maintained a glittering salon where Proust regularly came. In 1910 her daughter Madeleine, a model for Gilberte, married the Comte de Lauris, a model for Saint-Loup.

PLANTEVIGNES, Marcel (1889–1966). Son of a tie manufacturer. Proust met him in Cabourg in August 1908 when he was on holiday, and entertained him in his room at the Grand Hôtel every evening for long, confidential conversations. But Plantevignes did not keep them secret, and Proust sent him a haughty letter breaking off the relationship. His father came to see Proust, who considered himself seriously slandered and challenged the other to a duel without a word of explanation. In fact, a young girl had called Proust a pervert and Plantevignes had not come to his defence. They eventually made up the quarrel, and Octave, the young dandy in *Jeunes Filles*, is partly based on Plantevignes. His memoirs, *Avec Marcel Proust*, came out in 1966.

POLIGNAC, Edmond, Prince de (1834 – 8 August 1901). Son of Charles x's minister 'Ultra', he was a lordly character with a passion for music, painting and books. In 1865 he won first prize for composition at the Paris Conservatoire. He posed beside Charles Haas for Tissot's painting *Le Cercle de la rue Royale* in 1867. Proust used to say he was like 'a disused dungeon converted into a library'. Robert de Montesquiou and his cousin the Comtesse Greffulhe arranged his marriage on 15 December 1893 to the rich and musical Winnaretta Singer, who was thirty years his junior. In his studio in the rue Cortambert he would have large orchestras and choirs perform the music he composed. It was during one of their receptions that Proust heard Fauré's sonata. Proust used a remark of Polignac's for Bergotte: 'What can you do, as Anaxagoras said, life is a journey!' The musical career of Baldassare Silvande is based on Polignac's. In 1901 Proust attended his funeral, and remembered its grandeur when he came to describe Saint-Loup's funeral.

POLIGNAC, Princesse Edmond de, *née* Winnaretta Singer (USA, 1865 – London, 1943). Daughter of a rich American industrialist married to a Frenchwoman (Isabelle Boyer). She was passionately interested in music, and at the age of 16 met Gabriel Fauré, who was to remain a loyal friend. In 1887 her first marriage to Monsieur de Scey-Montbéliard took place, but it did not last and was annulled by Rome in 1892. After her marriage in 1893 to Prince Edmond de Polignac (see above) they moved in the highest social circles and were great patrons of the arts. In 1899 Maurice Ravel dedicated his *Pavane pour une infante défunte* to her. They bought the Palazzo Manzoni in Venice in 1900. In Paris, their house in the avenue Henri-Martin became the venue for annual art exhibitions where Winnaretta showed some of her own work; she also acquired several pictures by Monet. The couple were very friendly with Wagner, and went to stay at Bayreuth every summer. Proust went to see her on 31 August 1901, a few days after her husband's death; he saw her again in 1903 at the Princesse Hélène de Caraman-Chimay's house. She had just finished the translation of Thoreau's *Walden*, which he had wanted to do with Antoine Bibesco. In *Le Figaro* of 6 September 1903 he published 'Le Salon de la Princesse Edmond de Polignac' under the pen-name 'Horatio'. In 1907, after an absence of two years, Proust reappeared at her salon on 11 April to hear the first performance of Reynaldo Hahn's *Bal chez Béatrice d'Este*, and invited her to his first dinner party at the Ritz on 1 July. He saw her for the last time in 1922, at Madame Hennessy's party. Until 1929, she financed Serge Diaghilev's enterprise (she had had the idea of a Ballets Russes season since 1908), and she subsidised many composers – Stravinsky, Satie, Poulenc and Ravel among them – until her death in 1943. She endowed the Fondation Singer-Polignac, which is in her town house at 43 avenue Henri-Martin (now Georges-Mandel).

POLIGNAC, Pierre, Comte de (born Kerscamp, 24 October 1895). In March 1920, this friend of Proust's (whom he met in 1917) married Charlotte Grimaldi, adopted daughter of the Prince of Monaco. In June the then Prince Consort paid a visit to Proust, who found him 'even nicer than when he was Polignac'. But the following month Proust was annoyed when he did not subscribe to the de luxe edition of *Jeunes Filles*. The Comte de Nassau, who marries the Grand Duc de Luxembourg to 'the only daughter of another prince in his family', is an unflattering reflection of Polignac.

POREL, Jacques (born Paris, 25 March 1893). Son of the actress Réjane and the actor and theatre director Porel. He met Proust at Cabourg in 1911. In 1917 he had to leave the army (he was gassed at Ypres). That year, he dined at the Ritz with Proust and the Princesse Soutzo. Proust used to call him 'lightweight Porel'. He married Anne-Marie Duval-Foulc on 11 March 1918. When Proust lived in the rue Laurent-Pichat, from June to October 1919, Porel was living with his mother, and they were neighbours. After he moved out, Proust stayed in touch with him and in 1920 they met at a party where Vines was playing Debussy. On Réjane's death (13 June 1920) Porel asked Proust to write a piece for the *Nouvelle Revue Française*, but Proust was too ill. On 19 November 1922, Porel came to Proust's deathbed and slipped on to his finger a ring that Anatole France had given Réjane after the première of *Lys Rouge*. He was one of the originals of Berma's son-in-law.

PORTO-RICHE, Georges de (Bordeaux, 20 May 1849 – Paris, 4 September 1930). Playwright. He was a regular guest at the salons of Princesse Mathilde, Madame Aubernon, Madame Straus and Princesse Alexandre Bibesco, and was also entertained by the Prousts. In 1920 he became the administrator of the Bibliothèque Mazarine where Proust had held a post when young. In 1923 Porto-Riche was made a member of the Académie Française.

Works: *Le Vertige* (1873), *Un drame sous Philippe II* (1875), *Les Deux fautes* (1878), *La Chance de Françoise* (1889), *Amoureuse* (1891), *Les Malefilâtre* (1904), *Le Vieil Homme* (1911), *Zubiri* (1912), *Le Marchand d'estampes* (1917), *Les Vrais Dieux* (1929).

POTOCKA, Comtesse Nicolas, *née* Emmanuela Pignatelli (1852–1930). Proust first met her at the party on 30 May 1894 at the Pavillon Montesquiou. Her aristocratic salon was a meeting-place for Blanche, Bourget, Dr Pozzi, Maupassant and Jean Béraud. Proust was also a guest. The Comtesse was called 'the siren' and also, like Madame Verdurin, 'the boss'. Proust devoted an article to her in *Le Figaro* of 30 May 1904, signed 'Horatio': 'Le Salon de la Comtesse Potocka'. At the turn of the century she moved out to Auteuil to devote herself to her greyhounds. This cruel and beautiful woman died there abandoned by everyone, and was eaten by rats.

POUQUET, Jeanne (Paris, 7 August 1874 – Saint-Médard-d'Excideuil, 14 July 1961). In May 1881, when she was 7, Nadar photographed Jeanne Pouquet dressed up as a fortune-teller. Several years later, when she had become a pretty young blonde, Proust met her at Madame Arman de

Caillavet's house; she had just become engaged to her son Gaston. Proust was instantly drawn to this girl who seemed 'as clear as a spring' (as he later wrote), and despite her engagement he courted her fiercely. He tried in vain to get hold of a photograph of her, as the narrator did with Gilberte: 'In order to obtain one I stooped to plaguing the Swanns' friends and even some photographers; this did not achieve what I wanted, but it meant I had made friends forever with some very boring people.' Jeanne married Gaston Arman de Caillavet on 11 April 1893, and Proust soon stopped loving her. Their daughter Somine (1894–1968), who later married André Maurois, became the model for Mademoiselle de Saint-Loup: 'Formed of the very years I had lost, she seemed like my Youth.' Widowed in January 1915, Jeanne went back to her maiden name at the end of the war when she married her cousin, Maurice Pouquet. Widowed a second time, she died in the Dordogne, at the Château d'Essonvieras.

POURTALÈS, Comtesse Edmond de, *née* Méanie de Bussière (1832?–1914). Proust saw her at the party on 30 May 1894 at the Pavillon Montesquiou. She had been one of the beauties of the Second Empire and posed among the Empress Eugénie's ladies-in-waiting in the famous picture by Winterhalter. The Comtesse invited Proust and Hahn to her salon, which included the Faubourg Saint-Germain circle as well as grand figures of European courts such as the Princess Metternich. She also entertained Proust's sworn enemy, Gustave Schlumberger.

PRÉVOST, Marcel (Paris, 1 May 1862 – Viane, 8 April 1941). Writer. A former student at the École polytechnique, he was an engineer until 1890 when he devoted himself entirely to literature. In 1905 Louisa de Mornand acted in *Les Demi-vierges*, one of his novels adapted for the stage. At a party given by the Comtesse de Mun in 1922 he wanted to greet Proust, but when he mentioned the fact that their admirers confused their names, Proust replied crisply and in a loud voice that such people made the mistake 'only initially'. According to Céleste Albaret Proust had not forgiven Prévost for having once written an article criticising him.

Works: *Le Scorpion* (1887), *Chonchette* (1888), *Mademoiselle Jauffre* (1889), *Laura* (1890), *La Confession d'un amant* (1891), *L'Automne d'une femme* (1893), *L'Heureux ménage* (1900), *Les Vierges fortes* (1900), *Lettres à Françoise* (1902).

RADZIWILL, Constantin, Prince (31 July 1850 – 1920). Member of a great and flamboyantly wealthy family of Polish origin, he was well known for his homosexual habits and his twelve handsome and energetic valets (to each of whom he had given a pearl necklace). In *Papillotes mondaines*, Montesquiou said: 'To speak of women would be uncivil / In the house of Constantin Radziwill.' Like the Prince de Guermantes in his later years, or the old Prince de Foix, he enjoyed the company of rough young men.

RADZIWILL, Léon, Prince (Château d'Ermenonville, 6 September 1880–1927). Son of the above, nicknamed 'Loche'. He was 23 when Proust met him at the end of 1902, after Bertrand de Fénelon had left for the Constantinople embassy. 'He was as broad as he was high, and he looked more like a block than a statue.' On New Year's Day 1903 he gave Proust an inkwell inscribed: 'A true friend is a sweet thing.' But the break came soon enough. One winter evening in 1903, alone in the dining room of Prince Radziwill's château in Ermenonville, Proust wrote a hurtful character sketch of his friend which was not published until 1927. Léon's voice was 'hilariously slow, with a fake good humour which seemed clogged by stupidity and naïvety'. Once this emotional storm had blown over, the friendship regained an even keel. Léon remained one of Proust's most regular visitors, like Reynaldo Hahn and Antoine Bibesco. He was the model for the Prince de Foix's son.

RÉGNIER, Henri de (Honfleur, 28 December 1864 – Paris, 23 May 1936). Poet. Like Proust, he was a member of the 'Académie canaque' in 1892; in 1895 he married its organiser, Marie de Hérédia. On 9 June 1897 he fought a duel with Montesquiou after a quarrel about the fire at the Bazar de la Charité. In September 1908 Proust took exception to an article by Régnier about pasticheurs which did not mention him: 'He has listed all the pasticheurs of the moment, even idiots, but not me.' He took his revenge in a stinging pastiche of Régnier's rococo prose which appeared in *Le Figaro* on 6 March 1909. Proust then received a generous letter from the poet: 'I think it is very like me.' In 1920, Régnier was one of the group of friends – Barrès and Léon Daudet among them – who took steps to make sure Proust was awarded the Cross of the Légion d'honneur.

REINACH, Joseph (Paris, 30 November 1856 – Paris, 18 April 1921). Politician. A lawyer, head of Gambetta's office in 1881, secretary of the Ligue des patriotes until 1886, he was elected member of parliament for the Basses-Alpes in 1889. Proust met him in 1896 through Madame Straus; he was 25 and Reinach, who was 40, considered him a sophisticate. At the Straus's house in October 1897 he proclaimed Dreyfus's innocence: Jules Lemaitre and Gustave Schlumberger left the party. Under his influence Madame Straus's salon became the headquarters of the pro-Dreyfus faction, and he himself played an important part in Captain Dreyfus's rehabilitation. Proust wrote to him during this time. From 1915 to 1919 he used the pen-name 'Polybe' for his daily column in *Le Figaro* about the war (in which he had lost his son and his son-in-law). On 27 July 1917 he dined at the Ritz with Proust, Paul Morand and the Princesse Soutzo. Proust made a sarcastic remark about him on this occasion: 'He always seems rather like Consul, the monkey who could smoke, dine in a restaurant and pay the bill, and from time to time a glimmer of something almost human would pass across his face.' When he died in 1921 Proust suggested to Jacques Rivière a 'comic obituary' for the *Nouvelle Revue Française*, but Rivière turned the idea down with alacrity. Reinach was one of the models for Brichot, who (like him) writes pretentious articles about the war.

RÉJANE, Gabrielle Réju, known as Réjane (Paris, 1856 – Paris, 1920) Actress. In 1874 she was awarded second prize at the Conservatoire. She began her career at the Vaudeville theatre in 1875, and later married its director, Porel (they divorced in 1904). She created the role of *Germinie Lacerteux* by Edmond de Goncourt in 1888. Proust invited Madame Straus, her son Jacques Bizet and Jacques Baignères to the première of this play, which caused a scandal. In 1905 she acquired the Nouveau-Théâtre, which became the Théâtre Réjane. Proust became properly acquainted with her when he moved in to the fourth floor of her town house, where he lived from June to October 1919, but the idol of his youth was by then an old woman with a bad heart. She died on 13 June 1920, while she was making the film of *Miarka* by Jean Richepin. The character of Berma was partly based on her.

RENAN, Ernest (Tréguier, 28 February 1823 – Paris, 2 October 1892). Writer and philosopher. Proust paid him a visit on 17 January 1889 and after a long conversation Renan gave him an inscribed copy of *La Vie de Jésus* (which had had great success on its publication in 1863). Proust wrote a pastiche of Renan on 28 March 1908 in *Le Figaro*. Bergotte's spiral nose belonged to him, and the invocation of Koraï was suggested by *Prière sur l'Acropole* (published in 1883).

RISLER, Édouard (Baden-Baden, 23 February 1873 – Paris, 22 July 1929). French pianist. In 1895 he accompanied Proust's poem sequence, *Portraits de peintres*, which was recited at Madame Lemaire's house with music by Reynaldo Hahn. Proust admired him, and when he gave a grand dinner at the Ritz in 1907 he asked Risler to come and play instead of Fauré, who was ill. He played Chopin, Couperin, Fauré and, at Proust's request, the overture to *Die Meistersinger* and the death of Isolde from *Tristan und Isolde*. He inspired the character of the pianist Dechambre in *A la Recherche*.

RIVIÈRE, Jacques (Bordeaux, 15 July 1886 – Paris, 14 February 1925). Writer. Educated by the Jesuits in Bordeaux, then at the lycée Lakanal, he met the writer Alain-Fournier (1886–1914) and married his sister. From 1910 he was a contributor to the *Nouvelle Revue Française*, and its editor from 1919 until his death. He considered Proust one of the greatest French writers, and Proust, for whom he acted as intermediary in his negotiations with Gaston Gallimard, valued him highly. In a letter dated 7 February 1914, Proust expressed his delight at having found 'a reader who realises that my book is a dogmatic work and a structure!' In 1920, when he was suffering from neurasthenia and had financial problems, he was worried about his pregnant wife's health; Proust sent him to his cousin, Dr Roussy, who advised him without charging any fee. On 30 September Proust managed to get the Blumenthal Prize of 12,000 francs awarded to him. He also supported his novel *Aimée*, which was dedicated to Proust, for the Balzac Prize, but Rivière refused to let Proust talk to Léon Daudet about him, which cost him the prize.

Works: *Études* (1912), *L'Allemand* (1918), *Aimée* (1922), *A la trace de Dieu* (1925), *De la sincérité envers soi-même* (1943), *Nouvelles Études (1947)*.

Correspondence: Avec Alain-Fournier (1905–14), *Avec Paul Claudel* (1907–24), *Avec Marcel Proust* (1914–22).

ROBERT, Louis de (Paris, 5 March 1871 – Sannois, 1937). Writer. Proust met him in about 1898 when he worked for the Edison company. The Dreyfus affair was at its height, and they attended the Zola trial together. In March 1911, Proust got in touch with him again: Robert was by then an invalid. He had won the Prix Fémina in 1909 for his psychological novel *Le Roman d'un Malade* – the work brought them closer. Proust talked to him about the beginnings of *A la Recherche*: 'I've been working on a long project I call a novel, because it isn't contingent on memory [?]' (L. de Robert, *Comment débuta Marcel Proust*, p. 20). Proust later asked his advice about publishers. On 10 February 1913, Robert received this reply from his friend Humblot, to whom he had recommended Proust: 'I may be narrow-minded, but I cannot understand how someone can take thirty pages to describe how he tosses and turns in bed before getting to sleep.' A few months later, when Proust learnt that Robert was having emotional difficulties, he offered his help: 'I have not only reconciled friends to each other, but also lovers and marriages.' Robert was the first person to read the whole of *Swann*, and Proust called him 'Swann's first friend'. In November 1913 Robert suggested he submit his book to Colette, but without success. In 1919 Proust asked for his support in the Prix Goncourt. Robert left two accounts of their friendship: *Comment débuta Marcel Proust* (1925) and *De Loti à Proust* (1929).

ROCHAT, Henri. A young Swiss employed at the Ritz who went to work for Proust as his secretary at the beginning of 1919. In fact his main function was to entertain him, and they played countless games of draughts together (as the narrator did with Albertine). But Proust gradually became bored with him. In 1921 he asked his friend Horace Finaly, the director of the Banque de Paris et des Pays-Bas, to find Rochat a job in Buenos Aires, and Henri left for the Argentine on 4 June. He was Proust's last major love affair. Like Albertine, he had 'an astonishing natural bent for painting' and, like Morel, 'magnificent handwriting spoilt by the grossest spelling mistakes'.

ROSTAND, Maurice (Paris, 26 May 1891 – Ville-d'Avray, 1968). Writer. When Proust was looking for a publisher, Maurice Rostand wrote recommending him to Fasquelle, who published his father, the poet Edmond Rostand (1868–1918). Early in 1913 Rostand wanted to meet

Proust, who suggested a rendez-vous at six o'clock in the morning in front of Nôtre-Dame. Rostand declined the invitation, but continued to write enthusiastic letters. In the end Proust asked him to supper at Larue's (at about midnight) one evening in May, after a performance by the Ballets Russes. Afterwards, Proust and Rostand went back to the boulevard Haussmann where Proust read him the proofs of *Swann*. On 26 December Rostand wrote an article for *Comœdia* which was so extravagant in its praise of the work it made Proust furious (he compared Proust to Pascal, Shakespeare and Leonardo da Vinci).

SAGAN, Boson, Prince de (Paris, 1832 – Paris, 1910). Boni de Castellane's uncle. An arbiter of taste who frequented the foyer of the Comédie-Française (a fashionable meeting-place) with his friends Robert de Fitz-James, General de Galliffet, Charles Haas and Louis de Turenne. In 1908 he suffered an attack of paralysis and was consigned to a wheelchair, like Charlus. Part of his first name was borrowed for the Duc de Guermantes.

SAGAN, Princesse Boson de, *née* Jeanne Seillière (1839–1905). She came from a family of self-made barons of the Second Empire, and was related to Madame Aubernon and Baron Doäzan. She married the Prince de Sagan in 1859. In Trouville, in summer, Proust often visited her house, the Villa Persane, and her seaside walks inspired the description in *A la Recherche* of the Princesse de Luxembourg's walks in Balbec, escorted by a little black servant. In 1885 she gave a famous ball which Charles Haas and the Chevignés attended in animal costumes. She ended her life insane.

SAINT-PAUL, Diane, Marquise de, *née* Feydeau de Brou. Daughter of an upper-class family, her salon in the rue Nitot was a meeting-place for the whole of Faubourg Saint-Germain society. Every Thursday she gave brilliant concerts, which Proust often attended. Her acid tongue and high spirits earned her the nickname 'Serpent of the sonatas'. Montesquiou said of her that 'it was equally annoying for paganism and for Christianity that she should be called both Diana and Saint-Paul'. In his article on Madame Lemaire's salon which appeared in *Le Figaro* in 1903, Proust described Madame de Saint-Paul recruiting future guests (as Madame de Saint-Euverte does at the Princesse de Guermantes' party). She was the main model for Madame de Saint-Euverte.

SAINT-SAËNS, Camille (Paris, 9 October 1835 – Alger, 16 December 1921). Composer. A child prodigy and piano virtuoso, student at the Conservatoire, in 1871 he founded the Société nationale de musique with Bizet, Fauré, Franck, Lalo, Duparc and Massenet. He taught Reynaldo Hahn, and shared his sexual inclinations. Proust met him with Hahn at Madame Lemaire's in Dieppe in August 1895. To please Hahn, Proust wrote two articles on Saint-Saëns in *Le Gaulois* (they appeared on 14 January and 14 December 1895); their tone was appreciative but conveyed some reservations: 'Saint-Saëns makes archaism present his credentials to modernity; little by little he brings the value of original imagination to the common ground between the two, through the erudite, singular and sublime properties of his musical expression; he is a musical humanist.' However, his music supplied the 'little phrase' of Vinteuil's sonata. It may have been at Madame Lemaire's that Proust first heard Saint-Saëns' piano and violin sonata in D minor; he became obsessed by the principal theme of the first movement. He often asked Hahn to play the sonata to him when he visited him in his room at 6 rue du Cirque. In *Jean Santeuil*, Françoise – the hero's mistress – plays the Saint-Saëns piece, identified by its real name.

SAINT-VICTOR, Claire de. Daughter of the famous critic Paul de Saint-Victor (1827–81) and a fierce supporter of Dreyfus, she was nicknamed 'Nôtre-Dame de la Révision'. Madame Aubernon said her salon was 'the mirror of mine'. She was one of the models for Madame Verdurin.

SALIGNAC-FÉNELON, Bertrand, Comte de (1878 – 17 December 1914). Proust met him in the autumn of 1901 through Antoine Bibesco, with whom he was friendly. In the secret society he formed with the Bibesco brothers, his nickname was 'Nonelef' (an anagram of Fénelon). From the start Proust tried to encourage rivalry between Antoine and Bertrand, for his own ends, but he did not succeed. According to George D. Painter, Proust went to Coucy with the Bibesco brothers, Robert de Billy, Lauris and Fénelon on 28 March 1902 (Good Friday). In the dungeon, Proust seized Fénelon's arm, and the latter cheered him up by singing the 'Good Friday' passage from Parsifal (as Saint-Loup does for the narrator in *A la Recherche*). At about the end of May, Fénelon made a spectacle of himself at Larue's: he walked along the back of the seats to bring Proust his coat (Proust described the scene in *Jean Santeuil* with Bertrand de Réveillon, and later with Saint-Loup in *Le Côté de Guermantes*). On 3 October 1902 he and Proust left for Holland. But this journey, although of great emotional importance, was not a success, as he wrote to his mother on 17 October from Haarlem: 'I have been alone since yesterday. I am in such a disastrous emotional state that I am worried I shall ruin poor Fénelon's trip with my depression, so I have let him have a breathing-space away from my moans and groans!'

On his return, Fénelon was appointed attaché to the French embassy in Constantinople. Before he left, he went to see Proust with Georges de Lauris; Proust, who was in a very excitable state, flew into a rage with him and trampled on his hat (a scene which reappears in *Guermantes* when the narrator squashes Charlus's hat). Later, their love changed to deep friendship. In *A la Recherche* Proust describes Saint-Loup (who was based on Fénelon) as 'the most intelligent, good, brave being, unforgettable to anyone who knew him'.

In August 1914 Fénelon, who was then a diplomat in Christiana, volunteered. At the first battle of the Artois on 17 December 1914, he was reported missing at Mametz. The news of his death was not confirmed until much later, and it was announced in *Le Figaro* on 15 March 1915 (only his wallet was ever found). Like Saint-Loup, Bertrand de Fénelon was homosexual, and Proust only understood this very late. 'Proust did not invent it – his information came from the most reliable sources – the ravishing young man with blue eyes, darling of the turn-of-the-century society ladies, on whom Saint-Loup was based, was thoroughly versed in heterodox practices, or rather, in what we called in the slang of those days "bimétallisme".' (Paul Morand, preface to *Le Visiteur du soir, op. cit.*).

SAUSSINE, Henri, Comte du Pont de Grault (Bézins, 4 October 1859 – 1949). A dilettante, amateur musician and music critic. In his salon at 16 rue Saint-Guillaume Proust met the pianist Delafosse in 1893. At the Salle Érard on 5 May 1894, the latter played Saussine's *Fantaisie* as an accompaniment to Montesquiou's poems *Les Chauves-souris*. Proust probably also met Fauré through Saussine, and it was under his influence that Proust learned to appreciate Wagner and César Franck.

SCHEIKÉVITCH, Marie (1884–1964). She was the daughter of a Russian aristocrat and the divorced wife of Pierre Carolus-Duran, son of the painter. Barrès nicknamed her 'Our Lady of the Sleeping-cars'. In 1912 Reynaldo Hahn asked her to recommend Proust to her lover Adrien Hébrard, the director of *Le Temps*, whom she called 'Nounou'. In mid-August, she sought Proust out at the Grand Hôtel in Cabourg with Gaston Calmette. They had two conversations. Madame Scheikévitch became a faithful friend of Proust's and played a part in launching *Swann*. Proust may have been thinking of her when he created the character of Madame Timoléon d'Amoncourt in *Sodome et Gomorrhe*. In November 1913 she finally persuaded Hébrard to send Élie-Joseph Bois to interview Proust after the publication of *Swann* and to run an article by Paul Souday the following month. In about November 1915, Proust covered the blank pages of his friend's copy of *Swann* with the famous résumé of the whole story of Albertine. After a dinner at the Crillon in November 1917 their relationship became strained because of some unpleasant remarks Madame Scheikévitch made. In 1922, in a gesture of reconciliation after his death, she asked Céleste to return to her the cigarette-lighter made of two English pennies that she had given Proust in 1917, and which he mentions in *A la Recherche*. In 1935, Plon published her *Souvenirs d'un temps disparu* and her 'Marcel Proust et Céleste' appeared in *Œuvres libres* in 1960.

SCHIFF, Mr and Mrs Sydney. Sydney Schiff (1871–1946) and his wife Violet, *née* Beddington, were a rich and intelligent English couple, patrons of writers and artists. Sydney, who was a talented novelist under his pen-name Stephen Hudson, had dedicated his novel *Richard Kurt* to Proust in 1919, before he met him. He was to translate *Le Temps retrouvé* into English after Scott-Moncrieff's death. They had read *Swann* with great enthusiasm in London during the war. In the correspondence that covers the years from April 1920 to September 1922, Proust calls Mrs Schiff 'Violet angel' and 'hidden, scented, marvellous flower'. In the year of the Goncourt Prize Sydney Schiff made Proust the useful suggestion of publishing an extract of his book in the July number of the review *Art and Letters*. Proust saw them at the Ritz on 2 May 1922 and invited them to the rue Hamelin with his sister-in-law Marthe and Suzy, his niece. The Schiffs invited Suzy to England, to the indignation of Proust, who considered her too young to visit such a distant country.

On 18 May, after the first performance of Stravinsky's *Fox*, the Schiffs gave a grand supper in honour of Stravinsky, Diaghilev, Picasso, Joyce and Proust.

SCHLUMBERGER, Gustave (Guebwiller, 17 October 1844 – Paris, 1929). Byzantine historian. He was fiercely anti-Dreyfus, and he quickly disappeared from Madame Straus's salon in October 1897. In 1908, Proust planned to write an article against his recent academic nominations: 'Schlumber (sic) seems to me a national disgrace, the triumph of all that is base and stupid' (letter dated 15 June 1908 to Madame Straus). At the Princesse Murat's party on 22 June, Proust took his revenge on Schlumberger in a childish fashion: he walked 'in front of him twenty times without saying good day', repeating: 'I shall say good day to him when he says good day to Madame Straus; she couldn't care less but I could' (letter to Madame Straus of 22 June). Their antipathy was mutual, and in *Mes souvenirs*, which appeared in 1934, Schlumberger declared Proust's work to be 'completely incomprehensible'.

SCHWARTZ, Gabrielle. A friend with whom the young Proust played in the Champs-Élysées. On the boulevard Bineau tennis-courts at Neuilly in the summer of 1891 she was photographed with Proust, who was holding his racket like a guitar. She later married Lucien Klotz, the Minister of Finance.

'SEM' (Georges Goursat, known as Sem), (Périgueux, 23 November 1863 – Paris, 1934). Cartoonist. In 1900 he published a collection of caricatures called *Les Sportsmen* which made him famous in artistic and literary circles. Like Montesquiou, Proust admired his work. When on holiday in Normandy in the summer of 1907, Sem tried to dissuade Proust from his esteem for the Italian primitives. 'Sem and Helleu who are *very intelligent* have both tried separately to persuade me that primitive art is worthless' (letter to Georges de Lauris of 27 August 1907).

Works: *Un pékin sur le front* (1916), *La Ronde de nuit* (1928). He illustrated Georges Courteline's *Messieurs les ronds-de-cuir*.

SERT, José-Maria (Barcelona, 24 December 1876 – Barcelona, December 1945). Spanish painter, son of a rich industrial family from Barcelona. He came to Paris where his studio was on the top floor of the luxurious town house he owned in the rue Barbet-de-Jouy (before he moved to the avenue de Ségur). In 1914 he married Misia Godebska, who had already been divorced twice, from Thadée Natanson and Alfred Edwards. He was a great admirer of Tiepolo (1696–1770), who was his inspiration, and every year he went to Venice to see the Dolfin palace and to Wurtzburg, where the artist painted *Les Quatre Parties du monde de la résidence*. In 1914 he designed the costumes for *La Légende de Joseph*, a ballet by Diaghilev (who was very friendly with his wife); Proust admired the costumes enormously, and compared them to the Fortuny and Carpaccio dresses the narrator buys for Albertine.

SOUTZO, Princesse Dimitri, *née* Hélène Chrissoveloni (Galatz, Romania, 5 February 1879 – Paris, 26 February 1975). A princess of Greco-Romanian origin. On 4 March 1917 Proust was introduced to her at Larue's by her future husband, Paul Morand. They developed the habit of dining several times a week in her apartment at the Ritz. He kept up a long correspondence with her, which Morand published in *Le Visiteur du soir*. It was to her that Proust spoke, in November 1918, of the 'miraculous, dizzying Peace'. She features in his revised pastiche of Saint-Simon, at the end of the year, as 'the only woman, unfortunately for me, who can make me leave my retreat'.

STANDISH, Madame Henry, *née* Hélène des Cars (1847–1933). Madame Greffulhe's friend and first cousin. The Faubourg Saint-Germain nick-named her 'Missis' and Queen Alexandra imitated her in everything. She had been the mistress of General Galliffet and the future Edward VII. Proust mentions her under her real name in *Sodome et Gomorrhe*: 'It would take a lesson to explain to certain stupid young people why Madame Standish is at least as great a lady as the Duchesse de Doudeauville.' On 24 May 1912 she was in Madame Greffulhe's box at the Vaudeville theatre, and Proust noticed how elegantly dressed she was. He muddled up the evenings when he told Madame Gaston de Caillavet about it: 'One night Madame Greffulhe took me to the Opéra with Madame Standish to see a performance by the Monte Carlo ballet. I learnt that they had two very different, quite opposite ways of approaching elegance in dress' (letter of July 1912). He made use of this contrast when he described the outfits the Princesse and the Duchesse de Guermantes wore to the Opéra in *Le Côté de Guermantes*.

STRAUS, Émile (1844–1929). A rich Jewish lawyer friendly with Joseph Reinach, and possibly the illegitimate brother of the Rothschilds. In 1889 he married Geneviève Halévy (1849–1926), the widow of Georges Bizet. At first, Straus thought that Proust was a bad influence on his stepson, Jacques Bizet (who had introduced Proust to his mother's salon), but later paid him a reconciliatory visit in the boulevard Malesherbes. In 1914 he examined the contract between Proust and Grasset at the time of the negotiations with N.R.F. He and his wife looked after the sale of Proust's furniture in November 1917 and November 1918. He stayed a loyal friend to Proust all his life, and kept up a substantial correspondence with him; Proust also had a high regard for Straus. He was a collector of pictures (Gustave Moreau, Pissarro, Monet, Eugène Boudin), and had acquired his love of impressionists from Geneviève Straus. An important model for Swann: like the character, Straus devoted his large fortune to his beautiful wife's clothes and social position (he appears in *Jeunes Filles* when Swann, like him, glances into his wife's salon from behind a curtain). He was also a model for the Duc de Guermantes: he prized his wife's wit and adored her even though she sometimes made him jealous.

STRAUS, Madame Émile, *née* Geneviève Halévy (1849–1926). Daughter of the composer Jacques-Fromental Halévy (1799–1862), who wrote *La Juive*. On 3 June 1869 she married Georges Bizet (1838–75), her father's former student in composition classes at the Conservatoire, composer of *Carmen* (1874) and *L'Arlésienne* (1872). They had one son, Jacques. After Bizet's death in 1875, she married Émile Straus in 1889. Her looks, clothes and wit were all equally charming. In 1888 Proust, who had been a friend of her son's since the lycée Condorcet, began to visit the round salon in the boulevard Haussmann where Madame Straus entertained the Faubourg Saint-Germain set and the artistic and literary world. She remained a very close friend of Proust's even after he completely lost touch with her son Jacques, and exchanged many letters with him. In 1908 she made him a gift of the little notebooks which he used for the manuscript of *A la Recherche*. In November 1922 she lost Proust and her son Jacques within a fortnight of each other, and she never recovered from the blow. She herself died four years later. Proust used some of her characteristics for the Duchesse de Guermantes, who is famous for her witty repartee in *A la Recherche*.

TRARIEUX, Gabriel (born in Bordeaux, 17 December 1870). Symbolist poet. He was a friend of Proust and Robert de Billy's at the École des sciences politiques in 1890. The following year he features in the photograph taken on the boulevard Bineau tennis-courts in Neuilly, where Proust is at the feet of Jeanne Pouquet. Proust probably met André Gide for the first time through Trarieux, who also helped with the production of *Le Banquet* from March 1892 to March 1893.

TURENNE, Louis, Comte de Turenne d'Aynac (1843? – Paris, 3 December 1907). A habitué of the salons of Madame de Chevigné, Madame Straus, Princesse Mathilde and Comtesse Greffulhe, an intimate friend of Charles Haas and the Prince of Wales, he was the epitome of the 'cercleux' (the members of the most fashionable sets) of the time. Like Bréauté, who was based on him, he considered himself an art lover. Proust mentions his monocle in the dedication to Lacretelle: 'Monsieur de Palancy's monocle really belongs to poor dear Louis de Turenne [...]. The Turenne monocle then passes to Monsieur de Bréauté in *Le Côté de Guermantes*, I think.'

ULRICH, Robert (born about 1881). Nephew of Félicie Fitau, the Prousts' old cook. He was intermittently employed as Proust's secretary in the boulevard Haussmann until 1 July 1907, and he reappeared briefly in Cabourg in 1909. He turned up at the boulevard Haussmann one afternoon in July 1913, unemployed and hungry: Proust telephoned Jacques Bizet's wife to find him a job. Joseph Périgot, Françoise's valet in *Le Côté de Guermantes*, is partly based on him.

VAUDOYER, Jean-Louis (Le Plesses-Robinson, 1883 – Paris, 1963). Writer. From 1910 onwards he supported the Ballets Russes in *La Revue de Paris*, and interested Proust in this new artistic movement. He wrote a brilliant article in *L'Opinion* in May 1921 on the exhibition of Dutch art at the Jeu de Paume: he was deeply interested in art criticism before devoting his time to literature. At 9.15 a.m. on 24 May, Proust sent his chauffeur Odilon to fetch him to go to the Dutch exhibition; while they were there, Proust suffered an attack of dizziness, and Vaudoyer took his arm and steered him towards Vermeer's *View of Delft* (Proust remembered this when he wrote Bergotte's death scene). None the less, he was strong enough to accompany Vaudoyer to the Ingres exhibition in the rue de la Ville-l'Évêque.

Works: *L'Amour masqué* (1908), *La Bien-Aimée* (1909), *La Maîtresse et l'amie* (1912), *La Reine évanouie* (1923), *Raymonde Mangematin* (1925), *Les Délices de l'Italie* (1924), *Beautés de la Provence* (1926), *Peintres provençaux* (1947), *L'Italie retrouvée* (1950).

VUILLARD, Édouard (Cuiseaux, 11 November 1868 – La Baule, 21 June 1940). Painter. A former pupil at Condorcet and friend of Antoine Bibesco, he often visited Princesse Alexandre Bibesco's salon, as did Bonnard and Odilon Redon. In June 1903 he made a sketch of Proust, the Bibescos and their friends at dinner in Ermenonville. The following year, Proust tried to get hold of the sketch, which he considered a 'unique coincidence of his admirable talent, which so often fertilises my memory, and a moment of perfect happiness in my life' (letter to Antoine Bibesco dated 28 March 1904). Proust went to visit the artist in his studio when he was on holiday in Cabourg in 1907. He told Hahn: 'He said, with great intensity, "a chap like Giotto, don't you think, or perhaps a chap like Titian, don't you think, knew just as well as Monet, don't you think, a chap like Raphael, etc.". He says chap about once every twenty seconds but he is a rare being' (letter of September 1907). Elstir, who uses the same expressions in *Jeunes Filles*, was based on him, among other painters.

WAGRAM, Princesse Alexandre Pouthier de, *née* Berthe de Rothschild. In December 1893 Proust received invitations from the Princesse de Wagram and her sister the Duchesse de Gramont. It was a foothold in the salons of the Faubourg Saint-Germain, even though they were both slightly déclassé, as they were born Rothschilds. At the Princesse de Wagram's in 1894 Proust first met the Comtesse Greffulhe with her hairstyle of 'Polynesian grace'.

WARU, Gustave, Comte de. Madame de Chevigné's nephew. In 1893 he became acquainted with Proust, who was doing everything in his power to get to know the Comtesse. Proust thought he looked like a bird – a characteristic of Saint-Loup and the Guermantes family. In June he asked Waru to the dinner he gave for his ten best friends in the boulevard Malesherbes.

WHISTLER, James Abbott McNeill (Lowell, Massachusetts, 10 July 1834 – London, 17 July 1903). American painter. A friend of Montesquiou and of Blanche's who painted two portraits of Montesquiou in 1891; Montesquiou adopted his bearing and his expressions. In 1897 Hahn introduced him to Proust at Méry Laurent's. 'I only met Wisthler (sic) myself on one occasion, when I made him say something good about Ruskin! and kept his very nice grey gloves which I have since lost' (letter of February 1905 to Louisa de Mornand). Proust was fascinated by the painter, who had been Ruskin's declared adversary since their famous lawsuit in 1878. On 15 June 1905 he visited the Whistler exhibition at the École des beaux-arts. In *Swann* he describes one of his pictures, *The Opal Beach*, which Legrandin sites close to Balbec. Whistler was among the models for Elstir, whose name comes partly from his.

WILDE, Oscar (Dublin, 16 October 1854 – Paris, 20 November 1900). Irish writer. Oscar Wilde was in Paris in the spring of 1894 and visited Madame Straus's salon; Proust dined with him at Madame Arman de Caillavet's. According to Fernand Gregh: 'They eyed each other with a complicated kind of curiosity.' Wilde also paid a visit to 9 boulevard Malesherbes where, like Charlus in the narrator's home, he made disparaging remarks about the furniture, to Proust's great displeasure. Charlus may have been slightly coloured by Wilde's decadence, and Morel by that of the beautiful and equivocal Lord Alfred Douglas, who dogged Wilde's footsteps in the offices of *La Revue blanche* in the rue Lafitte. Charlus himself refers to Wilde in *Sodome et Gomorrhe*: 'I don't recall which man of taste it was who replied, when asked which event in his life had touched him most deeply: "The death of Lucien de Rubempré in *Splendeurs et misères*."' The 'man of taste' was Wilde, who made that reply in *Intentions*, which was translated in 1906.

YEATMAN, Léon (1873–1930). Proust met him in 1893 and invited him to the famous dinner for his friends in June of the same year. Yeatman was an excellent mimic, and from 18 to 20 March 1897 he imitated Proust's voice in the three performances of the show Jacques Bizet organised to parody *Les Plaisirs et les jours*, entitled *Les Lauriers sont coupés*. He was passionately pro-Dreyfus, and signed the *Manifeste des cent-quatre*. In 1900 Proust saw the Yeatmans often. At the beginning of February they were astonished to be woken up by Proust's father's footman, whom Proust had sent to ask them where the heart of the poet

Shelley was buried. Proust and Yeatman visited the church of Saint-Wolfran at Abbeville in September 1901, to help with Proust's articles on Ruskin. Yeatman's uncle was Maurice Barrès' electoral agent.

YTURRI, Gabriel d' (Tucuman, 1868 – Paris, 6 July 1905). He was born in Argentina and emigrated to Paris at the age of about 15. The Baron Doäzan discovered him working behind the counter at the Grands Magazins du Louvre, and made him his secretary until Montesquiou took him away. Proust, who knew him well through his relationship with Montesquiou, often wrote to him. D'Yturri accompanied Montesquiou on a trip to the United States in February 1903, and Proust compared them to St Paul and Timothy. On 6 July 1905, d'Yturri died of diabetes in Neuilly; on two occasions Proust had sent his mother to enquire after him, but the second time she arrived too late: he had just died. On 27 June 1908 Montesquiou gave a public reading of 'Le Chancelier des fleurs', in memory of his secretary. Proust was annoyed not to be invited to the ceremony, and complained to Montesquiou in a letter a few days later.

II

The Work

CHAPTER ONE

List of Proust's Works

A la Recherche du temps perdu

The novel is difficult to summarise, as impressions and memories are as important as events. Moreover, the play of memory gives the action a time sequence which is not linear. And Proust, whose constant pre-occupation was to establish and demonstrate general principles and to draw abstractions, constantly intervenes in the plot and shatters it.

The cycle comprises seven works or sections: *Du Côté de chez Swann* (1913), *A l'ombre des jeunes filles en fleurs* (1919), *Le Côté de Guermantes* (1920–21), *Sodome et Gomorrhe* (1921–22), *La Prisonnière* (1923), *Albertine disparue* or *La Fugitive* (1925), *Le Temps retrouvé* (1927).

OVERALL SUBJECT The story of a life from childhood to maturity; this life is illuminated by a literary vocation. Each of the seven parts corresponds to a stage in the life, a moment in time, a place and a precise milieu, as well as characters the narrator finds revealing. These different moments lead up to the final revelation of the work to be accomplished, marked by the seal of time. *Le Temps retrouvé* thus brings the progression to 'the most objective and credible of conclusions'.

GENESIS From 1895 (the year he began *Jean Santeuil*) until his death in 1922 Proust never stopped working on the project which became *A la Recherche*. After 1908 (when he abandoned *Contre Sainte-Beuve*) he set to work on it in real earnest.

ORIGINALITY The narrative writing in *A la Recherche* is unique. Its formal originality was not conscious, however: Proust simply wished to carry his artistic beliefs to their natural conclusion. *Jean Santeuil* and

Contre Sainte-Beuve both contain scenes and characters which are later fleshed out for their reappearance in *A la Recherche*. The preface to *Contre Sainte-Beuve* mentions the importance of involuntary memory, founded on the correlation between time and memory which is so important in the work. According to George D. Painter, Proust actually experienced the episode with the madeleine (which might also have been a biscuit) on 1 January 1909. Whether this event took place or not, the discovery – one which Chateaubriand had already used – remains fundamental to the overall plan of *A la Recherche*.

The work follows a precise directional line: the opposition between Time lost and Time recaptured which assures a symmetrical effect. Proust also wrote a part of the last section at the same time as the first. The whole novel plays on the complementary oppositions of art and reality, the child and the adult world, the world and its representation. Proust wrote: 'People fail to recognise that my books have a structure, but one with a span wide enough so that the rigour of this structure, to which I have sacrificed everything, will be slow to reveal itself.' He was inspired by the great cycles, Balzac's novels and Wagner's operas. Each section is as much independent as it is integral to the whole. The joyful parts at the beginning, like *Jeunes Filles*, call up the sombre sections at the end, like *Sodome et Gomorrhe*. The whole structure rests on a single character who is simultaneously the narrator and the central hero, whom Proust presents in the first person, 'I', or in the third person, 'Marcel'. This gives a temporal and spatial unity to the story, but also ensures its mobility and the ease with which it evolves by the diversity of viewpoint. Originally, *Le Temps perdu* balanced *Le Temps retrouvé*. When it was to be published by Grasset, it was a triptych: *Le Temps retrouvé* was preceded by *Swann* and *Le Côté de Guermantes*, which subdivided to form *Sodome et Gomorrhe*, which in turn underwent the same process. *La Prisonnière* and *La Fugitive* came out of *Sodome et Gomorrhe III. A la Recherche*, which seems to end with the revelations of *Le Temps retrouvé* through constant progression, is also a return to deep sources through the help of 'anamnesia'. The loop closes back on itself with the last page of the work.

The narrator becomes a writer to describe a narrator who becomes a writer. As in Balzac, characters appear and disappear in reality and in memory, seen from ever-changing viewpoints. They summon each

LIST OF PROUST'S WORKS 235

other up. Gilberte, who is reminiscent of Odette, merges into Albertine. Proust also makes use of metaphors and signs, 'winks' as Auguste Anglès has it. Situations and themes are set up to repeat themselves: failed love, society parties, jealousy, bereavements, homosexual encounters. This game of correspondences ends in *Le Temps retrouvé*. The reality of people and things at last appears at the end of the journey.

CHRONOLOGY OF *A LA RECHERCHE* (as reconstructed by Willy Hachez)

1879. Marriage of the narrator's parents. Swann meets Odette. 30 January: Grévy becomes President of the Republic. 18 December: Paris-Murcie fête. End of 1879: Swann and Odette 'do a cattleya' (make love, in their private language).

1880. The relationship between Swann and Odette deteriorates. June: Swann hears the musical phrase again at the Saint-Euverte party. July: The narrator is born. October/November: Gilberte (the daughter of Odette), Albertine, Morel, Mademoiselle Vinteuil and the *'jeunes filles en fleurs'* are born. End of 1880 – early 1881: Odette goes on a Mediterranean cruise lasting two years.

1881. At the beginning of the year: Swann meets Madame Cottard on an omnibus; she tells him that Odette adores him. His jealousy assuaged, he leaves for Combray to see Madame de Cambremer-Legrandin.

1885. The narrator and his mother pay a New Year visit to Aunt Léonie, who always spends the winter in Paris. He has to give a 5-franc piece to Françoise.

1888. He goes to see his Uncle Adolphe, who is entertaining Odette that day; because of this affair the uncle is excluded from the family circle and no longer welcome at Combray.

1889. Swann marries Odette.

1890. The narrator has to go to bed without his goodnight kiss from his mother when Swann comes to stay with Aunt Léonie at Combray.

1892. Holidays at Combray. He goes for walks in the direction of Tansonville, where he sees Gilberte, and towards Guermantes, where he never reaches the château. His attention is caught by two ladies. He attends the wedding of Dr Percepied's daughter at Combray and sees the Duchesse de Guermantes. In Paris, he goes to see Madame Swann.

1894. Vinteuil's daughter is living a scandalous life with her female friend. The narrator, who is 14, masturbates and discovers sex for the first time on Aunt Léonie's sofa with one of his cousins. Aunt Léonie dies in the autumn; he inherits from her. He reads Augustin Thierry. Françoise, Aunt Léonie's servant, goes to work for his parents.

1895. Early in the year: the narrator, who is now 15, wants to visit Florence and Venice, but has to give up the idea because of ill health. He meets Gilberte in the Champs-Élysées. He goes to see Berma at the theatre. Monsieur de Norpois dines with his parents, and talks of King Théodose's visit.

1896. 1 January: the narrator suggests to Gilberte that they build their friendship afresh, but the relationship deteriorates after a happy beginning. October: He goes out again with Gilberte and his parents and meets Princesse Mathilde during Nicholas II's visit to France (7 October). At this time (he is 16), Bloch takes him to a brothel.

1897. 1 January: the narrator realises he has not managed to capture Gilberte's heart. First part of the year: he is 17, and part of Odette's circle. He treasures the memory of the month of May. June/July: he goes to Combray for Aunt Léonie's mother's funeral, walks in the country-side and observes the scandalous life Mademoiselle Vinteuil and her female friend have been leading at Montjouvain since Vinteuil's death. August: he meets the *jeunes filles en fleurs* at Balbec. November: the Dreyfus affair begins with the publication of the '*bordereau*', the note listing secret documents which the anonymous writer was willing to sell to the Germans. The narrator's parents move house. He goes to the Opéra and sees the Duchesse de Guermantes. He falls in love with Madame Swann and the Duchesse de Guermantes in turn.

1898. 13 January: the Esterhazy trial opens. 14 January: Zola publishes *J'accuse*. Picquart's first arrest. From 7 to 23 February: Zola sentenced. He appeals, but is sentenced again in July. June: after his grandmother's death the narrator goes into mourning for six months, and does not resume his social life until December. Winter: he attends a dinner given by the Duchesse de Guermantes.

1899. He is invited to a party by the Princesse de Guermantes. He discovers the link between Charlus and Jupien. 3 June: Picquart is released from prison.

1900. Under doctor's orders, the narrator (who is now 20) leaves for Balbec, where he stayed in 1897. Monsieur de Charlus meets the 20-year-old Morel, who is doing his military service in Doncières. Morel is invited to play Debussy's *Fêtes* at La Raspelière. The narrator and Albertine are guests of the Verdurins (twenty years after Swann and Odette). May: Sarah Bernhardt plays *L'Aiglon*. The narrator stays at Balbec until 15 September. After that: Albertine lives with him in Paris.

From *La Prisonnière* onwards, Proust had no time to synchronise his chronology. One must therefore make out an internal chronology (the ages of the characters) and an external one (historical events that occurred after the dates established by the internal chronology).

1901. The narrator lives with Albertine. Winter: visit to the Duchesse de Guermantes. Charlus is 62. Albertine leaves the narrator for good. He talks about Rosita and Doodica, whom Barnum was showing at the time. Spring: Albertine runs away and dies in an accident. He begins to forget Albertine on All Saints' Day.

1902. Beginning of the year: conversation with Andrée. Spring: stay in Venice. He sees the aged Madame de Villeparisis and Monsieur de Norpois, now over 80. He falls for a glass-seller of 17 (Albertine's age in Balbec). In Venice, a singer sings *O Sole mio* (which was written in 1901). Gilberte announces her marriage to Robert de Saint-Loup. Summer: third stay in Balbec. Gilberte is pregnant.

1903. Gilberte gives birth to a girl (Mademoiselle de Saint-Loup in *A la Recherche*). He does his military service.

1904–1914. The narrator lives in a nursing home a great deal of the time.

1907. The Eulenbourg affair.

1909. The Ballets Russes.

1914. Gilberte leaves for Combray because of the war.

1916. Beginning of the year: Saint-Loup dies at the front, his funeral is at Combray. Monsieur Verdurin dies, and his wife later marries the Duc de Duras, then the Prince de Guermantes who has been ruined by the revolution in Bavaria.

1918. November: the emotional and nostalgic walk in the Bois de Boulogne.

1919. Early in the year: the narrator is ill, 'flu is everywhere. The episode of the madeleine, which reminds him of Combray. May/June: returning from a nursing home, he pays a morning visit to the Princesse de Guermantes. He is 39; he meets the Duc de Guermantes, who is 83, and asks to see Mademoiselle de Saint-Loup (who is 16). He decides to write *A la Recherche*; it is the best day of his life (the worst was the evening in 1890 when his mother refused to kiss him goodnight).

Because of the war, Proust had to abandon his planned division of the work into twenty-year periods (the fixed points are Odette's age and the afternoon party at the Princesse de Guermantes, which had to be displaced from 1912 to 1919).

1879. Swann loves Odette. The narrator is not yet born.

1899. Swann is dying. The narrator is at the height of his social career.

1919. Swann has been forgotten and the narrator is introduced to his granddaughter. The narrator devotes himself to his work, which brings Swann back to life.

DU CÔTÉ DE CHEZ SWANN First section of *A la Recherche*, published in 1913. The first edition ran to 513 pages, and the flyleaf announced the last part of the two-volume work to be published in 1914. It is simultaneously a huge preface to *A la Recherche* and its provisional conclusion, with the narrator's first disappointments. It consists of three parts.

Part I: 'Combray'. This begins with the narrator's long awakening, recreating a world by evoking the bedrooms he has known like so many stages of his existence. The first memories of Combray are recalled through anamnesia, with the scene of the goodnight kiss, the small family clan and Swann. Then Combray emerges as a whole through the phenomenon of involuntary memory sparked off by the madeleine soaked in tea. Characters who appear include: Uncle Adolphe and Odette, Berma, Bloch, Swann's daughter and Françoise in the kitchen. The evocation continues with the 'two ways', one the path that runs alongside Swann's property, the other known as the Guermantes way. The first serves as a pretext for the poetic passage about the mayflowers, the strange behaviour of Gilberte at Tansonville and the cruel scene between Mademoiselle Vinteuil and her woman friend. This portrayal of a childhood full of disturbed feelings and sensuality is accompanied by an allusion to the narrator's guilty habits in 'the little room that smelt of orris-root'. The Guermantes way presents the Monet-like landscape of river and waterlilies. It is also the opportunity for the Duchesse de Guermantes to make her entrance. Proust makes his first reference to the narrator's vocation in the episode of the steeples at Martinville. This first part ends as the narrator wakes up.

Part II: 'Un amour de Swann'. This section retraces an episode that occurred before the narrator was born. He depicts the birth of Swann's passion for Odette, and his jealousy over her. It is also the first description of Parisian society, with the Verdurins' 'little clan'. Proust sets his first major society scene at a party given by Madame de Saint-Euverte where the Guermantes are seen. It shows the effect of the phrase from Vinteuil's sonata on Swann's love, now seen as an illness. A dream finally rids him of it. The section ends with Swann's departure for Combray.

Part III: 'Noms de pays: le nom'. Made up of three very short sections. The first is a reverie on the poetry of place-names, the pretexts for imaginary journeys; the second tells of the narrator's games in the Champs-Élysées, when he was smitten by Gilberte. The third shows him much later, when he finds himself in the Bois de Boulogne on the eve of war. Times have changed: 'The reality I knew no longer exists.'

A L'OMBRE DES JEUNES FILLES EN FLEURS The second section of *A la Recherche*, published in 1919 and much augmented since the 1912 version shown to Grasset which then constituted Proust's first volume. It consists of two parts.

Part I: 'Autour de Madame Swann'. Following on from the last part of *Du Côté de chez Swann*, this links up with the childhood love between

Marcel and Gilberte. However, Proust gives the characters a new orientation, which he announces in the subtitle: 'A break in the narrative: old friends in new aspects – The Marquis de Norpois – Bergotte'. Swann, a highly talented dilettante much altered by marriage, has adopted a bourgeois lifestyle, and his chief concern is now the social rise of his wife Odette, whose salon is beginning to be talked about. The characters who stand out are Bergotte, who brings to mind Anatole France, the great doctor Cottin and the diplomat Norpois, who dines with the narrator's parents. Norpois goes to see Berma in *Phèdre*, on the advice of the ambassador. He often visits the Swanns, where he listens to the Vinteuil sonata. At one of their lunches Marcel at last meets Bergotte, who reawakens his sense of vocation. His passion for Gilberte dies, as another subtitle indicates: 'How I cease for the time being to see Gilberte: a first tentative sketch of the pains of parting and of the irregular progress of forgetting.' He becomes gradually more detached thanks to 'the heart's periods of remission' – 'Les intermittences du coeur' was an early title for the novel.

Part II: 'Noms de pays: le pays'. The subtitle, 'First stay at Balbec; girls by the seaside', establishes the essential theme: two years later, the narrator is cured of his passion for Gilberte and leaves for Balbec with his grandmother and Françoise, their maid. The train journey, then the description of the Grand Hôtel, follow on from each other. The grandmother meets an old friend, Madame de Villeparisis, who takes Marcel for walks. During one of them the sight of three trees at Hudimesnil makes him remember his literary vocation, as the Martinville steeples had earlier. Madame de Villeparisis also introduces her nephew Robert de Saint-Loup to the narrator, and he meets another Guermantes, the strange Baron Charlus, at the same time. After Mademoiselle de Stermaria and the milk-maid, he discovers the *'jeunes filles en fleurs'* (Albertine Simonet, Andrée, Gisèle) on the esplanade at Balbec. Of the three he likes Albertine best, 'at times a bacchante', at times 'well brought up'. He meets with rejection when he tries to kiss her. He then pays a visit to the painter Elstir: Monsieur Biche from the 'Verdurin clan'; like Bergotte, he symbolises art, and once again urges Marcel to create. But the bad weather drives the summer visitors back to Paris; before leaving, the narrator again evokes the bedroom where he lay sick, seeking external sensations.

LE CÔTÉ DE GUERMANTES Third section of *A la Recherche* (published in 1920–21). Made up of two long parts; only the second is divided into chapters. The central theme (initiated in *Jeunes Filles*) is the narrator's introduction to the Faubourg Saint-Germain.

Part I: 'Le Côté de Guermantes I'. Begins with his family's move to an apartment in the Guermantes' town house. At the Opéra, where Berma is performing, Marcel is able to watch the aristocratic society which fascinates him. Every morning he loiters, waiting for a sight of the Duchesse de Guermantes, whom he thinks he loves, while his friendship with Saint-Loup is becoming less important. He leaves for Doncières to visit Robert in his barracks; he is hoping to arrange an introduction to the Duchesse, who is Robert's aunt. Proust recycles the garrison scenes and the episode of the grandmother's voice on the telephone from *Jean Santeuil.* Through this, he begins to discuss the Dreyfus affair. In spring, the narrator meets Saint-Loup with his mistress, the actress Rachel. Another large society gathering features in this first part, the afternoon party given by Madame de Villeparisis. This provides a chance to describe a rather mixed social milieu, where Odette is among the guests even though the Duchess does not address a word to her. On the way out of the reception, Charlus offers to act as guide to the narrator. This first part ends with the grandmother being taken ill in a public convenience in the Champs-Élysées.

Part II: 'Le Côté de Guermantes II'. Subdivided into two chapters.

Chapter 1: 'My grandmother's illness – Bergotte's illness – The Duke and the Doctor – My grandmother's decline – Her death.'

Chapter 2: 'Albertine's visit – Prospect of a rich marriage for some of Saint-Loup's friends – The Guermantes' display of wit in front of the Princesse de Parme – Strange visit to Monsieur Charlus. – I understand his character less and less – The Duchess's red shoes.'

This chapter, which is much more substantial than the first, sees both Saint-Loup's break with Rachel and the narrator's reconciliation with Albertine. Although he no longer loves her, the narrator is to be a guest at the Duchess's table; he will have plenty of time to contemplate the Elstir paintings. But he has lost his illusions about that world. During a visit he pays Charlus, the Baron suddenly throws himself into an incomprehensible violent rage, which is followed by an equally mysterious calm. At the end of *Guermantes*, Marcel learns that he is to receive an invitation from the Princesse de Guermantes, whose salon is even more exclusive than her cousin the Duchess's. Swann tells the Duchess of his approaching death, but his old friend brushes him aside because she does not want to miss a dinner party. This volume emphasises the narrator's dedication to high society, and his disillusionment. The heroes of Combray disappear. Their grandmother has just died, and Swann's death follows shortly. *Sodome et Gomorrhe* and its 'race of men-women' is announced in the last pages.

SODOME ET GOMORRHE Fourth section of *A la Recherche* (published in 1921–22). It has two parts of unequal length.

Part I: 'Sodome et Gomorrhe I'. 'Introducing the men-women, descendants of those of the inhabitants of Sodom who were spared by the fire from heaven.' This follows directly on from the last pages of *Guermantes*. In the Hôtel de Guermantes' courtyard, the narrator spies on the seduction ritual which Charlus and the tailor Jupien perform. He thus discovers the Baron's predilections and launches into the important theme of the 'race of men-women'.

Part II: 'Sodome et Gomorrhe II'. This is divided into four chapters:

Chapter 1: The chapter opens with the Princesse de Guermantes' party. The narrator's devotion to society is coupled with statements about the ravages of time, which he will reiterate with greater insistence in *Le Temps retrouvé*. After the party Albertine visits the narrator; he feels a 'terrible need' for her. In the hope of meeting the Baronne Putbus's maid, he leaves for Balbec, where he discovers 'the heart's intermittent feelings'. The memory of his grandmother arouses sad feelings. He asks Albertine to join him there.

Chapter 2: This is the longest chapter. The narrator analyses his love for Albertine and describes the jealousy he feels at the first hint of homosexuality in her. In Balbec he encounters Charlus, who is at the height of his passion for Morel. These characters all attend the party the Verdurins give at La Raspelière, an estate they have rented from the dowager Marquise de Cambremer.

Chapter 3: The evolution of Charlus's love for Morel and the narrator's for Albertine, are covered in this chapter. The journey in the Norman train that carries the 'little clan' to the Verdurins' evokes another wave of memories, the poetry of the stations, or characters like

Monsieur de Crécy, Odette's former husband, whom she ruined. But disenchantment claims the narrator, and he considers abandoning his plan to marry Albertine.

Chapter 4: To illustrate the 'intermittent feelings', he tells of the narrator's break with his mistress, then the renewal of his passion by the news (which tortures him) of strange bonds between Albertine and Mademoiselle Vinteuil and her friend. The narrator takes her back to Paris immediately, and announces his forthcoming marriage to his mother.

LA PRISONNIÈRE Fifth section of *A la Recherche* (published in 1923, after Proust's death). Its earlier title was 'First part of Sodome et Gomorrhe III'. Although in its original form the text had no breaks, it can be divided into three parts:

The first retraces the episode of 'Albertine's imprisonment', from which the book takes its name. Proust describes the young girl's sleeping body, watched by the narrator. In its power to calm the hero, Albertine's kiss is reminiscent of his mother's. He is increasingly jealous, and asks Andrée to keep a watchful eye on his mistress. Having bought a pianola for Albertine, he plays Vinteuil's sonata while musing on the attitudes of nineteenth-century artists towards their work. The narrator is about to hear the news of Bergotte's death at the Vermeer exhibition.

In the second part, the narrator goes to the Verdurins' party, where Charlus has organised a concert in honour of Morel, who wants to play an unpublished work, Vinteuil's septet. Once again, the music arouses the narrator's sense of vocation. Madame Verdurin causes a quarrel between Morel and Charlus, and the latter has to leave the party, helped by the Queen of Naples. He falls seriously ill.

The third part describes the end of Albertine's time with the narrator, before she runs away. The jealous scenes caused by suspicion become more frequent, as do the reflections on 'Gomorrhe'. During one of these quarrels, the narrator has a premonition of his mistress's death. Albertine's taste in clothes reveals her aesthetic disposition: she wears Fortuny dresses inspired by Carpaccio. She also plays Vinteuil. The narrator can talk to her about Dostoyevsky and Thomas Hardy. He thinks of her as 'a mighty goddess of Time' because she encourages him in 'the search for the past'. But one morning Françoise tells him that 'Mademoiselle Albertine has gone': he is seized with anguish.

LA FUGITIVE Sixth section of *A la Recherche*, which was published in 1926: the printing was finished by 30 November 1925 and the edition went on sale at the beginning of January 1926. It was first subtitled 'Second Part of Sodome et Gomorrhe III', then called *La Fugitive*, then *Albertine disparue*. In its original form the text is unbroken. It begins by describing Albertine's flight to Touraine to stay with her aunt, Madame Bontemps. The narrator, miserable without her, sends Saint-Loup as an emissary and asks Andrée to move in with him, but a telegram from Madame Bontemps tells him the news of Albertine's death in a riding accident. The narrator gradually recovers. He goes to meet Gilberte, now Mademoiselle de Forcheville, which briefly awakens his love for her; then Andrée gives him more information about Albertine's homosexuality, which the narrator, who is already in the process of forgetting her, takes calmly. At length, he leaves for Venice. During the journey he reads a telegram with a mistake in the signature which makes him think it is from Albertine (who would therefore be alive). He feels no joy at the idea. On the way to Paris he hears of the marriage of Gilberte, the real author of the telegram, to Saint-Loup. The narrator then goes to see them in Tansonville. He also discovers, to his sorrow, about Saint-Loup's liaison with Morel. The stay at Tansonville continues in *Le Temps retrouvé*.

LE TEMPS RETROUVÉ Seventh section of *A la Recherche* (published in 1927). Proust originally intended to call this last volume *L'Adoration perpetuelle*. Even though the text is unbroken in its original form, it falls into three parts, of which only the last, about the Princesse de Guermantes' afternoon party, justifies the title of the book.

The first part describes the narrator's stay in Tansonville, where he finds that the two 'ways' or 'directions' of his childhood converge. He finally understands the gesture Gilberte made at their first meeting. His vocation is once again thrown into question by reading a passage from the Goncourts' *Journal* – in fact a pastiche by Proust. He feels unable to write. Marcel then departs to a nursing home for several years.

In the second part, the narrator comes back to Paris and comments on the changes in society and fashion. Gilberte tells him that Combray is occupied by the Germans. He has a long discussion with Saint-Loup. On nocturnal walks through Paris Marcel meets Charlus, much aged and now pro-German, who attacks the propaganda articles written by Norpois and Brichot. He comes across him again being flagellated in a brothel owned by Jupien which Saint-Loup frequents. The latter dies as a hero at the front. The narrator leaves to spend several years in a nursing home once again.

The third part evokes the famous 'afternoon party' given by the Princesse de Guermantes, which itself subdivides into two sections: 'L'Adoration perpetuelle' and 'Le Temps retrouvé' (until 1911 this was called 'Le Bal des têtes'). The first section describes the narrator's return to Paris, still uncertain about his literary vocation. On the way to a social engagement with the Princesse de Guermantes, he meets Charlus, who is now out of favour. Then his involuntary memory is again set in motion by a trip on the uneven paving stones outside the Hôtel des Guermantes. He recaptures the time he has lost, and understands at last all the signals he has received. He can interpret them in his work. The trials he has faced until then have only developed his mind and provided him with material. At the 'bal des têtes' given by the Princesse de Guermantes – in fact Madame Verdurin, who has married the Prince – the narrator subjects the characters to minute scrutiny and registers their metamorphosis by time. Berma has been abandoned by everyone and Oriane, the Duchesse de Guermantes, has lost her society audience. Odette has become the Duc de Guermantes' mistress. Only Mademoiselle de Saint-Loup, the daughter of Robert and Gilberte, brings the narrator's youth back to him. The concluding pages delineate his literary and artistic vocation precisely: he must create a work of art to fix the past forever. He goes away to work on it through the night, ill and misunderstood. It will be completed with its keynote of time, the last word in *A la Recherche*.

La Bible d'Amiens

A translation of the book by John Ruskin, published in 1904 by Mercure de France, with notes and a preface by Proust (who dedicated the work 'tenderly' to the memory of his father). The preface brings together two articles Proust wrote in 1900: one, 'Pélerinages ruskiniens' ('Ruskinian pilgrimages') in *Le Figaro* of 13 February; the other, 'Ruskin à Nôtre-

Dame d'Amiens', in the April issue of *Le Mercure de France* (the latter piece was dedicated to Léon Daudet). It outlines Proust's aesthetic and declares what will always be his critical method: 'In the bringing together of different works we can establish common features whose sum makes up the artist's physiognomy.' This method should also rediscover the writer's 'spiritual life', and the idea justifies the system of notes which try to use a judicious selection of quotations to capture Ruskin's 'original, specific activity'.

Proust's preface consists of three chapters. The first, 'Nôtre-Dame d'Amiens in Ruskin's eyes', tells of Proust's first journey to Amiens and describes the cathedral that gives its name to the work. The second, 'John Ruskin', traces the old age and death of this 'man of genius', whose greatness lies more in the strength of his doctrines than in the content of his books. The last chapter, 'Post-scriptum', expresses Proust's reservations about the 'Ruskinian idolatry' which confuses beauty with truth. He ends by saying that to penetrate the soul of a great master allows one to 'become fully conscious of what one feels oneself'.

Chroniques

A third volume of collected writings which appeared after Proust's death, in 1927, through the efforts of his brother Robert. It brings together various youthful pieces and texts from the first ten years of the century which were not included in either *Les Plaisirs et les jours* or *Pastiches et Mélanges*, as well as later pieces written up to 1921. They are essentially circumstantial pieces about prominent personalities or salons, as was the fashion. The society chronicler's finesse looks forward to, or recalls, the acumen which runs throughout *A la Recherche*.

The first part – 'Les Salons. La Vie de Paris' – sets the social world and the arts in context. 'Un Salon historique. Le Salon de S.A.I. la princesse Mathilde', which appeared in *Le Figaro* of 25 February 1903, prefigures her portrait in *A la Recherche*, with her good nature and her literary and society acquaintances. Proust's homage to the illustrator of *Les Plaisirs et les jours*, 'La cour aux lilas et l'atelier des roses. Le Salon de Madame Madeleine Lemaire' (*Le Figaro*, 11 May 1903), begins with a pastiche of Balzac. 'Le Salon de la princesse Edmond de Polignac' (*Le Figaro*, 6 September 1903) gives an early version of Saint-Loup's funeral in that of the composer Edmond de Polignac, which he describes in a tone borrowed from Shakespeare. Proust also mentions Fauré's first sonata and Rameau's *Dardanus*. Oriane de Guermantes already seems to make an appearance in the guise of 'the queen beauty, Comtesse Greffulhe, laughing and splendid'. 'Le Salon de la comtesse d'Haussonville' (*Le Figaro*, 4 January 1904) describes Coppet and its owners in the manner of Renan; 'Le Salon de la comtesse Potocka' (*Le Figaro*, 13 May 1904) alludes to Stendhal, Balzac and Saint-Simon, as well as to the hostess's old literary and musical acquaintances, who include Barrès, Montesquiou, Maupassant, Fauré and Hahn. Proust describes her retreat to Auteuil, where, like Hecate, she lived out her days, surrounded by her greyhounds. 'La Comtese de Guerne' (*Le Figaro*, 7 May 1905) is the last salon, and the first section ends with an obituary of Gustave de Borda.

The second part, 'Paysages et Réflexions', contains 'Journées de lecture' and extracts from *A la Recherche*. 'Notes et souvenirs' and 'Critiques littéraire', the last two chapters, contain some pages on Ruskin and the Gothic churches with 'Pèlerinages ruskiniens en France' and 'La mort des cathédrales'. Among the articles of literary criticism, 'A propos de Baudelaire' presents a measured but decisive attack on the symbolists. 'Les Éblouissements' and 'A propos du "style" de Flaubert' reveal Proust's powerful analytical abilities. Since *Jean Santeuil* his style has gained in strength and precision of imagery, giving a foretaste of the style later to be found in the novel.

Contre Sainte-Beuve

This work was published for the first time in 1954 by Bernard de Fallois, then in 1971 by Pierre Clarac and Yves Sandre. Both editions are incomplete or incorrect. The first, from 1954, combines critical and aesthetic reflections with the novel, as Proust wished, but the text is truncated and lacks organisation. The second, dating from 1971, contains only the critical writings.

It was a project which originated in 1908. In a letter to Georges de Lauris, Proust was uncertain about the form it should take – 'an article in classic form, Taine's essay less well done' – or the account of a morning with his mother: 'Mummy would come to my bedside and I'd talk to her about the article on Sainte-Beuve I want to write, and I'd develop the ideas for her.' This conversation would certainly have been at the end of the work. According to a letter of the summer of 1909 to Alfred Vallette, the editor of *Le Mercure de France*, the 'novel part' ran to '250 or 300 pages', and the long discourse on Sainte-Beuve, 'the critical part', 125 pages. The book was given its title, *Contre Sainte-Beuve*, by Bernard de Fallois, in acknowledgement of the critical text, but this might not be considered entirely appropriate, as the work presages the fictive auto-biography of *A la Recherche*.

At the beginning the hero wakes in the morning, as in the later novel, and waits for his mother. He then recalls his childhood in Combray; the bedtime scene and the two walks are already included. The seaside town of Querqueville, where he had stayed with his grandmother, conjures up his meeting with the Marquise de Villeparisis and his budding friendship with Jacques de Montargis. His mother then intervenes, bringing him a newspaper in which one of his articles is published. The memory of a journey to Venice with her wells up in his mind, while noises from the street and the rays of sun on the balcony provide another reality. He and his mother begin a discussion which suggests the world of the Guermantes. The narrator is in love with the Comtesse. Swann is in love with Sonia. He also alludes to 'young women, half-glimpsed and longed for', and to the Verdurin clan with a courtesan, a pianist and a doctor. He lusts after Mademoiselle de Quimperlé or de Caudéran, the peasant girl from Pinsonville and the Baronne de Picpus's chamber-maid. Charlus emerges too, in the guise of the Marquis de Gurcy or de Guercy, the florist Borniche's lover. In the 'long chat' which follows, Proust essentially attacks Sainte-Beuve's method of identifying the work with the person who wrote it, and of aiming 'to surround oneself with every possible piece of information on a writer, to collect his letters, to question the people who knew him'. For Proust, the interior self 'which produces the work' differs utterly from the exterior self which society can observe. In the course of his opposition to Sainte-Beuve, the novelist constructs a brilliant piece of literary criticism on Baudelaire, de Nerval and Balzac.

Jean Santeuil

An unfinished autobiographical novel written between 1895 and 1899. André Maurois found it among Madame Mante-Proust's papers, and in 1952 Bernard de Fallois published it with Gallimard under this title, which is the name of the principal character. It was produced in three volumes, with a nineteen-page preface by André Maurois. Pierre Clarac re-edited it for the Pléiade edition of 1971. From all the evidence, it seems that it would never have been published as it was, for it was still at the 'rough draft' stage, full of imperfections and repetitions, and containing passages with no real links between them. Proust said of it: 'Can I call this book a novel? It's less than a novel, perhaps, and yet much more: it's the very essence of my life with nothing added.' In fact, this story, which sets out to be 'true', passes into fiction. In the 'Introduction', the narrator presents an early version of Bergotte, the writer C. who at his death leaves an unpublished manuscript in which Jean Santeuil (otherwise known as Marcel Proust) is the hero.

It is a forerunner to *A la Recherche* from the start. Jean Santeuil's mother doesn't come to say goodnight to him, to 'toughen him up'. The hero's childhood years follow, with his love for Marie Kossichef (the future Gilberte) whom he meets in the Champs-Élysées, pages on his reading and his thoughts at Étreuilles, which is none other than Illiers. *Jean Santeuil* becomes the *Bildungsroman* that the story 'Violante ou la mondanité' (printed in *Le Banquet* in 1893) pointed to. The 'chapters' deal with the lycée; philosophy classes; then Jean's entrée into society through his new friend Henri de Réveillon, who introduces Jean into his parents' house; military service; the first pangs of love and jealousy the hero feels. He is also concerned about politics because of the Dreyfus affair.

Proust addresses questions of aesthetics through the painter Bergotte and Saint-Saëns' little phrase. The novel ends with the death of his father and some reflections on the ineluctable passage of time, which look ahead to *Le Temps retrouvé*: 'The creation of life and death, the creation of time never stopped.'

In fact, all the elements of *A la Recherche* were already at hand, but Proust hadn't yet mastered them. He vacillated endlessly between autobiography and fiction. Besides, his style, which bears traces of *Les Plaisirs et les jours* and of the great models of the seventeenth and nineteenth centuries, is not yet completely formed. The sentences are long but do not have the firmness and definition we find in *A la Recherche*.

CHRONOLOGY OF *JEAN SANTEUIL* (as reconstructed by Willy Hachez):

1878. Middle of the year: Jean Santeuil's birth.

1884. At the age of 6, Jean cries in bed at night, missing his mother's goodnight kiss.

1885. His parents, who want to bring him up to be manly, consult a doctor.

1891. At 13, Jean is in love with Marie Kossichef, whom he meets in the Champs-Élysées.

1892. January–February: Jean is sad because his young girlfriend is ill and cannot come out. 20 March: His parents separate him from Marie and send him to take lessons with Monsieur Jacomier until August. After the holidays, he goes to college. During his youth he often spends holidays in Étreuilles.

1893. October: Jean goes to Henri-IV. He is taken by a bigger boy 'to see the girls'.

1895. Now 17, Jean goes into 'Philosophie' and makes friends with Henri de Réveillon. He meets Duroc, head of Hanotaux's cabinet. He quarrels with his mother. The Armenian massacres are being debated in parliament.

1896. July: End of his year in 'Philosophie'. He goes to do his military service.

1897. August–September: First stay at Réveillon. October: Jean returns to Paris to study law, but leads a busy social life and does not attend his course.

1898. February: He goes to hear the Zola trial. He is invited to dinner by Madame Marmet. July: He fails his first law exam and decides to take a political science course. August–September: Stay at Beg-Meil. End of the year: Second stay at Réveillon; from there he goes to Provins.

1899. Life in high social circles. He conceives a passion for Madame S. (Françoise) which dies soon afterwards. August–September: Stay in Savoie. His love affairs become more numerous.

1900. He is in love with Charlotte for six months. Bored with his society existence, he regrets the 'lost time' since he left school. His parents are getting older; time is flowing irresistibly past.

Pastiches et Mélanges

A collection of prose pieces, journalistic articles and prefaces written at different times, published by Gallimard in 1919.

Pastiches. The Lemoine Affair. July 1908 saw the eruption of a scandal surrounding Lemoine, a French engineer who had extorted more than a million francs in gold from Sir Julius Wernher, president of De Beers, by claiming that he could manufacture diamonds. Proust described the exploit in *Le Figaro* in February and March 1908. This book contains nine different versions of the event, each written in the style of a different author: *I Dans un roman de Balzac; II L'Affaire Lemoine par Gustave Flaubert; III Critique de roman de M. Gustave Flaubert sur l' 'Affaire Lemoine' par Sainte-Beuve, dans son feuilleton du Constitutionnel; IV Par Henri de Régnier; V Dans le journal des Goncourt; VI 'L'Affaire Lemoine' par Michelet; VII Dans un feuilleton dramatique de M. Émile Faguet; VIII Par Ernest Renan; IX Dans les Mémoires de Saint-Simon.*

The book also contains pastiches Proust did not publish, describing the affair in the manner of Sainte-Beuve, Chateaubriand, Maeterlinck and Ruskin, and a 'Pastiche de *Pelléas et Mélisande*'. Proust was a talented observer, and here proves himself to be a marvellous comic author who does not hesitate to laugh at himself and his translations in his pastiche of Ruskin.

Mélanges. These more austere pieces are in quite another mode; they are grouped in three sections. The first, 'En mémoire des églises assassinées' ('In Memory of Murdered Churches'), describes the destruction of the Great War. It consists of a series of articles on Norman churches and on Ruskin: *Les Églises sauvées*; *Les Clochers de Caen*; *La Cathédrale de Lisieux*. The *Journées de pèlerinage* and *John Ruskin* were written in 1900 to accompany his translation of *The Bible of Amiens*. The study entitled 'La Mort des cathédrales' (which appeared in *Le Figaro* of 16 August 1904) had taken issue with the move to separate the Church and the State. The second section consists of only one article – 'Sentiments filiaux d'un parricide' ('Filial Feelings of a Parricide') – a meditation on madness which appeared in *Le Figaro* on 1 February 1907.

The last section is made up of 'Journées de lecture', an article published in *La Renaissance latine* on 15 June 1905 under the title 'Sur la lecture', which was the preface to Proust's translation of *Sesame and Lilies*.

Les Plaisirs et les jours

Proust's first book, published by Calmann-Lévy in June 1896. It was illustrated with watercolours by Madeleine Lemaire, and also contained four piano pieces by Reynaldo Hahn and a short preface by Anatole France. (He had to be entreated to write it, and said of Proust in the preface: 'There is something of a depraved Bernardin de Saint-Pierre and of an innocent Petronius in him'.) The book was dedicated 'To my friend Willie Heath, who died in Paris on 30 October 1893'; the fore-word that accompanied this dedication (written in July 1894) alludes to the death and particularly to the illness that would shape Proust's future life. In choosing the title 'Pleasures and Days' Proust was parodying the Greek poet Hesiod (eighth century BC), author of *Works and Days*.

This collection brought together the essence of what Proust had published up to that time, loosely organised (the process of presenting the public a second time with articles that had already appeared in the press was to become common during this era; Proust inaugurated it with this book). The decadent pieces that make up the volume had been published, two or three years earlier, in journals like *Le Banquet*, *Le Gaulois* or *La Revue blanche*. However, three studies published in *La Revue blanche* were not included: 'Avant la nuit' (which would have been out of place) and the story 'L'Indifférent'. The pieces are grouped according to type: pastiches, stories, pen-portraits, prose poems and verse. The poems are placed in the middle of the collection, and grouped under the title 'Portraits de peintres et de musiciens'. The order here is not chronological but circular, as it would later be in *A la Recherche*. Thus the first story, 'La Mort de Baldassare Silvande', corresponds to the last, 'La Fin de la jalousie', which describes the death of Honoré. The pieces are linked to each other, and some characters reappear in several of them, without necessarily being the same person, or contrast with each other in two halves of the same work (like Violante and Honoré, or Madame de Breyves and the 'young girl'). The mood of the first part is pessimism at the disintegration of personality; that of the second, optimism about the intervention of art and the hereafter.

The stories 'La Mort de Baldassare Silvande, Vicomte de Sylvanie' describes the slow decline of the young Alexis's uncle, a dilettante from the nobility struck by general paralysis. Just before he dies the sound of church bells sets off the process of involuntary memory and makes him relive his childhood with his mother. Apart from the evocation of personal memories, Proust was influenced by Tolstoy's description of Prince André's death in *War and Peace*.

'Violante ou la mondanité' explores how the 'eternal life' of a young girl in society is 'gradually narrowed down to nothingness' by the futility of worldly pleasures. The fate of Oriane and the young Marcel will be the same.

'Mondanité et mélomanie de Bouvard et Pécuchet' begins a long series of pastiches and provides an example of the young Proust's fin-de-siècle tastes in music and reading.

'Mélancolique villégiature de Madame de Breyves' describes the pangs of love the heroine feels for the young Monsieur de Laléande. The story points the way for 'Un amour de Swann', and it is at Trouville (the future Balbec) that Madame de Breyves goes into a decline.

'La Confession d'une jeune fille' tells of a young girl's suicide after she caused her mother's death by succumbing to her lover in front of her. Several themes of *A la Recherche* are here in embryo: cruelty (which will reappear with Mademoiselle Vinteuil); maternal love and the goodnight kiss; lack of willpower, and sexual initiation by a 'depraved' young cousin.

'Un dîner en ville' gives a first sketch of the little Verdurin clan of *A la Recherche*. The character of Honoré is reminiscent of that of Swann.

'La Fin de la jalousie' depicts Honoré's death. Only on his deathbed can he transcend his jealousy. In a letter of 1913 to Robert de Flers, Proust makes the link with 'Un amour de Swann'.

Short pieces These are grouped under the titles 'Fragments de la comédie italienne' and 'Les Regrets, rêveries couleur du temps'. These are also preliminary sketches for *A la Recherche*. Themes explored here are: love, in 'Critique de l'espérance à la lumière de l'amour'; music, in 'Éloge de la mauvaise musique', and memory in 'Tableaux de genre du souvenir'. Portraits of snobs are drawn in 'Personnages de la comédie mondaine'.

Sésame et les lys

A work by Ruskin translated and annotated by Proust, published by Mercure de France in 1906 with a shorter but more literary preface than the one in *La Bible d'Amiens*, dedicated to the Princesse Alexandre de Caraman-Chimay, *née* Hélène de Brancovan. Like *Jean Santeuil*, it contains recollections of childhood reading. Proust expresses his opposition to the 'predominant role that Ruskin assigns to reading in this little work'. For 'we cannot receive the truth for anyone'. We must pass beyond this 'honey ready prepared by others' and make it our own. Proust ends by discussing the poetry of the past which is offered by the language of the ancient authors.

Letters

The following quantities have been recorded: In 1893 (period of social life): 65 letters. In 1905 (his mother's death): 186 letters. In 1913 (publication of *Swann*): 190 letters. In 1915 (wartime): 135 letters.

It is obviously difficult to assess the exact total of Proust's correspondence, as letters have been lost or destroyed. But with an average of 150 letters a year after 1890, it is possible to estimate the total number at about 5000. By examining each year's accounts, despite the difficulty of placing the letters chronologically, since Proust rarely took the trouble to date them other than by the day of the week, it emerges that he generally wrote between one and three letters a day. In 1912, his correspondence doubled compared to the years 1910 and 1911, which shows that he was working less on his novel, by now well advanced.

On 10 December 1919, after he won the Goncourt Prize, he wrote a letter to his niece to thank her for her congratulations, and told her – to excuse his brevity – that he had 870 letters to reply to.

PROUST'S CORRESPONDENTS Agostinelli (Alfred); Amphitryon (Italian officer); Antoine; Antoine (Mme); Astruc (Gabriel); Ballot; Bardoux (Jacques); Barney (Mlle Natalie Clifford); Barrès (Maurice); Beaunier (André); Bélugou (Léon); Berry (Walter); Bibesco (Prince Antoine), (Prince Emmanuel), (Princesse Georges-Valentin); Billy (Robert de), (Mme Robert de); Bizet (Jacques); Blanche (Jacques-Émile); Blum (René); Boulenger (Jacques), (Marcel); Bourges (Elémir); Boylesve (René); Brach (Paul); Brun (Louis); Caillavet (Gaston Arman de), (Mme Gaston Arman de), (Mlle Simone de); Calmette

(Gaston); Catusse (Anatole), (Mme); Chevilly (Pierre d'Humilly de); Clermont-Tonnerre (Duchesse de); Colette; Copeau (Jacques); Crémieux (Benjamin); Curtius (Ernst-Robert); Daireaux (Max); Daudet (Léon), (Lucien); Desjardins (Dr Abel); Dreyfus (Robert); Duplay (Maurice); Duvernois (Henri); Faure-Biguet (J.N.); Fénelon (Bertrand de); Flers (Robert de), (Marquise Robert de); Fould (Eugène); France (Anatole); Franklin (Alfred); Gaillard-Lacombe (V.); Gallimard (Gaston); Gauthier-Villars (H.); Gautier-Vignal (Comte Louis); Gide (André); Godebska (Misia); Grasset (Bernard); Gregh (Fernand); Gueritte (Mme T.J.); Guiche (Duc Armand de); Guillouin (René); Hahn (Reynaldo); Hauser (Lionel); Hayman (Mme Laure); Hennessy (Mme Jean); Lacretelle (Jacques de); Lang (André); La Rochefoucauld (Comte Gabriel de); Lauris (Comte Georges de), (Mme Georges de); Lavallée (Pierre); Lemaitre (Jules); Mâle (Émile); Marais (Paul); Martin-Chauffier (Louis); Maugny (Comte Clément de), (Comtesse); Mauriac (François); Maurras (Charles); Montesquiou (Comte Robert de); Morand (Paul); Mornand (Mlle Louisa de); Nahmias (Albert); Nantois (Mme de); Noailles (Comtesse Mathieu de); Nordlinger (Mlle Marie); Oncieu de la Batie (Comte Victor d'); Pierrebourg (Baronne A. de); Porel (Jacques); Porto-Riche (Georges de); Proust (Dr Adrien), (Mme Adrien); Robert (Louis de); Rosny aîné (J.-H.); Salignac-Fénelon (Bertrand, Comte de); Sassoon (Sir Philip); Schiff (Sydney; pseudonym Stephen Hudson), (Mme Sydney); Scheikévitch (Mme); Souday (Paul); Soutzo (Princesse Hélène); Straus (Émile), (Mme Émile); Trax (Georges de; pseudonym Fr Fosca); Ullmann (Constantin); Vaudoyer (Jean-Louis); Vettard (Camille); Weil (Mme Nathé); Yeatman (Léon); Yturri (Gabriel d').

PUBLISHED CORRESPONDENCE In 1970, Philip Kolb undertook the task of editing all Proust's existing correspondence. He chose a strict chronological order, without giving preference to any one recipient. Until then editors had favoured a volume for each correspondent. This was the case with the general correspondence Robert Proust published with Plon from 1930 to 1936. The series began with the numerous letters to Robert de Montesquiou. Although this classification has the advantage of getting closer to the character of each recipient through Proust's attitude to them, Philip Kolb's method allows the reader to follow the different stages of the writer's life more precisely.

UNPUBLISHED OR LOST LETTERS These are mostly love letters. Proust's niece, Madame Mante-Proust, never wished to acknowledge the writer's homosexuality. She always gave the same answer on the subject: 'As you can well imagine, he didn't have time to worry about things like that.' Whatever the truth might have been she burnt a large part of the passionate correspondence between her uncle and Reynaldo Hahn. Letters Proust exchanged with Albert Le Cuziat were dispersed after the writer's death. The tenant of the Hôtel Marigny, who owned several hundred, used to sell them to his clients at a small price in the 1920s. He also gave some to his doctor and his friends. Sacha Bernard, a distant relation of Berlioz, who knew Proust at the same time as the young Comte Gautier-Vignal, lost a small buckskin bag containing his correspondence with Proust – about 80 letters – on a train from Grenoble. As for the letters to his grandfather, they were snapped up by a collector and are still unpublished.

NATURE OF THE CORRESPONDENCE The length of the letters varies from a few words to several pages. It depends on the recipient, on Proust's state of health, on the time he had available, and on the purpose of the letter. The handwriting and the crossings-out also reflect the physical state of this perpetually sick man. In general the writing is broad and very legible, unencumbered by crossings-out, but this was not so in the last six months of Proust's life. Particularly in the letters to Jacques Rivière, when they are not written by Céleste Albaret, the handwriting is totally different. He could hardly form a few lines in minuscule writing. Sometimes they are no more than brief notes. His letters occasionally also contain table seating plans, such as the one to Robert de Billy on 9 June 1893, and there are a number of drawings in the letters to Reynaldo Hahn. Proust had no illusions about his talents as a draughtsman. He wrote to Gallimard: 'I can't even draw.' For this reason he refrained from illustrating letters to less intimate friends.

Throughout his correspondence, Proust's orthography is sometimes bizarre, notably for proper nouns. He neglects most of the conventions. He abbreviates certain words, omits some accents, some hyphens, and even the circumflex on the imperfect subjunctive. He almost always writes 'peut'être' instead of 'peut-être'. He often uses a dash to indicate a new paragraph. Often, too, his letters were written by his secretaries, which increased the spelling mistakes and lack of punctuation. For two years Henri Rochat made his presence felt with his beautiful handwriting, but he spelt the name of Sainte-Beuve 'Saint-Beuve'. He confused the infinitive with the past participle, and the verb 'est' with the conjunction 'et'.

STYLE The style varies according to the period, the subject matter and the recipients. The precious, fin-de-siècle style he used with Robert de Montesquiou in 1893 is in direct contrast to the pathetic, rambling letters addressed to Jacques Rivière in November 1922. With his closest friends, notably Reynaldo Hahn, he didn't worry about adopting a style. From September 1904 onwards he and Hahn used a bizarre language dear to Hahn, and which he used with all his close friends; in imitating his puerile fantasies Proust endowed them with a fund of humour and ingenuity. Despite his illness and his unhappy love affairs, Proust filled his letters with humour and poetry, and he often tried to put across an idea or impression that is later found in almost the same form in the novel. His envelopes, notably those he sent Cocteau, sometimes had the address written in the form of a poem.

SUBJECT MATTER Every conceivable subject is touched on in the course of Proust's correspondence. Financial problems, with Lionel Hauser; society intrigues with Robert de Montesquiou; long descriptions of his physical condition with his mother. His disappointments in love, especially when Agostinelli disappeared in 1914, are frequently mentioned. But one of his main aims was to gather information for his novel, and he asks all his correspondents for endless details about food, clothes or medicine. Sometimes, particularly with Jacques Rivière, Louis de Robert and Georges de Lauris, he reveals the hidden meanings and the composition of his novel. Through his letters to Reynaldo Hahn or Madame Straus, we can follow the whole genesis of *A la Recherche*, and keep abreast of his progress and the development of the characters. In reading them we find many evocations that prove significant for the novel, but in a primitive, less worked form. This whole correspondence, revealing as it does the writer's day-to-day life and the progress of his work, is an indispensable tool for the understanding of Proust and of *A la Recherche*.

CHAPTER TWO

Dictionary of
the Main Characters in
A la Recherche

In a dedication to Jacques de Lacretelle, Proust wrote: 'There are no keys to the characters in this book, or rather there are eight or ten for each one; just as for the church at Combray, my memory lent me many churches as "models". I couldn't tell you which they are. I can't even now remember whether the landscape was taken from Saint-Pierre-sur-Dives or from Lisieux. Some of the stained glass is certainly partly from Évreux, partly from La Sainte-Chapelle and Pont-Audemer.'

THE FOUR GENERATIONS IN *A LA RECHERCHE*
1820: The grandmother; Madame de Villeparisis; the Marquis de Norpois; Madame de Cambremer.
1850: The parents; Françoise; the Duc de Guermantes; Charlus; Swann; Odette; Legrandin; Brichot; the Verdurins.
1880: The narrator; Gilberte; Albertine; Charles Morel; Saint-Loup; Albert Bloch; Mademoiselle Vinteuil.
1900: Mademoiselle de Saint-Loup.

ADOLPHE, Uncle. Brother of the narrator's grandfather. His valet was the violinist Morel's father; Morel made a great cult of him. He quarrelled with his friend Swann over Odette, and with the narrator's family when the narrator met 'the lady in pink' at his house. Models: Louis Weil, Proust's great-uncle (main characteristics); Jules Amiot, Proust's uncle (a few characteristics).

AGRIGENTE, Prince d'. Known as 'Gri-Gri' by the Swanns. He is seen in Odette's box. In *Sodome et Gomorrhe*, this tall, thin man with dull eyes is, oddly enough, taken for a flashy foreigner by a hotel servant. *A la Recherche* specifies that 'the Prince d'Agrigente was descended from the House of Aragon', which had held the crown of Sicily. The Prince is in fact from Poitiers. His château, the one he occupies at least, does not belong to his family, but to the family of his mother's first husband, and is just about equidistant from Martinville and Guermantes. At the Princesse de Guermantes' afternoon party, the narrator finds him very ill and transformed by old age.

AIMÉ. Maître d'hôtel of the Grand Hôtel in Balbec, then of a Parisian restaurant in *Jeunes Filles*. He tells the narrator about Albertine's double life, which intensely displeases him. In *Le Fugitive*, Aimé also reveals Saint-Loup's homosexuality to the narrator. Models: Olivier Dabescat, maître d'hôtel of the Ritz; Hector, maître d'hôtel at the Hôtel des Réservoirs; and Charles from Larue's.

ALBARET, Céleste. A character in *Sodome et Gomorrhe*, who becomes 'postwoman' to the Grand Hôtel in Balbec with her sister, Marie Gineste. The narrator makes friends with her, charmed by 'her curious genius for language'. Françoise, who is jealous of her, calls her 'the wheedler'. Model: Proust's housekeeper Céleste Gineste (1891–1984), who married Odilon Albaret in 1913.

ALBERTINE. Albertine Simonet was part of the 'little band' of *jeunes filles en fleurs* whom the narrator catches sight of on the esplanade at Balbec. He is attracted to her because of her slangy language, her dark looks, with plump cheeks and green eyes, her impudence and her toughness. She is sporty, and rides a bicycle. Marcel meets her again in Elstir's studio. He also sees her dancing with Andrée at the Incarville casino. Back in Paris he thinks about marrying her, but ends up asking her to come and live with him, despite his mother's opposition. When he discovers Albertine's relationship with Mademoiselle Vinteuil and Andrée, he becomes jealous. The painful scenes make Albertine leave for Touraine, to stay with her aunt, Madame Bontemps, where Saint-Loup goes to attempt to persuade her to return. She refuses, and the narrator sends her a pleading telegram. At the same moment he receives one from Madame Bontemps announcing his mistress's death in a riding accident. Marcel's sadness and jealousy, which has been revived by further evidence of Albertine's homosexual liaisons, both fade into forgetfulness during his journey to Venice.

Commentators have always questioned whether Albertine was the narrator's mistress in the full sense. In *Sodome et Gomorrhe*, he says he accomplished this in Balbec 'with great indifference'; several pages earlier, however, he says it happened in Paris. But some people believe that he was never in fact her lover, as this passage from *La Prisonnière* seems to state: 'Besides, Albertine horrified me by saying I was right to give her her due and say that I wasn't her lover, because in any case, she added, "it's true that you aren't". Perhaps I wasn't, completely, but should I then assume that all the things we did together were things she had also done with all the other men whose mistress she had sworn to me she never was?' Main model: Alfred Agostinelli, Proust's chauffeur. According to Élisabeth de Gramont, Proust took her first name from the Comtesse Jean de Montebello, a friend of Robert de Montesquiou's. Other models: Albert Nahmias, Albert Le Cuziat, Henri Rochat, Marie de Chevilly, Louisa de Mornand, Mary Finaly.

ALBON, Monsieur d'. A character in *Le Temps retrouvé* who was a member of the Guermantes set, whose wit he admired.

ALIX, 'Marquise du Quai Malaquais'. She frequented Madame de Villeparisis' salon in order to steal away her guests. Main model: Madame de Chaponay, who, like Alix, wore her white hair dressed high like Marie-Antoinette. First name: That of the Vicomtesse Alix de Janzé, *née* Choiseul.

Ambassadress of Turkey. She appears in *Guermantes* and *Sodome et Gomorrhe*. The narrator sees her at the Duchess's house, then with the Princesse de Guermantes, and remarks on her malevolence and snobbery.

AMBRESAC, Mademoiselles d'. Characters in *Jeunes Filles*, relations of Madame de Villeparisis. The narrator meets them at Balbec, where they do not get on with Albertine.

AMBRESAC, Madame d'. In *Guermantes*, she attends Berma's performance in *Phèdre* at the Opéra; she takes off the Duc d'Aumale's coat at the beginning.

AMONCOURT, Madame Timoléon d'. In *Sodome et Gomorrhe* she goes to a party given by the Princesse de Guermantes, where she talks to the Duchess about Ibsen and D'Annunzio, to the Duke's displeasure.

ANDRÉE. The member of the 'little band' the narrator likes most, apart from Albertine. She is as knowing and complex as the latter, her nature encompassing both perversity and real goodness. Marcel asks her to chaperone Albertine, but he comes to have doubts about the nature of the relationship between the two. He remembers seeing them holding each other close when dancing at the Incarville casino. Later, Andrée admits her liaison with Albertine to the narrator. Her faults of character – jealousy and sourness – intensify over the years. She ends up marrying Octave, whom she shamelessly slandered in Balbec. In *Le Temps retrouvé*, she becomes Gilberte de Saint-Loup's best friend. Models: Anna Agostinelli (Proust's chauffeur's mistress), Jeanne (wife of Paul Iribe).

ARGENCOURT, Comte d'. He first appears in *Guermantes* at a reception given by Madame de Villeparisis, where he talks about Maeterlinck to the Duchesse de Guermantes, whom he admires. He is anti-Dreyfus, and is rude to Bloch. After this party he meets Charlus and the narrator in the street. At the Princesse de Guermantes' afternoon party in *Le Temps retrouvé*, he has the odd appearance of someone made up to look like an old man.

ARPAJON, Madame d'. The naïve mistress of the Duc de Guermantes. In *Guermantes*, the Duchess denigrates her to the Princesse de Parme. In *Sodome et Gomorrhe*, she goes to a party given by the Princesse de Guermantes where she shows her jealousy of the Duchesse de Surgis, who has supplanted her in her lover's affections. To Grand-Duc Wladimir's great delight, Madame d'Arpajon is soaked by a fountain. She entertains Madame Swann but snubs Madame Verdurin. She appears greatly aged at the famous afternoon party given by the Princesse de Guermantes in *Le Temps retrouvé*; later, Bloch confuses her death with that of the Marquise d'Arpajon.

AUBERJON, Duchesse Gisèle d'. In *Guermantes*, Madame de Villeparisis recommends her to the Duchesse de Guermantes to help with her tea party.

BALLEROY, Madame de. In *La Prisonnière*, she is the great-aunt of the Duchesse de Guermantes' niece. She sends the narrator a love-letter, but he is too upset by Albertine's departure to reply to it. Name: Proust visited the Château de Balleroy, near Bayeux, in 1907.

Barrister from Cherbourg. He proudly entertains the Cambremers to dinner while on holiday in Balbec. In *Sodome et Gomorrhe*, the narrator hears of his death during his second stay in Balbec. Model: Maître Ployel, the lawyer the Prousts met in Évian.

BAVENO, Marquise de. In *Guermantes*, the Princesse d'Épinay tells her about the punning nickname given to Charlus, 'Taquin le Superbe' ('Tarquin the Great' – *taquin* also means 'tease').

BEAUSERGENT, Madame de. Madame de Villeparisis' sister. Like her, she wrote her Memoirs which, together with Madame de Sévigné's, are the favourite reading matter of the narrator's grandmother. Her voluminous works are reminiscent of Madame de Boigne's. Swann mentions her in the pastiche of the Goncourts' *Journal*. Model: None. She is an entirely imaginary character.

BEAUSERGENT, Marquis de. Nephew of the above, who wrote her Memoirs for him. In *Guermantes*, he is in Madame de Cambremer's box at the Opéra for Berma's performance in *Phèdre*. When the narrator sees him at the Princesse de Guermantes' afternoon party in *Le Temps retrouvé*, he is greatly changed by arteriosclerosis. Model: The Marquis d'Osmond, for whom his aunt, the Comtesse de Boigne, wrote her Memoirs.

BEAUTREILLIS, General de. An anti-Dreyfus general who appears in *Guermantes*.

BELLERY, Madame de. The Duchesse de Guermantes' aunt in *La Prisonnière*.

BELLOEUVRE, Gilbert de. A charming but stupid young man who often visits Balbec. The narrator describes him in retrospect in *La Fugitive*.

BERGOTTE. A central character who is the personification of the novelist in *A la Recherche*, as Vinteuil is the musician and Elstir the painter. Bloch first tells the narrator about him in *Swann*. Bergotte's friendship with

Gilberte intrigues the narrator; she gives him a booklet on Racine by the writer. In *Jeunes Filles*, Norpois criticises his private life and disparages his talent. When the narrator meets him at the Swanns', he is surprised by his goatee beard and his snail-shell nose. In *Guermantes*, Bergotte enjoys the Duchesse de Guermantes' salon. Although ill himself, he often visits the narrator when the latter's grandmother is ill. He suffers from insomnia and nightmares. He shuts himself away at home, pouring contempt on the world. But his work gradually becomes less successful. One of the most famous passages in *La Prisonnière* describes his death. In the midst of an attack of uraemia, he gets up to go and see Vermeer's *View of Delft* in an exhibition of Dutch painting, and falls down dead while staring at a 'small expanse of yellow wall'. Proust is in fact describing an illness which overcame him in 1921 in the Jeu de Paume. Models: There are many – Anatole France, whom Proust knew well from Madame Arman de Caillavet's salon (in *Jean Santeuil*, Bergotte, the painter and sculptor, was based on him; in an early version the character was called Berget); John Ruskin (Bergotte reveals to the narrator, as Ruskin revealed to Proust, 'the secret of the beauty and truth that were already half-felt'); Bourget; Bergson; Darlu; Daudet; Barrès; Renan and Lemaitre (for a few traits). But in creating the writer Proust probably drew most strongly on his own contradictions and personal experience.

BERMA. In *Swann*, Swann talks about her to the narrator when he is going to see her in *Phèdre*. Norpois praises her lavishly. The narrator sees her again at the Opéra in *Guermantes*, and then has a better understanding of the talent of the actress, who is no more than 'a window opening on to a masterpiece'. In *Le Temps retrouvé*, when she is old and suffering from a fatal illness, she goes back to playing Phèdre to pay for her daughter's extravagances. She gives a tea-party in honour of her daughter and son-in-law, but no one comes, since they all prefer to go to the Princesse de Guermantes' (who is in fact Madame Verdurin). Proust describes this 'funerary meal', where the tragedienne sits almost alone at her table eating 'forbidden cakes slowly and solemnly, with an air of carrying out funeral rites'. Her daughter and son-in-law shamelessly abandon her for the Guermantes' party. Models: Sarah Bernhardt, Réjane and perhaps Mademoiselle Bartet.

BERMA (daughter of the actress). A character in *Le Temps retrouvé*. Model: Madame Jacques Porel, Réjane's daughter-in-law, who was not a heartless snob.

BERMA (son-in-law of the actress). Model: Jacques Porel, who was Réjane's son and a friend of Proust's. He adored his mother. In *Le Temps retrouvé* Proust forgot the transposition, and called Berma's daughter and son-in-law her 'son and daughter-in-law'.

BERNARD, Nissim. One of the most typical Jewish characters in *A la Recherche*; Bloch's great-uncle. He entertains the narrator and Saint-Loup at his magnificent villa. However, despite his prestige, his great-nephew makes him a laughing-stock. In *Sodome et Gomorrhe*, Proust gives a humorous account of his homosexual misadventures in the corridors of the Grand Hôtel at Balbec. In *La Prisonnière*, he lends Morel 5000 francs, through Bloch's intervention. Model: The very rich Baron Horace de Landau, Madame Finaly's uncle. First name: From the banker Nissim de Camondo.

BERNIER Charlus's valet in *Guermantes*.

BLANDAIS, Madame. Member of a respectable middle-class circle in Balbec who annoys the Cherbourg barrister by her interest in the actions of the hotel guests in *Jeunes Filles*. The narrator talks about her at Doncières.

BLATIN, Madame. At the beginning of *A la Recherche*, the narrator meets her in the Champs-Élysées for the first time. She knows Gilberte. Marcel is taken in by her false good nature, then discovers that she is unctuous and pretentious. His mother and, later, the Swanns confirm this. Odette tells a story at her expense about a Singhalese man she saw in the zoological gardens: to her 'Hello, negro' he replied: 'I'm a negro – but you're a camel!'

BLOCH, Albert. A middle-class Parisian Jew and friend of the narrator's, whose parents don't like him and order him out of the house. He first tells the narrator about Bergotte in Combray. Charlus compares him to the portrait of Mohammed II by Bellini. In *Guermantes*, he is introduced to the Marquise de Villeparisis at one of her receptions, and shows his lack of manners and education. He talks bitterly about Saint-Loup, with whom he is friendly, to the narrator. They discuss the Dreyfus affair with Norpois without managing to discover his views. Later, in Doncières, the narrator introduces him to Charlus, who finds him interesting. At the beginning of *La Prisonnière*, Bloch arranges for his uncle Nissim Bernard to lend Morel 5000 francs, which earns him the hatred of Morel, who becomes anti-Semitic. In *Sodome et Gomorrhe* Bloch, who is passionately pro-Dreyfus, gets Swann and the Prince de Guermantes to sign petitions supporting Colonel Picquart. He meets the narrator and Saint-Loup in 1914. Bloch displays both his fear of going to the front and his vulgarity. During the war his reputation as a playwright rises. In *Le Temps retrouvé*, the narrator hardly recognises him at the Princesse de Guermantes' afternoon party: he has changed his name to Jacques du Rozier, wears a monocle and affects 'English chic'. Models: His name probably comes from a signatory of the *Manifeste des cent-quatre*, a Professor at the École polytechnique in Buenos Aires; Pierre Quillard (a poet Proust met at Mallarmé's), who used the same Homeric jargon; Léon Brunschwicg, a philosopher and old friend from Condorcet; Horace Finaly; Francis de Croisset, Madame de Chevigné's son-in-law, from whom Proust borrowed the anglomania and icy cool of Bloch's later appearances.

BLOCH, Monsieur Salomon. Father of the above. He meets the narrator in Balbec and invites him to dinner with Saint-Loup. He gives his opinion of Bergotte, and displays his avarice. On his death, his son makes a cult of his memory. Model: Hugo Finaly, a rich Jewish banker whom Fernand Gregh compared to Polonius in *Hamlet*.

BONTEMPS, Monsieur. Albertine's uncle. A former Dreyfusard disliked by the Faubourg Saint-Germain, he was known as a hard-liner during the war. An influential politician, he became head of the Department of Public Works. He appears mostly in *Le Temps retrouvé*.

BONTEMPS, Madame. Wife of the above and Albertine's aunt. She visits Madame Swann in *Jeune Filles*. Odette invites her to dinner with the Prince d'Agrigente and the Cottards. Albertine does not like her very much. She is keen for her niece to marry the narrator, and allows her to live with him. But during a visit to the narrator in *La Prisonnière*, she tells him certain things about Albertine's life which reveal her lies and reawaken Marcel's jealousy. It is to her house that Albertine runs, and the narrator sends Saint-Loup there in an attempt to get her to return to him. Later, she tells the narrator the news of Albertine's death. During the war her salon and that of Madame Verdurin become important. She is reminiscent of a queen of the Directoire period.

BORANGE. Grocer at Combray in *Swann*. Model: Madame Damoiseau, grocer in Illiers.

BORODINO, Prince de. He appears in *Jean Santeuil*. In *Guermantes* he is a captain of cavalry in Doncières, and allows Saint-Loup to let the narrator spend the night in the barracks. Later, he gets him leave to go to Bruges. Madame de Villeparisis dislikes him. Model: Captain Walewski, Napoleon's great-nephew and Proust's superior officer in Orléans. His mother had been Napoleon III's mistress (like the Prince de Borodino's mother).

BRÉAUTÉ-CONSALVI, Hannibal, Marquis de. In *Swann*, he appears at Madame de Saint-Euverte's, where the narrator is struck by his monocle. His close friends call him 'Babal', because of his first name. During a party at the Duchesse de Guermantes', he takes the narrator for the organist, Monsieur Widor, and then the new attaché from the Swedish delegation. Proust stresses his status in society even though he claims to loathe the social world. Bréauté is considered very erudite, gives stupid advice which is much heeded, and talks about botany to the Duchess. He becomes Odette's lover in *Sodome et Gomorrhe*. Long after his death, his old friend Oriane calls him a 'snob'. Models: Comte Louis de Turenne and the Marquis Henri de Breteuil, who wore monocles and considered themselves art connoisseurs.

BRICHOT. Professor at the Sorbonne, who appears at the beginning of the novel at the Verdurins' house, where he stands out because of his pedantic comments on etymology. Monsieur Verdurin praises him extravagantly although his wife doesn't hesitate to criticise him. She also separates him from Madame Cambremer, with whom he is in love; he goes almost blind and becomes addicted to morphine in the wake of his great distress. Despite his friendship with Charlus, he is an accomplice of Madame Verdurin's in the Baron's 'execution'. She calls him 'Chochotte'. In 1914 Brichot writes pretentious articles on the war for *Le*

Temps; they increase his fame but earn him the mockery of Charlus and Madame Verdurin. Models: Brochard, a philosophy teacher at Condorcet, then at the Sorbonne, who was known for his pedantry and endless speeches. He was a guest at Madame Armand de Caillavet's salon; he also became blind and paralytic. Joseph Reinach was the model for his articles about the war.

Butchers' boys. There are several in *A la Recherche*. The first appears in *La Prisonnière*: he weighs choice cuts of beef and look like 'a beautiful angel at the Day of Judgement, ... weighing souls and separating the good from the evil'. The second, who makes his appearance in *Le Temps retrouvé*, is Françoise's new butcher boy, her protégé, a 'shy and blood-stained young man' whom she tries to prevent going off to the war. The last, also in *Le Temps retrouvé*, is a young dairyman Jupien recruits into his brothel. He suggests him to Charlus as a replacement for Maurice, pretending he is a butcher's boy, a 'killer of cattle, a man of the slaughter-houses'.

Butler (of the narrator). In *Le Temps retrouvé* he tortures Françoise with his gloomy predictions about the war, and has little admiration for Saint-Loup's conduct at the front.

CAMBREMER, Marquis de. A Norman nobleman, nicknamed 'Cancan', who owns the Château de Féterne near Balbec. He is ugly, with a nose squashed sideways, and amiable in a banal way. In *Sodome et Gomorrhe* he and his wife visit the Verdurins. At La Raspelière he shows his admiration for Cottard. He takes an interest in the narrator's fits of breathlessness and, although an anti-Semite, makes polite remarks about a Jewish colonel. He later quarrels with the Verdurins. At the Guermantes' party in *Le Temps retrouvé* the narrator notes how he has changed 'by the addition of enormous red pockets to his cheeks'. Name: It comes from a small village in Normandy, near Lisieux; it provides Charlus with a rude pun in *Sodome et Gomorrhe*.

CAMBREMER, Zélia, Dowager Marquise de. *Née* Du Mesnil La Guichard. A good musician. She appears at Madame de Saint-Euverte's party, where Swann and the Princesse des Laumes laugh at her name. She has few acquaintances in the Faubourg Saint-Germain and the Duchesse de Guermantes doesn't like her. In *Sodome et Gomorrhe* she entertains the narrator during his second stay in Balbec. He practises his mimicry when talking about art. Unlike her daughter-in-law, whom she compares to an 'angel', she is an admirer and good interpreter of Chopin. She has many children: Madame de Gaucourt, who like Marcel suffers from asthma, is one of them. She survives the war and lives to a great age. Models: The Princesse de Brancovan, an excellent interpreter of Chopin; the Château de Féterne, the Marquise's house, is based on her villa Bassaraba in Amphion. Madame d'Haussonville (for some characteristics).

CAMBREMER-LEGRANDIN, Renée-Élodie, Marquise de. Sister of Legrandin de Méséglise. She is cultured and intelligent, despises Chopin and Poussin and prefers *Pelléas et Mélisande* to *Parsifal*. Married to the son of the dowager Marquise de Cambremer, she is as snobbish as her brother and dreams of being included in the Guermantes set. Her tragedy is not to be introduced into aristocratic circles. She visits the Verdurins, disdainfully, and criticises their move to La Raspelière, which they have rented from her mother-in-law. She eventually quarrels with them. She was in love with Swann, and inspired a great passion in Brichot. In *Le Temps retrouvé*, Saint-Loup considers her pretentiousness and impertinence 'idiotic'. The Marquise becomes indifferent to the friendliness of the Duchesse de Guermantes, who is now seeking her out, and so loses all her social standing. Model: The Comtesse d'Haussonville, who was also a model for her mother-in-law.

CAMBREMER, Léonor de. The Cambremers' son who inherits Legrandin's intelligence and his grandmother's musical gifts. In *La Fugitive*, to his mother's great displeasure, he marries Jupien's niece, whom Charlus has adopted and who has thus become Mademoiselle d'Oloron. In *Le Temps retrouvé* we learn of the predilections he shares with Charlus and his uncle Legrandin, whom he physically resembles.

CAMUS. Combray grocer in *Swann*. Model: Monsieur Légué in Illiers, supplier to the Amiots' Ernestine. There was another grocer in the little town whose name was Camus.

CAPRAROLA, Princesse de. In *Sodome et Gomorrhe* she visits Madame Verdurin to entice away some of the 'elements' of her salon. The 'patronne' finds her intelligent.

CARTIER. A character in *La Prisonnière*, a friend of La Trémoïlle and de Bréauté whom the Duchesse de Guermantes finds boring.

CÉLINE, Aunt. Sister of the narrator's grandmother. At the beginning of the novel she stands out because of the incomprehensible fashion in which she thanks Swann for sending wine to them in Combray.

CHARLUS, Palamède de Guermantes, Baron de. Younger brother of Basin, Duc de Guermantes, and Madame de Marsantes, Saint-Loup's mother. His close friends call him 'Mémé' and his sister-in-law Oriane, in one of her witticisms, nicknames him 'Taquin le Superbe'. He has all the qualities and the vices of his kind. His aristocratic haughtiness (he always expresses himself with great emphasis) is combined with extreme refinement, a feminine sensitivity and a brilliant mind. 'What's more, being very intelligent, the conversation of an intelligent man meant little to him', Proust wrote. The narrator sees him for the first time in the park at Tansonville with Gilberte. He is dressed in twill, and has 'eyes which popped out of his head' (*Swann*). He is a friend of Swann's, and in Combray he passes for Odette's lover when he accompanies her on outings. The narrator later meets him in Balbec and takes him to be a lunatic. Madame de Villeparisis introduces them, and Charlus later pays the narrator a friendly visit in his room. Later still, after a party given by the Marquise in Paris, they leave together and the narrator notices his strange behaviour with a drunken coachman. Through Saint-Loup the Baron invites himself to see the narrator, and makes an incomprehensible scene which is followed by a partial reconciliation.

In *Sodome et Gomorrhe*, Marcel discovers his real nature, the key to his ambiguous personality, through the seduction scene he witnesses between Charlus and the tailor Jupien. At a party given by his cousin – who has a violent passion for him – Charlus, who is hiding his depraved tastes less and less, asks to be introduced to Madame de Surgis-le-Duc's young sons, whose beauty has caught his eye. The narrator later encounters him at Doncières station, where he is meeting Morel, the violinist who becomes his new protégé. When he visits the Verdurins at La Raspelière, they make the mistake of giving the Marquis de Cambremer the place of honour. He becomes an intimate of the 'little clan', believing that they know nothing of his habits. In the event the narrator records his crushing downfall, while depicting his undeniable artistic gifts. Cruelty and madness are mixed in him. He is sometimes accompanied by 'apaches', but with Bichot strips pederasty of any mythological or literary prestige. He makes Morel write gossip-column pieces that compromise the Comtesse Molé but converses with enthusiasm about Balzac's *Secrets de la princesse de Cadignan*. He dines with a footman at the Balbec hotel and plays a Fauré sonata with the sensitivity of a great master. One moment he is the aesthete, making enlightening comments on Balzac and the artists, the next a little powdered lord so interested in women's clothes he is called 'the dressmaker'. In *La Prisonnière*, at the concert he gives at the Verdurins', the Baron quarrels with Morel because of an intrigue 'la patronne' sets up. He is deeply distressed, and retires on the arm of the Queen of Naples. After this upset Charlus falls very ill, and is reduced to frequenting Jupien's seedy hotel where he gets Maurice, who looks like Morel, to flagellate him. During the war Charlus, who is the son of a Bavarian duchess, makes no secret of his German sympathies, and criticises the articles Brichot and Norpois write. He is arrested at Morel's instigation, then released. He has adopted Jupien's niece, whom he first intended for Morel. He gives her the title Mademoiselle d'Oloron and marries her to the young Cambremer, who shares his tastes. The narrator sees him later in the Champs-Élysées, with a beard and white hair that make him look like King Lear. He is diminished by illness, and he is exaggeratedly polite to Madame de Saint-Euverte, whom he used to criticise so savagely. The narrator can hardly make out what he is saying, but his memory and intelligence are unaffected.

Some of Charlus's repartee: In *Sodome et Gomorrhe*, in reply to Madame Verdurin's apologies for having placed him on her left at the dinner table, he said: 'It's of absolutely no consequence, *here*!' Madame Verdurin later defiantly asked him if he knew a ruined nobleman whom she could employ as concierge in her town house; Charlus replied: 'Yes ... yes, I think so ... but I wouldn't advise it ... I should be worried for you that any elegant visitors would not go further than the concierge's lodge.'

Models: Robert de Montesquiou gave him his general bearing, with his impenetrable and frightening façade, his pride, his insolence, and his undoubted artistic talents. But Charlus also reveals the influence of: Baron Doäzan, combed and powdered and in love with a Polish violinist; Comte Aimery de La Rochefoucauld, known for his haughtiness and his sharp witticisms; Oscar Wilde; Prince Boson de Sagan and Comte Joachim Clary, both afflicted with paralysis at the end of their lives; and the writer Jean Lorrain.

CHARMEL. Charlus's footman in *Guermantes*. His name comes from Réjane's concierge in the rue Laurent-Pichat.

CHÂTELLERAULT, Duc de. He visits Madame de Villeparisis in *Guermantes*. The smell of appleblossom gives him hayfever. Charlus does not seem to hear his greeting. At the Princesse de Guermantes' party in *Sodome et Gomorrhe*, he recognises the usher as the young man he accosted in the Champs-Élysées; an incident inspired by Albert Le Cuziat and the young Comte de S. At the Guermantes' afternoon party in *Le Temps retrouvé*, the narrator sees him as 'a little old man'.

Chauffeur. The narrator's chauffeur drives him with Albertine. Model: Alfred Agostinelli, whom Proust engaged in 1907, and perhaps Odilon Albaret.

CHAUSSEGROS, Madame de. She appears briefly with the narrator in *Guermantes*.

CHAUSSEPIERRE, Madame de. The Duchesse de Guermantes does not greet her at the Princesse's party in *Sodome et Gomorrhe*. At the beginning of *La Prisonnière* the narrator describes her modest life and small concerts.

CHAUSSEPIERRE, Monsieur de. He is elected President of the Jockey Club over the Duc de Guermantes at the beginning of *La Prisonnière*.

CHENOUVILLES, The. The Cambremers' cousins. At the opening of *Sodome et Gomorrhe*, the Cambremers go to dinner with them. Their name is pronounced 'Ch'nouville'.

CHEVREGNY, Monsieur de. The Cambremers' cousin, an occasional passenger on the 'little train' in *Sodome et Gomorrhe*. He shows his poor literary taste and his arrogance.

CITRI, Marquise de. In *Sodome et Gomorrhe* she goes to the Princesse de Guermantes' party and criticises everything.

COIGNET, Charlus's valet in *Guermantes*.

COTTARD, Dr. A doctor who is 'better than Potain' and Dr du Boulbon's rival. Although he holds the rank of senior clinician, he shows his stupidity in the Verdurin salon, reveals a taste for ready-made phrases, repeats inept puns and enquires about proper names. Later, however, Proust's pastiche of the Goncourts' unpublished *Journal* praises his finesse and distinction. He becomes a Colonel in the medical services during the war and dies of overwork. Models: Many different doctors in Dr Adrien Proust's entourage, such as Dr Doyen, a brilliant surgeon but an uneducated man, Auguste Broca, a surgeon, and Professor Guyon, a urologist and Robert Proust's teacher, all known for making puns. Another disciple of Proust's father, Cotard, gave the character his name, together with Dr Cottet of Évian. Dr Pozzi, as volatile as Cottard, and Comte Albert Vandal, with his pince-nez and his involuntary tic in the eye, might also have been models.

COTTARD, Madame. Like her husband, she is a member of the Verdurin clan. She reveals her lack of culture to Swann during a dinner when she talks about bad but fashionable plays. Later, in an omnibus, she tells him of Odette's love for him. In *Jeunes Filles* she visits Odette de Crécy, who has become Madame Swann. When the narrator's grandmother is ill, she recommends her 'lady-in-waiting' to his parents. In *Sodome et Gomorrhe*, she unexpectedly falls asleep while visiting the Verdurins at La Raspelière. Model: Dr Pozzi's wife, just as keen on her wifely duty and just as betrayed by her husband as Madame Cottard.

COURGIVAUX, Monsieur de. At the Guermantes' afternoon party in *Le Temps retrouvé* he seems incredibly rejuvenated to the narrator.

COURVOISIER, Vicomte Adalbert de. A shameless pervert presented as a good husband in *Le Temps retrouvé*.

COURVOISIERS, The. The Guermantes' nephews and relations by marriage, with some difference and some resemblances. They feature mainly in *Guermantes*.

CRÉCY, Pierre de Verjus, Comte de. Odette's former husband, whom the narrator meets at Balbec in *Sodome et Gomorrhe*. He is a bankrupt and erudite nobleman but he lacks discretion. Model: The old Marquis

Antoine de Castellane (1844–1917) whom Proust met in Cabourg in 1908.

CRÉCY, Odette de: see SWANN, Odette.

CRIQUETOT, Comtesse de. A relation of the Cambremers; Proust learns of her existence by the announcement of her death in *Sodome et Gomorrhe*.

Curé at Combray. In *Swann*, he 'even intended to write a book on the Parish of Combray'. Model: The old Abbé of Illiers, Canon Joseph Marquis, great amateur historian and etymologist. In 1907 Canon Marquis published a huge learned tome entitled *Illiers*. He went to visit Aunt Amiot as the Comray curé visits Aunt Léonie.

DECHAMBRE. Madame Verdurin's favourite pianist in *Sodome et Gomorrhe*. Brichot announces his death, while hiding the news from her. Model: Édouard Risler, Proust's friend and Madame Lemaire's favourite pianist.

DELAGE, Suzanne. In *Guermantes*, Madame Bontemps mistakenly believes her to have been a childhood friend of the narrator's.

DELTOUR, General. Secretary to the President of the Republic who attends Morel's concert at the Verdurins' in *La Prisonnière*. Charlus puts pressure on him to award his protégé a decoration.

DIEULAFOY, Professor Georges. He is present at the grandmother's deathbed in *Guermantes*. Model: Professor Dieulafoy (1839–1911), a doctor and acquaintance of Princesse Mathilde's.

DU BOULBON, Dr. A doctor Bergotte recommends to the narrator in preference to Cottard in *Jeunes Filles*. He comes to see the grandmother at the start of her illness. Models: Dr Le Reboulet, doctor to the Faubourg Saint-Germain (for his society status). Dr Laboulbène, Dr Proust's guest (for part of his name). Dr Alfred Chambon (born in Odessa in 1870), doctor at the Grand Hôtel in Cabourg. In 1921 Proust also told Léon Daudet that there was in him 'something of the Brissaud kind of doctor, more an eloquent sceptic than a clinician'.

DUCRET. Charlus's valet in *Guermantes*.

DURAS, Duchesse de. Highly praised by Charlus, she is present at the concert Morel gives at the Verdurins' in *La Prisonnière*.

DURIEUX, Mademoiselle. She invites Albertine to tea in *Jeunes Filles*.

E., Professor. A doctor. In *Guermantes* he sounds the grandmother's chest after reciting some poetry. He displays his pessimism and bad grace. Some time later the narrator meets him at the Princesse de Guermantes' where he hears the news of his former patient's death. Model: Dr Édouard Brissaud, as for Cottard.

ÉGREMONT, Vicomtesse d'. In *Guermantes* she acts as a servant for the Princesse d'Épinay during a reception.

ELSTIR. Painter and regular guest at Madame Verdurin's salon; she calls him 'Monsieur Biche', and he presents himself as a mediator. He meets Saint-Loup and the narrator at the Rivebelle restaurant in *Jeunes Filles*. Marcel later goes to visit him in his studio, where he learns that Elstir once painted Odette's portrait in male dress. He finds Albertine there; she is a friend of the painter's. At Doncières, Saint-Loup talks of Elstir as an extraordinary art critic, but the Duc de Guermantes, who owns several of his pictures and invites the narrator to admire them in *Guermantes*, finds him overpriced and ends up exchanging the paintings for a 'daub'. Madame Verdurin is furious that he left the 'little clan' and criticises him harshly. Despite this, Elstir is the only person to care about Verdurin's death in *Le Temps retrouvé*. Models: Gustave Moreau (for some of his mythological pictures); Monet (for his seascapes and cathedrals); Renoir (for his *Déjeuner des canotiers*); Alexander Harrison, seascape painter (in 1896, Proust and Marie Nordlinger visited him in his studio, and Marie later wrote: 'I never thought I was having tea with Elstir'); Vuillard, whom Proust met in his studio in Cabourg. Name: Perhaps a combination of the names of Helleu and Whistler.

ELSTIR, Madame. In *Sodome et Gomorrhe*, Madame Verdurin calls her a trollop. Model: Madame Helleu, adored by her husband.

ÉPINAY, Princesse d'. She appears in *Guermantes* and *Sodome et Gomorrhe*. She is delighted to entertain the Duchesse de Guermantes and makes her repeat her pun about 'Taquin le Superbe'. Later she visits Odette and is surprised by her social success.

EUDOXIE, Queen. She appears in *La Prisonnière*. The wife of King Théodose. During an official reception she chats for a long time with her friend Madame de Vaugoubert, to the detriment of the French ministers' wives. This episode ruins her husband's diplomatic career. Model: An incident like this occurred in 1901 during a reception for the Empress Alexandra given by Madame de Montebello.

EULALIE. Aunt Léonie's smiling confidante and informer in *Du Côté de chez Swann*, disliked by Françoise.

FAFFENHEIM, Prince von. In *Le Côté de Guermantes*, he visits Madame de Villeparisis and manoeuvres himself next to Norpois, trying to get elected to the Académie des sciences morales. At the Duchesse de Guermantes' house, where he is known as 'Prince Von', he tells the narrator some secrets, talks about Rachel and praises the intelligence of the German emperor who doesn't like Elstir's paintings. He tells the anecdote of the 'old archaeologist'. In *Sodome et Gomorrhe* he is believed to support Dreyfus's cause. Model: Charles Ephrussi (also a model for Swann), who like Faffenheim pronounced 'Madame' as 'Matame'.

Father (of the narrator). In his dressing-gown he looks like the painting of Abraham by Benozzo Gozzoli. Cold and solemn by nature, he is irritated by the narrator's tender feelings for his mother, but shows some intelligent sympathy when he lets his wife stay with their son one night. He is passionately interested in meteorology, endlessly checking the temperature at Combray. A difficult character, he quarrels with Uncle Adolphe about the 'lady in pink' whom the narrator meets at the latter's house and with Bloch. His wife admires the sense of direction he shows in the walks around the little town he makes her take with Marcel. His later efforts to obtain from Legrandin some precise information about Balbec or a word of introduction to the Cambremers are in vain. In *Jeunes Filles*, this 'Director at the Ministry' (probably the Ministry of Foreign Affairs, since he is a colleague of Norpois's) invites Norpois to dinner; he talks about diplomacy but the narrator is aware of his naïvety. Much later, the narrator realises that his father's apparent coldness hides a deep sensitivity; as he ages, he becomes more and more like him. Model: Proust's father.

FÉRÉ, Monsieur and Madame. The Cambremers give a dinner party in their honour in *Sodome et Gomorrhe*.

FEZENSAC, Madame de. The Duchesse de Guermantes' aunt in *La Prisonnière*.

FLORA, Aunt. The narrator's great-aunt who joined her sister Céline in thanking Swann in a strange way for sending some wine to them at Combray.

FOGGI, Prince Odon. Madame de Doudeauville's brother-in-law, who goes to Venice with Norpois and Madame de Villeparisis in *La Fugitive*.

FOIX, Prince de. Father of Saint-Loup's friend, a client of Jupien's whose death causes sadness in *Le Temps retrouvé*. Model: Prince Constantin Radziwill, father of Loche, Proust's friend.

FOIX, Prince de. Son of the above. In *Guermantes* he goes to the same restaurant as the narrator and Saint-Loup on the day of the great fog. There is a rumour about his forthcoming marriage. Model: Loche Radziwill, Prince Constantin's son (a few traits).

FORCHEVILLE, Comte de. A nobleman of Norman origin whose family claims to be older than the La Rochefoucaulds. At the beginning of *Swann* Odette introduces him to the Verdurins. He proves to be stupid and vulgar. He orders his brother-in-law Saniette out of the house. With Madame Verdurin's help he becomes Odette's lover, and inspires deep jealousy in Swann, who dreams about him in the guise of Napoleon III. In *La Fugitive*, after Swann's death, he marries Odette and adopts her daughter Gilberte, who becomes Mademoiselle de Forcheville. He squanders a large part of his fortune. At his death, Odette describes him as a mediocrity, and claims she could only ever love intelligent people like Swann or the Duc de Guermantes.

FORESTELLE, Marquis de. He is seen at Madame de Saint-Euverte's; he stands out because of his monocle. He owns a château near Pierrefonds, where Swann considers paying him a visit at the beginning of *A la Recherche*.

FORESTIER, Robert. A character in *Guermantes* whom Madame

Bontemps wrongly believes to have been a childhood friend of the narrator's.

FOSTER, Miss. The third of the marriageable heiresses the Prince de Foix and his friends discuss in a restaurant in *Guermantes*.

FRANÇOISE. Born about 1830, she first appears as Aunt Léonie's cook in Combray. A peasant woman with a mixture of cruelty and nobility in her, she looks like a statue in the porch of Saint-André-des-Champs. She teaches the narrator the grammatical rules of old French and how to pronounce certain words. She is very attached to her mistress, and suffers a 'savage grief' at Aunt Léonie's death. She then goes to work for the narrator's parents, and takes him to the Champs-Élysées. In *Jeunes Filles* she deploys her talents as a cook for Norpois with her famous *boeuf à la gelée*. She accompanies the narrator and his grandmother to Balbec. She proves a lucid judge of Marcel's friends, Bloch and Saint-Loup, and is unsurprised by the relationship between Charlus and Jupien. At the opening of *Guermantes*, she regrets leaving Combray for Paris. During the grandmother's illness she cares for her devotedly but her reflections are a source of irritation. She detests Albertine when the latter moves in with the narrator, and tries to arouse his suspicions with enigmatic remarks that he would understand it all 'one fine day'; she hates him spending money on his mistress. One day he finds her looking through his papers. In *La Prisonnière*, she none the less tries to get Albertine to stay. She is jealous and exclusive, and also shows her displeasure at the narrator's friendships with Marie Gineste and Céleste Albaret. During the war she is tormented by the maître d'hôtel who wants to 'throw her a pip', when she is worrying about getting her nephew, who is later killed at the front, exempted from military service. She learns of Saint-Loup's death with a mixture of sorrow and cruel curiosity. In *Le Temps retrouvé* she comes to understand the narrator's work with 'a certain intuition for her task'. She 'had arrived at a sort of instinctive comprehension of literary work, which was more accurate than that of many more intelligent people'. She helps to organise the manuscript. Models: Ernestine Gallou, who remained in Illiers where she worked for Monsieur Amiot and his wife (Aunt Léonie); she was also Ernestine in *Jean Santeuil*. Also some of Proust's own servants, like Félicie Fitau, Céline Cottin and Céleste Albaret.

FRANÇOISE, daughter of. Marguerite appears in *Guermantes* with her repertoire of slang which disconcerts the narrator. She helps him with the typing of his book. Fifteen years later, in *Le Temps retrouvé*, she doesn't seem to have aged. Model: (partly) Yvonne Albaret, Céleste's niece, who completed the typing of *La Prisonnière* and *La Fugitive*.

FROBERVILLE, Colonel de. General Froberville's nephew who attends the Princesse de Guermantes' party in *Sodome et Gomorrhe*. He talks to de Bréauté and the Duchess and is delighted to hear that she is not going to Madame de Saint-Euverte's garden party.

FROBERVILLE, General de. Friend of the Princesse des Laumes and of Swann's. In *Swann*, the narrator notices his monocle at Madame de Saint-Euverte's. Models: General de Galliffet (a friend of Charles Haas): Comte Léon de Tinseau, 'a fake man of letters, a real brute', an habitué of the Duchesse de Gramont's parties (for the monocle).

FURCY, Comtesse de. An American who makes an appearance at the Guermantes' afternoon party in *Le Temps retrouvé*. She commits a gross error about the name Forcheville.

G. (writer). He visits Madame de Villeparisis in *Guermantes*. The Duchesse de Guermantes sees him as a pleasant friend rather than a man of letters.

GALLARDON, Marquise de. While a guest at Madame de Saint-Euverte's she tries to persuade the Princesse des Laumes to visit her, but she is snubbed. The Duchesse de Guermantes calls her 'a poisonous old woman'. At the Princesse de Guermantes' party in *Sodome et Gomorrhe*, she unsuccessfully introduces her nephew to Charlus.

GALOPIN, Monsieur. Combray pastry-cook from whom Madame Goupil buys a tart. Name: in reality, Galopin was a doctor in Illiers whose daughter was called Madame Goupil.

GAUCOURT, Madame de. Monsieur de Cambremer's sister. She suffers from asthma, and her brother tells the narrator about it in *Sodome et Gomorrhe*.

GILBERTE. The daughter of Swann and Odette. The first time the narrator sees this little blonde girl is in the park at Tansonville; she makes a gesture which seems to him indecent, then disappears. He sees her again later in the Champs-Élysées and plays 'prisoner's base' with her. She gives him a booklet on Racine by Bergotte. The narrator is upset that the Swanns don't like him. He waits impatiently for a letter; finally she writes to him while she is ill. He then goes to tea with her and notices how like her parents she looks. But her sweetness towards her father is only superficial: Gilberte is heartless. He writes to her in vain after a quarrel, and little by little he frees himself from the memory of her. Much later, in *La Prisonnière*, he discovers that she was having a liaison with a young man at the time; he is upset by this duplicity, but feelings of indifference win out. At the beginning of *La Prisonnière* he catches sight of a young girl who looks like Gilberte; the porter at the Hôtel de Guermantes says her name is 'Déporcheville'. He sends a telegram to Saint-Loup, who had known a Mademoiselle d'Éporcheville in a brothel, but Saint-Loup corrects his mistake. He finally meets her while visiting the Guermantes. It is in fact Gilberte, now called Mademoiselle de Forcheville because her mother's second husband has adopted her. She is a snob, and dreams of being a guest of the Duchesse de Guermantes, where she is at last invited to lunch. Once there, she lies about not knowing Lady Israëls and is happy to forget her father and her own Jewish origins. Later, she tells the narrator the news of her marriage to Saint-Loup; he visits them at Tansonville where he rediscovers his childhood. Gilberte no longer cares about her position in society. Saint-Loup is unfaithful to her. In *Le Temps retrouvé* she confesses Albertine's sexual habits. After her husband's heroic death, she retires to Tansonville which is invaded by the Germans. She becomes Andrée's friend. The narrator sees her again at the Guermantes' afternoon party, thickened and looking like her mother. She talks movingly to him about Saint-Loup's strategic theories and shows her contempt for the Princesse de Guermantes (formerly Madame Verdurin) and even for the Duchesse de Guermantes. She introduces the narrator to her daughter, Mademoiselle de Saint-Loup. She looks so like her parents that she awakens in the narrator memories and feelings of time gone by which help him to start writing. Models: Antoinette Faure, Marie Bénardaky, Jeanne Pouquet, Suzette Lemaire and Madame Georges de Lauris.

GINESTE, Marie. The narrator meets her during his second stay in Balbec, in *Sodome et Gomorrhe*. She is one of the two 'postwomen' (the other is her sister, Céleste Albaret) whom Françoise is jealous of. Model: Céleste Albaret's spinster sister.

GISÈLE. One of the 'little band' of young women the narrator sees on the esplanade. Albertine thinks her 'boring' and Andrée 'cruel'. She leaves for Paris to prepare for an exam; the narrator tries to go with her and help her with her French composition, but without success. He meets her again in Passy, in *La Prisonnière*. Later, Andrée tells him: 'I know her faults but she is still my best friend and the person I feel most fond of.'

GOUPIL, Madame. Dr Percepied's daughter. In *Swann*, the narrator first sees the Duchesse de Guermantes at her wedding. She buys a tart from the pastry-cook Galopin. At the beginning of *Sodome et Gomorrhe* she writes to the narrator to congratulate him on an article.

GRANDMOTHER (of the narrator). She is known as Madame Amédée, from her husband's first name, but her own name is Bathilde. She was born about 1820. She loves nature and fresh air; the provincial society of Combray considers her a little 'batty'. Her goodness and serenity are obvious. She and the narrator's mother form 'the pure stock' of Combray. She is an unbiased judge of people, finding Jupien's niece 'perfect' and the Prince des Laumes, future Duc de Guermantes, 'common'. She does not like Bloch, but she appreciates Swann's good taste. Her favourite authors are Madame de Sévigné, whom she loves to quote, and George Sand, whose novels she gives her grandson. For her, as for Sand, virtue resides in nobility of spirit. Her artistic tastes, which influence the narrator's, make her choice of presents subtle and refined. At the beginning of *Jeunes Filles* she accompanies the narrator to a performance of *Phèdre* by Berma. She is worried about his 'lack of willpower', but his illness moves her to give in to his every whim. On Swann's advice she takes the narrator to Balbec for some good sea air. They feel a deep tenderness for each other. They let each other know they are awake, each morning, by knocking on the partition between their bedrooms. A childhood friend, Madame de Villeparisis, introduces her to her nephew, Robert de Saint-Loup, who wants to take her photograph. She takes pains to look younger, which amuses her grandson. In *Guermantes*, she is walking in the Champs-Élysées with the narrator when she has a stroke. He takes her to Professor E., on her return she has to take to her bed. She is dying. Dr Dieulafoy comes to verify that the end is close. When she does die, her grandson feels no grief, but the memories that come back to him during his second stay in Balbec make him very distressed. He calls this delayed grief 'the heart's intermittent reactions'. His grandmother also comes back to him in dreams. Her daughter comes to look more and more like her. Later, thinking about her death and Albertine's and reproaching himself for his selfishness, the narrator has the impression that 'his life is tarnished by a double murder'. Models: His mother and his maternal grandmother, Madame Nathé Weil.

GRANDFATHER (of the narrator). Monsieur Amédée. In *Swann* he is a less appealing character than his wife, and he represents the prejudices of bourgeois Combray (he is passionately interested in marriages and genealogy). He is suspicious of Bloch, the narrator's young Jewish friend, and starts quoting lines from Racine's *Esther* or singing tunes from Halévy's *La Juive* when he is mentioned. He was once one of Swann's father's best friends, but he no longer sees Swann because of his marriage to Odette, and he discusses that liaison when out for a walk with his son and grandson. He also used to know the Verdurins, whom he now mistrusts. He recently quarrelled with his brother, 'Uncle Adolphe', because he entertained the narrator at the same time as 'the lady in pink'. His grandson, who adores his grandmother, hates to see her in misery when his grandfather drinks cognac, which he is forbidden. His conventional attitude to his wife's death comes as a surprise. Model: His maternal grandfather Nathé Weil (even though in *A la Recherche* the grandfather is anti-Semitic).

GREAT-AUNT (of the narrator). 'The only rather vulgar person' in the family. She owns the Combray house, and leaves her money to a niece she has quarrelled with. At the beginning of *Swann* she enjoys teasing the narrator's grandmother and Swann.

GROUCHY, Comte de. In *Guermantes* he is late for a dinner party at the Guermantes', and the Duchess gives him a cool greeting.

GUERMANTES, Basin, Duc de. The Guermantes are a mixture of several famous families such as the La Rochefoucaulds, the Clermont-Tonnerres, the Noailles, the Polignacs and the Gramonts. Basin (born in 1836) is the 12th Duc de Guermantes and the 17th Prince de Condom; during his father's lifetime he was the Prince des Laumes. He is Charlus's brother. He married his cousin, Oriane, and although he enjoys her wit and intelligence he has been unfaithful to her since the day after their marriage. In her *Memoirs* his aunt, Madame de Beausergent, described him as a child as 'an adorable model of juvenile virtues'. He has changed a great deal, and the narrator's grandmother, who knows of this description, finds him 'common' when she finally meets him. The narrator is eager to meet him (Norpois has spoken highly of him) and he sees him making a solemn entrance at his aunt the Marquise de Villeparisis' house; but he too is soon disillusioned. Later he sees him often, as the Duc lives in the same town house as the narrator's parents. He is unlikeable and offhand. But he becomes friendly with the narrator's father, and makes a courteous visit of ceremony when the grandmother is dying. An anti-Dreyfusard of long standing, he is strongly opposed to the views of Swann and of his nephew, Saint-Loup, then suddenly switches his allegiances completely. He soon receives the narrator with bogus humility and shows him his paintings by Elstir, whose beauty he cannot appreciate. He is closed to art and insensitive to everything. He hears of the death of his cousin, 'Mama' d'Osmond, when he is on the point of leaving for a costume ball; he decides to ignore the news and shouts: 'No, no, they're exaggerating, they're exaggerating!' He chooses not to believe in Swann's incurable illness. The only thing that can touch him is a sartorial mistake: his wife's 'red shoes'. The marriage is in a sorry state; the Duc keeps a number of mistresses. After Madame d'Arpajon, he takes up with Odette, whose daughter Gilberte is to marry his nephew and heir, Saint-Loup. He makes condescending remarks to his future daughter-in-law about her past relationship with Swann, which was very close. During the war, he is anglophile and 'anti-Caillautiste'. In *Le Temps retrouvé*, he retains his majesty in old age, looking more and more like his brother Charlus without suffering the same decline. He maintains his whimsical tyranny over his wife. Although Odette laughs at him, she remains his mistress and cares for him, but the liaison is held against him. He is beaten by Chaussepierre for the Presidency of the Jockey Club and is unable to get a seat in the Académie des beaux-arts. And so the glory of the Guermantes passes away. First name: That of the 2nd lord of Illiers. Models: Émile Straus; Comte de Greffulhe; Duc Agénor de Gramont. Boson de Talleyrand-Périgord, Prince de Sagan (whose first name also inspired the character's) was a model for him as well as for Charlus; the Comte d'Haussonville's old age suggested that of the Duke.

GUERMANTES, Oriane, Duchesse de. Born in 1842, wife of the above, she was the Princesse des Laumes before her father-in-law died. Her maiden name was also Guermantes. Some of her relations call her Oriane-Zénaïde or Marie-Sosthène. The narrator first sees her in the Combray church in *Swann*. He is disappointed in her appearance, but nevertheless falls in love with her. Her conversation, which he over-hears 'like a deliciously French popular song', conveys 'a pure French grace that can no longer be found in the speech or the writing of the present day'. The Duchess – very elegant, very Parisian – lives in a wing of the Hôtel de Guermantes, where the narrator's parents also live. He sees her go by in the street every day. He soon stops loving her, but still finds her company very enjoyable. He goes to see her so that she can advise him on the clothes Albertine ought to wear. During the Dreyfus affair the Duchess never takes politics into account in her salon; her rivals accuse her of letting the demands of high society take precedence over the national interest. Her haughty and contemptuous character is gradually revealed: the Guermantes wit is unsparing of Madame de Gallardon or Madame de Chaussepierre. She never allows Swann's wife or daughter in her house during his lifetime, despite her close friendship with him. With the passage of time, old grudges are forgotten. The Duchess becomes friendly with Madame de Cambremer and Rachel, whom she boasts of having brought out into society. She believes that Bloch was 'born in the world to which she herself belonged and had been dandled on the knees of the Duchesse de Chartres'. *Le Temps retrouvé* thus traces her social decline, a result of new acquaintances and a dulling of her famous wit. She appears with dyed hair, surrounded by bad company, her husband openly unfaithful with Odette. She begins to hate Gilberte, her rival's daughter; she calls her the 'little horror' and claims that she was not even sorry when her husband died. She too becomes a *déclassé* Guermantes. Models: The Comtesse de Chevigné (for her husky voice, her elegance and her bird-like profile); the Comtesse Greffulhe, who was mainly a model for the Princesse de Guermantes (for her good looks); Madame Straus and the Duchesse Alain de Rohan, who was the Princesse de Léon before her father-in-law died (for their witticisms); Madame Standish, the Comtesse Greffulhe's friend (for the austere chic of her clothes; she is like the Duchess when she makes a dazzling appearance at the Opéra with the Princess, in *Guermantes*; Madame de Goussencourt, châtelaine of Saint-Eman, whom Proust saw on Sundays at mass in Illiers.

GUERMANTES, Gilbert, Prince de. The Duc de Guermantes' cousin. He appears in *Guermantes* as a passionate anti-Semite and a grandee so obsessed with the rules of etiquette that he seats his wife on his left because she comes from a less illustrious family than his. He walks slowly, and greets the narrator in a formal manner. His deepest convictions and his sexual habits are revealed in *Sodome et Gomorrhe*: he takes Swann to the bottom of his garden and admits that he believes Dreyfus to be innocent; a valet unmasks the tastes he has in common with his cousin Charlus. The Prince tries unsuccessfully to make an assignation with Morel at the brothel in Maineville. At the afternoon party in *Le Temps retrouvé* the narrator learns that the Prince has been widowed and ruined by the fall of the German kingdoms; he has married Madame Verdurin. He has a white beard in old age, his manner is still stiff and his slow walk now seems leaden, but he greets his guests with the goodheartedness of 'a king of the fairies'. Models: Comte Aimery de La Rochefoucauld (who set great store by matters of etiquette and breeding); Prince Constantin Radziwill (who had the same predilections); Louis de Talleyrand-Périgord (who married a rich widow, Madame Cecilia Blumenthal, in 1917).

GUERMANTES, Marie-Hedwige, Princesse de. Born a Bavarian duchess, she married the Prince de Guermantes. The Faubourg Saint-Germain calls her Marie-Gilbert. She is a complete contrast to the Duchesse de Guermantes, her cousin by marriage, in beauty, elegance, wit and temperament, as the narrator notices when he meets the Princess for the first time in the Duchess's box at the Opéra. The Princess is languid; her sparkling cousin considers her 'a bit idiotic'. Her parties are thronged by the Faubourg, but are 'killingly boring'. She is supposed to be in love with Charlus, who treats her badly but talks about her to the narrator as the most beautiful woman in the world. After her death the Prince marries Madame Verdurin, also a complete antithesis of the Duchess. Models: Comtesse Henri Greffulhe (with her sculptural beauty, topaz eyes and sumptuous clothes, in contrast to the more sober attire of Madame de Chevigné or Madame Standish, both models for the Duchess); Comtesse Jean de Castellane, *née* Marie-Hedwige, a Bavarian duchess.

HERWECK, Monsieur d'. A Bavarian musician. In *Sodome et Gomorrhe*, the Duchesse de Guermantes introduces him to her husband, who is furious to meet such an insignificant person.

HEUDICOURT, Madame Zénaïde d'. In *Le Côté de Guermantes*, her cousin the Duchesse de Guermantes denies that she is either malicious or witty. Bréauté mentions her avarice. She owns Vicomte de Bornier's manuscripts.

HOWSLER. The brother of Madame Verdurin's coachman who has to leave his job because of Morel's intrigues, in *Sodome et Gomorrhe*.

HUNOLSTEIN, Madame de. In *Le Côté de Guermantes*, the Prince de Guermantes refuses to have her as a guest at the foot of the stairs. Her nickname is 'Petite' because of her enormous size.

IÉNA, Prince and Princesse d'. In *Le Côté de Guermantes*, the Duchesse de Guermantes praises their Empire furniture. Although he agrees about the furniture, Charlus questions their right to their title.

IMBERT, Madame. A woman from Combray whose asparagus is praised in *Du Côté de chez Swann*.

ISRAËLS, Lady Rufus. Swann's aunt. In *La Prisonnière*, she has her card conveyed to the Duchesse de Guermantes, who mendaciously denies knowing her; Gilberte does the same.

JUPIEN. A tailor whom Madame Verdurin claims is an ex-convict. He keeps a shop in the courtyard of the Hôtel de Guermantes where the narrator's parents live. In a scene in *Sodome et Gomorrhe*, the narrator spies on his 'meeting' with Charlus, which he compares to a bumblebee fertilising an orchid. Morel and the Baron regularly come to 'have tea' with Jupien. Jupien is in fact a fund of knowledge and talents through 'little bits of reading done by chance'. He is devoted to Charlus, and helps him find his protégé in the brothel at Maineville where Morel has an assignation with the Prince de Guermantes. Jupien also tells the narrator about Morel's liaison with Saint-Loup. In *Le Temps retrouvé*, during the war, he becomes the proprietor of a brothel where Charlus is flagellated. Later Jupien looks after the Baron, who has a stroke and almost goes blind. Models: Gabriel d'Yturri (Montesquiou's factotum); Mineguishi (the Japanese valet of the old, impotent and half-blind Comte Clary); Albert Le Cuziat (proprietor of the Hôtel Marigny), who supplies the model for Jupien's last phase. Place: On the ground floor at 9 boulevard Malesherbes the tailors Eppler, and Sandt and Laborde, had shops side by side.

JUPIEN (niece of). A young dressmaker called Marie-Antoinette, whom the narrator's grandmother finds charming and believes to be Jupien's daughter. She falls for Morel, who asks for her hand but then breaks off with her, abusing her because she made a 'mistake' in her youth. Charlus adopts her and gives her the title of Mademoiselle d'Oloron. She marries the young Cambremer, but dies a few weeks after her wedding. The announcement of her death carries the names of almost all the characters in *A la Recherche*, from the most prestigious to the most humble.

'KING' of a small island in Oceania. In *Jeunes Filles*, he is reminiscent of Jacques Lebaudy, son of a sugar millionaire who bought a piece of land in the Atlas mountains and proclaimed himself Emperor of the Sahara.

LAMBRESAC, Duchesse de. She is noticeable for her way of greeting people in *Sodome et Gomorrhe*.

LAU D'ALLEMANS, Marquis du. In *La Fugitive*, the Duchesse de Guermantes remarks on his offhand manners.

LAUMES, Prince and Princesse des. See GUERMANTES (Basin, Duc de and Oriane, Duchesse de).

Lawyer from Paris. He accompanies Madame de Cambremer and her daughter-in-law to Balbec in *Sodome et Gomorrhe*. He is an art-lover who prefers Le Sidaner to Elstir; he promises to invite the narrator to meet Le Sidaner.

LÉA. A young actress the narrator surprises dressed as a man in the Champs-Élysées with Gilberte. He sees her again looking very elegant at the races in Balbec. Léa is the girlfriend of Bloch's cousin. Knowing her to be 'Gomorrhean', Marcel worries about her friendship with Albertine and tries to dissuade the latter from going to see her perform at the Trocadero. Shortly afterwards, he comes across a very crude letter from Léa to Morel, which confirms her tastes despite her love for Morel. He also learns from Albertine that they went on a journey together. Model: Ginette Lantelme, a lesbian actress who stayed at the Grand Hôtel in Cabourg at the same time as Proust.

LEBLOIS DE CHARLUS, Comte. In *Sodome et Gomorrhe*, this homonymous baron is blamed for some things of which Charlus is guilty.

L'ÉCLIN, Madame de. This character in *Le Côté de Guermantes* is nicknamed 'starving belly'. Her hair is worn in bands which entirely hide her ears.

LEGRANDIN. A provincial scholar, a burgher of Combray born in 1850, son of a friend of the narrator's great-aunt. Eaten by snobbery, he pretends not to know the narrator and his father on the way out of church, at the beginning of *Du Côté de chez Swann*. He recommends a stay in Balbec for the narrator and his grandmother, but not for his sister, who is married to a local nobleman, the Marquis de Cambremer. In *La Fugitive*, he takes to calling himself Comte de Méséglise and makes friends with Charlus, whose habits he shares. Théodore, the boy grocer from Camus' shop, is his 'protégé'. His snobbery is at last satisfied when his name features on the wedding announcement of his nephew Cambremer and Mademoiselle d'Oloron, Jupien's niece and Charlus's adopted daughter. He becomes close to Bloch, now the famous writer Jacques de Rozier. At the Guermantes' party at the end of *A la Recherche*, the narrator sees how old and wraithlike he has become. Models: Georges Rodier (a dilettante Proust knew through Madame Lemaire); Henri Cazalis (society doctor, poet under the name Jean Lahore).

LÉONIE, Aunt. Daughter of the narrator's great-aunt and widow of

Uncle Octave, known as 'Madame Octave'. In *Du Côté de chez Swann*, the narrator and his parents stay with her in Combray during the holidays. The faithful Françoise obeys her with fearful respect. She never leaves her bed, and receives the curé and her old servant, Eulalie, Françoise's rival, in her bedroom. Aunt Léonie watches everything that goes on in the rue de l'Oiseau. Her dream is to go as far as Tansonville, but she dies before it is fulfilled. At the end of her life, the narrator realises his similarities to this relation he calls 'the bad fairy of heredity'. She leaves him her money and her furniture, which ends up in Jupien's brothel. It is sometimes difficult to distinguish this character from the great-aunt, often referred to as 'my aunt'; a confusion Proust himself makes. Model: Madame Jules Amiot, Proust's aunt in Illiers.

LEROI, Madame Blanche. A friend of Madame de Villeparisis who appears in *Le Côté de Guermantes*. She is more elegant and refined than her friend, and she keeps a rival salon which the Marquise refers to disdainfully. Models: Madame 'Cloton' Legrand (for some features); Madame Laure Baignères (for her repartee).

LÉTOURVILLE, Duchesse de. In *Le Temps retrouvé*, when she is herself convalescent, she is disagreeably surprised to find Charlus very ill.

LÉTOURVILLE (the young de). He attends the Guermantes' afternoon party in *Le Temps retrouvé*. He has written the narrator a letter that surprises him. Model: The Marquis Illan de Casa-Fuerte, a young friend of Proust's.

LÉVY, Esther. Bloch's cousin. She catches Albertine's eye in the Incarville casino. Her liaison with the actress Léa causes a scandal at the Grand Hôtel in Balbec. In *La Prisonnière* the narrator, in a fit of jealousy, suspects Albertine of having had a relationship with her.

Lift operator in the Grand Hôtel in Balbec. In *Sodome et Gomorrhe* he makes an attempt to be elegant but gives himself away through his incorrect pronunciation and his silliness. He comes to warn the narrator about Madame de Cambremer's visit, mangling the name. He has a cold, and coughs under Marcel's nose. In *Le Temps retrouvé* he enlists in 1914.

LUXEMBOURG, Duc de. The father of Mademoiselle d'Entragues, whom Saint-Loup wanted to marry in *La Fugitive*.

LUXEMBOURG, Her Highness the Princesse de. In *Jeunes Filles* she meets Madame de Villeparisis in Balbec, who introduces her to the narrator and his grandmother. She offers them presents as if they were animals in a zoo. The hotel guests mistake her for a courtesan. Models: The Princesse de Sagan, *née* Marguerite Seillière (in Trouville she went for walks, like the character, accompanied by a 'little negro dressed in red satin'); Princesse Albert de Monaco, *née* Heine.

Manager of the hotel in Balbec. In *Sodome et Gomorrhe*, he comes to collect the narrator at the station for his second stay in Balbec. He is noted for his faults in pronunciation.

MANCHESTER, Duchesse Consuelo de. She goes shopping in London with her friend the Duchesse de Guermantes; her death is announced in *La Prisonnière*.

'MARQUISE, La'. She runs the public conveniences in the Champs-Élysée in *A l'ombre des jeunes filles en fleurs*, and congratulates herself on 'choosing her circle'. Françoise is sure she is a real marquise.

MARSANTES, Comtesse Marie-Aynard de. The Duc de Guermantes' and Charlus's sister, widow of a President of the Jockey Club killed in 1871, Saint-Loup's mother. She cannot accept his liaison with Rachel, who takes her revenge by talking about her cruelty about Dreyfus and evoking a false etymology of her name: 'mater semita'. In *Guermantes*, the narrator is appreciative of her antiquated vocabulary. After first excluding Odette Swann from her circle, she ends up by accepting her and trying to impose her on the Guermantes, to the Duchess's great indignation. She marries her son to Gilberte, who inherits a lot of money from her father, and later stops them divorcing. In *Le Temps retrouvé*, the Duc de Guermantes, who has become Madame de Forcheville's lover, meets his mistress in her house.

MAURICE. An inmate of Jupien's brothel who looks curiously like Morel and who flagellates Charlus in *Le Temps retrouvé*. Charlus is thrilled to hear the young jeweller confess to a crime he probably did not commit.

Milkmaid. Françoise brings her to the narrator in all innocence, in *La Prisonnière*; he intends to give her a letter to deliver, but sends her away with a generous tip.

MOLÉ, Comtesse. Madame Verdurin calls her the Comtesse de Molé. She leaves her card at the Duchesse de Guermantes' one morning, in *Guermantes*. Charlus, who does not like her, gets Morel to slander her in the press. It causes her death. However, the Comtesse appears again in *Le Temps retrouvé* when she issues an invitation to the narrator, who avoids it.

MONSERFEUIL, General de. In *Le Côté de Guermantes*, the Duchesse de Guermantes refuses to speak to him on behalf of Saint-Loup, and sneers at his never-ending attempts to be elected to parliament.

MONTERIENDER, Comtesse de. She is noted for an absurd remark about Vinteuil's sonata: 'It's the best thing since table-turning!' at Madame de Saint-Euverte's party in *Swann*. Model: Madame de Galbois, Princesse Mathilde's lady-in-waiting, who was known for her stupid remarks.

MONTMORENCY, Éliane de. Charlus talks to Madame de Mortemart about her at the Verdurins', in *La Prisonnière*.

MONTPEYROUX, Comtesse de. The Guermantes circle nickname her 'Petite', because of her obesity, but this never annoys her. She appears in *Guermantes*.

MOREAU, A.-J. Known as 'A.J.' in the narrator's father's ministry. In *Guermantes* he gives Marcel a ticket for a performance of *Phèdre*.

MOREL, Charles, called Charlie. (In the manuscripts Proust did not correct, he was also called Bobbie Santois.) A handsome and talented violinist, son of Uncle Adolphe's valet, who is by turns obsequious and rude to the narrator. Through some murky scheming, he gets the Verdurins' coachman sacked. He is engaged to Jupien's niece, but insults her and breaks it off suddenly. He borrows money from Bloch's uncle, then considers taking him to court. He first meets Baron Charlus at the station in Doncières when he is doing his military service in the band of an artillery regiment, in *Sodome et Gomorrhe*. He uses the Baron, playing up to his homosexual tastes without really sharing them. He begs the narrator not to reveal his father's profession when he is introduced to the Verdurins, at La Raspelière, where his virtuosity is admired. However, Morel shows his ignorance by playing a tune by Meyerbeer which he thinks is by Debussy. His dinner at Saint-Mars-le-Vêtu with the Baron confirms his social success. Even though Charlus finds out about his (failed) rendez-vous with the Prince de Guermantes in the brothel at Mainevile, he continues to love Morel and dreams of getting him the Légion d'honneur. With this in mind, he organises a musical evening at the Verdurins' where Morel plays Vinteuil's unpublished septet. The hosts, hurt by the Baron's haughty attitude, persuade the violinist to break off his relationship with his protector. His ingratitude and hatred continue throughout the war: he and Madame Verdurin get the newspapers to publish defamatory remarks about the pro-German sentiments of old Guermantes. Morel refuses any conciliation with him later, out of fear; besides, in a posthumous letter to the narrator Charlus claims he would have killed Morel if he had ever seen him again. From then onwards, Morel takes up with Saint-Loup, who shares his uncle's tastes, and is supported by him and even by his wife Gilberte. The narrator discovers that Morel used to supply Albertine with young laundrymaids, after he had abused them himself. Unknown to anyone he is a deserter, and at the end of the war he is arrested, but released thanks to a letter from Saint-Loup. He then re-enlists, and comes back unharmed and decorated. In *Le Temps retrouvé*, the narrator sees him again at the Prince de Guermantes', illustrious and well respected. He recalls the moments he spent with the narrator in Balbec nostalgically; with the passage of time, this brings no feelings but the poetry of memory. Models: The young pianist Léon Delafosse (Montesquiou's protégé, who was equally ambitious but less cruel); Lord Alfred Douglas, Wilde's companion (for his perversity); Henri Rochat, Proust's secretary: he had broken off an engagement with a concierge's daughter, which probably suggested the episode of Morel's engagement. Proust was also inspired by Baron Doäzan's adventure with a Polish violinist.

MORIENVAL, Baronne de. In *Le Temps retrouvé*, she asks Gilberte, after a recital given by Rachel, if *Les Deux Pigeons* is by La Fontaine.

MORTEMART, Madame Marie-Thérèse de. In *La Prisonnière*, she has a long conversation with Charlus about Éliane de Montmorency at the Verdurins'.

Mother (of the narrator). She seems the double of the narrator's grandmother; they are very much alike. They are both great readers of Madame de Sévigné. However, his grandmother's idealism is in contrast to his mother's realism, which is tempered by great kindness. At the beginning of *Swann*, when the narrator cannot go to sleep without his goodnight kiss from her, she spends the night beside him reading *François le Champi*. Another day, she makes him taste a madeleine dipped in tea: the narrator's childhood in Combray resurges from an incident like this. On her mother's death, she comes to resemble her more and more and gives herself up to a 'cult of sorrow' in *Sodome et Gomorrhe*. As in real life, Marcel and his mother go to Venice together in *La Fugitive*.

NAPLES, Queen of. A dethroned and penniless queen who appears at Morel's concert at the Verdurins' in *La Prisonnière*. She comes back by chance to collect her fan and witnesses the scene against Charlus; she offers him her arm when he is leaving. Model: Marie-Sophie-Amélie, sister of the Empress Elisabeth of Austria, wife of François II, who was, until 1861, the last King of Naples. She later lived in Neuilly in a retirement imposed by poverty.

Narrator, The, or 'Marcel' (called by this name twice in *La Prisonnière*). The main character in *A la Recherche*. Apart from 'Un amour de Swann', which is written in the third person (Proust had thought of continuing in this narrative mode for the rest of *A la Recherche*), the whole story is lived by him, sometimes as a witness, sometimes as its hero. Is he Proust himself? The incidents he relates are often so closely based on Proust's own life that it is tempting to think he must be Proust (as in *Sodome et Gomorrhe*, when he describes himself: 'I, this strange human being who, while waiting for death to deliver him, lives behind closed shutters, knows nothing of the world, stays as still as an owl and, like an owl, can only see clearly in the darkness'). In a letter to Lucien Daudet Proust puts an end to the confusion by stating clearly that the book is definitely a novel, not an autobiography (besides, he masters the use of 'I' in the same way that he uses the other characters). He also gave some of his own characteristics to other characters, such as Swann, Charlus, Bergotte, Elstir, Octave and Vinteuil.

The narrator, a young middle-class Parisian, must have been born about ten years later than Proust. The first image we have of him is as an insomniac who spends most of the night recalling 'our long-ago life in

Combray at my great-aunt's house, in Balbec, in Paris, in Doncières, in Venice, in other places too, which I will remember, the people I knew in each place, what I saw in them, and what I was told about them.' His parents live in Paris and spend their holidays in Combray, where his father was born. He tells of what he was in the past and lives through three great passions: for Gilberte Swann (in *Jeunes Filles*); for the Duchesse de Guermantes, a purely platonic love (in *Guermantes*); and for Albertine (the most important amorous episode, which runs from *Sodome et Gomorrhe* to *La Fugitive*). The narrator toys with the idea of writing, but is unsure of his talent. Each time he gives up the idea, 'privileged moments' lasting no time at all, intuitive flashes, encourage him to write. He analyses these flashes and, as a consequence, describes all the spoilt moments which, by going before, constitute 'lost time'. The novel the reader has in his hands is therefore the book the hero is going to write. Thus the end of the book, which is the result of his reflections and leads to his decision to write, in fact predates the beginning of the story, which is the history of his vocation.

NASSAU, Comte de. In *Guermantes*, the Princesse de Luxembourg's nephew who will inherit the title of Grand-Duc de Luxembourg. In a restaurant and at the Duchesse de Guermantes', the narrator hears malicious gossip about him. Model: Comte Pierre de Polignac, husband of the Duchesse de Valentinois, the Prince of Monaco's adopted daughter and heiress.

NAUSSAU, Princesse de. 'Great society courtesan'. See ORVILLERS, Princesse de.

NIÈVRE, Princesse de. In *La Fugitive*, she plans to marry her son to Gilberte Swann, while denying the intention for fear of her cousin, the Duchesse de Guermantes.

NOÉMIE, Mademoiselle. In *Sodome et Gomorrhe*, an inmate of the Maineville brothel who receives Charlus then keeps him waiting.

NORPOIS, Marquis de. A former ambassador who appears in *Jeunes Filles*. The narrator's father, who is his colleague at the Ministry of Foreign Affairs, places his hopes of being elected to the Institute in him, and asks him to dinner. Norpois enjoys Françoise's *boeuf à la gelée* and expresses pedantic opinions on Berma, the Comte de Paris, Bergotte, Madame Swann and the narrator's literary essay. Since he considers poets to be 'flute players', he discourages him from becoming a writer and advises him to join the diplomatic service. The narrator sees him again at Madame de Villeparisis' house; he was once her lover. Norpois mentions his father's candidacy to him, holding out little hope. Norpois talks to Bloch about the Dreyfus affair with such judicious balance that he manages to avoid giving any precise opinion at all. Later, the narrator is astonished to hear from the Duchesse de Guermantes that Norpois praised him highly. He sees him again as an old man, many years later in Venice, with Madame de Villeparisis. In the best traditions of diplomatic language, he confides his ambition to go into politics, despite his age. He does manage to plot with Prince Odon Foggi to get a post in Constantinople, where he previously left an excellent reputation. During the 1914 war he wrote pompous newspaper articles riddled with his usual rhetorical clichés; the supporters of Caillaux considered him senile, and Charlus mocked him. In this, his fate was curiously similar to Brichot's. Models: Comte Benedetti, an habitué of Princesse Mathilde's salon (like Norpois, he was French ambassador to Berlin in 1870); Comte de Fleury, ambassador to St Petersburg (lover of Comtesse Sophie de Beaulaincourt, the chief model for Madame de Villeparisis); Jean Guillemin, embassy attaché; acquaintances of Dr Proust's at the Foreign Office, Gabriel Hanotaux, Arman Nisars or Camille Barrère (ambassador to Quirinal). Proust based Norpois's opinions on articles by François Charmes which he transcribed: Charmes was the leader writer for *La Revue des deux mondes* in 1895. Some aphorisms of Norpois's are: 'All roads lead to Rome, but the road from Paris to London, on the other hand, must pass through St Petersburg'; 'Obviously, leaving the service is an evil worse than the plague, because everyone dies of it when one is stricken'; 'What are the Chinese doing? They seem to be playing for time, as if that were not the best means of wasting it . . .'

OCTAVE (the Verdurins' nephew). Son of a rich industrialist, a golfer, slightly consumptive, a dandy and a socialite: he appears in Balbec as Albertine's companion. One of his expressions gives him the nickname: 'I'm in a fix'. In *Jeunes Filles*, the narrator remarks on his ignorance and is amazed by his peremptory judgements of Madame de Cambremer and

Madame de Villeparisis. Although he is slandered by Andrée he ends up by marrying her, to the despair of Rachel, whose lover he was. He becomes a writer of talent, justly famous despite rumours that his wife and some 'negroes' were supposed to have written his books. For Octave, art is so personal that he cannot talk about it. During the war he is exempted from military service because of his illness. He becomes a misanthropist, refusing to see anyone except those he considers worthy of interest. Models: Various young men Proust met in Cabourg (such as the artist Léonce de Joncières or Marcel Plantevignes); Jean Cocteau (the dandified artist); in his later guise, Octave is reminiscent of Proust himself.

ORSAN, Monsieur d'. At the beginning of *A la Recherche*, Swann suspects his friend of being Odette's lover.

ORVILLERS, Princesse Paulette d'. Natural daughter of the Duc de Parme. In *Sodome et Gomorrhe*, she holds a rather false social position. She seems to be one and the same as the Princesse de Nassau. Model: The Marquise d'Hervey de Saint-Denis, natural daughter of the last reigning Prince of Parma.

OSMOND, Amanien, Marquis d'. Cousin of the Duc de Guermantes, nicknamed 'Mama'. When Osmond is dying, the Duc de Guermantes refuses to be given the news, because he doesn't want to miss the party to which he has been invited; when he learns of the death, he shrugs his shoulders, says 'They're exaggerating! They're exaggerating!' and goes off to the party. Name: From the Marquis d'Osmond, great-nephew of the Comtesse de Boigne and a friend of Proust's.

PALANCY, Monsieur de. In *Swann*, the narrator sees him with his monocle at Madame de Saint-Euverte's house. He meets him again at the opening of *Guermantes* at a performance of *Phèdre* at the Opéra. Model: According to Proust himself, in his dedication to Lacretelle, 'Monsieur de Palancy's monocle is taken from poor dear Louis de Turenne'.

PARME, Princesse de. The narrator is introduced to her at a party at the Guermantes'. Despite her great name and vast fortune, she had been unsuccessful in inviting the Duchesse de Guermantes to an evening of

Chinese shadows. She is especially amiable towards the narrator; he thought he detected the scent of a bunch of violets about her, because of her name. He describes the ceremony with which the Duchess's guests treat her; he also notes how the Princess jostles her lady-in-waiting. In *La Fugitive*, she entertains the narrator's mother without taking any notice of her at all, but the next day pays her a visit lasting three hours. She is also seen to be complicit in the marriage between the young Cambremer and Jupien's niece, hinting that the latter is in fact Charlus's daughter. Model: Princesse Mathilde (for some features), although she appears in person in *A la Recherche*.

PERCEPIED, Dr. A Combray doctor. It is from his car, in *Swann*, that the narrator has the revelation about the steeples of Martinville. Percepied meets Vinteuil near the cemetery where he has been weeping on his wife's grave. Name: From the postman in Illiers. Model: Dr Galopin of Illiers.

PERDREAU, Abbé. In *Swann*, he is the priest at Combray. He is mentioned only once, when Aunt Léonie sees her niece through the window. Name: From a priest at Saint-Jacques in Illiers in the eighteenth century.

PÉRIGOT, Joseph. Françoise's young footman in *Guermantes*, who borrows books from the narrator. He writes an indiscreet letter to his family.

Philosopher from Norway. A member of the Verdurins' 'little clan' in *Sodome et Gomorrhe*. The narrator comments on his efforts to speak French. The conversations Marcel has with him echo the discussions about insomnia between Bergson and Proust which Edmond Jaloux witnessed in September 1920. Model: The Swedish philosopher Algot Ruhe, Bergson's translator and author of a review of *Du Côté de chez Swann* in *Var Tid* in 1917. Proust wrote to Rivière: 'I hope that eminent Swede won't recognise himself in the Norwegian philosopher in *Sodome* II, but I am worried that he might.'

PIERRE, Monsieur. A character in *Guermantes*. 'Historien de la Fronde', an habitué at the salon of Madame de Villeparisis, whom he flatters. He shows his shyness and is exaggeratedly polite to the Duchesse de

Guermantes. He is especially ignorant of botany. The Duc de Guermantes ridicules him after a discussion of the word 'mentality'.

POIRÉ, Abbé. Father-confessor to the Faubourg Saint-Germain in *Sodome et Gomorrhe*. The Princesse then the Prince de Guermantes ask him to say masses for Dreyfus. Model: The Abbé Mugnier.

POMMELIÈRE, Marquise de la. Nicknamed 'Apple' ('La Pomme'). The Princesse de Guermantes talks to the narrator about her in *Sodome et Gomorrhe*.

PONCIN, Monsieur. First President of the Court of Appeal in Caen. In *Jeunes Filles*, he is holidaying in Balbec; several years later, in *Sodome et Gomorrhe*, he is awarded the medal of Commander of the Légion d'honneur. He pretends to be pleased when the narrator returns to Balbec, and shows equally hypocritical regret at the grandmother's death. Model: Monsieur Gougeon, first President of the Besançon Court of Appeal, whom Proust met in Évian.

PONCIN, Madame. Wife of the above. In *Jeunes Filles*, she belongs to a bourgeois set in Balbec. She gives mistaken reports about the Princesse de Luxembourg.

PORTEFIN, Berthe, Duchesse de. In *Guermantes*, Madame de Villeparisis recommends her to the Duchesse de Guermantes to help serve the tea.

POULLEIN. The Guermantes' footman. In *Guermantes*, the Duchess changes his day off to prevent him seeing his fiancée.

POUSSIN, Madame. 'Lady from Combray' seen at Balbec in *Sodome et Gomorrhe*. The narrator nicknames her 'You must tell me all about it'.

PUTBUS, Baronne. In *Sodome et Gomorrhe*, the narrator discusses Baronne Putbus's maid with Saint-Loup; he is infatuated with her. Knowing that the Baronne has been invited to La Raspelière by the Verdurins, he sends a message from Balbec asking about her servant. We discover that Baronne Putbus is one of Princesse Sherbatoff's three friends, together with Madame Verdurin and the Grand-Duchess Eudoxie. Elstir, disguised as a butler at the Verdurins', whispers indecent suggestions to her.

RACHEL. The narrator meets her first in a house of assignation where she is known as 'Rachel when from the Lord' after the great tune from Halévy's opera *La Juive*. At the start of *Guermantes*, he sees her again, now an actress and Saint-Loup's beloved mistress. Scenes between the lovers take place increasingly often at the theatre or in restaurants. At the time, her performances are considered interesting, but the Duchesse de Guermantes does not appreciate them and laughs at her. The Guermantes disapprove of Saint-Loup's liaison with this Jewish actress. Rachel breaks off the relationship in the end and becomes the mistress of Octave, with whom she is in love, but the young dandy abandons her without compunction to marry Andrée. Saint-Loup himself marries Gilberte, who tries to be like Rachel, knowing that her husband still loves the actress. Many years later, in *Le Temps retrouvé*, she has grown old and ugly but has become famous, and an intimate friend of the Duchesse de Guermantes. At the Guermantes' afternoon party, where she recites some poetry, the narrator has difficulty recognising her before Bloch enlightens him. Rachel is spiteful about Berma, and rude to her rival's daughter and son-in-law. Models: Mademoiselle Marsy (a young actress, Boni de Castellane's mistress); Émilienne d'Alençon (a *demi-mondaine* kept by Jacques d'Uzès); the actresses Ginette Lantelme (who was also a model for Léa) and Louisa de Mornand (Louis d'Albufera's mistress) lent a few features. Probably also Liane de Pougy, Méry Laurent and Cléo de Mérode. First name: The same as one of the servants of Proust's friend Louisa de Mornand.

RAMPILLON, Madame de. In *Swann*, the Duchesse de Guermantes calls her 'the appalling R.', and in *Sodome et Gomorrhe* ridicules her decolletage at a party given by the Princesse de Guermantes.

RÉMI. Swann's coachman, who looks like the 'doge Lorédan'. In *Swann*, Odette dislikes him and wants to have him dismissed.

RISTORI, Madame. An Italian tragic actress Madame de Villeparisis disparages in *Guermantes*.

ROSEMONDE. One of the 'little band' in *Jeunes Filles*. The narrator meets her during his second stay in Cabourg. Albertine has been the paying guest of her parents in Incarville.

ROUSSEAU, Madame. Her death in Combray is announced at the beginning of *Swann*.

SAINT-CANDÉ, Monsieur de. The narrator thinks about his monocle during Madame de Saint-Euverte's party in *Swann*. Model: 'for Monsieur de Saint-Candé's monocle I had in mind the one worn by Monsieur de Bethman, not the German – although it was partly that originally – Hottinguer's relation [. . .]'. (Dedication to Jacques de Lacretelle, in A. Maurois, *op. cit.*).

SAINT-EUVERTE, Marquise Diane de. In *Swann*, she gives a musical evening at which General de Froberville, the Duchesse de Guermantes, then Princesse des Laumes, and Charles Swann are guests. At this party Swann hears the sonata by Vinteuil which awakens his love for Odette. Later, in *Sodome et Gomorrhe*, the Marquise goes to a party given by the Princesse de Guermantes in order to recruit guests for her garden-party the following day. Charlus is abusive about her; she replies in a cowardly way. After the war, she meets the Baron – now decrepit and paralysed – in the Champs-Élysées, and he greets her humbly. Model: Marquise Diane de Saint-Paul. Name: From an Orléans street near Proust's lodgings during his military service.

SAINT-EUVERTE, the young Madame de. Wife of a grandson of the above, *née* La Rochefoucauld. The narrator meets her at the Guermantes' afternoon party in *Le Temps retrouvé*. She imitates Madame Récamier by dressing in a sumptuous Empire dress and lounging on a chaise-longue; she symbolises the remoteness and continuity of time.

SAINT-FERRÉOL, Madame de. In *Guermantes* Saint-Loup, at Madame de Villeparisis' house, pretends not to know who she is, but the Duchesse de Guermantes offers to pay her a visit.

SAINT-FIACRE, Vicomtesse de. The narrator sees her in *Le Temps retrouvé*, at the Guermantes' afternoon party, disfigured by cocaine.

SAINTINE. 'Once the flower of the Guermantes circle'. In *La Prisonnière* Charlus criticises his marriage to a woman from 'the middle classes cross-bred with minor nobility'.

SAINT-JOSEPH, General de. In *Guermantes*, the Duchesse de Guermantes praises him at the expense of General de Monserfeuil.

SAINT-LOUP-EN-BRAY, Robert, Marquis de. (In the first notebooks, Proust called him Montargis.) Son of the Comtesse de Marsantes. The narrator meets him in Balbec in *Jeunes Filles*. He walks elegantly across the hotel dining room; his skin and blond hair are touched by the sun, and his eyes – from one of which a monocle keeps falling – are the colour of the sea. His stylish clothes might make him seem effeminate, if he were not also well known for his adventures with women. His great-aunt, Madame de Villeparisis, introduces him to the narrator and his grandmother; at first he displays only haughty indifference towards them, but suddenly makes friends with the narrator. He is attracted by socialist doctrines and appears to despise his class. The narrator later goes to Doncières, where Saint-Loup, a career officer, is posted. He dines with friends and discourses brilliantly on 'the art of war'. While on leave in Paris, he take the narrator to a restaurant with his mistress Rachel, where in a fit of jealousy he punches a journalist who is rude to the young actress. But the liaison upsets his family, and when he is posted to Morocco he breaks off the relationship; he also tells Swann that his enthusiasm for Dreyfus has cooled. In *La Fugitive*, after several brilliant marriage plans, he marries Gilberte, daughter of the same Madame Swann he had refused to be introduced to previously. His disdain for the social world grows stronger and stronger, and – since he shares the sexual tastes of his uncle Charlus – he becomes friendly with Morel. He believes he sees a resemblance between Morel and Rachel, to whom he goes on paying enormous sums. When the narrator visits him in Tansonville, he notices how much Saint-Loup has come to enjoy deceit, and how his sensibility has diminished. In August 1914, Saint-Loup enlists; he writes the narrator a letter from the front that contains liberal cultural views mixed with interesting remarks about strategy. He also talks of the unsuspected courage shown by men of humble backgrounds, which gives him a better understanding of the great epics of history. During his last leave, he goes to meet Morel at Jupien's hotel, and loses his Croix de Guerre there. Two days later he is killed at the front while protecting his men's retreat; he has become a true Guermantes again. He is buried at Combray. The narrator stresses that he bore no bitterness towards the enemy: the last time he saw him, Saint-Loup was singing a Schumann *lied* in German. Name: Probably inspired by a village near Illiers, and by others in Seine-et-Marne such as

Saint-Loup-de-Naud or Bourg-en-Bray. Models: Lieutenant de Cholet (Proust's commanding officer in Orléans); Gustave de Waru (the nephew of Madame de Chevigné, whom Proust met in 1892); Boni de Castellane; the group of 'young Dukes' including Bertrand de Fénelon, Gabriel de La Rochefoucauld and the Marquis d'Albufera (who recognised himself in Saint-Loup in 1921 and quarrelled irrevocably with Proust).

SAINT-LOUP, Mademoiselle de. The daughter of Gilberte Swann and Robert de Saint-Loup. She appears in *Le Temps retrouvé*, when her mother introduces her to the narrator. He notices her resemblance to her parents, and comments on the feelings and memories of childhood she evokes. Model: Simone, the daughter of Gaston de Caillavet and Jeanne Pouquet, later Madame André Maurois.

SANIETTE. An archivist; faithful hanger-on of the Verdurins, for whom he is a scapegoat. He is shy, yet lacks discretion; he tries hard to please. During one dinner party he invents a ridiculous story about the La Trémoïlles and is snubbed by Swann. Forcheville, his brother-in-law, throws him out of the Verdurins' house. The narrator meets him in the little train at Balbec in *Sodome et Gomorrhe*. The Verdurins are very unwelcoming to him at their party because he tactlessly announces Princesse Sherbatoff's death. He suffers a stroke when he hears that he is ruined; unknown to everyone, the Verdurins then offer to give him a small income. He dies a few years later, attended by Cottard. Although a fervent Catholic, Saniette was a 'revisionist' during the Dreyfus affair. Name: It may have been taken from the Condorcet physics teacher Monsieur Seignette, who taught Proust in Class 2.

SAUMOY, Guy. An adventurous and original young man who visited Balbec regularly. The narrator describes him retrospectively in *La Fugitive*.

SAZERAT, Madame. Aunt Léonie's neighbour in Combray, where she appears with her dog. Eulalie persists in calling her Madame Sazerin. In *Guermantes* she stays in Paris on several occasions, but her Dreyfusism keeps her apart from the narrator's family. When Marcel meets her in Venice she asks him to point out Madame de Villeparisis, once the mistress of her father, whom she ruined.

SHERBATOFF, Princesse. For a long time the narrator is puzzled about her identity, then one day recognises her as a fat and vulgar woman he had seen two days earlier. Yet she enjoys a firm position in society and used to be very beautiful; her anti-snobbery, however, is only apparent. She is the prototype member of the Verdurins' 'little clan' and a great friend of Madame Verdurin, whom she takes to the theatre. She advises the narrator and Brichot not to talk about the death of Dechambre, the pianist, in front of Madame Verdurin, for fear of reawakening her grief. Marcel eventually quarrels with her. Saniette gives the Verdurins the news of her death, but they have no feelings about it because they held her in very little esteem. Through the Goncourts' *Journal* it is discovered that she was supposed to have 'fired a shot at the Archduke Rudolph at point-bank range'.

SIDONIA, Duc de. A Spanish grandee who appears at a party given by the Princesse de Guermantes in *Sodome et Gomorrhe*; he has a long conversation with Charlus, whose sexual habits he shares.

SILISTRIE, Princesse de. In *La Fugitive*, she tries to marry off her son to Gilberte Swann.

SKI (short for VIRADOBETSKI). A Polish painter and sculptor whom the narrator meets on the little train at Balbec in *Sodome et Gomorrhe*. He is a friend of the Verdurins', a pianist when the mood takes him, and superficially gifted in all the arts. He enjoys fantasy, and teases Brichot about 'his little eye for the women'. It is he who reveals Charlus's sexual habits to Cottard. He thinks that the Baron is of lowly origins, but is unconcerned about the mistake when he is informed of it. Much later, at the Guermantes' afternoon party, the narrator sees him again, looking like a dried-up fruit. Model: Frédéric de Madrazo (known as 'Coco', one of Madame Lemaire's regular visitors), a second-rate painter who also played the piano and sang when he felt so inclined.

SOUVRÉ, Marquise de. In *Guermantes*, the Duc de Guermantes refuses the Princesse de Parme's request for an invitation for her. The narrator meets her at the Princesse de Guermantes' party.

STERMARIA, Mademoiselle Alix de. She has lost her mother and is holidaying in Balbec with her father when the narrator notices her in

Jeunes Filles and dreams of love on an island in Brittany with her. Saint-Loup meets her in Tangiers and asks Marcel to write and invite her to dinner. She is on the point of accepting the narrator's offer in the Chalet du Bois, but after an anxious wait he learns to his great disappointment that she has cancelled.

STERMARIA, Monsieur de. Alix's father, a country squire from Brittany who displays his arrogance and vulgarity in Balbec, where he is on holiday. He nevertheless introduces himself to the chief barrister, like him a friend of the Cambremers'.

SURGIS-LE-DUC, Marquise or Duchesse de. In *Sodome et Gomorrhe*, she appears at the Princesse de Guermantes' party where the Duc de Guermantes, her lover, takes her up into a gallery for a better view of the fountain. She is warmly welcomed by Charlus, to whom she introduces her sons; later, when she discovers the truth about Charlus, she forbids them to see him. After Swann's explanations her name loses its poetic ring in the narrator's eyes.

SURGIS, young Comte or Marquis Arnulphe de. The younger son of the above, whose good looks are equalled only by his stupidity. His mother introduces him to Charlus at the Princesse de Guermantes' party.

SURGIS, Victurnien de. Older brother of the above, whose good looks he shares. After an introduction by his mother in *Sodome et Gomorrhe*, Charlus is very taken with him.

SWANN, Charles. Son of a Jewish exchange broker, neighbour and friend of the narrator's family, whom he visits in the garden at Combray. He owns a large estate at Tansonville where he lives with his former mistress Odette de Crécy, now his wife, and their daughter Gilberte. As his house stands near Méséglise, the narrator's family are in the habit of referring to 'Swann's way' or 'the Guermantes way' on their Sunday walks. He has acquaintances in Parisian high society, which the narrator's old aunts dispute; they are amazed that such a distinguished character could live near the wine market, that is, on the Ile Saint-Louis. As he knows Bergotte he has great prestige in the narrator's eyes, who sees him in the Champs-Élysées when he comes to fetch his daughter. Although Gilberte informs Marcel: 'My parents have taken against you', he nonetheless becomes close to the family. He listens with delight as Swann tells him about Balbec church, about Giotto, about Botticelli, Saint-Simon and Vermeer – on whom he is supposed to be writing a study, but it never materialises, as he is a dilettante. In his early love for Odette de Crécy, Swann had made use of his aesthetic sensibility, declaring she looked like Botticelli's *Daughter of Jethro*; to begin with, she was not 'his type of woman'. 'Un amour de Swann', at the beginning of *A la Recherche*, recalls this love affair. The scene of the cattleyas relates how Swann manages to get Odette's 'ultimate favours' in the carriage in which they were driving home by pretending to rearrange the flowers in her corsage.* Together one evening, they hear the 'little phrase' in the sonata by Vinteuil which becomes the *leitmotif* of their love; at Madame de Saint-Euverte's party, he hears it again, alone. He continues to see the Guermantes, who refuse to entertain Odette; later, though, he frequents the Verdurins, who open their doors to the former courtesan. After a time, their relationship becomes stale and Swann almost forgets about his mistress when she is not there, but his jealousy of Forcheville, whom he suspects of being Odette's lover, rekindles his passion and makes him explore Odette's stormy past. In this way Swann discovers her liaisons with other women in houses of assignation; he also goes to spy on her one evening outside the window, but mistakes the hotel. By the time he finally has proof of his mistress's treachery he no longer loves her, but he ends up marrying her. He is unfaithful to her, and, in *Jeunes Filles*, transfers all his affection to his daughter Gilberte. He continues to see the Guermantes, despite his Dreyfusism and his marriage. Oriane de Guermantes appreciates his elegance and wit; besides, according to the Faubourg he could have royal blood in his veins, because his grandmother was the Duc de Berry's mistress. In *Sodome et Gomorrhe* the Prince de Guermantes, during a party he is giving, takes Swann to the bottom of the garden; the other guests think the Prince is asking Swann to leave, whereas in fact he is confiding in him his secret conviction of Dreyfus's innocence. Swann also goes to see his old friend Oriane in the hope of introducing his wife to her, and tells her how little time he has to live. But the Duchess, who is due to go

---

*A cattleya is an orchid with large, highly coloured flowers. Swann often uses an expression full of undercurrents of private significance: 'to do a cattleya', meaning to make love.

out to a party, pretends not to believe in the seriousness of his illness and leaves him. He dies shortly afterwards. The narrator, with deep emotion, realises that he owes Swann both the content of his book and the decision to write it. Models: Nicolas Bénardaky, Marie's father (for Swann, father of Gilberte in the Champs-Élysées); Charles Ephrussi (for his knowledge of the arts) and Paul Hervieu (for his icy elegance); Émile Straus, who devoted his enormous fortune to his wife's clothes and social triumphs (his friends recognised him immediately in the scene from *Jeunes Filles* when the character casts a benevolent eye over Odette's guests from behind a curtain); Charles Haas (for his chief characteristics): he was a dandy, the son and grandson of Jewish exchange brokers, a friend of Montesquiou's and the Prince of Wales's (Madame Straus and Gabriel Astruc identified him immediately).

SWANN, Odette de Crécy, later Madame. The wife of the above, born in 1852. At the beginning of *A la Recherche*, she lives with Swann at Tansonville and is thought to be Charlus's mistress. The narrator's family do not receive her socially. The father and grandfather quarrel with Uncle Adolphe, who invited Marcel to his house at the same time as the 'lady in pink', his mistress, who, at the time, was the *demi-mondaine* Odette de Crécy.

'Un amour de Swann' relates the beginning of her liaison with Swann at the time she was part of the Verdurins' 'little clan'. Odette wanted to add Swann to her circle of acquaintances; he was introduced to her one evening at the theatre. Odette is tall and thin, whereas Swann only liked small, round, pink women. But he was to fall in love with her, and to say much later, at the end of their liaison: 'To think that I've ruined years of my life, that I've wanted to die, that I've suffered my greatest love for a woman I didn't like the look of, who really wasn't my type!' Besides, Odette is available: 'I am always free, I'll always be free for you.' He searches for her throughout Paris for a whole night. Gradually, the poor taste of her 'Japanese' decoration, her vulgarity and, above all, her propensity to tell lies are revealed. Forcheville may be her lover; Madame Verdurin encourages this liaison. Odette knows that Swann cannot do without her, and she leaves him and goes off to Bayreuth and on a cruise, journeys paid for by him. After numerous scenes, Swann eventually marries Odette, although he no longer loves her; she wants to make a break with her past. They have a daughter, Gilberte. The narrator sees Madame Swann, looking very elegant, in the allée des Acacias in the Bois de Boulogne; she has become 'as sweet as an angel'. But her husband dies before he succeeds in getting his friend the Duchesse de Guermantes to invite Odette to her house.

In *Jeunes Filles* Marcel, who is Gilberte's friend in the Champs-Élysées, is invited to their house by her mother and goes for walks with her. Bloch tells him he had an amorous episode with her in the Ceinture train, and Elstir tells him he painted her portrait as 'Miss Sacripant'. In *Guermantes*, she is a guest of Madame de Villeparisis, thanks to her anti-Dreyfus sentiments, although the Duchesse de Guermantes does not address a word to her: her salon, which formed around Bergotte as he was dying, is becoming more and more fashionable. Odette even goes so far as pretending not to know the Verdurins. The narrator discovers she was previously married to a Comte de Crécy, whom she ruined. After the death of Swann, whom she claimed to love madly, she marries Forcheville: she despises him but he adopts Gilberte. He runs through the enormous fortune left by Swann; nonetheless, Gilberte is still a rich heiress much sought after by the Faubourg Saint-Germain. Robert de Saint-Loup marries her and, in *La Fugitive*, proves to be a generous protector. Odette becomes the mistress of the Duc de Guermantes: she is shamelessly unfaithful to him, but also nurses him devotedly. At the Guermantes' afternoon party in *Le Temps retrouvé*, Odette 'defies the laws of chronology' and 'seems like a courtesan from times gone by, preserved forever'. But a little later she falls into a semi-senile state. Models: Proust's friend Laure Hayman (his great-uncle Louis Weil's mistress) is most reminiscent of Odette. But she was not unfaithful to Weil, and called Proust a 'monster' in an angry letter. There was also Madame Straus, Marguerite de Pierrebourg, who was separated from her husband and whom Hervieu met in Madame Aubernon's salon. Madame de la Béraudière, the old Comte Greffulhe's mistress, and a 'courtesan who was very beautiful at that time, called Clomesnil' whom Proust thought about 'for a moment, when she strolled about the pigeon-shoot' (dedication to Jacques de Lacretelle). Odette's Salon: Méry Laurent's salon, and the salon of another *demi-mondaine*, Madame de Loynes (Lemaitre's mistress), known for her anti-Dreyfus views; Madame Arman de Caillavet's salon, where Anatole France was a guest, was a model for Bergotte's presence.

SWANN, Mademoiselle. Daughter of the above two. See GILBERTE.

SWANN (father). Charles Swann's father, an exchange broker. *Du Côté de chez Swann* refers to his feelings of missing his wife.

THÉODORE (the young). A grocer's boy at Camus' who appears at the beginning of *Swann* as a chorister responsible for the upkeep of Combray church. He and his sister organise visits to the crypt. He plays forbidden games in the ruins of Roussainville, and appears as a bad character. In *La Prisonnière* he becomes coachman for one of Charlus's friends; his sister becomes Madame Putbus's maid. He writes the narrator a letter of congratulation on his article in *Le Figaro*. He ends up as a pharmacist in Méséglise, the 'protégé' of Legrandin. Models: Victor Ménard (an errand boy for the grocer Légué and a choirboy at Saint-Jacques d'Illiers); Agostinelli's letter about Proust's article 'Impressions de route en automobile' recalls Theodore's letter in *La Fugitive*.

THÉODOSE II. An Oriental sovereign on an official visit to Paris at the beginning of *A la Recherche*. Norpois comments on his speech at the Élysée. His brother dines with the Guermantes at Madame de Saint-Euverte's house. Model: Nicholas II's visit to Paris in October 1896.

TOURS, Vicomtesse de. The Duchesse de Guermantes notices her at the Princesse d'Épinay's, in *Guermantes*.

TRANIA, Princesse de. In *Le Temps retrouvé*, she is a guest of Madame de Forcheville who has become the Duc de Guermantes' mistress.

TROMBERT, Madame. An acquaintance of Madame Swann in *Jeunes Filles*.

Twins (the). Servants in the Grand Hôtel in Balbec, with faces like tomatoes. Although twins, their habits differ. Models: The twins at the Ritz whom Proust introduced to his friends the Schiffs. One of them left for Switzerland with Lord Northcliffe.

VALCOURT, Madame Édith de. She attends at the concert Morel gives at the Verdurins', but is excluded from an invitation by Madame de Mortemart in *La Prisonnière*.

VALLENÈRES, Monsieur. An archivist, manager and occasional secretary to Madame de Villeparisis in *Guermantes*. He is anti-Dreyfus and respects Bloch.

VARAMBON, Madame de. The Princesse de Parme's lady-in-waiting. Her stupidity and naïvety become obvious when she takes the narrator to be a relation of Admiral Julien de la Gravière. The Duchesse de Guermantes reminisces about her in *Le Temps retrouvé*. Model: Baronne de Galbois, Princesse Mathilde's lady-in-waiting, as Proust himself confirms in *Chroniques*.

VAUDÉMONT, Marquis Maurice de. One of the two young noblemen who, with an actress and her lover, form a separate group in *Jeunes Filles*. He invites the narrator to dinner, using one of the young people as a go-between.

VAUGOUBERT, Marquis de. French ambassador to King Théodose who is praised by Norpois for his diplomacy, and who reveals his homosexuality in remarks to Charlus during a party given by the Princesse de Guermantes. In *Le Temps retrouvé* he is distraught about losing his son in the war. Model: Marquis de Montebello, French ambassador in St Petersburg.

VAUGOUBERT, Marquise de. Wife of the above. She attends a party given by the Princesse de Guermantes. In *Sodome et Gomorrhe* she is described as looking very masculine and being very dominant in the household. In *La Prisonnière*, she brings her husband into diplomatic disgrace by monopolising the attention of Queen Eudoxie, her friend, at the expense of the French ministers' wives, during King Théodose's second visit. Model: Madame de Montebello, wife of the Marquis de Montebello, a diplomat. During Nicholas II's second visit to France in 1901, Madame de Montebello (then ambassadress to Russia) went to a lunch party in honour of the sovereigns in Compiègne. When the Empress Alexandra took off her hat, all the ladies present did the same except for Madame de Montebello, whose hat and hair-do were in one piece (she had false curls attached to the hat). It was said that Monsieur de Montebello's recall in 1902 was not unconnected with this incident.

VAUGOUBERT. Son of the above two. He was wounded seven times in the war before being killed.

VÉLUDE, Vicomtesse de. Sister of the Comtesse de Montpeyroux, and equally fat; always known as 'Mignonne' in the Guermantes' circle. She appears in *Guermantes*.

VERDURIN, Gustave. The pastiche of the Goncourts' *Journal* at the beginning of *Le Temps retrouvé* reveals that this undynamic character, who is henpecked by his wife, is in fact a great art critic, a contributor to *La Revue* and author of a book on Whistler, 'a lover of all refinement, and of all the beauties of the painted form'. He was one of the first to discover and support Elstir, who considers him 'the brain who had conceived the most accurate vision of his painting'. After his marriage, he stopped writing because of morphine addiction. He and his wife are 'at home' every Wednesday in their apartment in the rue Montalivet, then in their town house on the Quai Voltaire. He rents a country house in Normandy, La Raspelière, where the 'little clan' gathers every summer. Verdurin is cruel in his treatment of Saniette, but also reponds generously when he hears that this man, the butt of everyone's jokes, is bankrupt. His social hypocrisy is remarkable. He prides himself on his knowledge of the aristocracy, but wrongly accords Cambremer precedence over Charlus. When Saniette tells him of the death of one of the 'faithful', Princesse Sherbatoff, Verdurin, who wants to go to a party, uses a witticism of the Duc de Guermantes': 'You're exaggerating!' He enjoys quarrels which allow him to dominate the 'little clan' more completely. He dies during the war, shortly after Cottard; Elstir is the only person who misses him. Models: Albert Arman de Caillavet (whose wife twisted him round her little finger); Émile Straus.

VERDURIN, Madame. 'Boss of the little clan'. Wife of the above. Through a combination of *savoir-faire* and ruthlessness she makes her salon one of the most highly regarded in Paris. Politics and art interest her equally. During the Dreyfus affair she is anti-clerical and revisionist, attending the trial at Madame Zola's side and entertaining Picquart and Laborie in the evenings. Brichot, Cottard, Ski, Elstir, Saniette and the Princesse Sherbatoff are all among her 'faithfuls'. She considers high society personalities 'bores', and distrusts Swann's elevated acquaintances. She tries to thwart his love affair with Odette. As the Cambremers' tenant at La Raspelière, Madame Verdurin pretends not to want to mix with them. The *petite bourgeoise* Madame Bontemps, wife of a civil servant and Albertine's aunt, is her great friend. She invites the writer Bergotte to her salon, but is more interested in painting and music. Later, the pastiche of the Goncourts' *Journal* reveals that she was Fromentin's 'Madeleine' and the favourite model of Elstir. The clan calls Elstir 'Monsieur Biche'; Madame Verdurin boasts that she taught him the name of every flower; he quarrels with her after her marriage. She is authoritarian, and makes Brichot break off his affair with the laundry-maid who was his mistress. Although she knows Normandy better than the Cambremers, she is indifferent to the beauty of landscape. After trying to get Charlus to join the 'little clan', she decides to make Morel break with the Baron during a musical evening at which Charlus's guests show how off-hand their attitude towards him is. During the concert, the narrator describes with some humour how she can only express her admiration for Vinteuil's music in physical terms: it makes her 'cry', or 'sneeze her head off'. Her salon is transformed by the appearance of the Ballets Russes; Stravinsky, Straus and the dancers meet at her suppers. She goes to the Opéra with the Princesse Your-beletieff, and begins to open her doors to the Faubourg set: the Guermantes, the d'Haussonvilles and the Comtesse Molé, whom she accords a spurious title. Madame Verdurin, like Madame Bontemps, becomes one of the reigning queens of the wartime Paris society that is reminiscent of the Directoire. But she pursues Charlus with obstinate hatred, claiming that he, and the Queen of Naples, are spies: 'If we had an energetic government,' she says, 'all that lot would be in a concentration camp.' Her nephew Octave, later a remarkable writer, becomes one of the ornaments of her salon. During a difficult period, when she was suffering from being unable to have croissants for breakfast, she has some delivered thanks to an order from Cottard. 'She had a croissant again for the first time the day the newspapers reported the sinking of the *Lusitania*.' After Monsieur Verdurin's death, she marries the bank-rupt Duc de Duras, and appears in *Gotha* under the name 'Sidonie, Duchesse de Duras, *née* des Baux'. Widowed again, she marries the Prince de Guermantes. From then onwards she holds a pre-eminent position in the Faubourg Saint-Germain set, and at the famous after-noon party in *Le Temps retrouvé* she leads the applause for Rachel, who recites to her guests. Models: Madame Albert Arman de Caillavet, for her authoritarian manners; she also was at home on Wednesdays and felt herself persecuted by 'bores'. Madame Aubernon resembled her in being witty and ruthless (in her salon Proust met Dr Pozzi, the model for Cottard, the pedant Victor Brochard, model for Brichot, and Baron Doäzan, the hostess's cousin, one of the main models for Charlus); her country house, called 'Coeur Volant', inspired La Raspelière. Madame Lemaire (who was known as 'the boss' and who nicknamed the painter Clairin 'Chochotte', as Madame Verdurin does Brichot); Madame Ménard-Dorian, Jacques de Lacretelle's aunt, and Madame de Saint-Victor (both known for their pro-Dreyfus salons); Madame Cecilia Blumenthal (a rich widow who married Louis de Talleyrand-Périgord in 1917).

VILLEMANDOIS, Marquis de. In *Le Temps retrouvé*, he has completely forgotten his past enmity towards the narrator.

VILLEMUR, Madame de. She is introduced to the painter Detaille at the Princesse de Guermantes' party in *Sodome et Gomorrhe*.

VILLEPARISIS, Marquise de. *Née* Mademoiselle de Bouillon, about 1820, she is the aunt of the Duc and of the Duchesse de Guermantes. She is a childhood friend of the narrator's grandmother, whom she meets in Balbec. She is very friendly, and affects a simple lifestyle, inviting the narrator and 'Madame Amédée' to come for drives and discussing her literary opinions with them. She showers the narrator with presents, and introduces him to her great-nephew Saint-Loup. Marcel also meets her nephew, Charlus, at her house. Once a great beauty, she had a stormy youth and 'married beneath her'. As with the Duchesse de Guermantes in later years, her 'hereditary thirst for spiritual nourish-ment' may have lowered her position in Faubourg society. At a party she gives in Paris, the narrator meets Norpois, the Marquise's lover, Saint-Loup, Charlus, the Duchesse de Guermantes and the Comtesse de Marsantes. Bloch knocks over a vase of flowers that Madame de Villeparisis was painting; when he is ready to take his leave, she pretends to be asleep so that she doesn't have to speak to him. In *Sodome et Gomorrhe,* the narrator meets her in the little train at Balbec and has a long conversation with her, thus offending the Princesse Sherbatoff. Many years later he sees her in Venice with Norpois, aged and unrecognisable. Models: Comtesse Sophie de Beaulaincourt, Boni de Castellane's great-aunt; she too had difficulty in regaining her place in society after a youthful mistake. Old and ugly, her face flushed crimson and wearing thick spectacles, she looked like the character Madame Sazerat, whose father was ruined by the Marquise, spotted in Venice. Madame de Beaulaincourt and Madame Lemaire both painted flowers. The character's Memoirs were inspired by Madame de Boigne's; Madame Finaly, who took Proust for drives in Normandy in 1892, was a further model.

VINTEUIL, Monsieur. The narrator's great-aunts' old piano teacher, who has retired with his daughter to Montjouvain, near Combray. In *Swann,* he shows his harsh opinions of 'young people of the worst kind' and his great love for his daughter, whose 'Gomorrhean' habits upset him deeply. Swann hears his sonata played at the Verdurins'; one 'little phrase' from the piece becomes the *leitmotif* of his love for Odette. Although his work is still little known, Vinteuil's name wields a certain prestige. The narrator later hears the musician's masterpiece, the unpublished septet, at Madame Verdurin's. While a 'prisoner', Albertine plays him parts of it on the pianola. Through this music, the narrator (and thereby Proust) finds 'proof of the irreducably individual existence of the soul'. Models: There are many models for the character's talent (though not for his personality): César Franck ('80 per cent', according to Louis Beauchamp), Claude Debussy, Gabriel Fauré, Camille Saint-Saëns, Vincent d'Indy.

VINTEUIL, Mademoiselle. Daughter of the above. She has a bad reputation in Combray. She is shy, looks like a boy and has a deep voice. She causes her father suffering, but he adores her nonetheless. The narrator's parents meet her coming out of church in *Swann.* One day after the musician's death, the narrator is hidden close to the Montjouvain house and inadvertently witnesses a sadistic scene in which Mademoiselle Vinteuil and her woman friend profane her father's memory by spitting on his photograph. This friend, who is older than her, is musically very gifted; the composer considered her 'a superior woman with a great heart'. She helps his daughter decipher the illegible notes of his unpublished works. In fact the narrator discovers that their cruelty may be no more than 'simulated wickedness' in people who are naturally good. In *Sodome et Gomorrhe*, the narrator is staggered to discover Albertine's intimacy with the two friends; he does everything he can to prevent her seeing them at the Verdurins' musical evening. But he also knows that despite the suffering they have caused him, the two young women have also revealed to him, through their work on Vinteuil's compositions, 'the promise that something other than oblivion exists, and that that something is realisable through art'. Models: The daughter of the composer Ernest Guiraud, and Juliette Joinville d'Artois, who lived alone at Mirougrain, near Illiers, during Proust's childhood.

VIRADOBETSKI. See SKI.

VIRELEF, Madame de. In *La Fugitive*, she hesitates to invite Gilberte Swann and the Duchesse de Guermantes to her box at the Opéra.

YOURBELETIEFF, Princesse de. Young sponsor of the Ballets Russes; she attends a performance with her friend Madame Verdurin in *La Prisonnière*. Model: Misia Godebska, a friend of Stravinsky and Diaghilev.

CHAPTER THREE

Dictionary of Places in
A la Recherche

BALBEC In his youth, Proust had been sent to Normandy with his grandmother. He was well acquainted with the Channel beaches – Trouville, Dieppe and Cabourg – whose popularity had increased by the spread of the railways and the fashion for sea-bathing. Cabourg's fortunes rose in the nineteenth century through the efforts of Monsieur Durand-Morambeau, a businessman who paid 100,000 francs for about 125 acres of land to the west of Dives and gave the town its initial plan. This became Balbec, the bathing resort in *A la Recherche* (which Proust had first considered calling Briquebec, Querqueville, Criquebec or even Bouillebec, as can be seen in the margin of his notebook number 32). Here, the narrator meets Albertine and the 'little band'. Other models for Balbec were Évian, where Proust's parents spent their holidays, and Beg-Meil, in Brittany, where Proust stayed with Reynaldo Hahn. Beg-Meil gave Balbec its Celtic atmosphere. For Legrandin, Balbec is 'part of the ancient geological framework of our land, the end of the earth, the true country of the Cimmerians, a dismal coastline notorious for all the shipwrecks in its perpetual fog' (*Du Côté de chez Swann*). The centrepiece of the resort is the Grand Hôtel, which is reminiscent of the Hôtel des Roches-Noires at Trouville, the Splendide in Évian, the Grand Hôtel in Cabourg and even the Ritz in the Place Vendôme. Balbec, like Venice, is one of those names which delight the narrator in his imagination before he sees them in reality.

CANTELOUP (Wood). See CHANTEPIE (Forest).

CARQUETHUIT In *Jeunes Filles*, Elstir advises the narrator to visit this place, near Balbec, rather than the Pointe du Raz: 'I know of nothing else like it in France, it is more like certain aspects of Florida.' Elstir paints *Le Port de Carquethuit*, which is a combination of *Plymouth* and *Scarborough* by Turner.

CARQUEVILLE A small town in Normandy where Madame de Ville-parisis takes the narrator and his grandmother in her car, in *Jeunes Filles*. Model: Criqueboeuf, near Honfleur, which also had a church covered in ivy.

CHAMPIEU An imaginary village near Combray which features in *Swann*.

CHANTEPIE (Forest). This forest, which is close to Balbec, is called Canteloup in *Jeunes Filles*, and Chantepie in *Sodome et Gomorrhe*. Monsieur de Cambremer hunts there and the narrator goes for drives through it, first with Madame de Villeparisis and then with Albertine. Name: From the Château de Chantepie, not far from Cambremer in Normandy.

COMBRAY The native town of the narrator's family, and the place where his first holidays are spent. It gives its name to the first chapter of *A la Recherche*, in which Proust evokes the little garden where Swann's bell could be heard tinkling. Then Combray springs up complete with its atmosphere, inhabitants, church and belltower, brought to mind by the cup of tea. It is the first evocation of the world of the Guermantes, whose property borders the little town, and of the narrator's childhood universe with its two symbolic walks. Along the walk that goes 'Swann's way' he first sees Gilberte, on the bank at Tansonville. Images of happiness and peace follow: the lilacs and the hawthorn, Uncle Adolphe's little play, Françoise's delicious meals. In Aunt Léonie's garden, the narrator reads Bergotte for the first time and discovers the magic of names with the Combray priest. Name: From a small village of 300 people about 31 kilometres south of Caen (Calvados), and from the town of Combres, 14 kilometres from Illiers. Model: Until 1913, Proust had sited Combray in the Chartres area, just where Illiers stands, 24 kilometres from Chartres (which had a population of 2,997 in 1880). In

1914 he placed it between Reims and Laon, near the battle zone; the Germans were to occupy a part of it.

CREUNIERS, Les. A cliff near Balbec which looks like a pink cathedral in one of Elstir's paintings. In *Jeunes Filles*, Andrée takes the narrator there on the day of the game of 'ferret'. This is a real place, which was the object of one of Proust and Mary Finaly's walks in 1892.

DONCIÈRES A garrison town close to Balbec. Saint-Loup, who is serving in the army there, often travels from one place to the other in a horse-drawn carriage. The narrator pays him a visit and stays at the Hôtel de Flandre. The town is described exactly: its streets, the place de la Republique where Captain de Borodino lives, the cathedral, the station – Doncières-la-Goupil – and the station restaurant where he dines with his friend. It is at Doncières that Saint-Loup becomes Madame de Cambremer's lover. Albertine also goes there with the narrator. Morel, the violinist, is doing his military service there when he meets Charlus on the station platform. Name: That of a village in Lorraine, near Épinal. Models: Orléans (Proust's garrison town, with its cathedral, its cobbled streets and misty countryside); Fontainebleau (where Proust stayed with Léon Daudet in 1896; it was there that he had the telephone conversation with his mother which gave rise to the episode of the 'telephone girls', 'the High Priestesses of the Invisible'; Fontainebleau was also the garrison town of Proust's friends Daniel Halévy and Louis de la Salle, whom he went to visit in the autumn of 1893); Versailles (where in the autumn of 1906 and 1908 he lived in the Hôtel des Réservoirs, model for 'the eighteenth-century *petit palais*' where the narrator lives in Doncières). In *Jean Santeuil*, the garrison town is first Fontainebleau, then Provins, and finally Orléans.

DOVILLE (also spelt DOUVILLE). Terminus of the little train to La Raspelière. This small village actually exists in the department of La Manche.

FÉTERNE The Dowager Marquise de Cambremer's country house. Name: From a little village called Féternes, near Thonon. Model: The Villa Bassaraba, belonging to the Princesse de Brancovan, in Amphion on the shores of Lake Leman.

GUERMANTES, Château de. In *A la Recherche*, it stands 10 leagues from Combray. Name: From a château in Seine-et-Marne, 3 kilometres from Lagny-sur-Marne. It was designed by Le Nôtre and built in the reign of Louis XIV. The original owners, Claude and Pierre Viole, were succeeded in 1698 by Paulin Prondre, a tax collector in Lyon who repossessed the deeds of the property. Guermantes remained the fief of the Pondres until 1920 when Jules de Lareinty (François de Pâris's grandfather) sold it. On 23 May 1909, Proust asked Georges de Lauris in a letter 'whether the name Guermantes belonged to the Pâris family or if it was extinct and could be used by a literary man', for (he added in 1910) he wanted to use it absolutely freely, both to 'glorify' and 'besmirch' it. He went to spend a few hours there with his friend François de Pâris after the book's publication; Pâris had also told him a number of anecdotes about the history of Guermantes. The property was later bought by a timber merchant, who sold it to the Hottinguer family. Models: The Château de Gossaincourt at Saint-Éman, not far from Illiers, with its pepperpot turrets. The Château de Villebon (dating from the fourteenth century) in a small village to the north of Illiers, which had a courtyard with rough paving stones like the ones that set in motion the last experience of involuntary memory in *A la Recherche*. It belonged at the time to the Marquis de Pontoi de Pontcarré; it now belongs to Monsieur de la Raudière. In the first version of the novel, the name Villebon was used instead of Guermantes. The Château de Bayeux, which Proust visited in 1907. Like the Château de Guermantes, it was famous for the tapestries by François Boucher that were exhibited there.

GUERMANTES WAY In the area around Combray, the Guermantes way was one of the narrator's favourite walks. Model: The little village of Saint-Éman near Illiers. The Saint-Éman 'way' resembled the Guermantes way: a river with flowering waterlilies.

HUDIMESNIL In *Jeunes Filles*, while walking around Balbec, the narrator sees three trees near the village of Hudimesnil which produce in him the same feelings of happiness he had experienced on seeing the Martinville steeples.

MARTINVILLE-LE-SEC A place near Combray whose two steeples are described when the narrator goes for a drive with Dr Percepied. He writes an article about them, which the Duc de Guermantes neglects to read in *Guermantes*. Proust apparently wrote this essay for *La Revue lilas* in 1888, although it may have been inspired by the rickety steeples in Caen that he saw on his trip through Normandy in 1907. At the time he published 'Impressions de route en automobile' in *Le Figaro*, which could correspond to the narrator's article. Model: Probably the Marché-ville area, because of its name and its situation just outside Illiers.

MÉSÉGLISE WAY The opposite direction to the Guermantes way, the Méséglise-la-Vineuse way (also called Swann's way, since one had to pass Swann's property to get to the village of Méséglise) was the second of the narrator's favourite walks. The countryside was typical of flatlands. The Duc de Guermantes represents the district in the Chambre. Name: Almost the same as that of the small hamlet of Méréglise, near Illiers.

MIROUGRAIN A farm near Combray belonging to Aunt Léonie. She enjoyed the thought that if there were a fire in her house in Combray she could go and spend the summer with her family in 'her pretty farm at Mirougrain, where there was a waterfall'. Model: A country house called 'Le Rocher de Mirougrain' in Illiers, in the direction of Saint-Éman. A mysterious young woman, Juliette Joinville d'Artois (who was perhaps a model for Mademoiselle Vinteuil), lived there.

MONTJOUVAIN The house near Méséglise in which Vinteuil and his daughter lived. In *Swann*, the narrator, lying on a bank overlooking the house, witnesses a sadistic scene between Mademoiselle Vinteuil and her woman friend. Name: There is a mill on the Thironne, not far from Illiers, called Montjouvin. Model: The Mirougrain country house, with its steep slope and its pond.

LA RASPELIÈRE A property near Balbec which the Dowager Marquise de Cambremer lets to the Verdurins. Name: Taken from La Rachepelière, a hamlet near Illiers. Models: 'Les Frémonts', the Baignères' villa in Trouville, with its 'three views'; 'Coeur Volant', Madame Aubernon's country house in Louveciennes, perched on a hill; Madame Aubernon's 'Manoir de la Cour Brulée' in Trouville; Madame Straus's 'Clos des Mûriers' in Trouville; the Château de Réveillon (which belonged to Madame Lemaire) for the interior decoration, which combined real and painted flowers.

RIVEBELLE A seaside resort in Normandy that Estir once used to visit. In Rivebelle, Saint-Loup and the narrator have dinner at a restaurant whose dining room Proust compares to an aquarium. Name: An amalgamation of Riva-Bella, near Cabourg, and Belle-Rive, beside Lake Geneva.

ROUSSAINVILLE-LE-PIN A small place mentioned in *Swann*, on the road to Méséglise, famous for its castle keep in the woods; in the rain it looks as if it is being 'chastised like a village in the Bible'. Some fighting took place there in 1914. Name: The real Roussainville is a hamlet 1½ kilometres south of Illiers with neither ruins nor woods. Le-Pin comes from Bailleau-le-Pin, another village to the north-east of Illiers.

SAINT-ANDRÉ-DES-CHAMPS A church near Combray. In *Swann*, the faces of Françoise and Théodore look like carvings in its porch. Models: Notre-Dame-des-Champs at Châteaudun and the church of Saint-Loup-de-Naud. Originally Proust probably had in mind the porch of Chartres, the essence of whose Gothic carving he wanted to distil. In describing the carvings he also made use of *L'Art religieux du XIIIe siècle en France* by E. Mâle.

SAINT-HILAIRE A church in Combray which was to be destroyed during the war. The narrator first sees the Duchesse de Guermantes there, sitting in a chapel dedicated to Gilbert le Mauvais (the chapel of the Virgin in Saint-Jacques d'Illiers). Name: From an Illiers church demolished during the Revolution. Model: 'Some of the stained-glass windows are undoubtedly from Évreux, others from La Sainte-Chapelle and Pont-Audemer' (Dedication to Jacques de Lacretelle).

TANSONVILLE Swann's property near Combray which the narrator's parents have not visited since his marriage to Odette de Crécy. In *Swann*, Marcel sees Gilberte and Charlus for the first time there, then says farewell to the hawthorn on the bank that runs beside the house. The Saint-Loups move there, in *La Fugitive*, and the narrator goes to spend a few days with them. The house is taken over by the Germans in 1914. Name: From the Château de Tansonville, 3 kilometres from

Illiers. Model: The Pré Catelan garden (belonging to Proust's uncle Jules Amiot) provided the white gate, the lilacs, the 'Archers' House' where the caretaker lives (this was in fact a small gazebo Jules Amiot had built in his park), the Tansonville bank and the hawthorn hedge. Proust's nocturnal walks with Madeleine Lemaire at the Château de Réveillon in 1894 suggest the narrator's night-time walk with Gilberte at Tansonville at the beginning of *Le Temps retrouvé*.

THIBERZY In the Combray region. When the kitchenmaid in *Swann* is about to have a baby, a midwife is fetched from Thiberzy.

VIEUXVICQ In the Combray region. In *Swann*, its belltower seems to stand next to the steeples of Martinville when the narrator goes for a drive with Dr Percepied. Model: A small town to the south of Illiers.

VIVONNE The waterlilies in this river are evoked by the narrator's cup of tea at the opening of *Swann*. It is part of the walk along the Guermantes way, a typical river landscape. Name: Similar to the Thironne, one of the tributaries of the Loir, near Tansonville. Model: The Loir.

CHAPTER FOUR

Principal Themes in Proust's Work

Proust and his World

Snobbery

Proust has often been criticised for devoting too much of *A la Recherche du temps perdu* to 'society'. But is Racine blamed for depicting princesses, or Molière for the fact that Acaste is a Marquis and Alceste a Comte? In his book *Hommage à Marcel Proust*, Paul Valéry wrote: 'What in itself is known as "society" is made up of symbolic figures. Each character features in it in order to personify an abstract notion. It is necessary for powerful influences to come in contact with each other; somewhere, *money* has to talk to *beauty, politics* must be tamed by *elegance, literature* and *good breeding* should entertain each other to tea. As soon as a new force is recognised, its representatives appear at "society" gatherings before very much time elapses. The movement of history can be reasonably well recorded in the successive reign of different social types in the drawing rooms and at the hunts, weddings and funerals of the nation's supreme tribe. All the abstract concepts I mentioned are represented by individuals who are what they are, and the resulting contradictions and complications can only be observed in this small theatre.'

In *Jean Santeuil*, society figures are described in the characters of the Duc and Duchesse de Réveillon. But Proust is not yet sufficiently detached from his subject to describe it effectively: we have to wait several chapters to meet the Duc de Réveillon. In *Jean Santeuil* Proust himself revels in the delights of high society, and wants us to share them in the chapter 'La première de Frédégonde', when the hero takes his revenge on Madame Marnet, who has cancelled an appointment with him, by appearing at the Opéra in the company of the King of Portugal.

His snobbery also comes from the fact that he adores great names, with all their aesthetic and historical associations. In *Les Plaisirs et les jours*, Madame Lenoir succumbs to the delights of self-gratification, like Proust: 'Since the rich and glorious names of the past had such singular power over her sensitive soul, the intense pleasure she felt was equally disinterested whether she was dining with princes or reading memoirs of the *ancien régime*.'

In *Sésame et les lys* (1906), Proust began to transcend his snobbery. In a note he denounced 'the sophisms which intelligent people produce from the arsenal of their intellect to justify their basest tendencies. This is equivalent to saying that becoming more intelligent creates less right to be so. Quite simply, different people live side by side in the breast of each of us, and the life of more than one superior being is often no more than the co-existence of a philosopher and a snob.' In the preface to the work, he wrote: 'To enjoy someone's company because he had an ancestor in the Crusades is pure vanity. Intelligence has nothing to do with it. But to enjoy someone's company because his grandfather's name crops up in Alfred de Vigny or Chateaubriand, or (an irresistible lure for me, I confess) because his family crest appears in the Grande Rose of Nôtre-Dame d'Amiens, that is where intellectual sin begins.'

In *A la Recherche*, the world of high society is better analysed. According to Émilien Carassus, Proust passed beyond snobbery as a guiding principle in his life to a sense of snobbery as something conquered. Like Madame Lenoir in *Les Plaisirs et les jours*, he realised that 'his snobbery was only in his imagination, and was, moreover, his entire imagination'. He overcame it by an awareness of two things: 'On one hand, the aristocracy offered certain real advantages, and their company afforded an intellectual like himself as much if not more richness than the company of other intellectuals who were no more stimulating to his interior life; on the other hand, the time he had wasted was not absolutely gone: in his secret self, and thanks to the resurgence of the past in his memory, he could use the play of illusions – and disillusion-ment – to nourish his literary creativity. Proust did not free himself from snobbery and fear by bringing lucid judgements to bear on aristocratic society, but by bringing lucid judgement to bear on the nature of his own vocation' (É. Carassus, *Le Snobisme et les lettres françaises*, p. 570). If he then learnt to judge society people according to their true worth, it was no longer as social and aesthetic phenomena but according to how the experience of time spent in their company nourished the imagination and the life of the mind. Proust inverted the process of snobbery, no longer attached to predetermined criteria, the beauty of a name or its illustrious history, but to the deep knowledge of the individual and the deep substance of his impressions.

The Salons

In *A la Recherche*, the narrator observes the social strategies of the Faubourg. Its hierarchy is tempered by politeness, apart from a certain vulgarity of expression or attitude used to display hostility to the bourgeoisie – the Duc de Guermantes' brusque greeting to the musician he despises at the risk of getting 'a tremendous punch in the guts', or the horrific stories told about the Duchess in front of Legrandin. Bourgeois morality is banned from the salons. The Duc de Guermantes' behaviour with his mistress Madame d'Arpajon does not trouble Oriane at all. It is social dilemmas, not moral decisions, which can threaten to lower the tone. To entertain, one must have a name; then the assessment of the salon is established 'according to the people the mistress of the house excludes rather than those who visit her' (L. Pierre-Quint, *op. cit.*, p. 141). For this reason, being excluded from a fashionable salon is felt to be the worst of punishments.

Principal scenes of society life in the salons. Madame de Villeparisis' afternoon party, the Duchesse de Guermantes' dinner, the Princesse de Guermantes' evening party, dinner at the Verdurins' at La Raspelière, the Verdurins' musical evening in Paris and the afternoon party given by the Princesse de Guermantes in *Le Temps retrouvé*. These very long scenes were the parts of the work most substantially redrafted between 1914 and 1922.

The Prince and Princesse de Guermantes' salon. The most prestigious. Its ceremony is probably based on Princesse Mathilde's. Royal and Imperial Highnesses flock together, but the salon's splendour is equalled only by the boredom which afflicts it.

The Duchesse de Guermantes' salon. More open than the above. The Duchess passes for a woman of letters by inviting artists or writers to her dinners, but she limits them to one per evening so as not to spoil her salon's reputation.

Madame de Villeparisis' salon. A little *déclassé*, it is at the bottom of the ladder.

The nobles who frequent the salons seem to stand at the pinnacle of the social hierarchy. In fact, their chief preoccupation is to outdo each other in climbing the social steps the salons represent. The salons' apparently fossilised and static rituals of precedence hide perpetually shifting patterns of intrigue. Thus the salons form and reform, fill up, improve or destroy themselves – as when the Princesse de Parme tries to steal the Duchesse de Guermantes' guests.

Through his innate sense of observation, Proust discovered the organic unity of each salon, the 'coterie' or 'clan', a group of people who have the 'same way of judging small things', the same turn of wit. The 'Guermantes wit' crystallises their coterie. The most closed to all innovation is the Courvoisiers' salon, but Proust also commented on its lack of culture. Even in *Jean Santeuil*, salon conversation is an uninterrupted stream of platitudes, entirely concerned with social intrigues or questions of etiquette.

The 'Cercles'

Cercle des Ganaches. Founded in 1819, also called the Cercle littéraire, it included generals and bankers.

Cercle de l'Union. Founded in 1828 on the inspiration of the Duc de Guiche, Jean Greffulhe and Urbain Sartoris. It was situated at 11 boulevard de la Madeleine from 1856 to 1948. Talleyrand was among the first members.

Other members included Prince Radolin (German ambassador to Paris from 1901 to 1910), Comte R. de Khevenhüller-Metsch (Austro-Hungarian ambassador to Paris from 1903 to 1911), General de Galliffet, General Lyautey (joined in 1900). Proust's friend Armand de Guiche dissuaded him from standing for membership. Various characters in *A la Recherche*, such as the Duc de Guermantes, are members of the Union (they are often also members of the Jockey Club). The Union, which was originally very exclusive, later became more eclectic than the Jockey; there were notably more foreign members. But the ballot rules for admitting candidates were very severe (one black ball cancelled twelve white ones, instead of six, as at the Jockey Club).

Jockey Club. Founded in 1833 under the name 'Cercle de la Société d'Encouragement'; it took the name Jockey Club in 1903. From 1863 to 1924 it was situated at 2 rue Scribe. Proust would have liked to join, but after Charles Haas's death in 1902 his candidature was impossible. Charles Haas himself had been refused four times from 1865 onwards (this was a record), but was allowed in on the fifth occasion because of his conduct during the war of 1870 (he was put up by the Comte de Saint-Priest and the Comte Albéric de Bernis on 21 January 1871).

Many of the characters in *A la Recherche* are members: the Guermantes, the Prince d'Agrigente, Charles Swann. When the President of the Jockey Club dies, the Duc de Guermantes (the longest-standing vice-President) expects to be elected, but to everyone's surprise he is beaten by Monsieur Chaussepierre, the deputy vice-president. 'It's hard for the Duc. He claimed to be above failure of that sort, assuring everyone, besides, that he owed it to his old friendship with Swann. In fact, he never got over it [...] What is more, the Duc could not bear anyone to talk about the Dreyfus affair "which had brought so much misfortune", he used to say, even though he only really felt one of the consequences: his failure to win the presidency of the Jockey Club.' Later, in *Le Temps retrouvé*, the Duke is again beaten because of his liaison with Madame de Forcheville (the former Odette Swann). For the same reason, he is unable to get a seat in the Académie des beaux-arts; at about the same time, Monsieur de Charlus obtains neither the presidency of the Union nor that of the Société des amis du vieux Paris.

Cercle Agricole. Founded in 1835 by a group of landowners, with the aim of refining agricultural techniques and developing the associated industries.

Cercle de la rue Royale. In 1855, the Jockey merged with the Nouveau Cercle or Cercle des Moutards, which dated from 1847 and was made up of young members of the legitimist aristocracy. Old members of the Nouveau Cercle, unhappy about the merger, then organised the Cercle de le rue Royale, which was absorbed by the Cercle Agricole in 1865 because of financial difficulties. A new Cercle de la rue Royale was therefore founded. In 1916, this too joined up with the Cercle Agricole and moved in to the latter's premises, but kept the name Nouveau Cercle de la rue Royale. In 1946, members of the Cercle de l'Union artistique, called the Épatant, joined it and it then called itself simply Nouveau Cercle. Its statutes laid down that half its members should be French and half foreign.

The picture of the Cercle de la rue Royale painted by James Tissot in 1868 (2.15m × 3.30m) shows Comte A. de La Tour-Maubourg, the Marquis du Lau, Comte Étienne de Ganay, Comte J. de Rochechouart, C. Vansittart, the Marquis de Miramon, Baron Hottinguer, the Marquis de Ganay, Gaston de Saint-Maurice, Prince Edmond de Polignac, the Marquis de Galliffet and Charles Haas.

On 10 June 1922 *L'Illustration* printed a reproduction of the picture which Paul Brach sent to Proust, who thanked him and mentioned the people it showed, particularly Polignac and Saint-Maurice, 'the only two apart from Haas I knew personally'. The painting now belongs to descendants of Baron Hottinguer's, to whom it was awarded in a lottery.

Polo. Founded in 1892 by the Vicomte de La Rochefoucauld in the Bois de Boulogne. Proust was a member, but never went there (it's said he once caught a cold there and never went back).

Servants

As in Molière, high society and the servant class went together. They had the same rituals. Domestic servants participated in the life of the leisured class, of which they were a fragment. The degree of specialisation among servants rendered them unable to do any other work. The arrogance of the Princesse de Guermantes' 'usher' and the pride shown by Aimé, the maître d'hôtel of the Grand Hôtel in Balbec, are sufficient indication of their participation in their masters' sense of superiority. The Faubourg was swarming with them; that was Swann's first impression at Madame de Saint-Euverte's party. Before penetrating 'society', he crosses another no less impressive 'society', the 'straggling mob' of footmen.

In *Jean Santeuil*, the élitism that characterises Proust's idea of society is already apparent. The writer C.'s occasional companion, the lighthouse-keeper, knows his place, and 'in the simplicity of his respect knew whether to tiptoe away or to stay and chat to C. when he needed it, thus helping the delicate blossoming of a work he will never know anything about'. Proust was convinced of the gulf between the creator and the man of the people. A servant had to tend to all the needs of a master who was completely insensitive to anything concerning the servant. C.'s behaviour towards the young sailor shows this: 'During the evening, he often sent the servant to wake the ship's boy who was already asleep in his bed and make him get up'. For Proust, as for C., there were two breeds: masters and servants.

In *A la Recherche*, the ordinary people as such (those described by Zola or Balzac) do not exist, apart from the strange Jupien, who is hardly representative of the working classes. There are only the people of the household. Proust describes them with as much attention as he does their masters, for the two make up a whole entity. These servitors also bring the narrator treasures of language and good sense. They do not come from the industrial cities but from the countryside, a privileged place in Proust's mind. For him, a lover of contrasts and opposites, illiteracy and poetry were one. There is the case of Françoise, with her highly-flavoured speech mannerisms, and the two Balbec 'postwomen' recently arrived from their native Massif Central. Morel, the peverse creature whose origins were a millstone round his neck, constitutes a different example. But his out-of-the-ordinary physique allowed him to reverse roles in his relationships with his titled worshippers (J. Canavaggia, *Proust et la politique*, p. 33). He teaches Charlus to place art above the social hierarchy.

This other 'society' gives a better understanding of the Faubourg Saint-Germain from which, in the end, it scarcely differs. It has the same sets of feelings based on hate, cowardice and arrogance. It also has the same archaic language and the same lack of culture. Thus Françoise is close to the Duchesse de Guermantes. Servants, as the narrator's maid shows him, live with their fate: 'As long as the world goes round, you see, there will be masters to make you jump and servants to do their whim.' They can only be inexorably bound together.

Social Relationships

A la Recherche takes place on two levels: that of encounters in the social world, the surest way of losing oneself and never attaining the other, and that of creation, of the decoding of signs, which allows the other to be experienced in an indirect way, through writing which reconstitutes the world. Parties, dinners, afternoon parties and society scenes follow each other, all elevated to the status of an institution. But, through an apparent paradox, the many opportunities of contact they offer do not help to achieve any knowledge of other people. A person is either deliberately secretive, like Charlus, or exists solely through the 'social' eye that rests on him. He is 'a creation of other people's thoughts'; he is condemned to death; he no longer exists. Such is the case with Swann or Madame Sherbatoff. The danger is to accept the mask society imposes and to give way to snobbery, since it is 'the admiration in other people of all that is independent of their personality' (*Jean Santeuil*).

In the social comedy it is conversation, considered 'superficial ramblings' in *Jeunes Filles*, that most alienates the individual from himself. Like Oriane, Swann, the eternal dilettante, gives up on creativity. He will never write his essay on Vermeer; 'When open to others for conversation, we are to a certain extent closed to ourselves' (*Jeunes Filles*). Soon, society conversation and salon manners, like the Guermantes wit, become reduced to a series of signs, pieces of mimicry like Madame Verdurin with her head in her hands, to the detriment of individuality. The 'faithful' of the 'little clan' are 'shaped [...] on the same model'; they are no more than elements of a group or coterie.

The world of society sterilises the creative man. This happens to the narrator when he encounters it in *Guermantes*, and loses 'the sense which makes us consider something as merely a performance, and comes to believe in it as if it were a unique being.' To create and to know oneself, it is essential to avoid all society and any group. Charlus manages this for a time when he leaves the Guermantes for the Verdurins, as does the narrator when he grows closer to the great mediators, Elstir and Vinteuil, the solitary musician from Combray, both almost unknown in society.

As early as 1900 Proust expressed this truth in an article in *Le Figaro*. He developed it in *Le Temps retrouvé*: 'In their work as in life, people [...] should be strongly [...] individual. It is when they are most absolutely themselves that they can best express the universal soul.' In *Contre Sainte-Beuve*, he also states: 'A book is the product of a different self to the one we display in society.' Like Baudelaire, Proust uses artistic creation as a means of discovering the essence of human beings and of things; communication is achieved through the intermediary of writing.

Proust and the Individual

Love

Love occupies a special place in *A la Recherche*. As Proust pointed out to Jacques Rivière, the story contains three great passions: Swann's for Odette, and the narrator's for Gilberte then for Albertine. These three reflect each other, with points in common as well as dissimilarities, especially in their outcome. Although one of the love affairs ends in marriage, another in a break-up and the third in death, they nevertheless have an ending in common: the hero's indifference to his passionate feelings, an indifference that marks his cure. In *A la Recherche* love is seen as stifling, possessive and rarely reciprocated: it often leads to loneliness and the perversions that entails. It is also interchangeable – the narrator comments that he could just as easily have loved Andrée as Albertine. The element of chance comes at the birth of passion, when the woman is unknown, at the moment of instantaneous desire. At first Odette was not Swann's 'type'. By contrast, the narrator's love for Gilberte is born of a violent physical attraction. Desire passes, before or after love. 'Once upon a time,' Swann says, 'one dreamed of capturing the heart of the woman one was in love with; later, feeling that you had a woman's heart was enough to make you fall in love' (*Du Côté de chez Swann*).

Swann's love for Odette prefigures the novel's other romantic episodes in all its details. At the start of his love, Swann dreams of conjugal peace: 'It would be so nice to have a little person with whom you could be sure to find that rare thing, some good tea!' The narrator also wishes Gilberte could be 'an obliging and comfortable collaborator who could help me with my work in the evenings'. Imagination and art are the chief servants of passionate feelings. Odette looks like Botticelli's *Daughter of Jethro* and so arouses Swann's desire. The narrator desires Gilberte from the beginning, and because she is a friend of Bergotte's and visits the fascinating Norman churches with him, 'the charm of all the ideas that cathedrals evoked in me, the charm of the hills of the Ile de France and the Norman plains reflected back on to the image I formed of Mademoiselle Swann: I was ready to fall in love with her. Of all the things love needs to come into being, the most conducive is our believing that the other person has an unknown life which their love will allow us to penetrate.'

The other person's absence from the place where we expect to find them also stimulates passion. The narrator is tormented by the notion that he might not find Gilberte in the Champs-Élysées or Albertine on the esplanade at Balbec: 'But to unleash this sadness, this sense of the irreparable, this anguish which prepares for love, one must [...] risk the impossible' (*Jeunes Filles*). In the same way, Swann searches for Odette for a whole night. Uncertainty and a sense of the unknown provoke a love whose character is in fact purely subjective. 'One doesn't love a woman because one respects her qualities, but because one knows nothing about her' (M. Raymond, *Proust romancier*, pp. 130–1). The jealousy caused by not knowing how the loved one is spending their time, the 'fugitive being', persecutes Swann (like Honoré in 'La Fin de la jalousie' in *Les Plaisirs et les jours*). The heroes of *A la Recherche* are caught in a vicious circle. Suspicion engenders jealousy, which gives rise to suspicion. 'What is terrible is not knowing' (*Jean Santeuil*). To know the other person, they resort to the famous scenes of manic questioning, to 'probing chats' which increase the lover's misery because of the fragmentary revelations he achieves. The 'inquisitorial impulse that wants to know nonetheless suffers from knowing, and seeks to learn more' (*La Prisonnière*). But love uses jealousy to enforce a knowledge of the loved one, and of oneself. Jealousy is a spur to intellectual activity. Swann himself remarks that this curiosity is similar to 'that which he once felt for history'. And even though he is only interested in a single object, the lover can come to formulate general laws about love and the impossibility of communication between human beings.

Love, therefore, is an illness, and the writer uses a clinical vocabulary to describe it. He talks of 'symptoms', of 'cancer', of 'pain in the heart'. The cure for it is time, which heals naturally, and old age, which diminishes our sensitivity. The interim solution is to lock the loved one away in order to have her entirely for oneself: this is the theme of *La Prisonnière*. Albertine is then thought of 'more as a domestic animal than as a young girl'; this brings the narrator peace and security. But still, jealousy and suffering are not far away, and the real cure only comes with the indifference wrought by time.

Memory and Oblivion

The whole of *A la Recherche* rests on memory. Its hero, the narrator, remembers, and he writes. Proust makes the well-known distinction between *intellectual memory*, the insipid and unattractive state of *anamnesia*, and *involuntary memory* which spontaneously releases highly coloured 'extra-temporal' moments from oblivion: 'the finest part of our memory is outside us [...] Outside us? Within us, properly speaking, but veiled from our own gaze, in a more or less prolonged state of oblivion. It is only thanks to that oblivion that we can occasionally regain the being we once were' (*Jeunes Filles*). In *A la Recherche* oblivion is seen as the best foundation for the miracles produced by emotional memory. Surging up from nothingness, the memories benefit from both 'the pressure of the imaginary and the consciousness of reality' (*Jean Santeuil*). The experience of the cup of tea unleashes the whole story of Combray. In *Le Temps retrouvé* other manifestations of involuntary memory – the crumpling of the napkin and the trip on the uneven paving-stones in the Guermantes courtyard – provoke the narrator's final decision to get down to work. He finally understands his vocation, which is to interpret all this by means of a work of art that will fix the time regained forever.

This literary procedure (which was not new, since Chateaubriand, Nerval in *Sylvie*, and even Fernand Gregh had used it) allowed Proust – despite his denying it in a letter of 1913 to Jacques Copeau – to make a virtuoso play on memory, toying with it like a dilettante. The 'intermittent reactions of the heart' are an example of the balance between memory and forgetting, caused by 'the anachronism that so often prevents the calendar of facts from coinciding with the calendar of feeling' (*Sodome et Gomorrhe*). In the novel, there are numerous variations on the way pain and relief from pain alternate in the characters' emotional lives.

Since he so enjoyed playing with the notion of time, Proust was tempted, at the beginning of *A la Recherche* (when the narrator wakes up in the opening pages of 'Combray') to abandon linear narrative in favour of presenting memories in the order in which they present themselves to the mind. Lost in time and space, with the bedrooms of his life turning in the darkness, the author can reorganise the world: 'A man asleep holds the thread of hours, the order of years and of worlds in a circle around him.' Nonetheless, this temporal discontinuity gives way to a story whose aim is to trace the history of a vocation. The experiences of involuntary memory in *Le Temps retrouvé* are simply events chronologically situated in the hero's psychic life, and not – like the experience of the *madeleine* and the cup of tea – the point of departure on a journey of exploration. The novel's central pivot is memory, and it becomes a brilliant set of variations on the theme of time.

Illness and Death

Proust's characters are no less sickly than their creator, although their afflictions are mostly at a psychic and psychological level. As the son and the brother of doctors, Proust makes use of a whole repertoire of therapeutic, pathological, surgical and psychological terms. He uses it to make a careful study of the progress of Charlus's erotomania and cerebrosclerosis, to describe Bergotte's death and the dying hours of the narrator's grandmother, which influenced his interior creative life deeply. The novel could also be summed up in terms of the slow degeneration of the characters caused by time, the inexorable inroads of a virus and the description of multiple perversions. The story of the narrator's physical and psychological ills merges with that of the novel.

Illness reveals character, as it does with the narrator and his grandmother. Proust often sets the indifferent strength of triumphant health against the helpless weakness of a sick person – like the radiant Françoise and the kitchenmaid in labour, or Swann announcing his fatal illness to the pitiless Guermantes. Proust also likes to stage-manage suffering with an obvious concern for theatrical effect, as with Berma's death at the end of *A la Recherche*. He stresses the symptoms of the illness and underlines their importance, thus giving a tragic dimension to the death of Saniette or Bergotte.

Proust often deals with death. In *Jean Santeuil*, he first evokes the future death of Jean Santeuil's parents, as if to make it happen: 'Selfishness, or perhaps the need for life itself, prevents us from spending too long thinking about the death of people precious to us. Such thoughts are dangerous and dismal, because out of terror of a death like this they anticipate it, and spread its pain over the time we have been given to enjoy their lives'. In *A la Recherche*, the narrator becomes acquainted with death by invoking his grandmother's. Every time Proust made corrections to his manuscript, he increased the images of death.

As in Montaigne, the idea of death is constant. It is a pure fact, about which one can do nothing. As with passion, Proust does not avoid this problem, which goes so far beyond the individual, nor can he resolve it. The only progress is to be able to stay calm in face of it. In *Le Temps retrouvé*, he writes: 'The idea of death settled in me forever [...] not that I liked death; I loathed it'. The idea impelled him to hurry in finishing his work.

Religion

For Proust, religion had a great deal to do with art. Under Ruskin's influence he came to appreciate the noble ceremonies of worship and the beauty of Gothic churches. His deep religious and Biblical knowledge were more use in providing harmony in his work than in sustaining him as a man. A sentence from *L'Imitation de Jésus-Christ* serves as the epigraph for 'Violante ou la mondanité' in *Les Plaisirs et les jours*. When Proust criticised the government's anti-clerical stance and condemned the separation of Church and State in 1904 in an article in *Le Figaro* called 'La Mort des cathédrales', he was reacting as an aesthete and disciple of Ruskin. His picture of Combray (or, earlier, of Étreuilles in *Jean Santeuil*) leaves an impression that is more poetic than religious, despite its church and 'the little streets [that] bore the names of saints'. He regarded the celebration of the Catholic mass as no more than a theatrical performance: 'One could say that a performance of Wagner at Bayreuth [...] pales in comparison with the celebration of High Mass in Chartres cathedral' ('La Mort des cathédrales').

If Proust believed in anything, it was in a vague but absolute eternity. His anguish shows in his work, when he describes a world crumbling and human beings in decline, but the fear of this general distintegration is dissolved by a deep sense of the eternal. This is a sense that the narrator in *A la Recherche* experiences in very brief flashes through the phenomenon of involuntary memory. He will transcend time by means of his work. Talking about *A la Recherche*, Albert Béguin stressed its 'mystic demands'; Henri Massis detected questions about resurrection, but the only expression of eternal life, for Proust, was the work of art. He discovered a form of salvation through creative ecstasy, revealing a world beyond the reach of time. This is how Bergotte's death in *La Prisonnière* should be interpreted: 'He was buried, but throughout the night of the funeral, in the lighted windows, his books stood three by three, keeping watch like angels with their wings spread, and seemed a symbol of eternal life for the one who was no more.' For Proust, salvation could only come through art: Bergotte's death in front of Vermeer's *View of Delft* is symbolically charged with light and hope.

Proust and his Time

Art

Proust was passionate about art, and there are countless references to works of art in his writing. According to him, art is born of life, and in every human being there exists a (more or less elevated) level at which life becomes creation. This creation – and this knowledge – remain inaccessible to the intelligence; that is why works of art cannot be adapted to theories. Proust condemned 'rationalisation' by saying: 'we go astray each time we fail to find the strength to force ourselves to put an impression through all the successive stages that will end in its being fixed forever, in the expression of its reality'. For beauty to have life, it must encounter a person capable not only of feeling but also of expressing it. The artist must be in a position, more than anything else, to 'free the hidden soul of things'.

JOHN RUSKIN (London, 1819 – Brantwood, 1900). English art critic. Son of a rich businessman, Ruskin studied in London (King's College) and Oxford (Christ Church College). He was a talented writer, and won the Newdigate Prize in 1839. He was a great admirer of Turner (1775–1851) and of medieval Italian art, and a defender of the pre-Raphaelites; from 1850 onwards he wrote for their periodical, *The Seed*. His aesthetic thought and philosophy of art led him to be considered the greatest art critic of his time from the age of 30. He taught history of art at Oxford from 1869 to 1878 and from 1883 to 1884. He was a close friend of Thomas Carlyle (1795–1881), who often inspired his work.

Works: Modern Painters (in five volumes, 1834–60), *The Seven Lamps of Architecture* (1849), *The Stones of Venice* (1851–3), *Pre-Raphaelitism* (1851), *The Political Economy of Art* (1857), *The Two Paths* (1859), *Sesame and Lilies* (1865), *Munera Pulveris* (1872), *Flux and Reflux* (1872), *The*

Bible of Amiens (1880–5), *Praeterita* (an unfinished autobiography 1885–9).

PROUST AND RUSKIN Abandoning the editing of *Jean Santeuil*, Proust – who was already well-versed in the French philosopher, Gabriel Séailles (1852–1922), and the German Friedrich Schelling (1775–1854) – immersed himself in John Ruskin.

Proust's enthusiasm can be partly explained by the interest French writers were showing at the time in English literature, 'sensations of art' and Venice. In 1893, Proust discovered Ruskin through the extracts published by *Le Bulletin de l'Union pour l'action morale*, a periodical founded a year before by the writer Paul Desjardins (1859–1940). At the end of 1896 he met Reynaldo Hahn's English cousin, Marie Nordlinger, who had already translated a chapter of Ruskin and who later helped him in his translation work. On 25 September 1899 he wrote to his mother from Évian to ask for Robert de la Sizeranne's book *Ruskin et la religion de la beauté*, which had come out in 1897. Proust was to devote himself wholly to Ruskin, augmenting his reading (which he did mostly in English, for lack of translations, and despite the fact that he had not mastered the language) with pilgrimages to French and Italian churches Ruskin had visited.

In October 1899, the critic Louis Canderax (1855–1940), literary editor of the *Revue de Paris* since 1894, commissioned him to write a study of Ruskin. Proust set to work in the Bibliothèque Nationale with his friend François d'Oncieu and began his first translations.

On 21 January 1900, Ruskin died; his death gave renewed topicality to studies devoted to him. In *La Chronique des arts et de la curiosité* on 27 January Proust published an obituary in which he did not stint in his praise: 'Director of the consciousness of his time, Ruskin was certainly that – but he was also its master of taste, and its guide to a sense of beauty'. On 13 February, *Le Figaro* printed Proust's 'Pèlerinages ruskiniens en France' in his honour. In April, *Le Mercure de France* published Proust's first major study, 'Ruskin à Nôtre-Dame d'Amiens' which provided material for his 85-page preface to *La Bible d'Amiens* in 1904. In August, *La Gazette des beaux-arts* published another piece by Proust entitled 'John Ruskin'. In 1906, the annotated translation of Ruskin's *Sesame and Lilies* appeared, preceded by a preface of 58 pages, 'Sur la

lecture', which had been published in *La Renaissance latine* of 15 June
1905. Ruskin provided Proust with a lofty definition of art and a
philosophy of the world whose mystical dimension we can interpret:
'Beauty is not an object of enjoyment, but [...] a reality infinitely more
important than real life.'

Yet, although Proust shared these aesthetic ideas overlaid with
spirituality, he was soon to detach himself from Ruskin. In November
1908 he wrote to Georges de Lauris, rather inaccurately: 'None of this
prevents Ruskin's work often being stupid, manic, irritating, false,
ridiculous'. There is a social dimension to Ruskin's thought which is
absent in Proust, who was then turning to another, equally aesthetic,
English philosopher, Walter Pater (1839–94). With him, according to
Anne Henry in her book *Marcel Proust: Théorie pour une esthétique*, 'egoism
was set against militant sermonising'. In his preface to *La Bible d'Amiens*
Proust had already transformed a 'work of social combat' into 'an
inoffensive tour guide'. He abandoned aesthetic socialism and rejoined
the ranks of the dandies, with Oscar Wilde (1856–1900), a disciple of
Pater, and the painter James Whistler (1834–1903), a sworn enemy of
Ruskin and Montesquiou. Although he remained forever convinced
of the supreme value of art, he would always dispute its humanism.

PAINTING Although he travelled very little (he knew the museums of
Venice and Holland, certainly, but had never seen those of Spain or
Germany), Proust knew a great deal about painting, from the Italian
primitives to Picasso, because in his eyes a picture was not an object to
be collected (as it was for Balzac), but the agent of the imagination. In
A la Recherche, great painters both real and fictitious are used as a
springboard for his aesthetic theories. Through the frescoes in Padua
showing 'Virtue' and 'Vice', Giotto – and the kitchenmaid in 'Combray'
– confront reality and abstraction in art. When Swann decides that
Odette looks like Botticelli's *Daughter of Jethro*, Proust touches on the
problem of Ruskinian idolatry, which confused the beautiful and the
real. But it is Elstir who guides the narrator on the path to his vocation
by revealing general laws of art to him through a new way of looking
at the world. For Elstir, metamorphosis replaces the metaphor in
literature. His *Port de Carquethuit* is the prototype example of this.

JOHANNES VERMEER (Delft, 1632 – Delft, 1675). Vermeer came from a family of lower middle-class business people, the son of a silk-weaver. Like Proust, he was asthmatic. He was apprenticed to a recognised master of the time, Leonaert Bramer (1595–1674), and then worked for the painter Carel Fabritius (1622–54), a former pupil of Rembrandt's. In April 1653 he married Catharina Bolnes, with whom he had fourteen children. The same year he was enrolled as a master in the Anvers guild. After the death of his father in 1655, he moved into his house – Mechelen – which stood on the market square in Delft. He was probably a picture dealer. On 15 December 1675 he died at the age of 43, leaving his family, including eight young children, in poverty. He was buried at the Old Church in the town.

Works: At present there are about 30 authenticated pictures by Vermeer (in 1947 the scandal over the forger Van Meegeren increased Vermeer's reputation: he was already very famous but not very popular). Among his best-known paintings are: *The Milkmaid* (c. 1658–60), *The Pearl Necklace* (c. 1662–3), *The Lacemaker* (1665), *The Guitar Player* (c. 1667–70).

The View of Delft (0.98m × 1.18m) hangs in the Mauritshuis Museum in The Hague. The picture was painted between 1658 and 1661, when Vermeer was less than 30 years old. It is one of his few pictures of the exterior world, rather than of domestic interiors. It shows an exact representation of the view of Delft from Schiekade: on the right, we can see the Rotterdam gate; in the centre, the Schiedam gate; and the tower of the Old Church, where Vermeer is now buried, appears in the dark area. It is even possible to identify the house from which Vermeer painted the picture.

This is the view Proust immortalised when he mentions the 'little expanse of yellow wall' – meaning the roof (on the right of the picture) to the left of the second small tower, lit by a shaft of sunlight that has broken through the clouds.

PROUST AND VERMEER Proust had a special admiration for Vermeer's painting (although it did not constitute a philosophical model, as many people have thought). In October 1902, during a trip with Bertrand de Fénelon, Proust had his first opportunity to see *The View of Delft* in The Hague. In May 1921, Proust visited an exhibition of Dutch art at the Jeu de Paume with Jean-Louis Vaudroyer. He suffered an attack of dizziness, which compelled Vaudroyer to take his arm and help him over to the picture. Of the painting, Proust said: 'Ever since I saw *The View of Delft* in the museum in The Hague, I've known that I had seen the most beautiful picture in the world.' In *A la Recherche*, Vermeer is used to stress Swann's dilettantism, as he will never write the study of him he plans, and Bergotte dies in front of *The View of Delft*.

PROUST AND RENOIR In *A la Recherche*, especially in *Jeunes Filles*, Proust uses numerous comparisons with pictorial works. In his view, painting has an advantage over literature: since it does not have to pass through the intermediary of language, it can have direct access to the sensibility. People have even commented on the 'impressionist style' used by Proust, a great admirer of Renoir, when, in the description of the picnic in *Jeunes Filles*, he conveys its fugitive quality by means of both pictorial and literary elements: 'For the most part, these young girls' faces were merged in the suffused pink of early dawn from which the real features have not yet burst forth. One only saw a delightful colour under which what would in a few years' time be a profile was not yet discernable.' Proust used impressionism to encapsulate the central problem of artistic creation: 'Nowadays, people of taste tell us that Renoir is a great eighteenth-century painter. But in saying that they forget the times and that it has taken a great deal, even in the middle of the nineteenth century, for Renoir to be hailed as a great artist. To succeed in being recognised as such, an original painter, any original artist, has to proceed like an oculist. The treatment with their painting, or their prose, is not always pleasant. When they have finished, the practitioner says: Now look. And suddenly the world (which was not just created once, but as often as an original artist has emerged) looks entirely different from before, but perfectly clear. The women going by in the street are quite unlike the ones we used to see, because now they are Renoirs, the Renoirs in which we once refused to see women' (*Le Côté de Guermantes*).

PROUST AND GUSTAVE MOREAU Proust also respected the symbolists, who were closer to his world, such as Gustave Moreau (1826–98). In 1902, the painter's house (at 14 rue de La Rochefoucauld) was made into a museum, thanks to Moreau's intimate friend and heir, Henri Rupp. Proust took a close interest in his work, not least because of

Montesquiou's admiration for him. He makes a number of references to his pictures, especially to *Le Jeune Homme et la Mort*, which is described as a 'masterpiece' in *Guermantes*, and in articles he wrote about Moreau. Proust was delighted by the intellectual and mythological aspects of Moreau's mysterious world, which put him beyond the reach of time and placed him 'at an uncertain moment that the canvas made eternal' ('Gustave Moreau' in *Nouveaux Mélanges*).

Proust was sensitive to many types of painters, and they inspired his work: the society painters like Paul Helleu or his friend Jacques Émile Blanche, Puvis de Chavanne, Bonnat, Jean Louis Forat, whom he met in the salons, Toulouse-Lautrec, whom he once saw in the offices of *La Revue blanche* in 1893, and, most of all, Édouard Vuillard, the closest to his own mental universe. They all contributed to the character of Elstir, as did Hokusai and Carrière, whom he admired. Elstir is the narrator's spokesman in recreating, like him, an individual world: 'Elstir's studio seemed to me like the laboratory of a sort of new creation of the world' (*La Prisonnière*).

Throughout his life, Proust remained curious about everything. He was a great connoisseur of museums, writing pieces on Rembrandt, Watteau, Monet and Chardin which were only published after his death under the title 'Portraits de peintres' in *Nouveaux Mélanges*. According to Colette Cosnier, in 'Gastronomie de Proust' (*Europe*, 1970): 'Some Proustian descriptions are exact transpositions of Chardin: the same bourgeois world, the same slightly bleak intimacy, the same everyday harmony and the same lack of lyricism ... How can we fail to compare the kitchenmaid to *La Ratisseuse de Navets*?' Excluding fictitious artists, Proust refers to about 250 painters in his work. Vermeer and Rembrandt being the most often mentioned.

Music

Proust always immersed himself in a musical atmosphere: he and his mother played the piano, and throughout his life he frequently attended concerts and performances. One of his relations, Louise Cruppi, entertained composers like Maurice Ravel, Nadia Boulanger and Florent Schmitt in her salon. She introduced Russian music to Paris and numbered Gabriel Fauré among her friends. Montesquiou and Saussine initiated Proust into the work of Wagner and César Franck. His friend Reynaldo Hahn, who often played the piano in his room in the boulevard Haussmann, enriched his musical knowledge (Proust had loved music before knowing very much about it). Hahn was an enthusiast of Massenet and Gounod, but loathed Wagner; his influence on Proust, however, did not seem decisive, for Proust wrote to him in 1895: 'The more legendary Wagner becomes, the more human I find him'. He appreciated the genius of Schumann and Beethoven, his favourite composer (according to Benoist Méchin), whose last sonatas and the final part of whose 15th quartet he particularly loved, but could also recognise that of Fauré (with whom he corresponded), Debussy and Wagner – the musician most often mentioned in *A la Recherche*. He was especially keen on *Tristan*, in which he saw 'the most sublime expression of expectation and desire', *Lohengrin*, where he savoured 'a sort of tenderness, a solemn sweetness in the pomp and the joy', and *Parsifal*.

Proust drew his concept of music from the German philosopher Schopenhauer (1788–1860), who believed it to be superior to all other art forms because it transcended both ideas and time. Throughout his work Proust talks of music with affection and penetration, until music and style become merged. In May 1895, he wrote to Suzette Lemaire: 'The essence of music is to awaken in us the mysterious depths of our soul (which are inexpressible in literature, or in general through any finite mode of expression which uses either words, and consequently ideas, or predetermined things and objects – painting, sculpture –) which begin at the point where the finite, and all the arts that have a finite objective, ends, the point where science ends, and which one could call religious.'

Proust was not swayed by fashion: it was not until nine years after its première, in 1911, that he discovered Claude Debussy's *Pelléas et Mélisande* through his 'théâtrophone' (a telephone connected to a microphone in the theatre which allowed him to hear a stage performance or concert at home). Gaston Poulet, talented violinist and leader of an orchestra, who came to Proust's apartment in the middle of the night to play César Franck's quartet, considered him a marvellous listener, 'simple, direct, with no attempt at punditry, like a man who drinks in the music without making a fuss about it' (*Bulletin de la Société des Amis de M. Proust*, No. 11, 1961, p. 423).

Music plays a vital role in the structure of *A la Recherche*. Through its links with the characters' interior lives, it allows them to know their emotional state and to live out their passions: Swann loves Odette, and the little phrase from the sonata by Vinteuil, which presided over the birth of their love, is its accompaniment until the end.

According to the writer Michel Butor, Vinteuil's septet – previously a quartet, quintet, then sextet – grew with the development of the work itself into four, five, six then seven sections. Vinteuil's piece appears in an early version of 1910 as Wagner's Good Friday music from *Parsifal*. Like Wagner, Proust used *leitmotif* in his narrative technique.

Proust used a number of models for Vinteuil's sonata. In 1913, he talked to Antoine Bibesco about the prelude to the first act of Wagner's *Lohengrin* (1850), and Fauré's *Ballade* (1881). In the long dedication he wrote Jacques de Lacretelle in a copy of *Swann* in 1918, he listed various references to real pieces for the 'little phrase' from the sonata (which in fact comes to represent music in its entirety): 'the charming but ultimately mediocre phrase from a sonata for piano and violin by Saint-Saëns, a musician I dislike [...] *L'Enchantement du Vendredi Saint* [...] Franck's sonata [...] the prelude from *Lohengrin* [...] a thing by Schubert' (André Maurois, *op. cit.*, p. xiii). The most important models are Saint-Saëns' sonata in D minor, for the little phrase, and Franck's sonata in A major for the whole work. The beginning of the septet corresponds to the first movement of Debussy's *La Mer*, but according to George D. Painter, more important models were Franck's quartet in D major and quintet in F minor.

Literature

In writing *A la Recherche* Proust spurned the traditional novel structure and chose a cyclical form, like Balzac in *La Comédie Humaine*. However, he very often refers to classic authors (mentioning more than 300 writers in the course of the book).* *La Prisonnière* contains a fine discussion of George Eliot, Dostoyevsky and Barbey d'Aurevilly (whose poetry of place Proust enjoyed). He borrowed the notion of involuntary memory from Gérard de Nerval (1808–55). It was in

---

* Proust often sent Céleste out to buy books from M. Fontaine, the local bookseller in the rue Laborde, near the church of Saint-Augustin.

'Sylvie' – one of the stories in Nerval's collection *Les Filles de feu* – that he found the interpolation of time in the story, as in Flaubert, of whom he said: 'The changes of time have an active or documentary nature. Flaubert was the first to rid them of parasitism, anecdotes and the dross of history. He was the first to set it to music.' *A la Recherche* is not so much a novel as a relection on its own structure, its own demonstration, as Proust had learnt from Tolstoy.

From the writers of the nineteenth and early twentieth centuries Proust drew other lessons. He considered the analytic novel, like Eugène Fromentin's *Dominique*, both 'insipid' and 'poor'. In *Guermantes* he attacked the 'prosaism' of Prosper Mérimée and fashionable writers like Pailleron, Henri Meilhac or Dumas *fils*; and he later took it out on Madame de Chevigné's son-in-law, Francis de Croisset, by depicting him in the character of Bloch in *Le Temps retrouvé*. He did not mince his words in criticising Ruskin, his former master, when condemning his images, like Maeterlinck's, as 'based on intellectual insincerity'. In the preface to *Tendres Stocks* in 1921, he was unsparing towards the style of Paul Morand, with his 'cliché-images', and that of Sainte-Beuve. He reproached Giraudoux for his rococo metaphors, which he later pastiched in *Guermantes*. For Proust an image had to be 'inevitable', like those of George Eliot.

Decisive influences. Robert de Montesquiou – and the writers he frequented – influenced Proust at the end of the nineteenth century. Although he spurned the novels of Paul Bourget, Proust nevertheless borrowed their evocations of works of art and pictorial references, and one of the characters in Bourget's *L'Émigré*, written in 1907, is a nobleman called Charlus. From Rémy de Gourmont, Proust borrowed the expression 'do a cattleya', which appears in Gourmont's novel *Sixtine*, published in 1890. He also enjoyed D'Annunzio, Baudelaire, Verlaine, the Comtesse de Noailles (who became the Vicomtesse de Réveillon in *Jean Santeuil*) and Mallarmé. In *Mallarmé et Proust*, Henri Mondor stresses Mallarmé's influence on *A la Recherche*. Yet Proust never fell into the decadent style of the time that Legrandin criticises in *Guermantes*: 'But you wouldn't like this, it isn't deliquescent enough, *fin-de-siècle* enough, for you; it's too straightforward, too honest. You need some Bergotte, as you've admitted, some gamey meat for the jaded palates of refined sensualists'.

Proust was skilled at dissecting the mechanics of a writer's style in order to parody it, like the pastiche of the Goncourts' *Journal* in *Le Temps retrouvé*. In this, he shows the perfect mastery of his art and the full measure of his borrowings.

Proust on Pierre Benoit: 'I don't know a single line of Pierre Benoit's. Léon Daudet occasionally writes that I am the leading French author – which gives me a certain satisfaction – and that after me comes Benoit – which destroys the satisfaction.'

On Flaubert and Balzac: 'In Flaubert's style, every aspect of reality is converted into a similar substance, a vast surface glistening monotonously. No impurities remain. Every surface has become reflective. Everything is depicted there, but by a process of reflection, without altering its homogeneous nature. Al that was different has been converted and absorbed. In Balzac, on the other hand, exist side by side all the undigested, as yet unconverted elements of a future style which is not yet in existence.'

On Gérard de Nerval: 'Never has a book moved me as much as Gérard de Nerval's *Sylvie*.'

On Charles Péguy: Proust criticised him for using 'ten ways of saying something, when there is only one'. 'I deplore poor Péguy's literary efforts and have never altered my opinion.'

On English literature: 'It is strange that, in all its very different guises, from George Eliot to Hardy, from Stevenson to Emerson, there is for me no literature that has a power comparable to that of English or American literature. Germany, Italy, very often France, all leave me cold. But two pages of *The Mill on the Floss* can make me weep. I know that Ruskin deplored the novel, but I can reconcile all these enemy gods in the Pantheon of my admiration.'

Politics

PROUST AND THE DREYFUS AFFAIR In 1898 Proust threw himself into the Dreyfus affair. Captain Alfred Dreyfus had been arrested four years earlier (in October 1894) and deported to Devil's Island, in French Guyana, in December of that year. An attaché to the General Staff of the French army, Esterhazy, had been accused by Colonel Picquart of being the author of the list of secret information which led to Dreyfus being convicted as a spy. He was acquitted in January 1898, after having been court-martialled. After the acquittal, Picquart was imprisoned in Mont Valérien fortress and Proust, through strenuous efforts, managed to get a copy of *Les Plaisirs et les jours* to him. On 13 January 1898, Émile Zola published an open letter defending Dreyfus, *J'Accuse*, in the journal *L'Aurore*. On 14 January, Proust put his signature to the 'intellectuals' manifesto' in the same journal, demanding that the trial be reopened. Zola was sentenced to a year in prison and a 3,000 franc fine, and Proust followed his trial at the Palais de Justice assiduously.

Like France itself, which was split in two by the affair, Proust felt divided by people close to him. On the one hand he leaned towards those who shared his conviction of Dreyfus's innocence, like Madame Straus, but on the other he came up against anti-Dreyfusards like his father, of whom he writes in *Guermantes*: 'My father, a friend of M. Méline's, was convinced of Dreyfus's guilt. Colleagues who had asked him to sign petitions in support of reopening the trial were angrily sent packing. He didn't speak to me for a week after he discovered that I had followed a different line of conduct.'

In *Jean Santeuil*, Proust describes the main events of the affair (which he had witnessed at the Palais de Justice). He devotes three chapters to it. During the Zola trial, where Jean goes every day and stays 'without a bite to eat, excited, impassioned, until five o'clock', Proust describes the events with an extraordinary dramatic sense. As Jean cannot get into the spectators' gallery, other witnesses describe to him the stormy sessions and furtive conversations in the courtroom which make him understand what is happening. But Jean is also pro-militarist. Proust himself remained a supporter of the French army all his life: 'Soldiers in civilian clothes are like gods disguised as mortals.' Colonel Picquart became a sort of intermittent apparition, a mythological hero in decline, glimpsed 'from time to time half-hidden by other people'. He seemed the epitome of a colonial conquerer with 'a spahi's light and rapid gait'. And Proust noted the 'intellectual probity' of the 'lover of knowledge' who was Dreyfus's champion. Later, he made the following comment: 'The Dreyfus affair nourished and sustained the French nation. France wallowed in it, unconsciously celebrating the marriage of drama and *café au lait* every morning.' But despite their appetite for the affair, the French people never held the key to the enigma. In a chapter entitled 'La Verité sur l'affaire Dreyfus' Proust described it as a very complicated story of espionage and counter-espionage from which even the incorruptible Picquart did not emerge without a blemish.

In *A la Recherche*, on the other hand, Proust was more concerned with depicting the reactions of the Faubourg Saint-Germain, using the affair as a catalyst that allowed him to analyse the deep feelings of each character. The events take place in a closed environment, the noble houses of the Faubourg. For this social group, 'after a Jewish captain had been indicted (whether or not it was justified), the entire army was indicated by the Jews, allied, horror of horrors, to the socialists'.

Attitudes of characters in A la Recherche to the Dreyfus affair

The Duc and Duchesse de Guermantes: anti-Dreyfus though not anti-Semitic, they were enthusiastic peddlers of gossip – 'Dreyfus's guilt can't be proved because he was the lover of the War Minister's wife'– or adopted a superficial social tone which was never personal – 'When one is the Marquis de Saint-Loup, one simply isn't pro-Dreyfus, my dear!' The Duke regretted the angry remarks he exchanged with Swann about the affair.

The Prince and Princesse de Guermantes: violently anti-Semitic from the start (much more so than their cousins), they are gradually converted to a pro-Dreyfus position. As the trial progresses the Prince becomes aware of certain illegalities (that the list was not by Dreyfus; the Henry document was a fake), and is no longer in doubt that the accused is innocent. His wife follows his views in this, and tells Swann about it. Swann is touched by their attitude, but nevertheless dissuades Bloch from asking them to sign the petition in support of Picquart: 'This is a charming man who has travelled thousands of miles to come over to our view [...] If he signed your list, he would compromise himself in the eyes of his own sort and he would be castigated because of us; he might come to regret taking us into his confidence and never do it again' (*Sodome et Gomorrhe*).

Baron de Charlus: In *Guermantes*, he explains his point of view to the narrator: 'The whole Dreyfus affair has been nothing but a nuisance: it is destroying society ... by the influx of Mr and Mrs Camel, Camelhouse, Cameldriver – complete unknowns whom I find even at my cousins' house just because they are part of the Ligue de la Patrie Française, or anti-Jewish, or something or other, as if a political opinion could give them some sort of social standing.'

Bloch: A Jew and passionate supporter of Dreyfus who attends the hearings of the Zola trial and shares his feelings about the day in restaurants in the evenings. 'Bloch thought he had chosen his pro-Dreyfus beliefs logically, although he knew that his nose, his skin and his hair had been imposed on him by his racial background' (*Le Côté de Guermantes*).

Swann: One of the few Jews (and proud of being so) accepted into Faubourg society. Despite his ardent pro-Dreyfus stance, he proclaims his attachment to the army by wearing the military medal he won during the war of 1870 throughout the affair. He refuses to sign the petition in support of Picquart because he does not wish to be associated with the anti-military campaign. However, the affair makes him regret spending years in the company of the aristocracy. It is difficult to define the narrator's own position, but it seems to resemble Swann's in its defence of a just cause.

Odette: Since she wants to make her way into society more than anything else, she takes advantage of the affair to become friendly with various members of the aristocracy, despite her conviction of Captain Dreyfus's innocence, and proclaims her nationalism at the expense of her husband's position. Accompanying her to dinner parties in the Faubourg Saint-Germain, Swann has no hesitation in making comments in a loud voice whenever she contrives to be introduced to a lady of nationalist persuasion: 'Now come along, Odette, you must be mad. Please calm down. It would be undignified of you to have yourself introduced to an anti-Semite. I forbid you to do so' (*Sodome et Gomorrhe*).

Madame Verdurin: Dreyfus's principal champion. She is Madame Zola's companion throughout her husband's trial, and she demands that all the regular guests at her salon should come out in favour of a retrial. And yet, at the beginning of *A la Recherche*, she declares herself to be anti-Semitic.

Saint-Loup: He upholds Dreyfus's innocence and spends his time with the pro-Dreyfus faction in Doncières, which brings wails of protest from his mother, the Comtesse de Marsantes. Later, it is made clear that this fiercely held position is due entirely to the fact of his love for Rachel, a Jewish actress and former prostitute. After his relationship with Rachel has ended he renounces his pro-Dreyfusism, declaring to Swann: 'It's a messy business [...] and I deeply regret having meddled in it. It had absolutely nothing to do with me. If I could start over again, I'd keep well out of it. I am a soldier and I support the army first and foremost' (*Sodome et Gomorrhe*).

Jewishness

The essential problem of the Dreyfus affair, which resounds throughout *A la Recherche*, is the integration of Jews into the Faubourg Saint-Germain. Bloch, who gets in almost as a thief in the night, and Swann, whose position is very uneasy during the Dreyfus affair, are always outsiders. Saint-Loup's mistress Rachel, who is described without much sympathy, does not free her lover from the prejudices of his kind, but makes him an outcast. When Charlus gives his point of view he brings up another burning issue, namely Zionism: 'I gather the newspapers are saying Dreyfus committed a crime against his country. That is what I understand them to be saying. I pay no attention to newspapers; I read them like I wash my hands. In any case, the crime is non-existent: your friend's compatriot would have committed a crime against his country if he had betrayed Judaea, but what has he got to do with France?'

This wariness of the 'accursed race' is felt as early as 'Combray', when the narrator's grandfather welcomes Bloch, the narrator's Jewish friend, with the ironic remark: 'On your marks, archers!' Later, the narrator's grandmother cuts the Jewish summer visitors in Balbec out of her circle of acquaintances, keeping only Madame de Villeparisis. The narrator shares her view when he admits to avoiding Bloch and his family in the Grand Hôtel, where they form a 'more picturesque than pleasant Jewish colony'. And the daughters of some other residents, 'beautiful, proud, mocking and as French as the statues of Reims would not have wanted to mix with that badly brought-up mob'. In remarks like this Proust shows his nationalism. He firmly describes his own family as very 'French', issue of the 'Combray breed, the breed that produced absolutely intact beings like my mother and grandmother', forgetting his descent from Auteuil Jews. There are only a few rituals that almost seem like folk customs, such as the incident of the broken vase between the narrator and his mother, which brings to mind the breaking of the cup in the Jewish wedding ceremony.

Three contrasting Jewish characters appear in Proust's work. In *Jean Santeuil*, Madame Marie: 'Even the most bigoted peasant would have been aware that the soul of a Jewish person like her would smell more sweetly to Our Lord than the souls of all the Christians, priests and saints.' Jean's mother becomes friendly with her, although 'Madame Santeuil came from a milieu which held the Jewish people in the very deepest distrust'. Madame Proust, the chief model for Madame Santeuil, was Jewish; she therefore appears both in the guise of the hero's mother and as Madame Marie.

In *A la Recherche*, Bloch and Swann are the absolute antitheses of each other. Bloch is a parody of a pretentious, arriviste Jew whom Proust mainly criticises for being ashamed of his religious and social background. He claims that he has 'detected under a microscope a minute quantity of Jewish blood in himself'. This caricature is matched by that of Charlus, whose utterances on the subject of Bloch only show up the absurdity of anti-Semitism. Swann, on the other hand, is the Jew Proust himself would have liked to be. They both managed to leave the Jewish bourgeoisie and penetrate Faubourg society; they are both pro-Dreyfus without denying military and patriotic values. Their closeness is also displayed in the aesthetic feelings and unhappy love affairs they share.

In effect, Proust and the narrator both oscillate endlessly between pride in belonging to the Jewish faith and shame at being one of the 'accursed race'.

The First World War

The army. It occupies an important place in *Le Temps retrouvé*: 'The German army and the French army behaved like individuals, but because they were giant assemblies the quarrel took on immense and magnificent proportions.' However, this grandiloquent tone is rare in *A la Recherche*, and the narrator speaks of his respect for the soldiers at the front and his disgust at the 'dodgers' with a sense of irony. While the people left at home like Madame Verdurin or Charlus give themselves over to a life of pleasure, in a capital city compared to Pompeii or Paris under the Directoire, the narrator stresses the heroism of Saint-Loup, who says of his men: 'If only you could see all those people, especially the ordinary people, the workmen, the shopkeepers, who never suspected what heroism lay hidden in them, and who would have died in their beds without having any idea of it'.

Proust is equally fascinated by the army in *Jean Santeuil*. But 'it was not a case of aesthetic attraction to troopers, whom homosexual mythology is quick to transform into old lags, as the Baron de Charlus is later bowled over by young men on leave from the war of 1914. It was a true devotion: Proust has no hesitation in comparing soldiers to gods who personify strength, and extolling the beauty of war, in short, indulging, like a fascist, in "hero worship"' (J. de Ricamont, Preface to J. Canavaggia, *op. cit.*, p. 6). Compared to them, Cottard as a reserve officer or Brichot and Norpois as patriotic short-story writers seem ridiculous. The Germanophile Charlus emphasises all the contradictions of this blinkered nationalism. Saint-Loup, enlisted in the most dangerous section of the army, the infantry, leaves an 'impression of something supernatural that all soldiers on leave basically give'. He is one of the 'escapees from the shores of death, to which they were to return'. Before going back to the front, he has a conversation with the narrator about the 'beauty of the aeroplanes that went up in the night'. 'And the sirens, are they Wagnerian? Which was quite natural, after all, very *Wacht am Rhein*; with the Kronprinz and the princesses in the Imperial box; one wondered if these were really aviators and not valkyries up in the skies!' Later, he dies a hero's death, the war having given him back both his nobility and his *raison d'être*, linked to his social class.

Peace. The narrator did not feel any sense of rejoicing at the peace, which only profited the politicians: 'Thanks to the feeding of the popular vote they've once again fished up the old trouts who always get re-elected.' The wheel has come full circle, to the sordid political intrigues of Monsieur Marie in *Jean Santeuil*, while Marcel dreams of a 'chamber of heroes' full of authentic political figures such as Saint-Loup would have been.

Some Quotes from Proust

ADOLESCENCE 'Adolescence is the only time one learns anything' (*Jeunes Filles*).

BEAUTY 'True beauty is so particular, so new, that it is not recognised as beauty' (*Guermantes*).

BELIEF 'Facts do not penetrate the world where our beliefs live' (*Swann*).

BOOKS 'A book is a large cemetery where on most of the graves one can no longer read the names' (*Le Temps retrouvé*).
   'True books must be the children not of daylight and conversation but of darkness and silence' (*Le Temps retrouvé*).

CRIME 'We forgive individual crimes, but not the participation in a collective crime' (*Guermantes*).

CRUELTY '... that indifference to the suffering one causes which, whatever other names it is given, is the terrible and permanent norm of cruelty' (*Swann*).

DESIRE 'Desire makes everything blossom, possession makes everything fade' (*Les Plaisirs et les jours*).

DIET 'There is only one thing more difficult than keeping to a diet, which is not imposing it on other people' (*Sodome et Gomorrhe*).

FLATTERY 'Flattery is sometimes just an outpouring of tenderness, and frankness just the spittings of bad temper' (*Les Plaisirs et les jours*).

FUTURE 'What we call our future is the shadow of itself that our past casts in front of us' (*Jeunes Filles*).
   'Sometimes the future is alive in us without our knowing it, and the words we believe false in fact sketch a future reality' (*Sodome et Gomorrhe*).

GOD 'However beautiful the monstrance, it is not until one closes one's eyes that one feels God passing by' (*Jean Santeuil*).

HABIT 'Habit is second nature; it prevents us from knowing the first, whose cruelties and enchantments it does not possess' (*Sodome et Gomorrhe*).

HAPPINESS 'What determines the happiness or unhappiness of our lives consists of things almost imperceptible to everyone else' (*Jean Santeuil*).

'Happiness is healthy for the body, but it is sorrow that develops the strength of the spirit' (*Le Temps retrouvé*).

HOMOSEXUALITY 'There were no abnormal people when homo-sexuality was the norm' (*Sodome et Gomorrhe*).

HOPE 'Hope is an act of faith' (*Les Plaisirs et les jours*).

IDEAS 'People consider to be clear those ideas that are confused to the same extent as their own' (*Jeunes Filles*).

JEALOUSY 'It's astonishing how jealousy, which spends its time making small suppositions that are false, has so little imagination when it comes to discovering the truth' (*La Fugitive*).
'There is no jealousy except of oneself' (*La Prisonnière*).

LIFE 'It is better to dream one's life than live it, especially because living it would be to dream it' (*Les Plaisirs et les jours*).

LOVE 'A man in love will be less happy to chat about love to Stendhal than about his mistress to his water-carrier' (*Jean Santeuil*).
'Physical love, so unjustly decried, forces every human being to display the very last dregs of goodness and self-denial he possesses, so that they glitter in the eyes of the immediate company' (*Swann*).
'One no longer loves anyone as soon as one falls in love' (*Swann*).
'She [Aunt Léonie] truly loved us; she would have been happy mourning us' (*Swann*).
'The most exclusive love for a person is always love for something else' (*Jeunes Filles*).
'Love causes [...] real geological upheavals in thought' (*Sodome et Gomorrhe*).
'Love is space and time made palpable to the heart' (*La Prisonnière*).
'In love, it is easier to give up a feeling than to break a habit' (*La Prisonnière*).
'It is wrong to speak of a bad choice in love, for as soon as a choice is made it is a bad choice' (*La Fugitive*).
'Loving is an unhappy ending like the ones in fairy tales, and there is nothing one can do about it until the enchantment is over' (*Le Temps retrouvé*).

MEMORY 'The best part of our memory lies outside ourselves, in a rainy breath, in the smell of a closed-up room or the smell of the first blaze of a fire' (*Jeunes Filles*).

MORALITY 'One becomes moral when one is unhappy' (*Jeunes Filles*).

MUSIC 'Music is perhaps the sole example of what might have been – if language, the formation of words and the analysis of ideas had never been invented – the communication of souls (*La Prisonnière*).

OLD AGE 'Old age is like death. Some people face it with equanimity, not because they have more courage than the rest but because they have less imagination' (*Le Temps retrouvé*).

OPINION 'A fashionable milieu is one in which each person's opinion is formed by the opinion of others. Is it formed in reaction to the opinion of others? Then it is a literary milieu' (*Les Plaisirs et les jours*).

PARADISE 'The real paradise is the paradise we have lost' (*Le Temps retrouvé*).

PARADOX 'Today's paradoxes are tomorrow's prejudices' (*Les Plaisirs et les jours*).

PAST 'Just like the future, it is not all at once but morsel by morsel that we taste the past' (*La Fugitive*).

PERSONALITY 'If someone else is like me, that means I am someone' (*Jean Santeuil*).
   'Our social personality is a creation of other people's thoughts' (*Swann*).

PLEASURE 'Nothing is more limited than pleasure and vice' (*Le Temps retrouvé*).

REALITY 'In order to make reality bearable we are all forced to harbour some little madnesses in ourselves' (*Jeunes Filles*).
   'Reality is only formed in memory; the flowers I am shown today for the first time do not seem to me to be real flowers' (*Swann*).

SILENCE 'Real art has nothing to do with so many proclamations; it is accomplished in silence' (*Le Temps retrouvé*).

SOUVENIRS 'We try to find in things that have become precious to us the reflection that our soul has projected onto them' (*Swann*).

STYLE 'For the writer as well as for the painter, style is not a matter of technique, but of vision. It is the revelation of the qualitative difference there is in the way the world appears to us (*Le Temps retrouvé*).

SUMMER 'Summer makes itself felt just as much by its flies and mosquitoes as by its roses and starry nights' (*Jean Santeuil*).

THEORIES 'A work of art in which there are theories is like an object that still has the price tag on it' (*Le Temps retrouvé*).

TIME 'Theoretically, we know that the world is turning, but in reality we do not notice it; the ground on which we walk seems not to move and we are content. It is the same with time in our lives' (*Jeunes Filles*).

'Novelists who count the days and years are fools. Every day may be the same for a clock, but not for a man. There are hilly and difficult days one takes an infinite amount of time to climb and sloping days one can freewheel down, singing' (*Chroniques*: 'Vacances de Pâques').

VICTIMS 'We love to create victims, but without putting ourselves entirely in the wrong, by letting them live' (*Le Temps retrouvé*).

WISDOM 'We do not receive wisdom, we have to discover it for ourselves, after a journey no one can make for us, and no one can spare us (*Jeunes Filles*).

WOMEN 'Let's leave the pretty women to the men with no imagination' (*Jean Santeuil*).

WORRIES 'There are times when a sort of beauty emerges from the multiplicity of worries that assail us' (*La Fugitive*).

WRITING 'It is as pointless to write specially for the people as for children. Whatever fertilises a child's mind, it is not a book of childish things' (*Contre Sainte-Beuve*).

CHAPTER FIVE

Proust's Style

In 1913, *Du Côté de chez Swann*, with its unexpected style and its long and difficult sentences, collided with literary prejudices. At the beginning of his reading of *A la Recherche*, Jacques de Lacretelle commented on: 'These long and labyrinthine sentences which, in his work, twine around reality to express everything it contains, these incidents and parentheses which, in his letters, weave around his correspondent a spider's web made up of compliments, scruples, a real need to come close and a prudent wish to veil himself' (Preface by J. de Lacretelle to A. Maurois, *op. cit.*, p. xii). The critic M. F. Vanderem in *Le Miroir des lettres* went as far as to indicate a way of reading Proust without being put off by his style: 'You begin the first week with twenty or so pages a day ... this is an absolute rule; do not rush ... You continue this for a week, at the end of which you add five pages a day ... And you will reach ... the end within a relatively short time ... with a pleasure that is ever more vivid and more penetrating.' Léon Pierre-Quint also told of his first reading of *Swann*. After a difficult first impression, 'I went back to the beginning; I was already used to Proust's twisting style; it seemed almost easy and enjoyable, like the very ornate keys which effortlessly open heavy coffer doors' (L. Pierre-Quint, *Marcel Proust: sa vie, son oeuvre*, p. 75).

In 1928, one of the best critics of Proust, Ernst Robert Curtius, defended 'the rhythm of Proust's style' which engendered 'a total coincidence of content and form': 'Proust's sentences have been criticised for being overloaded with relative clauses, weighed down with parentheses and thus stripped of harmony. Such critics do not realise that this apparent lack of harmony is in fact a new harmony which one must get used to in order to feel its charm [...] The whole sentence bursts forth, rocks backwards and forwards and then sinks away by fits and starts, in order to use its long-accumulated energy to make a brutal attack and grasp us by the heart. And the original beauty of the sentence resides in that it conveys to us an object, its image and the image of that image, all at once' (E. R. Curtius, 'Marcel Proust', *La Revue nouvelle*, 1928, pp. 70–1).

Proust himself explained in 1905: 'I am obliged to weave long lengths of silk as I spin them, and if I shortened my sentences they would be small bits of sentences, not sentences.' But he spurned tiresome and purely abstract sentences, choosing language that was 'provided with broad wings and softened with the finest feathers'. The writer thus ornamented his sentences with metaphors and images. Besides, the very long sentences only occupy a third of *A la Recherche* and are only used to convey the narrator's analytic monologues. Proust also knew how to use shorter sentences in tragic or comic descriptions, anecdotes or the retelling of dreams. What is more, he adapted his style to the language of each character and modified it according to different circumstances and dialogues. Charlus does not speak in the same way as Jupien, or even in the same way as Oriane, another Guermantes.

Although Proust's longer sentences are twice as long as average and so hark back to the traditions of the eighteenth century, they are also part of the techniques of the adventure novel, in that they keep the reader in suspense for their enormous span. After a lengthy wait, the key to the enigma is in the end of the sentence. The style itself is novel-like, because of the surprise it offers or through the unexpected image that adorns it. This effect does not depend on the variety of vocabulary, which according to Étienne Brunet's statistics is less extensive than Giraudoux's, but on the way it is used. Proust describes it more precisely in his notes for *Sésame et les lys* in 1905: 'We should consider words both as works of art whose deep meaning we must understand and whose glorious past we must respect, and as simple notes which have no value (in relation to us) except through the place we give them'. Through their elaborate architecture and their complex syntactical skeleton, 'these sentences are a microcosm that reflects the macrocosm of the novel, because they construct a world, dip into the unknown depths of being, and celebrate the soul set free' (J.-Y. Tadié, *Proust*, p. 113).

The most famous sentence is the first sentence of *A la Recherche*: 'For a long time, I used to go to bed early.' The first word (*Longtemps*) makes a pair with the last three words of *A la Recherche* (*dans le Temps*) to bring the wheel full circle. This sentence was used by Roland Barthes in 1982 as the title of a lecture he gave at the Collège de France.

The most contentious sentence is in *Du Côté de chez Swann*: 'She offered up to my lips her sad, pale and faded forehead along which, at this early morning hour, she had not yet arranged her false curls, and where the vertebrae showed through like the points of a crown of thorns or the beads of a rosary [...]'. The obscure metaphor in this sentence was in part responsible for N.R.F.'s refusal to publish Proust's novel in 1912. Gide explained his reasons, on 11 January 1914, in a letter he wrote Proust: '... as bad luck would have it, my eye immediately lit on the cup of camomile on page 62, then stumbled on the sentence on page 64 (the only one in the book I don't clearly understand [...]) where a forehead with vertebrae showing through it is mentioned'. (His page numbers correspond to the Grasset edition of 1913.) Generations of readers and editors have subsequently grappled with the sentence, which Philip Kolb attempted to explain in 'Une énigmatique métaphore de Proust' (*Europe*, 'Centenaire de Marcel Proust', August–September 1970, pp. 141–51).

The longest sentence in *A la Recherche* is to be found in *La Prisonnière*: 'Sofa swirled up from a dream between the new and very real armchairs, small chairs covered in pink silk, carpet brocaded by card table elevated to the status of person since, like a person, it had a past, a memory, keeping in the cold shadow of the Quai Conti salon the tan from sunning in the windows of the rue Montalivet (whose time it knew as well as Madame Verdurin herself) and in the glass doors at Doville, where it had been taken and where it looked out all day long beyond the flowery garden to the deep valley of the   * while awaiting the moment when Cottard and the violinist would play their piece together; bouquet of violets and pansies in pastels, present of a great artist friend, since dead, only surviving fragment of a life now gone without trace,

---

* This blank space is intentional; it featured in the original manuscript.

summing up a great talent and a long friendship, recalling his attentive and gentle gaze, his fine hand greasy and limp while he painted; pretty clutter, mess of presents from the faithful which followed the mistress of the house everywhere and ended up assuming the imprint and fixity of a character trait, a line of destiny; profusion of bunches of flowers, of boxes of chocolates whose blossoming, here as below, was systematised according to an identical mode of flowering: curious interpolation of strange and superfluous objects which never lose a sense of having just come out of the box in which they were given and which remain forever what they were to begin with, New Year's presents; all these things so that isolating others was impossible, but which for Brichot, veteran of the Verdurins' parties, had that patina, that bloom of things which conjures up their spiritual double, giving them a sort of depth; all this, scattered about, sang before him like so many keynotes that awoke in his heart beloved resemblances, confused reminiscences, and which partitioned and outlined the drawing room in which they were now dotted here and there as on a beautiful day a patch of sunlight frames the atmosphere, the furniture and the carpets, chasing from a cushion to a vase, then to a stool with a musty smell of perfume, with a play of light that made the colours stand out, and which sculpted, evoked, spiritual-ised, brought to life in a form that seemed the ideal image, transmitted through all their successive houses, of the Verdurins' salon.'

CHAPTER SIX

Critical Comment

The Press

LES PLAISIRS ET LES JOURS (published 12 June 1896). Apart from a few favourable reviews, the reception was poor, and this luxury edition illustrated with watercolours by Madeleine Lemaire passed almost unnoticed. The public found in Proust an affinity with Anatole France, whose preface to the book formed the first major critique of Proust's work. It stressed his 'agile, penetrating and truly subtle intelligence' and his 'marvellous powers of observation'.

Very few articles appeared: one in *Le Figaro* of 9 June 1896; one in *Le Gaulois* of 12 June and one in *Le Temps*. Proust was already breaking away from the style of *La Revue blanche* by using longer and more incisive sentences; he was flexing his muscles for *A la Recherche*. But his old classmates from Condorcet – among them Léon Blum in *La Revue blanche* on 1 July, and Fernand Gregh in *La Revue de Paris* on 15 July – reproached him for being a dilettante and social butterfly. Charles Maurras was the only one who already regarded Proust as a classic author, and emphasised the purity of his style in *La Revue encyclopédique* of 12 August. In 1897, the following year, Jean Lorrain wrote a scathing piece under the pseudonym 'Raitif de La Bretonne' in *Le Journal* of 3 February: it led to his duel with Proust three days later. The book was unsuccessfully submitted for an Académie prize in 1898.

LA BIBLE D'AMIENS (translation published in 1904) and Sésame et les lys (translation published in 1906). Marcel Proust's translations of these two works by John Ruskin aroused little enthusiasm. The only people to comment were Bergson (perhaps because of their family ties), Albert Sorel (Proust's old teacher) and the critic André Beaunier in *Le Figaro*. In 1987, when *La Bible d'Amiens* was reissued, Alain Bosquet wrote in *Le Figaro*: 'It is a sort of history lesson, at once precise and hallucinatory, with an equally luminous and vibrant treatise on architecture thrown in. Sometimes, the text strays into a declaration of love for France and for Amiens cathedral. [...] Ruskin's English is majestic and biting, tenacious and scathing, solemn and full of Biblical furies. Without betraying the sense of a single syllable, Proust has made of it a lyrical and seductive prose, full of tender insinuation and minute delicacies.'

DU CÔTÉ DE CHEZ SWANN (published 14 November 1913). In *Excelsior* of 23 November 1913, Jean Cocteau compared this to 'a giant miniature, made up of mirages, superimposed gardens, the interplay of space and time, large fresh brushstrokes in the style of Manet'. Lucien Daudet, writing in *Le Figaro* on 27 November, hailed *Swann* as a masterpiece, with a style that he called 'simple, because of its invisible complexity'. Paul Souday, who devoted a whole feature to it in *Le Temps* of 10 December, gave the book most publicity despite his equivocal critical judgement. He mentioned the large number of 'inaccuracies' and took him to task for the 'naïvety' of 'Un Amour de Swann', while recognising 'valuable elements from which the author could have created an exquisite little book'. Pierrefeu, in *L'Opinion*, criticised him for 'defying analysis'; the *Journal des Débats* for being 'too abstruse'; and Maury for writing a bad version of Bourget. Rachilde, in *Le Mercure de France* on 15 January 1914, confessed: 'I began this book with enthusiasm but ended up casting it aside with a feeling of dread, just as one might refuse to drink a sleeping-potion.' Proust defended himself in letters, and Blanche took issue with these critics in *L'Écho de Paris* on 15 April 1914. Maurice Rostand devoted a highly favourable article in *Comœdia* to *Swann*. Louis de Robert and Bernard Grasset considered entering the book for the Goncourt Prize.

A L'OMBRE DES JEUNES FILLES EN FLEURS (published 27 June 1919). Before the Goncourt Prize, he had only a few positive critical reactions, such as those of Abel Hermant, Binet-Vilmer and Vandérem. Meanwhile, Marbo spoke of 'chaos' and Billy of 'chatter'. The Goncourt Prize, which he was awarded through Léon Daudet's efforts, was seen by the left-wing press as an act of defiance. *L'Humanité* of 11 December 1919 censured Proust for his age: 'Make way for the old men!'; *L'Oeuvre* and *Le Populaire* accused him of having friends on the jury. In *Littérature*, Aragon wrote: 'No one would have believed a laborious snob could bring home such rich rewards.' But Paul Souday, in *Le Temps*, came to Proust's defence, as did two of the Academicians who had voted for him. Rosny senior accused the press of not having read *Jeunes filles* and Léon Daudet praised 'this powerful new novelist'. In the *Nouvelle Revue Française* of 1 January 1920 Jacques Rivière was severely critical of the 'daily press so often governed by preoccupations that are quite foreign to literature'. According to him, Proust rendered 'all the methods of the psychological novel' in a new form. The popular misconception of Proust as a valetudinarian and tedious writer was in the process of being formed. Rivière defended him once again in February, in 'Marcel Proust et la tradition classique'.

PASTICHES ET MÉLANGES (published 27 June 1919). When it appeared, at the same time as *Jeunes Filles*, this book received plaudits from *Le Figaro* and *Le Gaulois*. But in *Littérature* of October 1919, Philippe Soupault had no hesitation in writing: 'It is amazing [...] to find so little genius in one who displays so many talents.'

LE CÔTÉ DE GUERMANTES (published 21 October 1920). This time, the reviews in general were good. Yet Boulanger, writing in *L'Opinion*, accused Proust of snobbery, and Souday, in *Le Temps* of 4 November 1920, hurt him by calling him 'feminine'.

SODOME ET GOMORRHE I (published 2 May 1921). In 1921, Proust's subject matter startled conventional morality and shocked some homosexuals; Gide saw it as a over-pessimistic view of homosexuality. André Germain (the Baudets' brother-in-law) gave his opinions free rein in *Écrits nouveaux* and called Proust 'an old spinster, governess to some terribly upper-crust people, who would have gone to bed with a valet'. On the other hand, Edmond Jaloux and André Allard in the *Nouvelle Revue Française* came to his defence with the argument (which was to be extensively used) of 'Proust the moralist'.

SODOME ET GOMORRHE II (published 2 May 1922). Jacques Rivière won the day: Proust was now accepted as a classic author. Paul Souday liked the book and found the subject matter 'unnecessary, rather than truly scandalous'. In the *Nouvelle Revue Française* Allard still spoke of Proust's moralism, and Vettard compared him to Einstein.

LA PRISONNIÈRE (published in 1923). The praise for this book – from Sorel, Henriot, Lalou, Lanson, Bounoure, Mauriac – was unanimous. His old detractors bowed to the prevailing mood, ready to revert to their former opinions if the wind changed. This was to be the case with the next book.

ALBERTINE DISPARUE (published at the beginning of January 1926). Marius and Ary Leblond, in *L'Information*, condemned Proust's 'morbid psychology'. Gonzague Truc spoke of a 'paltry world' and Léon Daudet criticised his 'false picture of life'. Edmond Jaloux continued to support him, however, and compared him to Freud and Saint-Simon. Mauriac found the work 'admirable'.

Pierre Loewel, in *L'Avenir* of 27 January, wrote: 'The novel has not been revised since Proust's death, and it is full of useless repetitions and mistakes of detail.'

In *Le Temps* of 28 January, Paul Souday was equally severe. Like Kemp and Benoist-Méchin, he commented on Proust's 'progressive decline': 'The hero is a simpleton, who despite all his theories couldn't foresee Albertine's departure. As for the author, he uses without acknowledgement theories from Taine and Ribot, pushed to ludicrous extremes, common literary settings (those of *Le Lac, Le Souvenir, Tristesse d'Olympio*, of Stendhalian crystallisation), as well as theories from Schopenhauer.'

Benjamin Crémieux, in the *Nouvelle Revue Française* of 1 February, raised the question of the document's authenticity: '*Albertine disparue* "is only a draft" by which only "convinced Proustians" will be convinced. As such, this "rough outline" is a unique document for studying Proust's artistic method.'

Armand Pierhal wrote in *La Revue nouvelle* of 15 February: 'In the first volume the description of memory and forgetting is remarkable. There is an analogy with certain of Bach's chorales or with Wagner's use of *leitmotif*: the guiding themes here are "tirades made up of the special speech mannerisms of each character" which accompany each entrance.'

In *La Dépêche*, published in Toulouse on 19 February, Camille Mauclair accused both Gide and Proust of 'rotting the souls of others': 'Proust and Gide are obsessed with sexual perversion. The way in which Proust's genius, since his death, has come to be considered sacred, is a great mistake.'

LE TEMPS RETROUVÉ (1927). In *Le Temps* of 25 October Henriot criticised its 'sketchiness' and Souday its 'mistakes' and Proust's lack of 'conviction' in the passages about the war. However, on 10 December, Jaloux placed the accent on the cyclical structure of *A la Recherche*: 'The true greatness of Marcel Proust's work is only now becoming apparent [...] Many more years will have to pass before its intrinsic beauty is revealed in its entirety.'

The Intellectuals' View

Between the wars, the Surrealists were violently opposed to Proust. In March 1921, the periodical *Littérature* awarded him marks: Aragon gave him 0 out of 20, Breton 6 and Éluard 8. The first 'Surrealist manifesto' condemned both Proust and Barrès for being 'analytic'. The socially committed literature of the 1930s to 1950s held against him a failure to address the problems of his time. Leftist journals like *Europe* judged him to be 'outside society' in 1935; on 12 March 1937 *Vendredi* declared: 'Proust is dead, stone dead, and as distant from us as it is possible to be [...]'.

Jacques-Émile Blanche betrayed his friendship when, in *Les Nouvelles littéraires* of 21 July 1928, he only mentioned Proust's 'ferocity' and 'cynicism'. Daniel-Rops ticked him off for his 'rather sordid soul' in *Le Revue nouvelle* of April 1931. Official critics such as Billy or Lalou went along with contemporary opinion. *Le Divan* described him as 'forgotten', in March 1935, and *Le Mercure de France* said that 'Religion ... worshipped an idol'.

In 1947, *Les Temps modernes* and Jean-Paul Sartre accused Proust of being complicit with the forces of reaction. In 1949 Gaëtan Picon (who later changed his mind) wrote in his *Panorama de la nouvelle littérature Française*: 'If I say nothing of Proust, it is not because I know nothing about him or because I don't agree with him: it is because his work is distanced from us not merely in terms of years but by its very nature.'

Literary criticism thus ceased to be concerned with Proust's work until the 1950s. At that time, three events brought about a kind of rehabilitation, helped by the appearance of the *nouveau roman*: the publication of *A la Recherche de Marcel Proust* by André Maurois (1949); the publication of *Jean Santeuil* (1952) and that of *Contre Sainte-Beuve* (1954). Swayed by fashion, the critics now adored what they had once reviled. George D. Painter's biography of Proust (published in two volumes in England in 1959 and 1965, translated into French in 1963 and 1966) was enormously successful in France – even though it aroused controversy among some Proustians, who had no quarrel with the author's remarkable feat of documentation and synthesis, but with certain inferences about Proust's character and behaviour which he drew from *A la Recherche*.

By 1971, the centenary of Proust's birth, more than 600 publications on the writer and his work were in existence, and the flood of Proust studies has not diminished.

Opinions and Quotes on Proust

Hundreds of writers have given their verdict on Proust. The following is a small selection.

MAURICE BARRÈS: 'He attached an importance I find quite unreasonable to salon life, to individual relationships and to letters. Oh, Proust! Kind companion, what a phenomenon you were! And how easily I pass judgement on you! [...] He has become the French Meredith, the object of a passionate cult.'

JACQUES BENOIST-MÉCHIN: 'His vast cultural knowledge, his ever-lively intelligence and the almost tactile quality of his sensibilities allowed him to record a mass of psychological material and to interest himself in the most diverse aspects of life. He "wasted his time" with rare eclecticism. Day after day, he accumulated in his memory a myriad observations which he could just "regain" from the depths of himself. Not only did he fill his books with a crowd of characters, he also used them to express his ideas on all the arts – literature, drama, music, painting, architecture, even strategy – without ever giving the impression of writing "set pieces".'

MARTHE BIBESCO: 'Proust lived a life of nothing but love, passion and self-denial. His language is the language of a mystic.'

GEORGES CATTAUI: 'Each page of Proust's speaks to each one of us, and always at our own level. [. . .] In reading him, we become the readers of our selves.'

PAUL CLAUDEL (about *Du Côté de chez Swann*): 'A population of loafers and flunkeys [. . .]. In the course of those honourable years there were a number of events apart from Madame Verdurin's chatter and Monsieur de Charlus's love affairs.'

BENJAMIN CRÉMIEUX: 'Marcel Proust is the first writer to have made memory the foundation, the subject matter and the centre of a great work of art.'

ERNST ROBERT CURTIUS: 'He surpasses Flaubert in intelligence just as he surpasses Balzac in literary qualities and Stendhal in his understanding of life and beauty. [. . .] He has extended the domain of the human soul, and enriched the life of every one of us.'

LÉON DAUDET: 'In Marcel Proust could be found all the elements of a spoilt child, and, after he reached thirty, a spoilt old child: but he never was that, because his genius dispelled those elements – his genius, his personal dignity and his sense of the ridiculous.'

LUCIEN DAUDET: 'He searched the *Gotha* for the fine names he gave some of his characters, but moreover for relationships and ramifications which delighted him. In the same way, announcements of certain social events interested him as much as a novel in a single page, by the description of a family contained in the names, and the stories they told, often bringing together the most disparate and unexpected social circles. If he discovered that someone numbered a bishop, a duke and an ex-President of the Republic among his relations, he experienced a pleasure that he himself called Balzacian and which it would now be appropriate to call Proustian. A new person's appearance in a salon interested him intensely, as much because of the individual as because of the "social reason" they introduced, a new precipitating factor in the circle. A social sense was for him what a sense of direction is for certain birds. [. . .] He arranged human beings into groups and families with the delicacy and scruples of a scholar, as if he had a microscope and a pair of tweezers, putting each person into their particular place, worrying about possible errors, correcting his first classification when need be. [...] For a large number of people, the Duchesse de Guermantes, Madame de Sainte-Euverte and Madame de Cambremer are three "society ladies" differentiated only by being of different generations. For Marcel Proust they were three creatures as dissimilar as a hawkmoth, a geometrid moth and a white butterfly; in his hands they become three social examples with no shared characteristics.'

CHARLES DU BOS: 'His work is the most important thing to have happened in French literature for a long time.'

LOUIS GAUTIER-VIGNAL: 'Proust had every mental gift: intelligence, judgement, intuition, memory, imagination, poetic sense, sensibility. To these should be added his sense of humour. His ruling faculties were, undoubtedly, memory and imagination.'

ANDRÉ GIDE: 'If I now try to find the quality I most admire in this work, it is its gratuitousness. I don't know of a more useless work, nor one less anxious to prove something.'

EDMOND JALOUX: 'Will the man we most admire at the moment – the psychologist, the explorer of the unconscious – continue to dominate all the others? It is possible, but it is also unlikely. Future epochs will probably not share our taste for exceptional psychological states, and our curiosity about extremes cases. Perhaps [Proust] will be more admired as a character portraitist, or a social observer, or a poet: he has all that in him.'

HENRY JAMES (on reading Proust): 'I feel inconceivable boredom coupled with the most intense ecstacy it is possible to imagine.'

ROBERT KEMP: 'Personally, I would live on a desert island with him. I would live with Plato or with Montaigne; not with Descartes, Pascal or St John of the Cross ... With Stendhal? Perhaps. With Balzac, probably. But one can't imitate Balzac. He introduces you into his people, his city; he presents you with his creatures. Proust awakens the gift of creation. Under his example, you rethink your own thoughts [...]'

JOHN MIDDLETON MURRY: 'Whatever the author's intentions may have been, his work is by far the most meticulous dissection of modern consciousness that has ever been accomplished.'

ANAÏS NIN: 'Proust wrote from the depths of his soul about people who had none. His characters swim around in their own unconsciousness. [...] He is more alive in his senses and his passion for the smallest of life's details than a thousand so-called realists, because it is passion that recreates a flower, a leaf, a cathedral spire, a sunset, a meal. [...] Proust's life has flowed through me, has become part of my life. His thoughts, discoveries and visions visit me every year, bringing me every year more profound messages. There must be continuity.'

JACQUES POREL: 'Proust knew everything, but his viewpoint had not been deformed by erudition. He was simple, like an innocent boy, or pretended to be.'

JEAN-FRANÇOIS REVEL: 'It is true that Sainte-Beuve preferred Vicq d'Azyr to Stendhal, and one regretfully has to admit that Proust considered Maeterlinck, the Comtesse de Noailles and Léon Daudet to be geniuses, not Max Jacob, Apollinaire or Jarry. Some people make excuses for Proust by saying that his literary judgements were based on friendship; but this supposed excuse is in fact a further condemnation, because he was a writer who held the work of art to be a sacred thing, entirely separate from everyday life and everyday relationships, and these judgements are incorporated in *A la Recherche du temps perdu* itself.'

LÉOPOLD SÉDAR SENGHOR: 'An immense symphonic poem, that is how *A la Recherche du temps perdu* appears, with the different volumes taking the place of "movements".'

PAUL SOUDAY: 'Some people regard Proust as a great thinker and a profound psychologist, an ethical and aesthetic innovator, and all that this entails. He is none of those things.'

About *Du Côté de chez Swann*: 'This very long book is not easy to read. It is not only compact, but often obscure, and its obscurity has less to do with its depth of thought than its elocutionary overload [...] Add to this the fact that inaccuracies abound, that M. Proust's participles have, as a character of Labiche's said, a rotten nature, in other words they do not agree; that his subjunctives are no more conciliatory or disciplined, and cannot even defend themselves against the audacious interventions of the indicative ... However, M. Marcel Proust undoubtedly possesses great talent. He has an abundant imagination, very fine sensibilities, a love of landscape and the arts and a sharp sense of realistic and readily caricatured observation.'

About *A l'Ombre des jeunes filles en fleurs*: 'In our world of people in a hurry, absorbed in their work or pleasures, it is a matter of elementary prudence to adopt brevity of style if one wishes to be read. Many of M. Marcel Proust's critics have obviously given up on their reading and are taking their revenge for not having been able to get to the end. It is hard to read, certainly, not only because of its unexpected abundance but because of its often precious and tangled style. But it is at least certain that after some hesitation and distrust in the face of this mass of printed paper, if one decides to plunge in, one does not let go. [...] It is prolix but varied, often witty and brilliant, sometimes profound, and it always conveys the feeling of life.'

PAUL VALÉRY: 'Although I hardly know a single volume of Marcel Proust's great work, and although the very art of the novelist is almost unimaginable to me, I am nevertheless well aware, from the little of *A la Recherche du temps perdu* that I have had a chance to read, what an exceptional loss Literature has suffered; and not only Literature, but also that secret society which comprises, in each era, the people who give it its real worth.

'In any case, even if I had not read a line of his vast work, to find such widely differing minds as Gide and Léon Daudet united in their view of its importance would have been enough to assuage any doubts I might have had: such a rare meeting of opinion can only occur as close to absolute certainty as it is possible to be. We should rest assured: if they all say so at once, the sun is shining.'

MARTIN WALSER: 'A person reading Proust can feel like an atrophied example of humanity. One has the sense that until now one has hardly made any use at all of the full range of one's consciousness.'

VIRGINIA WOOLF: 'My great adventure was undoubtedly Proust. What is there left to write after that?'

Proust has often been compared to other writers. A few examples are given here:

Balzac, by Georges Gabory
Baudelaire, by André Rousseaux
Bergson, by Tibor Dénes
Chateaubriand, by Jean-Albert Bédé
Descartes, by Henri Bonnet
Dickens, by Paul Souday
Disraeli, by Georges Cattaui
Dostoyevsky, by E. Cabire
Einstein, by C. Vettard
Eliot, by Edmond Jaloux
Flaubert, by Paul Morand
Graça-Aranha (Brazilian aesthetician), by Valéry Larbaud
Heraclitus, by Paul Desjardins
La Bruyère, by Léon Daudet
Maine de Biran, by Camille Vettard
Marivaux, by Benjamin Crémieux
Meredith, by Maurice Barrès
Montaigne, by Élisabeth de Gramont and Albert Thibaudet
Rousseau, by John Middleton Murry
Saint-Évremond, by Léon Daudet
Saint-Simon, by Georges Gabory and Albert Thibaudet
Shakespeare, by Georges Cattaui
Spinoza, by Henri Bonnet
Stendhal, by Francis Birrel and José Ortega y Gasset
Taine, by Johannes Tielroy

CHAPTER SEVEN

Acquisition of Manuscripts

History

Since Proust's death, many collectors have sought out his manuscripts. From July to October 1922, Proust was negotiating with two buyers who both wanted to acquire the manuscript and the corrected proofs of *Sodome et Gomorrhe II*. Jacques Doucet (1853–1929) – an art lover who was famous for his collection of pictures (Manet, Van Gogh, Cézanne, Picasso) – offered 7000 francs in July; Proust hesitated because he knew that Doucet wanted to give his collection to the state. At the end of August, Serge André, owner of the *Revue du seizième siècle*, edited by Jacques Boulenger, offered 10,000 francs. But Proust died before the negotiations were complete. His manuscripts then passed into the hands of his brother Robert (until his death in 1935) and then to Robert's daughter, Suzy Mante-Proust. Some of the papers were unfortunately lost in the course of a move.

During the German occupation the manuscripts were sent to Bordeaux, then to the Mantes' estate at Valmante. In Bordeaux, Madame Mante-Proust's cousin, Monsieur Margerie, head of Paul Reynaud's office, wanted to have them taken to the United States, but she refused. In 1947, on her husband's death, she decided to put them in order, with the help of Bernard de Fallois, whom André Maurois had introduced to her: this is how the texts of *Jean Santeuil* and *Contre Sainte-Beuve* were discovered.

In 1961 Valéry Giscard d'Estaing, then Secretary of State for Finance, and Julien Cain, general administrator of the Bibliothèque Nationale, heard that Suzy Mante-Proust intended to let them go to the University of Illinois in Urbana in the USA. They arranged for them to be stopped at customs, and by a decree of 13 April 1962 (signed by Monsieur Michel Debré, the Prime Minister, and Monsieur Giscard d'Estaing) the Bibliothèque Nationale was given a subsidy of 1,100,000 francs to acquire them.

From 1962 onwards, considerable work was undertaken by the restoration and binding department of the Bibliothèque Nationale. The project was overseen by Madame Callu-Turiaf (an archivist and paleographer and former member of the École Française in Rome). The chief problem lay in the innumerable inserts that Proust loved, stuck like concertinas to the sheets of the notebooks (the longest of them was 1.40 metres in length). To ensure their conservation, silk chiffon was glued over the paper, which was of lesser quality than the notebooks themselves. Once properly recorded and analysed, the Proust estate was found to contain all the works of his youth: *Les Plaisirs et les jours, Jean Santeuil*, the translations of Ruskin, the *Pastiches, Contre Sainte-Beuve* and various different versions of *A la Recherche* in the form of manuscripts, typescripts and sets of proofs. But some of the notebooks, which were dispersed with the furniture after Robert Proust's death, were still missing.

In 1983, Monsieur Jacques Guérin – a collector who was a friend of Madame Robert Proust and a generous donor of objects belonging to Proust to the Musée Carnavalet – offered the Bibliothèque Nationale a batch of thirteen rough notebooks for *A la Recherche*, which completed the series of manuscripts. Since the price was extremely high, the Nationale bought four and suggested to the seller that he take the others to the procedure for 'dation en paiement' established by a law of 31 December 1968. The 'Commission d'agrément pour la conservation du patrimoine artistique national', set up by a decree of 27 October 1971, pronounced in favour of the 'dation' in the spring of 1984. The Proust estate is now complete, apart from a few autograph fragments and, more importantly, the letters kept by Philip Kolb in the Urbana, Illinois, University library in the USA.

The Proust Estate in the Bibliothèque Nationale

The basic material for *A la Recherche* is to be found in Proust's notebooks. The Bibliothèque Nationale's collection comprises:

62 school exercise books containing rough drafts of *Du Côté de chez Swann, A l'Ombre des jeunes filles en fleurs, Le Côté de Guermantes, Sodome et Gomorrhe, La Prisonnière, Albertine disparue* and *Le Temps retrouvé*.

20 school exercise books in a second group consisting of the definitive versions of *Sodome et Gomorrhe, La Prisonnière, Albertine disparue* and *Le Temps retrouvé*. They are numbered from i to xx and the last page of the twentieth book concludes with the word 'End'.

13 rough notebooks which previously belonged to Monsieur Jacques Guérin acquired in 1983 and 1984, thanks to a 'dation'. They are rough drafts for *A la Recherche*.

4 books of preparatory notes, which Madame Straus gave Proust in 1908 and which range from that date up to 1918. They are in a narrow format and cloth bound. The notes they contain are made up of a large number of reflections that were used in the writing of *A la Recherche*. A fifth notebook, which was used as a diary and for jotting down fragments, is in a private collection.

1 manuscript of about 200 pages containing an incomplete text of *Du Côté de chez Swann*.

1 exercise book containing the whole text of the death of Bergotte.

1 incomplete manuscript of *Le Côté de Guermantes*.

23 volumes of typescripts, more or less corrected by Proust; as well as 24 volumes of galley proofs and page proofs, some uncorrected, others covered with erasures.

1 file relating to Proust's schooldays, containing philosophy course material, essays, compositions and Latin translations.

Presentation of the Manuscripts

None of the notebooks really contains a sequential text. They are always in fragments of a few lines or several pages, often destined for several different sections of the narrative. The same notebook might have been written at different periods; the same text sometimes runs across several notebooks. They are therefore essentially working tools that Proust would use for a time, abandon more or less provisionally before going back to them, or perhaps dismantling them to share out the material between other notebooks.

There is a distinction between books of manuscript proper and draft notebooks, to which Proust sometimes gave names: 'Vénuste',

'Fridolin' or 'Babouche'. These contain several preliminary sketches for the same piece of text, with little difference between the various versions. Some are marked out by notes indicating the 'paramount importance' of one passage or another. Proust interpolated remarks on the progress of the project, announcing what was to come or summing up an episode, and decorated some of the drafts with caricatures and drawings. He sometimes makes brief notes, such as 'Express better', and sometimes writes out his instructions with great care. He also adds orders to be given to the servants, notes to jog his memory, fragments of correspondence to be inserted into the novel, telephone numbers, addresses, notes on books he has read, the characters' coats of arms and even (although infrequently) drawings. The final manuscript books, those containing *La Fugitive* and especially those for *Le Temps retrouvé*, are often in a very similar state to the rough notebooks.

The books themselves are exercise books of the type used in schools, covered with black moleskin, easy to carry and very flexible for writing half-propped up in bed. Each has between 60 and 100 ruled pages with a margin on the left. The latest ones, those written during the war, have cardboard covers and paper and binding of poorer quality. Normally Proust wrote only on the right-hand pages, and later used the margins for additions, which were made in smaller handwriting to fit the available space.

The multiple deletions and revisions often make for difficult reading. Proust sometimes used the left-hand pages as well, but as he always needed more space for his corrections, he used inserts ('paperoles'), which were originally Céleste Albaret's idea. She would stick additional sheets of paper on the bottom, or sometimes the top of the page; occasionally they were stuck on at the sides as well, or glued directly over the text to delete it. Folding these inserts into concertinas allowed even more space for the writing. But Céleste often muddled up the sheets. Moreover, the handwriting in the notebooks is not always Proust's own, as he sometimes dictated to a secretary: Albert Nahmias, or, after the war, Henri Rochat, who made numerous spelling mistakes, or Céleste herself, who wrote down just what she heard. But the essential difficulty in Proust's manuscript material remains one of textual organisation.

Appendices

Plan of Illiers

TO MIROUGRAIN, SAINT-ÉMAN & MARCHÉVILLE

Cemetery

TO CHARTRES

Railway Station

Viaduct

TO BROU

PLACE DU CALVAIRE

RUE DU CHEMIN DE FER

AVENUE DE LA GARE

TO BAILLEAU-LE-PIN & CHARTRES

RUE DE CHARTRES

PONT DU GUÉ BELLERIN

TO MÉRÉGLISE

CHEMIN DE HALAGE

RUE DE L'OISEAU FLESCHE

AUNT AMIOT'S HOUSE

PLACE LEMOINE

RUE FLORENT D'ILLIERS

CHURCH OF SAINT-JACQUES

TO ÉPEAUTROLLES & SAINT LOUP

SITE OF RUINED CHURCH OF SAINT-HILAIRE

PONT SAINT-HILAIRE

RUE SAINT-HILAIRE

TROIS MARIES

RUE DE BEAUCE

TO VIEUVICQ & BROU

CHEMIN DE HALAGE

Castle Ruins

CASTLE MEADOWS

RUE DES LAVOIRS

Laundry Tank

RUE DU CHEVAL BLANC

RUE DES FONTAINES

Boys' School

CHEMIN DE LA CROIX ROMVUE

RUE DES VIERGES

PASSERELLE

THE MALL

Pré Catelan

RAIDILLON (THE HAWTHORN PATH)

MAISON DES ARCHERS

RIVER LOIR

TO TANSONVILLE

TO ROUSSAINVILLE

½ mile

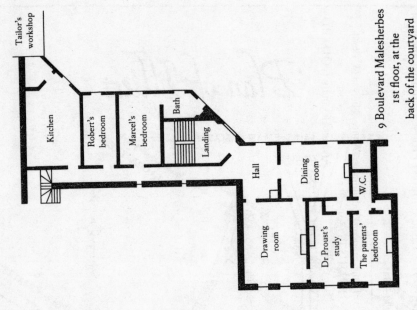

9 Boulevard Malesherbes
1st floor, at the
back of the courtyard

Tailor's workshop

Kitchen

Robert's bedroom

Marcel's bedroom

Bath

Landing

Hall

Dining room

W.C.

Drawing room

Dr Proust's study

The parents' bedroom

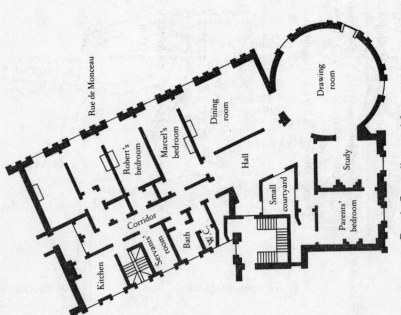

45 Rue de Courcelles – 2nd floor

Rue de Monceau

Kitchen

Robert's bedroom

Marcel's bedroom

Dining room

Corridor

Servants' room

Bath

W.C.

Hall

Small courtyard

Drawing room

Study

Parents' bedroom

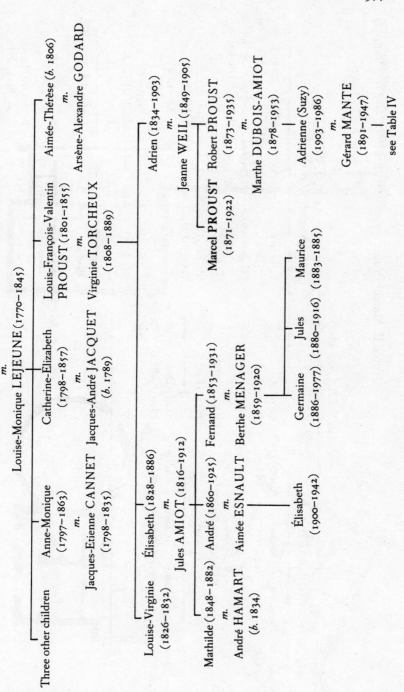

Table I: Marcel Proust's paternal ancestors

378

Table II: Marcel Proust's maternal ancestors (the Weil family)

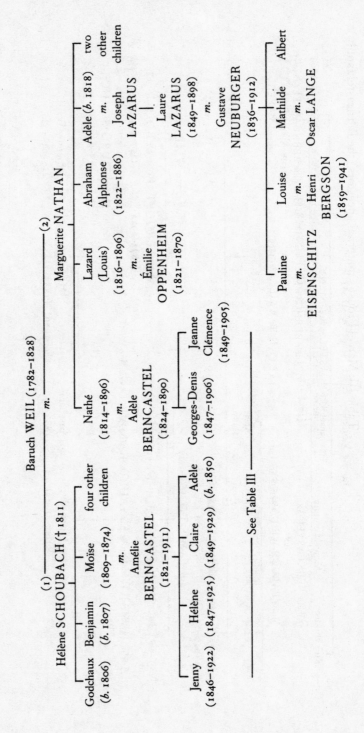

Table III: Marcel Proust's maternal ancestors (the Berncastel family)

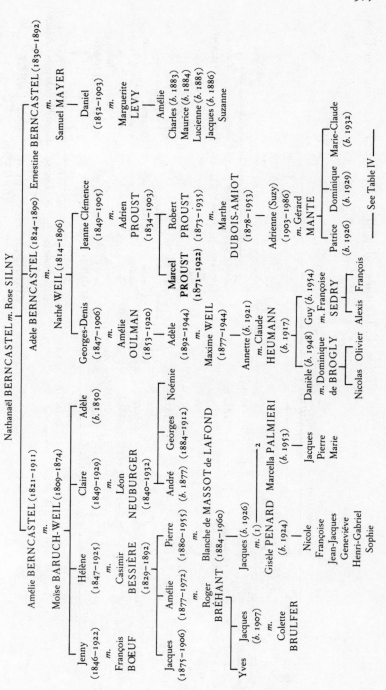

Nathanaël BERNCASTEL. *m.* Rose SILNY

Table IV: The Rostand family and Robert Proust's descendants

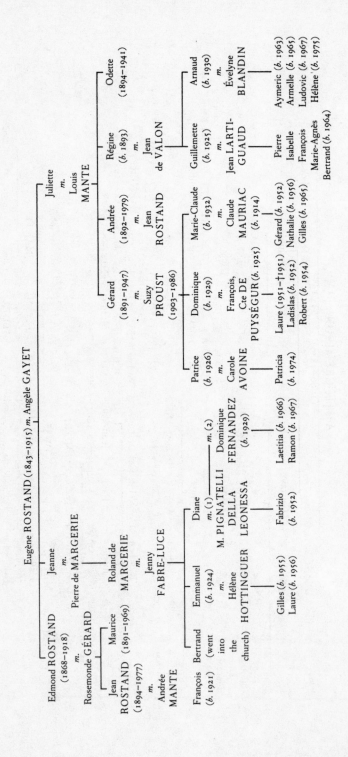

Table V: Adolphe Crémieux and his descendants

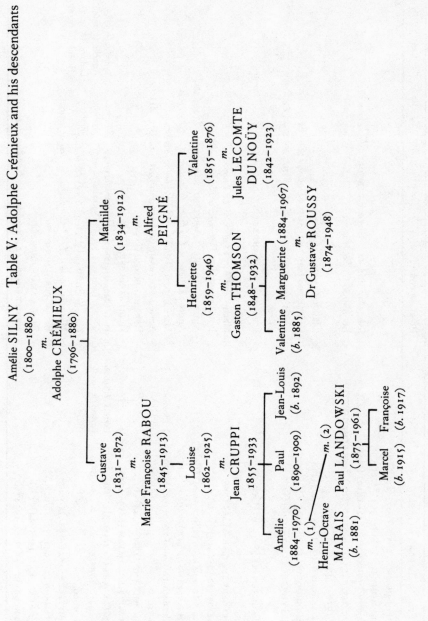

Literary Prizes in Proust's Time

Date	Nobel Prize for Literature (1901)	Prix Goncourt (1903)
1901	Sully PRUDHOMME (1839–1907) (Fr.).	
1902	Theodor MOMMSEN (1817–1903) (Ger.).	
1903	Bjørnstjerne BJØRNSON (1832–1910) (Norw.).	John-Antoine NAU (Eugène TORQUET), *Force ennemie*.
1904	Frédéric MISTRAL (1830–1916) (Fr.), José ECHEGARAY (1833–1916) (Sp.).	Léon FRAPIÉ, *La Maternelle*.
1905	Henryk SIENKIEWICZ (1846–1916) (Pol.).	Claude FARRÈRE, *Les Civilisés*.
1906	Giosuè CARDUCCI (1835–1907) (It.).	Jérôme and Jean THARAUD, *Dingley, l'illustre écrivain*.
1907	Rudyard KIPLING (1865–1936) (G.B.).	Émile MOSELLY, *Jean des Brebis, Terres lorraines, Le Rouet d'ivoire*.
1908	Rudolf EUCKEN (1846–1926) (Ger.).	Francis de MIOMANDRE (François DURAND), *Écrit sur de l'eau*.
1909	Selma LAGERLÖF (1858–1940) (Swe.).	Marius and Ary LEBLOND, *En France*.
1910	Paul HEYSE (1830–1914) (Ger.).	Louis PERGAUD, *De Goupil à Margot*.
1911	Maurice MAETERLINCK (1862–1949) (Belg.).	Alphonse de CHÂTEAUBRIANT, *Monsieur des Lourdines*.
1912	Gerhart HAUPTMANN (1862–1946) (Ger.).	André SAVIGNON, *Les Filles de la pluie*.
1913	Rabindranath TAGORE (1861–1941) (Ind.).	Marc ELDER (Tendron), *Le Peuple de la mer*.
1914	Not awarded.	Adrien BERTRAND (awarded in 1916), *L'Appel du sol*.
1915	Romain ROLLAND (1866–1944) (Fr.).	René BENJAMIN, *Gaspard*.
1916	Verner von HEIDENSTAM (1859–1940) (Swe.).	Henri BARBUSSE, *Le Feu*.
1917	Karl GJELLERUP (1857–1919) (Den.), Henrik PONTOPPIDAN (1857–1943) (Den.).	Henri MALHERBE, *La Flamme au poing*.
1918	Not awarded.	Georges DUHAMEL, Denis THÉVENIN, *Civilisation*.
1919	Carl SPITTELER (1845–1924) (Swiss).	Marcel PROUST, *A l'Ombre des jeunes filles en fleurs*.
1920	Knut HAMSUN (1859–1952) (Norw.).	Ernest PÉROCHON, *Nêne*.
1921	Anatole FRANCE (1844–1924) (Fr.).	René MARAN, *Batouala*.
1922	Jacinto BENAVENTE (1866–1954) (Sp.).	Henri BÉRAUD, *Le Vitriol de lune, Le Martyre de l'obèse*.

Literary Prizes in Proust's Time

Date	Prix Fémina (1904)	Grand prix de littérature (1911)	Grand prix du roman de l'Académie Française (1915)
1904	Myriam HARRY, *La Conquête à Jérusalem.*		
1905	Romain ROLLAND, *Jean-Christophe.*		
1906	Andér CORTHIS (Mlle Husson), *Gemmes et Moires.*		
1907	Colette YVER, *Princesses de science.*		
1908	Édouard ESTAUNIÉ, *La Vie secrète.*		
1909	Edmond JALOUX, *Le reste est silence.*		
1910	Marguerite AUDOUX, *Marie-Claire.*		
1911	Louis de ROBERT, *Le Roman du malade.*	Not awarded.	
1912	Jacques MOREL (Mme Edmond Pottier), *Feuilles mortes.*	André LAFON.	
1913	Camille MARBO (Mme Émile Borel), *La Statue voilée.*	Romain ROLLAND.	
1914	Not awarded.	Not awarded.	
1915	Not awarded.	Émile NOLLY.	Paul ACKER, for his work as a whole.
1916	Not awarded.	Maurice MASSON.	AVESNES, *L'île heureuse.*
1917	René MILAN (pseud.: Maurice LARROUY), *L'Odyssée d'un transport torpillé.*	Francis JAMMES.	Charles GÉNIAUX, for his work as a whole.
1918	Henri BACHELIN, *Le Serviteur.*	Mme Gérard d'HOUVILLE.	Camille MAYRAN, *Gotton Connixloo.*
1919	Roland DORGELÈS, *Les Croix de bois.*	Jérôme and Jean THARAUD.	Pierre BENOIT, *L'Atlantide.*
1920	Edmond GOJON, *Le Jardin des dieux.*	Edmond JALOUX.	André CORTHIS, *Pour moi seule.*
1921	Raymond ESCHOLIER, *Canegril.*	Comtesse de NOAILLES.	Pierre VILLETARD, *Monsieur Bille dans la tourmente.*
1922	Jacques de LACRETELLE, *Silbermann.*	Pierre LASSERRE.	Francis CARCO, *L'Homme traqué.*

Chronological Table of Art and Literature

Date	French Literature	Foreign Literature	Music and Art
1870	Flaubert: *L'Éducation sentimentale.* Hugo returns from exile and publishes the first French edition of *Les Châtiments.* Verlaine: *La Bonne Chanson.* Verne: *Vingt Mille Lieues sous les mers.* Died: Dumas père, J. de Goncourt, Lautréamont, Mérimée.	Rossetti: *Poems.* Dostoyevsky: *The Devils.* Died: Dickens.	Delibes: *Coppélia.* Duparc: *L'Invitation au voyage.* Fromentin: *Les Maîtres d'autrefois.* Cézanne: *Nature morte à la pendule.* Sisley: *Première Neige à Louveciennes.* Schliemann's excavation of Troy-Hissarlik began.
1871	Rimbaud: *Le Bateau ivre* (published 1883). Coppée: *Plus de sang.* Zola: *Rougon-Macquart* series with *La Fortune des Rougon* (→ 1893). Birth of: Valéry, Marcel Proust (10 July).	Carroll: *Through the Looking-Glass.* Eliot: *Middlemarch.* Meredith: *Harry Richmond.* Ostrovsky: *The Forest.*	Verdi: *Aida*, first performance at the opening of the Suez canal. Wagner: *Siegfried.* Morisot: *La Lecture.* Puvis de Chavannes: *Les Jeunes Filles et la mort.* Whistler: *The Artist's Mother.* Courbet's arrest. Fontaines Wallace in Paris.
1872	Leconte de Lisle: *Poèmes antiques.* Daudet: *Tartarin de Tarascon.* Zola: *La Curée.* (Charpentier buys *Les Rougon-Macquart.*) Died: Gautier. Birth of: Léautaud, R. de Flers, Bataille.	Butler: *Erewhon.* Hardy: *Under the Greenwood Tree.* Andersen: *Fairy Tales.*	Bizet: *L'Arlésienne.* Franck: *Rédemption.* Monet: *Le Pont de Westminster.* He moves to Argenteuil. Renoir: *Les Canotiers à Chatou.* Degas: *Le Foyer de la danse.*

1873	France: *Poèmes dorés.* Daudet: *Contes du lundi.* Rimbaud: *Une saison en enfer.* Zola: *Le Ventre de Paris.* Birth of: Péguy, Barbusse, Colette, Jarry.	Twain: *The Golden Age.* Tolstoy: *Anna Karenina* (→ 1877). Died: Manzoni.	Lalo: *Symphonie espagnole.* Lecocq: *La Fille de Mme Angot.* Concerts Colonne founded. Cézanne: *La Maison du pendu.* Monet: *Le Champ de coquelicots.* Pissarro: *Autoportrait.*
1874	Barbey d'Aurévilly: *Les Diaboliques.* Flaubert: *La Tentation de saint Antoine.* Féval: *La Ville vampire.* Gobineau: *Les Pléiades.* Huysmans: *Le Drageoir aux épices.* Rimbaud: *Les Illuminations.* Verlaine: *Romances sans paroles.* Died: Michelet.	Birth of: Hofmannsthal.	Saint-Saëns: *Danse macabre.* Grieg: *Peer Gynt.* Verdi: *Requiem*, dedicated to Manzoni. Wagner: *Götterdämmerung* L'École de Rome founded. Renoir: *La Loge.* Puvis de Chavannes: frescoes for the Panthéon in Paris. 1st Impressionist exhibition at Nadar's: Monet's *Impression, Soleil levant.*
1875	Déroulède: *Nouveaux Chants du soldat.* Erckmann-Chatrian: *Maître Gaspard Fix.* Sardou: *Le Haine.* Sully Prudhomme: *Tendresses.* Zola: *La Faute de l'abbé Mouret.* Died: Corbière.	Meredith: *Beauchamp's Career.* Tennyson: *Queen Mary.* James: *Roderick Hudson.* Died: Andersen. Birth of: Thomas Mann, Rilke.	The Paris Opéra opens. Bizet: *Carmen.* Fauré: *Sonate pour piano et violon.* Bartholdi: *Lion de Belfort.* Renoir: *Chemin montant dans les hautes herbes.* Burne-Jones: *The Mirror of Venus.* Birth of: Ravel, R. Hahn.
1876	France: *Les Noces corinthiennes.* Gobineau: *Nouvelles asiatiques.*	Swinburne: *Erechteus, a Tragedy.* Twain: *Tom Sawyer.*	Saint-Saëns: 1st Symphony in C minor Inauguration of the theatre at Bayreuth.

Contd over

Date	French Literature	Foreign Literature	Music and Art
1876	Huysmans: *Marthe*. Mallarmé: *L'Après-Midi d'un faune*. Died: Fromentin, G. Sand. Birth of: Jacob, A. de Noailles, Bernstein.	Dostoyevsky: *An Adolescent*. Turgenev: *Virgin Soil*.	Fantin-Latour: *L'Anniversaire*. Gauguin: *Sous-Bois de Viroflay*. Renoir: *Le Moulin de la Galette*. Moreau: *L'Apparition*.
1877	Daudet: *Le Nabab* Flaubert: *Trois Contes*. E. de Goncourt: *La Fille Élisa*. Hugo: *L'Art d'être grand-père*. Zola: *L'Assommoir*.	Collodi: *The Adventures of Pinocchio*. Meredith: *The Egoist*.	Saint-Saëns: *Samson et Dalila*. Massenet: *Le Roi de Lahore*. Marius Petipa: choreography for the ballet *La Bayadère*. Tchaikovsky: *Swan Lake*. Cézanne: *Autoportrait au chapeau de paille*. Degas: *L'Absinthe*. Manet: *Nana*. Rodin: *L'Âge d'airain*. Died: Courbet.
1878	Malot: *Sans famille*. Mistral: *Le Trésor du Félibrige*. Leconte de Lisle: *Poèmes barbares*. Sully Prudhomme: *Justice*. Zola: *Une page d'amour*. Birth of: Ramuz.	James: *Daisy Miller*.	Gounod: *Polyeucte*. Wagner begins *Parsifal*. Tchaikovsky: *Eugene Onegin*. Davioud and Bourdais: palais du Trocadéro. Garnier: Monte-Carlo casino. Whistler-Ruskin trial. Degas: *Danseuse au bouquet saluant sur la scène*.

1879

E. de Goncourt: *Les Frères Zemganno.*
Huysmans: *Les Sœurs Vatard.*
Loti: *Aziyadé.*
Vallès: *L'Enfant.*
Zola: *Nana.*

First Shakespeare festival at Stratford upon Avon.
Ibsen: *A Doll's House.*
D'Annunzio: *Primo vere.*
Strindberg: *The Red Room.*

Fauré: *Piano quartet in C minor.*
Carrière: *La Jeune Mère.*
Degas: *Miss Lola au cirque Fernando.*
Bouguereau: *La Naissance de Vénus.*
Dalou: *Le Triomphe de la République.*
Baron Jenney builds the Lister Building in Chicago.

1880

Les Soirées de Médan in which Maupassant publishes *Boule-de-Suif.*
Zola: *Le Roman expérimental.*
Died: Flaubert.
Birth of: Apollinaire.

Wallace: *Ben Hur.*
Tennyson: *Ballads.*
Ruskin: *The Bible of Amiens.*
Dostoyevsky: *The Brothers Karamazov.*

Franck: *Quintette.*
Manet: *Portrait d'Antonin Proust.*
Moreau: *Galatée.*
Böcklin: *L'Île des morts.*
Rodin: *La Porte de l'Enfer; Le Penseur.*
Galliera museum founded.
Died: Offenbach.

1881

Daudet: *Numa Roumestan.*
Flaubert: *Bouvard et Pécuchet.*
France: *Le Crime de Sylvestre Bonnard.*
Maupassant: *En famille; La Maison Tellier.*
Vallès: *Le Bachelier.*
Verlaine: *Sagesse.*
Birth of: Martin du Gard, Teilhard de Chardin, Larbaud.

Ibsen: *Ghosts.*
James: *Washington Square.*
Wilde: *Poems.*
Rossetti: *Ballads and Sonnets.*
Tagore: *Letters of a Traveller in Europe.*
Died: Dostoyevsky, Amiel.
Birth of: S. Zweig.

Sarah Bernhardt's triumphant tour of the USA.
Fauré: *Ballade pour piano et orchestre.*
Massenet: *Hérodiade.*
Saint-Saëns: *Septet in E flat.*
Gauguin: *Nu.*
Monet: *Débâcles* series.
Renoir: *Le Déjeuner des canotiers.*
Puvis de Chavannes: *Le Pauvre Pêcheur.*
Sargent: *The Lady of the Rose.*
Birth of: Bartok.

Contd over

Date	French Literature	Foreign Literature	Music and Art
1882	Becque: Les Corbeaux at the Comédie-Française. Goncourt: La Faustin. Halévy: L'Abbé Constantin. Huysmans: A vau-l'eau. Zola: Pot-Bouille. Birth of: Giraudoux, Vildrac.	Ibsen: An Enemy of the People. Whitman: Specimen Days. Died: Rossetti. Birth of: Joyce, V. Woolf.	Chausson: Poème de l'amour et de la mer. Lalo: Namouna. Wagner: Parsifal at Bayreuth. Manet: Le Bar des Folies-Bergère. Redon: Edgar Allan Poe. Musée des Arts décoratifs founded. Birth of: Stravinsky.
1883	Brunetière: Le Roman naturaliste. Hugo: La Légende des siècles (3rd series). Loti: Mon frère Yves. Maupassant: Une vie; Contes de la bécasse. Rollinat: Les Névroses. Villiers de l'Isle-Adam: Contes cruels. Zola: Au honneur des dames.	Björnson: Beyond Human Strength. Stevenson: Treasure Island. Died: Turgenev.	Chabrier: España. Delibes: Lakmé. Renoir: Les Grandes Baigneuses. Seurat: La Baignade à Asnières. Building of the Metropolitan Opera in New York. Gaudi: La Sagrada Familia in Barcelona (→ 1926). Died: Wagner, Manet.
1884	Mallarmé's first 'Tuesdays'. Bourges: Le Crépuscule des dieux. Daudet: Sapho. Huysmans: A rebours. Leconte de Lisle: Poèmes tragiques. Montépin: La Porteuse de pain. Moréas: Les Syrtes. Verlaine: Jadis et Naguère.	Meredith: Diana of the Crossways. Ibsen: The Wild Duck. Translation into French of Dostoyevsky's Crime and Punishment.	Franck: Prélude, Choral et fugue; Les Djinns. D'Indy: Sauge fleurie. Massenet: Manon. 1st Salon des Indépendants set up by Signac, Seurat, Cross. Cormon: Retour d'une chasse à l'ours à l'époque des cavernes. Puvis de Chavannes: Le Bois sacré.

	French literature	Other literature	Music & art
	Birth of: Chardonne, Duhamel, Paulhan, Supervielle.		Sargent: *Portrait of Mme Gautreau.* Whistler: *Portrait of Sarasate.* Rodin: *Les Bourgeois de Calais.*
1885	Becque: *La Parisienne.* Bourget: *Cruelle Énigme.* France: *Le Livre de mon ami.* Lorrain: *Modernités.* Mallarmé: *Prose pour Des Esseintes.* Maupassant: *Bel-Ami.* Died: Hugo, Vallès. Birth of: Guitry, Mauriac, Maurois, Romains.	Swinburne: *Marino Faliero.* Twain: *Huckleberry Finn.* Translation into French of Tolstoy's *Anna Karenina.* Birth of: D. H. Lawrence, Sinclair Lewis.	Franck: *Variations symphoniques.* Saint-Saëns: *Sonata in D Minor.* Massenet: *Le Cid.* Dujardin founds *La Revue wagnérienne.* Renoir: *Maternité.* Signac: *La Seine à Asnières.* Van Gogh: *The Potato-Eaters.* Pompon: *Canard appelant.* Richardson: Marshall Field Wholesale store in Chicago.
1886	Bloy: *Le Désespéré.* Courteline: *Les Gaietés de l'escadron.* Loti: *Pêcheur d'Islande.* Zola: *L'Œuvre.* Moréas: 'Symbolist' literary manifesto in *Le Figaro*'s supplement, 18 September. Birth of: Dorgelès, Alain-Fournier, Rivière.	James: *The Bostonians.* Stevenson: *The Strange Case of Dr Jekyll and Mr Hyde.* Vogüé: *Le Roman russe.* Tolstoy: *The Death of Ivan Illych.* Translation of Shelley's *Complete Works.*	Fauré: *2nd Quartet in G Minor.* Franck: *Sonata in A Minor.* Saint-Saëns: *Le Carnaval des animaux; 3rd Symphony in C Minor.* Bartholdi: *Statue of Liberty* (inauguration in New York harbour). Rodin: *Le Baiser.* Seurat: *Un dimanche d'été à la Grande-Jatte.* Died: Liszt.
1887	Antoine founds the Théâtre-Libre. 18/8: *Le Figaro* publishes 'Manifeste des Cinq' attacking Zola's *La Terre.* Hermant: *Le Cavalier Miserey.*	D'Annunzio: *Roman Elegies* (→ 1891). C. Doyle: *A Study in Scarlet.* Kipling: *Plain Tales from the Hills.* Strindberg: *The Father.*	Fauré: *Clair de lune; Requiem* (→ 1888). Gounod: *Messe à la mémoire de Jeanne d'Arc.* Satie: *Trois Sarabandes.* Verdi: *Otello.*

Contd over

Date	French Literature	Foreign Literature	Music and Art
1887	Loti: *Madame Chrysanthème.* M. Bashkirtseff: *Journal.* Verhaeren: *Les Soirs.* Died: Laforgue. Birth of: Cendrars, Jouve, Bourdet, Pourrat, Saint-John Perse.		Seurat: *La Parade.* Van Gogh: *Le Père Tanguy.* Single performance of *Lohengrin* at the Éden-Théâtre. Birth of: Le Corbusier.
1888	Barrès: *Sous l'œil des barbares.* Jarry: *Ubu roi.* Lemaitre: *Impressions de théâtre* (→ 1898). Maupassant: *Sur l'eau; Pierre et Jean.* Sully Prudhomme: *Le Bonheur.* Zola: *Le Rêve.* Died: Labiche. Birth of: Bernanos, Bosco, Jouhandeau, Lacretelle.	Chekhov: *The Bear.* Strindberg: *Miss Julie.* Fontane: *Dédale.* Birth of: K. Mansfield, E. O'Neill. Cazalis: *History of Hindu literature*	Debussy: *Deux Arabesques.* Mahler: *1st Symphony.* Lalo: *Le Roi d'Ys.* Satie: *Trois Gymnopédies.* Bonnat: *Le Cardinal Lavigerie.* Bernard: *Madeleine au bois d'amour.* Gauguin: *Le Christ jaune.* Ensor: *L'Entrée du Christ à Bruxelles.* Beltram: La Scala in Milan.
1889	Barrès: *Un homme libre.* Bourget: *Le Disciple.* Christophe: *La Famille Fenouillard.* Claudel: *Tête d'or* (published in 1890). France: *Thaïs.* Maeterlinck: *La Princesse Maleine.* Maupassant: *Fort comme la mort.* Rachilde: *Mr. Vénus Roman matérialiste,* (preface by M. Barrès).	D'Annunzio: *The Child of Pleasure.* Jerome K. Jerome: *Three Men in a Boat.* Stevenson: *The Master of Ballantrae.* Hauptmann: *Before Dawn.* Died: Browning.	Chausson: *Concert pour piano, violon et quatuor.* Franck: *Quartet in D Major.* Massenet: *Esclarmonde.* Tchaikovsky: *Sleeping Beauty.* Toulouse-Lautrec: *Au bal du Moulin de la Galette.* Van Gogh: *Champ de blé au soleil; Autoportrait à l'oreille coupée.*

	Verlaine: *Parallèlement.* First issue of *La Revue blanche.* Died: Barbey d'Aurevilly; Villiers de l'Isle-Adam. Birth of: Cocteau, Reverdy.		Puvis de Chavannes: frescoes in the Sorbonne and l'Hôtel de Ville in Paris (→ 1893). Exhibition by Gauguin and the Pont-Aven painters at the Café Volpini. Durand-Ruel opens an art gallery in New York.
1890	Daudet: *L'Immortel.* Mirbeau: *Sébastien Roch.* Porto-Riche: *Amoureuse.* Stendhal: *Vie de Henry Brulard* (posthumous). Zola: *La Bête humaine.* Birth of: Genevoix, Guéhenno.	Dickinson: *Poems.* Kipling: *The Light that Failed.* Translation of Tolstoy: *Kreutzer Sonata.* Translation of Ibsen: *Ghosts.*	Birth of ragtime in New Orleans. Debussy: *Cinq Poèmes de Baudelaire.* Fauré: *Cinq Mélodies.* Satie: *Trois Gnossiennes.* Mascagni: *Cavalleria rusticana.* Degas: *Les Danseuses bleues.* Beardsley: *Isolde.* Bing's Salon de l'Art Nouveau in Paris. Died: Franck, Van Gogh
1891	Barrès: *Le Jardin de Bérénice.* Gide: *Traité du Narcisse; Les Cahiers d'André Walter.* Huysmans: *Là-bas.* Renard: *L'Écornifleur.* Valéry: *Narcisse parle.* Verlaine: *Bonheur; Chansons pour elle.* Zola: *L'Argent.* Died: Banville, Rimbaud.	Hofmannsthal: *Gestern.* Hardy: *Tess of the d'Urbervilles.* Lagerlöf: *Gösta Berling.* Wilde: *The Picture of Dorian Gray.* Ibsen: *Hedda Gabler.* Died: Melville.	Fauré: *IIIe Valse-Caprice; La Bonne Chanson.* *Lohengrin* acclaimed at the Paris Opéra. Bonnard: *Femmes au jardin.* Monet: *Meules* series. Toulouse-Lautrec: *La Goulue au Moulin-Rouge.* Gauguin's first journey to Tahiti. Died: Seurat.

Contd over

Date	French Literature	Foreign Literature	Music and Art
1892	Barrès: *L'Ennemi des lois.* Claudel: *La Jeune Fille Violaine* (published in 1926). Curel: *Les Fossiles.* France: *La Rôtisserie de la reine Pédauque.* Maeterlinck: *Pelléas et Mélisande.* Montesquiou: *Les Chauves-Souris.* Verne: *Le Château des Carpathes.* Zola: *La Débâcle.*	C. Doyle: *The Adventures of Sherlock Holmes.* Hauptmann: *The Weavers.* D'Annunzio: *L'Innocent.* Ibsen: *The Master Builder.* Died: Tennyson, Whitman.	Tchaikovsky: *The Nutcracker Suite.* Massenet: *Werther.* Cézanne: *Les Joueurs de cartes.* Monet: *Cathédrales* series. Toulouse-Lautrec: *La Table au Moulin-Rouge.* Vuillard: *Sous la lampe.* The Munich 'secession'. Munch: *The Dance of Life*, 1st showing in Berlin causes a scandal. Birth of: D. Milhaud, A. Honegger.
1893	Lugné-Poe founds the Théâtre de l'Œuvre. Bourget: *Cosmopolis.* Claudel: *L'Échange.* Courteline: *Messieurs les ronds-de-cuir.* France: *Les Opinions de Jérôme Coignard.* Gide: *Le Voyage d'Urien.* Heredia: *Les Trophées.* Montesquiou: *Le Chef des odeurs suaves.* Samain: *Au jardin de l'infante.* Sardou: *Madame Sans-Gêne.* Verhaeren: *Les Campagnes hallucinées.* Died: Maupassant. Birth of: Drieu La Rochelle.	Shaw: *Plays Pleasant and Unpleasant.* (→ 1898). Hofmannsthal: *Fire and Death.*	Debussy: *Quatuor.* Puccini: *Manon Lescaut.* Verdi: *Falstaff*, his last opera. Tchaikovsky: *Symphonie pathétique.* Bourdelle: *Hommage aux morts.* Denis: *Les Muses.* Toulouse-Lautrec: *Jane Avril* (litho). Sisley: *Églises de Moret* series Vallotton: *La Valse.* Forain: *La Comédie parisienne.* Beardsley illustrates Malory's *Morte d'Arthur.* Horta: Tassel house in Brussels.

Contd over

1894			
	Barrès: *Du sang, de la volupté et de la mort.* France: *Le Lys rouge.* Gyp: *Le Mariage de Chiffon.* Louÿs: *Les Chansons de Bilitis.* Prévost: *Les Demi-Vierges.* J. Renard: *Poil de carotte.* Stendhal: *Lucien Leuwen* (posthumous). Zola: *Lourdes.* Died: Leconte de Lisle. Birth of: Céline, Rostand.	D'Annunzio: *The Triumph of Death.* Rilke: *Leben und Lied.* Sienkiewicz: *Quo vadis?* (translated 1900). Beardsley: *The Yellow Book.* Beckford: *Vathek* (preface by Mallarmé). Kipling: *The Jungle Book.*	Founding of the Schola Cantorum. Debussy: *Prélude à l'après-midi d'un faune.* Fauré: *VIᵉ Nocturne.* Massenet: *Thaïs.* Dvořák: *New World Symphony.* Rouault: *Jésus parmi les docteurs.* Le Douanier Rousseau: *La Guerre.* The French government refuses G. Caillebotte's bequest of Impressionist paintings. Guimard: The Castel Béranger in Paris. Died: Chabrier.
1895			
	Barbusse: *Les Pleureuses.* T. Bernard: *Les Pieds nickelés.* Gide: *Paludes.* Hervieu: *Les Tenailles.* Huysmans: *En route.* France: *Le Jardin d'Épicure.* Maurras: *Le Chemin de Paradis.* H. de Régnier: *Aréthuse.* E. Rostand: *La Princesse lointaine.* Verhaeren: *Les Villes tentaculaires.* M. Pottecher founds the Bussang People's theatre. Died: Dumas *fils.* Birth of: Éluard, Giono, Pagnol.	Gorky: *Chelkash.* Wilde's trial and sentence. Conrad: *Almayer's Folly.* Hardy: *Jude the Obscure.* Wells: *The Time Machine.* Tolstoy: *The Power of Darkness.*	Ravel: *La Habanera; Menuet antique.* D'Indy: *Fervaal.* R. Strauss: *Till Eulenspiegel.* Denis: *Les Pèlerins d'Emmaüs.* Moreau: *Jupiter et Sémélé.* Munch: *The Scream.* Horta: Hôtel Solvay in Brussels. 1st Venice Biennale. Auguste and Louis Lumière: 1st public showing of film: *L'Arroseur arrosé.*

Date	French Literature	Foreign Literature	Music and Art
1896	Estaunié: *L'Empreinte*. Fort: *Les Ballades françaises*. France: *L'Orme du mail*. He is elected to the Académie française. Gourmont: first *Livre des masques*. Montesquiou: *Les Hortensias bleus*. Renard: *Histoires naturelles*. Valéry: *La Soirée avec M. Teste*. Verhaeren: *Les Heures claires*. Died: E. de Goncourt, Verlaine. Birth of: Artaud, Breton, Montherlant, Tzara.	Hauptmann: *The Sunken Bell*. De Castro: *Salomé*. Weils: *The Island of Dr. Moreau*. D'Annunzio: *Virgin of the Rocks*. Chekhov: *The Seagull*.	Saint-Saëns: *5th Concerto*. Giordano: *Andrea Chénier*. Puccini: *La Bohème*. R. Strauss: *Thus Spake Zarathustra*. S. Bing opens the Galerie de l'Art Nouveau in Paris. Bonnard: *La Partie de cartes*. Gauguin: *Nave Nave Mahana*. Picasso: *Le Mendiant*. Redon: *Songes*. Méliès: *Escamotage d'une dame* at the Théâtre Robert-Houdin. 1st issue of the review *Jugend* in Munich.
1897	Barrès: *Les Déracinés*. Gide: *Les Nourritures terrestres*. Lorrain: *Monsieur de Bougrelon*. Loti: *Ramuntcho*. Péguy: *Jeanne d'Arc*. Régnier: *Les Jeux rustiques et divins*. Renard: *Le Pain de ménage*. Rictus: *Les Soliloques du pauvre* (ill. by Steinlen). Rostand: *Cyrano de Bergerac*. Died: A. Daudet. Birth of: Aragon, Soupault.	Wassermann: *The Jews of Zindorf*. Strindberg: *Inferno*. Maugham: *Liza of Lambeth*. Kipling: *Captains Courageous*. Lagerlöf: *Miracles of the Antichrist*. Rilke: *Crown of Dreams*. Wells: *The Invisible Man*.	Debussy: *Chansons de Bilitis*. Dukas: *L'Apprenti sorcier*. Massenet: *Sapho*. Toscanini at La Scala. Boldini: *Portrait de Robert de Montesquiou*. Mahler becomes director of the Vienna Opera (→ 1907). Klimt begins the 'secession' in Vienna. Gauguin: *Noa-Noa*. Rodin: *Balzac*. Deglane and Girault build the Grand Palais and the Petit Palais (→ 1900).

1898	Huysmans: *La Cathédrale.* Jammes: *De l'aube de l'angélus du soir.* Lichtenberger: *Mon Petit Trott.* Louÿs: *La Femme et le Pantin.* Samain: *Aux flancs du vase.* Zola: *Paris.* Died: Mallarmé. Birth of: Dabit.	Translation of Wagner: *Parsifal.* Blasco Ibañez: *La Barraca.* Conrad: *Nigger of the 'Narcissus'.* James: *The Turn of the Screw.* Shaw: *The Perfect Wagnerite.* Wilde: *Ballad of Reading gaol.*	Fauré: *Pelléas et Mélisande.* Messager: *Véronique.* Picasso in Paris. Cézanne begins *Les Grandes Baigneuses.* Monet begins *Les Nymphéas.* Marquet: *Nu fauve'?* Matisse: *Nu dans l'atelier.* Puvis de Chavannes: *Geneviève veillant sur Lutèce.* Exposition Nabi at Durand-Ruel's. Mucha: poster for *Médée* (performed by Sarah Bernhardt). Died: Moreau.
1899	S. Bernhardt gives her name to the Théâtre des Nations. T. Bernard: *L'Anglais tel qu'on le parle.* Curel: *La Nouvelle Idole.* Feydeau: *La Dame de chez Maxim's.* Gide: *La Prométhée mal enchaîné.* Mirbeau: *Le Jardin des supplices.* Moréas: *Les Stances.* Died: Becque. Birth of: Achard, Michaux, Ponge.	Translation of Kipling: *The Jungle Book* (by Robert d'Humières). D'Annunzio: *La Joconde.* Yeats: *The Wind Among the Reeds.* Tagore: *Sunset of the Century.* Chekhov: *Uncle Varya.*	Berlioz: *Prise de Troie* (première at the Opéra). Debussy: *Trois Nocturnes.* Ravel: *Pavane pour une infante défunte.* Schönberg: *La Nuit transfigurée.* Toulouse-Lautrec: *Cirque* series. Villon: *L'Ile d'amour.* Hennebique: 1, rue Danton; concrete architecture. L. Sullivan's architecture in Chicago. Klimt decorates Vienna university.

Contd over

Date	French Literature	Foreign Literature	Music and Art
1900	Barrès: *L'Appel au soldat.* Claudel: *Connaissance de l'Est.* Colette: *Claudine à l'école.* Mirbeau: *Journal d'une femme de chambre.* Péguy: *Cahiers de la quinzaine* founded. Ch.-L. Philippe: *La Mère et l'Enfant.* Prévost: *Les Vierges folles.* Régnier: *Les Médailles d'argile.* Rostand: *L'Aiglon.* Sarcey: *Quarante Ans de théâtre.* Died: Samain. Birth of: Chamson, Desnos, Dhôtel, Green, Prévert, Saint-Exupéry.	D'Annunzio: *The Flame of Life.* Conrad: *Lord Jim.* Strindberg: *The Dance of Death.* Tolstoy: *Resurrection.* Died: Wilde, J. Ruskin.	Charpentier: *Louise.* Ballets by Loïe Fuller. Puccini: *Tosca.* Schönberg: *Gurrelieder.* Sibelius: *Finlandia.* Monet: *Ponts de Londres* series. Exhibition of *Les Nymphéas* at Durand-Ruel's. Maillol: *Femme assise.* Bonnard illustrates Verlaine. Building of Alexandre III bridge. Gaudi: the Güell park in Barcelona (→ 1914)
1901	R. Bazin: *Les Oberlé.* Hervieu: *La Course au flambeau.* Lorrain: *Monsieur de Phocas.* Maurras: *Anthinéa.* Maeterlinck: *La Vie des abeilles.* Montesquiou: *Les Paons.* A. de Noailles: *Le Cœur innombrable.* Ch.-L. Philippe: *Bubu de Montparnasse.* Birth of: Leiris, Malraux.	Lagerlöf: *Jerusalem.* T. Mann: *Buddenbrooks.* Kipling: *Kim.* Chekhov: *Three Sisters.* Shaw: *Three Plays for Puritans.*	Ravel: *Jeux d'eau; Sonatine.* Ives: 2nd Symphony. Picasso: blue period. Klimt: *Judith I.* Bourdelle: *Masque tragique de Beethoven.* Maillol: *La Pensée.* Garnier plans an industrial city. Gallé founds the École des arts décoratifs in Nancy. Died: Verdi, Toulouse-Lautrec.

1902	Opening of the Académie Goncourt. Barrès: *Leurs figures.* Bloy: *Exégèse des lieux communs.* Bourget: *L'Étape.* Boylesve: *La Leçon d'amour dans un parc.* Curel: *La Fille sauvage.* France: *L'Affaire Crainquebille.*	C. Doyle: *The Hound of the Baskervilles.* D'Annunzio: *Francesca da Rimini.* Strindberg: *A Dream Play.* Gorky: *The Lower Depths.*	Debussy: *Pelléas et Mélisande.* Fauré: *Huit Pièces brèves.* Massenet: *Le Jongleur de Notre-Dame.* The review *Musica* founded. Picasso: *L'Étreinte.* Signac: *Sortie du port de Saint-Tropez.* Bonnard illustrates *Daphnis et Chloé.*
1902	Gide: *L'Immoraliste.* Maurras: *Les Amants de Venise.* A. de Noailles: *L'Ombre des jours.* Prévost: *Lettres à Françoise.* Régnier: *La Cité des eaux.* Died: Zola. Birth of: Aymé, N. Sarraute.		Méliès: *Voyages dans la lune.* Died: Tissot.
1903	Apollinaire: *La Chanson du mal-aimé.* Barrès: *Amor et dolori sacrum.* Courteline: *La Paix chez soi.* Huysmans: *L'Oblat.* Léautaud: *Le Petit Ami.* Mirbeau: *Les affaires sont les affaires.* Birth of: Queneau, Radiguet, G. Simenon.	D'Annunzio: *Laudes* (→ 1913). T. Mann: *Tristan.* Conrad: *Typhoon.* James: *The Ambassadors.* London: *The Call of the Wild.* Shaw: *Man and Superman.* Butler: *The Way of All Flesh* (posthumous).	Debussy: *Jardins sous la pluie.* Ravel: *Schéhérazade.* Satie: *Morceaux en forme de poire.* Caruso's debut at the Metropolitan Opera in New York. Schönberg: *Pelléas et Mélisande.* Gauguin: *Autoportrait.* Kandinsky: *Le Cavalier bleu.* Died: Whistler. The Perret brothers build with reinforced concrete in the rue Franklin in Paris.

Cond over

Date	French Literature	Foreign Literature	Music and Art
1904	Bataille: *Maman Colibri.* Bourget: *Un divorce.* Delarue-Mardrus: *Horizons.* Gourmont: *Promenades littéraires* (→ 1913). Rolland: *Jean-Christophe* (→ 1912). Verhaeren: *Toute la Flandre* (→ 1911).	Pirandello: *The Late Mattia Pascal.* Barrie: *Peter Pan* Chekhov: *The Cherry Orchard.* O. Henry: *Cabbages and Kings.* Died: Chekhov.	Fauré: *Impromptu pour harpe.* Roussel: *1st Symphonie.* Mahler: *Kindertotenlieder.* Puccini: *Madame Butterfly.* Schönberg: *1st quartet in D minor.* Derain: *Le Pont de Chatou.* Despiau: *Petite Fille des Landes.* Matisse: *Luxe, calme et volupté.* Mondrian: *Paysages hollandais* series.
1905	T. Bernard: *Triplepatte.* Gide: *Prétextes.* Montesquiou: *Professionnelles Beautés.* Péguy: *Notre patrie.* Pinchon plays Bécassine. Toulet: *Mon amie Nane.* Suarès: *Voici l'homme.* Leblanc plays Arsène Lupin (*Je sais tout,* 15 July). Died: Hérédia, Verne. Birth of: Sartre.	H. Mann: *Professor Unrat.* Wells: *Kipps.* Blasco Ibáñez: *The Horde.* C. Doyle: *The Return of Sherlock Holmes.* Rilke: *The Book of Hours.*	Debussy: *La Mer; Images.* Ravel: *Sonatine; Miroirs.* Falla: *La Vida breve.* Mahler: *7th Symphony.* Strauss: *Salomé* to Wilde's text. Picasso: pink period. First Fauvist exhibition at the Salon d'automne. Van Dongen: *Anita.* Brancusi: *Têtes d'enfant.* C. Claudel: *Paul Claudel.* Jourdain builds la Samaritaine. Die Brücke founded in Dresden.
1906	Barrès elected to the Académie française. Bordeaux: *Les Roquevillard.* Claudel: *Partage de midi.*	Galsworthy: *The Man of Property (The Forsyte Saga* → 1928). London: *White Fang.*	Fauré: *1st Quintet.* Ravel: *Histoires naturelles; Rhapsodie espagnole.*

	Loti: *Les Désenchantées.* Régnier: *Le Miroir des heures.* Died: Brunetière, Lorrain. Birth of: Beckett.	Sinclair: *The Jungle.* Lagerlöf: *Nils Holgersson.* Musil: *Young Törless.* Died: Ibsen.	Albéniz: *Iberia.* Derain: *Blackfriars.* Dufy: Trouville posters. Matisse: *La Joie de vivre.* Picasso: *Autoportrait; Portrait de Gertrude Stein.* Vlaminck: *Les Arbres rouges.* Blackton: first film cartoon, *Le Stylo magique.* Died: Cézanne.
1907	Bazin: *Le Blé qui lève.* Bernstein: *Samson.* Colette: *La Retraite sentimentale.* Leroux: *Le Mystère de la chambre jaune.* Mirbeau: *La 628 E 8.* A. de Noailles: *Les Éblouissements.* *L'Épatant* founded. Died: Jarry, Huysmans, Sully Prudhomme.	Gorky: *The Mother.* D'Annunzio: *More than Death.* Yeats: *Deirdre.* Hofmannsthal: *Letter from Lord Chandos.* Strindberg: *The Ghost Sonata.* Forster: *The Longest Journey.*	Dukas: *Ariane et Barbe-Bleue.* D'Indy: *Sonata* Debussy: *Poissons d'or.* Matisse exhibition in Berlin. Kahnweiler opens his gallery in the rue Vignon. Braque: *Grand Nu.* Rouault: *La Parade.* Le Douanier Rousseau: *La Charmeuse de serpents.*
1907	Birth of: Char, Vaillant.		Derain: *Les Baigneuses.* Picasso: *Les Demoiselles d'Avignon.* Maillol: *Pomone, Amants.*
1908	Barbusse: *L'Enfer.* Flers and Caillavet: *Le Roi.* France: *L'Île des pingouins.* Romains: *La Vie unanime.*	D'Annunzio: *The Ship.* Wassermann: *Caspar Hauser.* Sinclair: *The Metropolis.* Blasco Ibáñez: *Bleeding Sands.*	Ravel: *Ma mère l'Oye.* Saint-Saëns: music for the film *L'Assassinat du duc de Guise.* Berg: *Sonata*, op. 1.

Cond over

Date	French Literature	Foreign Literature	Music and Art
1908	*N.R.F.* founded. Forton creates *Les Pieds nickelés* in *L'Épatant*. Died: Coppée. Birth of: Brasillach, S. de Beauvoir.		Mahler: *Song of the Earth*. Cubist works by Braque and Picasso, working together. Bonnard: *Le Paon*. Monet: *Vues de Venise*. Chagall: *Nu rouge*. Montaner: Palace of Catalan music in Barcelona.
1909	Apollinaire: *L'Enchanteur pourrissant*, illustrated by Derain. Gide: *La Porte étroite*. Maeterlinck: *L'Oiseau bleu*. Birth of: Pieyre de Mandiargues, S. Weil. Marinetti's futurist manifesto in *Le Figaro*.	T. S. Eliot: *Portrait of a Lady*. Stein: *Three Lives*. London: *Martin Eden*.	Diaghilev's Ballets Russes in Paris with Pavlova, Nijinsky, Fokine. Falla: *Nuits dans les jardins d'Espagne*. Monet's *Nymphéas* exhibited at Durand-Ruel's. Delaunay: *Saint-Séverin*. Brancusi: *La Muse endormie*. Kandinsky: *La Montagne bleue*. Picabia: *Caoutchouc*. Nolde: *La Cène*. Bourdelle: *Héraklès archer*.
1910	Apollinaire: *Le Bestiaire ou Cortège d'Orphée*, illustrated by Dufy. Colette: *La Vagabonde*. Péguy: *Le Mystère de la charité de Jeanne d'Arc*; *Victor-Marie, comte Hugo*.	Tagore: *Gitanjali*. Rilke: *The Notebooks of Malte Laurids Brigge*. In Germany: the periodical *Der Sturm*. In Austria: the periodical *Der Brenner*. Died: Tolstoy, Björnson, M. Twain.	Debussy: first book of *Préludes*. Hahn: *La Fête chez Thérèse*. Puccini: *Girl of the Golden West* at the Metropolitan Opera, New York Stravinsky: *The Firebird*.

	Rostand: *Chantecler.* Roussel: *Impressions d'Afrique.* Died: Moréas, Renard. Birth of: Anouilh, Genet, Gracq.		Chagall à la Ruche: *Le Mariage.* Delaunay: *La Tour Eiffel.* Van Dongen: *La Femme au balcon.* Picasso: *Ambroise Vollard.* Perret: Théâtre des Champs-Élysées (→ 1913).
1911	Claudel: *Cinq Grandes Odes; L'Otage.* Larbaud: *Fermina Marquez.* Saint-John Perse: *Éloges.* Jammes: *Les Géorgiques chrétiennes.* Birth of: H. Bazin, Troyat.	Lawrence: *The White Peacock.* Conrad: *Under Western Eyes.* Mansfield: *In a German Pension.* S. Zweig: *The House Beside the Sea.* T. Mann: *Death in Venice.*	Debussy: *Le Martyre de saint Sébastien.* R. Strauss: *Der Rosenkavalier.* Stravinsky: *Petrouchka.* La Fresnaye: *Le Cuirassier.* Renoir: *Monsieur et Madame Durand-Ruel.* Klee illustrates *Candide.* Kupka: *Ordonnance sur verticale.*
1912	Barrès: *Gréco ou le Secret de Tolède.* Carco: *La Bohème et mon cœur.* Cendrars: *Pâques à New York.* Claudel: *L'Annonce faite à Marie.* Flers et Caillavet: *L'Habit vert.* France: *Les dieux ont soif.* Ghéon: *Le Pain.* Gide: *Le Retour de l'enfant prodigue.* Péguy: *La Tapisserie de sainte Geneviève et de Jeanne d'Arc.* Segalen: *Stèles.* J. et J. Tharaud: *La Fête arabe.*	Shaw: *Pygmalion.* Lagerlöf: *The Death-cart.* Died: Strindberg.	Hahn: *Le Dieu bleu.* Ravel: *Daphnis et Chloé* performed by the Ballets Russes, with *L'Après-Midi d'un faune.* Satie: *Véritables préludes flasques.* Prokofiev: *1st Concerto for piano and orchestra.* Schönberg: *Pierrot lunaire.* Delaunay: *Fenêtres* series. Bourdelle: *Apollon et les Muses.* Maillol: *Pomone.* Sauvage: tiered building in the rue Vavin. Died: Massenet.

Contd over

Date	French Literature	Foreign Literature	Music and Art
1913	J. Copeau opens the théâtre du Vieux-Colombier. Alain-Fournier: *Le Grand Meaulnes.* Apollinaire: *Alcools.* Barrès: *La Colline inspirée.* Cendrars: *Prose du Transsibérien.* Géraldy: *Toi et Moi.* Larbaud: *Journal d'A.-D. Barnabooth.* Martin du Gard: *Jean Barois.* Romains: *Les Copains.* Birth of: Camus, C. Simon.	Lawrence: *Sons and Lovers.* Gorky: *Childhood.*	Debussy: *Jeux; La Boîte à joujoux.* Roussel: *Le Festin de l'araignée.* Stravinsky: *Le Sacre du printemps.* Braque: *Femme à la guitare.* Duchamp: *Nu descendant l'escalier.* Gleizes: *La Ville et le Fleuve.* Malevitch launches Suprematism in Russia. Archipenko: *Nu cubiste.* Le Corbusier: La Chaux-de-Fonds house in Switzerland. Linder: *Max, victime du quinquina.* Feuillade: *Fantômas* series. Armory Show exhibition in New York.
1914	Bloy: *Le Pèlerin de l'absolu.* Bourget: *Le Démon de midi.* Carco: *Jésus la Caille.* Gide: *Les Caves du Vatican.* Hervieu: *Le destin est maître.* Leroux: *Chéri-Bibi.* Died: Alain-Fournier, Lemaitre, Mistral, Psichari, Péguy. Birth of: M. Duras.	London: *The Mutiny of Elsinore.* Joyce: *Dubliners.* O'Neill: *Thirst.* Shaw: *Common Sense About the War.*	J. Rouché: director of the Opéra de Paris (→ 1939). First performance of *Parsifal* at the Paris Opéra. Fauré: *Le Jardin clos.* Stravinsky: *Le Rossignol.* Delaunay: *Hommage à Blériot.* La Fresnaye: *L'Homme assis.* Utrillo: *Le Lapin agile.* Chirico: metaphysical interiors. Sant' Elia: Manifesto of futurist architecture. Setting up of the first great Hollywood film studios. Chaplin: *To Earn a Living* (his first film).

1915	Claudel: *Corona benignitatis Anni Dei.* Reverdy: *Poèmes en prose.* Rolland: *Au-dessus de la mêlée.* Died: Hervieu, Caillavet, R. de Gourmont, Pergaud.	Bunin: *The Gentleman from San Francisco.* Mayakovsky: *Cloud in Trousers.* Lagerlöf: *The Emperor of Portugal.* Woolf: *The Voyage Out.* Maugham: *Of Human Bondage.*	Debussy: *12 Études.* Falla: *L'Amour sorcier.* Vorticist exhibition in London. Futurist exhibition in Petrograd. Panama-Pacific Exhibition. Le Corbusier: Domino house. Feuillade: *Les Vampires; Les Mystères de New York.* De Mille: *Forfaiture.* Griffith: *Birth of a Nation.*
1916	Apollinaire: *Le Poète assassiné.* Claudel: *Le Père humilié.* Hémon: *Maria Chapdelaine* (posthumous). Montesquiou: *Les Offrandes blessées.* Tzara: *La Première Aventure céleste de M. Antipyrine.* Verhaeren: *La Belgique dévastée.* Died: Faguet, Verhaeren. Birth of: P. Emmanuel.	Blasco Ibáñez: *The Four Horsemen of the Apocalypse.* D'Annunzio: *Nocturnes.* Joyce: *A Portrait of the Artist as a Young Man.* Kafka: *Metamorphosis.* Essenin: *Poems.* Tagore: *The Home and the World.* Died: London, Sienkiewicz, James.	Poulet Quartet founded. Prokofiev: *'Classical' Symphony.* Webern: *4 Lieder.* Matisse: *Leçon de piano.* Soutine: *Les Harengs.* Picabia: *391.* Dadaist manifesto in Zurich. Feuillade: *Judex.* Died: Redon.
1917	Apollinaire: *Les Mamelles de Tirésias.* Delluc: *La guerre est morte.* Éluard: *Le Devoir et l'inquiétude.* Jacob: *Le Cornet à dés.* Soupault: *Aquarium.* Valéry: *Le Jeune Parque.*	Yeats: *The Wild Swans at Coole.*	Ravel: *Le Tombeau de Couperin.* Busoni: *Turandot.* Diaghilev mounts *Parade* with Satie, Picasso, Cocteau. Matisse: *Odalisques.* Chagall: *Double Portrait.*

Contd over

Date	French Literature	Foreign Literature	Music and Art
1917	Died: L. Bloy, Mirbeau.		Klimt: *Adam et Ève.* Picasso: *L'Italienne.* Modigliani: *Nu couché.* Died: Rodin, Degas. Chaplin: *The Immigrant.*
1918	Apollinaire: *Calligrammes.* Benoit: *Koenigsmark.* France: *Le Petit Pierre.* Giraudoux: *Simon le pathétique.* Mac Orlan: *Le Chant de l'équipage.* Maurois: *Les Silences du colonel Bramble.* Tzara: *Dadaist Manifesto.* Died: Apollinaire, E. Rostand.	Sinclair: *The Profits of Religion.* Mayakovsky: *Ode to Revolution.* Pirandello: *Right You Are.* Essenin: *Inonia.* Periodical *Roma futurista.*	Bartók: *Bluebeard's Castle.* Christiné: *Phi-phi.* Stravinsky: *Histoire du soldat.* Satie: *Socrate.* Fauré: *Sonate pour violoncelle et piano.* Poulenc: *Mouvement perpétuel.* The 'Six' founded in Paris. Gris: *L'Écossaise.* Soutine: *Autoportrait.* Modigliani: *Nus* series. Epoca exhibition in Italy with Chirico. Chaplin: *A Dog's Life.* Miró exhibition in Barcelona. Died: Klimt, Debussy.
1919	Benda: *Belphégor.* Breton: *Mont-de-piété.* Cendrars: *Du monde entier.* Gide: *La Symphonie pastorale.* Guitry: *Mon père avait raison; Pasteur.* Rolland: *Cola Bruignon.*	D'Annunzio: *Against One and All.* Essenin: *Manifeste imaginiste.* Periodical *Der Dada* in Germany. Brecht: *Drums in the Night.* Kafka: *The Prison Colony.* Wallace: *The Man Who Knew Too Much.*	Bartók: *The Marvellous Mandarin.* Ravel: *La Danse.* Milhaud: *Le Bœuf sur le toit.* Poulenc: *Le Bestiaire.* Strauss: *Die Frau ohne Schatten.* Matisse: *Le Compotier* (Carnegie Prize).